On Skidelsky's Keynes and Other Essays

On Skidelsky's Keynes and Other Essays

Selected Essays of G. C. Harcourt

G. C. Harcourt

Emeritus Reader in the History of Economic Theory, University of Cambridge;
Emeritus Fellow, Jesus College, Cambridge;
Professor Emeritus, University of Adelaide;
Visiting Professorial Fellow, University of New South Wales

palgrave
macmillan

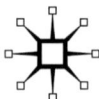

First published 2012 by
PALGRAVE MACMILLAN

Palgrave Macmillan in the UK is an imprint of Macmillan Publishers Limited,
registered in England, company number 785998, of Houndmills, Basingstoke,
Hampshire RG21 6XS.

Palgrave Macmillan in the US is a division of St Martin's Press LLC,
175 Fifth Avenue, New York, NY 10010.

Palgrave Macmillan is the global academic imprint of the above companies
and has companies and representatives throughout the world.

Palgrave® and Macmillan® are registered trademarks in the United States,
the United Kingdom, Europe and other countries.

ISBN: 978–0–230–28468–5

This book is printed on paper suitable for recycling and made from fully
managed and sustained forest sources. Logging, pulping and manufacturing
processes are expected to conform to the environmental regulations of the
country of origin.

A catalogue record for this book is available from the British Library.

Library of Congress Cataloging-in-Publication Data

Harcourt, Geoffrey Colin.
    On Skidelsky's Keynes and other essays / G.C. Harcourt.
      p. cm.
    Includes index.
    ISBN 978–0–230–28468–5 (alk. paper)
      1. Keynesian economics. I. Title.

HB99.7.H323 2011
330.15'6—dc23   2011024167

10 9 8 7 6 5 4 3 2 1
21 20 19 18 17 16 15 14 13 12

Printed and bound in Great Britain by
CPI Antony Rowe, Chippenham and Eastbourne

Contents

Tables

Figures

Acknowledgements

First, I would like to acknowledge the co-authors of some of the essays in these volumes: Stephanie Blankenburg, Avi Cohen, John Grieve Smith, Prue Kerr, Mehdi Monadjemi, Peter Nolan, Ajit Singh, Sean Turnell and Catherine Walston. One of the real pluses of the community of scholars is that co-authors are also such close and supportive friends. I am a very lucky person.

Second, I am most grateful to Janet Nurse, Jane Starnes and Grace Setiawan for being such wonderful, cheerful and uncomplaining typists, and to Ha (Viet Ha Nguyen) for handling so expertly my e-mails, and for research assistance.

The author and publishers wish to acknowledge with thanks the following for permission to reproduce copyright material:

The editorial team of *Economic and Political Weekly* for permission to reprint 'On Skidelsky's Keynes', *Economic and Political Weekly*, vol. 40, 19 November 2005, pp. 4931–46.

The editor of *The American Economist* for permission to reprint 'Political Economy, Politics and Religion: Intertwined and Indissoluble Passions', *American Economist*, vol. 42, Fall, 1998, pp. 3–18.

The editor of *Keio Economic Studies* for permission to reprint 'A Teaching Model of the "Keynesian" System', published in *Keio Economic Studies*, vol. 6, no. 2 (1969), pp. 23–46.

Taylor and Francis Group for permission to reprint 'On Keynes and Chick on Prices in Modern Capitalism', ch. 12 of Philip Arestis, Meghnad Desai and Sheila Dow (eds), *Money, Macroeconomics and Keynes: Essays in honour of Victoria Chick, Volume One* (London, Routledge, 2002), pp. 115–23.

Edward Elgar Publishing Ltd, Cheltenham, Glos. for permission to reprint 'On Specifying the Demand for Imports in Macroeconomic Models', in Philip Arestis, John McCombie and Roger Vickerman (eds), *Growth and Economic Development: Essays in Honour of A.P. Thirlwell*, Cheltenham, UK and Northampton, MA: Edward Elgar Publishing, 60–67.

Taylor and Francis Group for permission to reprint 'The Theoretical and Political Importance of the Economics of Keynes: Or, What Would Marx and Keynes Have Made of the Happenings of the Past 30 Years

Or More?' In Mathew Forstater, Gary Mongiovi and Steven Pressman (eds), *Post Keynesian Macroeconomics. Essays in honour of Ingrid Rima*, London and New York: Routledge, 2007, pp. 56–69.

The editor of the *Economic and Labour Relations Review* for permission to reprint 'The Rise and, Hopefully, the Fall of Economic Neo-Liberalism in Theory and Practice', *Economic and Labour Relations Review*, vol. 20, December 2009, pp. 1–6.

Orient Blackswan Private Limited, Hyderabad, India, for permission to reprint 'Price Theory and Multinational Oligopoly: Kurt Rothschild and Stephen Hymer Revisited' Originally published in *Post-Reform Development in Asia: Essays for Amiya Kumar Bagchi*, Orient Blackswan, 2009, pp. 263–88.

The editor of *History of Economic Ideas* for permission to reprint 'A Revolution Yet to Be Accomplished: Reviewing Luigi Pasinetti, *Keynes and the Cambridge Keynesians: A "Revolution in Economics" to Be Accomplished*, Cambridge, Cambridge University Press, 2007', *History of Economics Ideas*, vol. 17, 2009, pp. 203–8.

John Wiley and Sons Ltd. For permission to reprint 'The Collected Writings of An Indian Sage: Reviewing Alaknanda Patel', *Economica*, vol. 79, 2012, pp. 199–206.

John Wiley and Sons Ltd. for permission to reprint 'Keynes and the Cambridge School', ch. 22 of Warren J. Samuels, Jeff E. Biddle and John B. Davis (eds), *A Companion to the History of Economic Thought*, Malden, USA, Oxford, UK: Blackwell Publishing, 2003, pp. 343–59.

Edward Elgar Publishing Ltd., Cheltenham, Glos. for permission to reprint Geoffrey Harcourt (2007), 'What Is the Cambridge Approach to Economics?' in Eckhard Hein and Achim Truger (eds), *Money, Distribution and Economic Policy. Alternatives to Orthodox Macroeconomics*, Cheltenham, UK and Northampton, MA: Edward Elgar Publishing, pp. 11–30.

The editor of the *Economic and Labour Relations Review* for permission to reprint 'Markets, Madness and a Middle Way Revisited', *Economic and Labour Relations Review*, vol. 17, April, 2007, pp. 1–10. Corrected version in vol. 18, November, 2007.

Edward Elgar Publishing Ltd., Cheltenham, Glos. for permission to reprint Geoffrey Harcourt (2008), 'The Contributions of Tom Asimakopoulos to Post-Keynesian Economics', in L. Randall Wray and Mathew Forstater (eds), *Keynes and Macroeconomics after 70 Years, Critical Assessments of The General Theory*, Chapter 5, Cheltenham, UK and Northampton, MA: Edward Elgar Publishing, pp. 64–79.

John Wiley and Sons Ltd. for permission to reprint 'Keith Septimus Frearson 18 September 1922–2 February 2000: A Memoir and a Tribute', *Economic Record*, vol. 76, September 2000, pp. 297–300.

Continuum International Publishing Group, a Bloomsbury company, for permission to reprint 'Reddaway, [William] Brian, 1913–2002', in Donald Rutherford (ed.), *The Biographical Dictionary of British Economists*, Volume 2, K-Z, Bristol: Thoemmes Continuum, 2004, pp. 998–1003.

Oxford University Press for permission to reprint 'Sukhamoy Chakravarty, 26 July, 1934–22 August, 1990', *Cambridge Journal of Economics*, vol. 15, 1991, pp. 1–3 and 'David Gawen Champernowne, 1912–2000: In Appreciation', *Cambridge Journal of Economics*, vol. 25, July, 2001, pp. 439–42.

The editors of the *Royal Economic Society Newsletter* for permission to reprint 'Robin Matthews', *Royal Economic Society Newsletter*, Issue No. 151, Octoter 2010, pp. 17–18.

Third Millenium Information Ltd. for permission to reprint 'Economics: from Moral Science to Game Theory', in Peter Pagnamenta (ed.), *The University of Cambridge: An 800th Anniversary Portrait,* London: Third Millennium Publishing, 2008, pp. 168–71.

The Cambridge Faculty of Economics for permission to reprint 'Geoff Harcourt on Cambridge Economics' First Century', in *Cambridge Economics Alumni Newsletter*, Issue Number 2, Autumn, 2009, pp 4–6.

Introduction: On Skidelsky's Keynes and Other Essays

Some months before leaving Cambridge for our (Joan's and my) permanent return to Australia in July 2010 (we flew home on 30 July, our fifty-fifth wedding anniversary), I proposed to Taiba Batool that I put together a further volume of selected essays.[1] She suggested that I make it two volumes: hence these two good companions, *On Skidelsky's Keynes and Other Essays* and *The Making of a Post-Keynesian Economist: Cambridge Harvest. Selected Essays of G. C. Harcourt.*

This volume starts with the title essay, 'On Skidelsky's Keynes' (2005) (Chapter 1). I wrote this with Sean Turnell, whose fine Ph.D dissertation, Turnell (1999), I had examined some years before and with whom I had become a close friend. My suggestion that we write a review article of Robert Skidelsky's remarkable three volume biography of Keynes, Skidelsky (1983, 1992, 2000), led to four and more years of hard work by both of us. The article was published in 2005 in *Economic and Political Weekly (EPW)*, the influential and widely read Indian journal, due to the encouragement of Jayati Ghosh, my former Ph.D student in Cambridge and continuing friend. The version published here is unexpurgated – because of a word limit, we had to remove from the *EPW* version what we thought were choice and relevant asides. In the essay we outline the extraordinary span and scope of Skidelsky's achievement, set out our views on his evaluation of Keynes's many dimensional life and works, indicate the few places where we took issue with Skidelsky, for example, on Étienne Mantoux's assessment (1945; 1952) based on Lord Keynes of *The General Theory*, of Mr Keynes's Marshallian-Pigovian analysis of *The Economic Consequences of the Peace* (1919), and also side with Skidelsky against the hostile American response in the person of Brad de Long (2000, 2002), to the analysis in volume III of Keynes's and Britain's wartime and postwar activities and relationship with the USA.

1

The next chapter (Chapter 2) is an autobiographical essay I wrote for Michael Szenberg's *American Economist* series of eminent (don't laugh) economists' lives and philosophies (Harcourt (1998)). It was subsequently reprinted in the 2004 volume, *Reflections of Eminent Economists*, edited by Szenberg and Lal Ramratten. (The volume was a follow up to Szenberg's edition of his first selection of life philosophies of economists, Szenberg (1992).) Through the volume I was able to make contact with some wonderful human beings who also happened to be economists. In the essay I set out my evaluation of how economics should be done and taught, especially in the light of my post-Vietnam war views and my political, religious and economic views generally.

The next essay 'A Teaching Model of the "Keynesian" System' (Chapter 3), arose from lectures I gave in 1967 to the third year macroeconomics class at Adelaide. I had just returned from my first spell of teaching in Cambridge, 1964–66.[2] The course was dubbed 'Ackley in Algebra' (Ackley (1961)). I tried to follow Joan Robinson's insistence that we should distinguish between the analysis of differences (comparisons) and analysis of changes (processes) – sometimes I think I was somewhere in between in the course. It did allow me to introduce the class to Post-Keynesian, Kaleckian ways of thinking. At the same time I stressed to them that making relevant simplifying assumptions would take them back to models they had met in their first year classes.[3]

Of the next five essays, four are chapters I contributed to *Festschrifts* for four dear friends – Victoria Chick, Tony Thirlwall, Ingrid Rima and Amiya Bagchi. The first three essays are Post-Keynesian/Kaleckian in approach; they are reflections on the fundamental contributions of the three economists concerned to our understanding of how capitalist economies work. The chapter for Victoria Chick's volume (Chapter 4) arose out of my admiration for her 1983 book on *The General Theory* and her selected essays (Chick (1992)), 'must reads' for anyone who truly wants to understand the nature of Keynes's revolutionary contributions *and* what happens in the modern world. I was especially interested in the role of market and short-period prices as signals to decision makers in the processes by which the point of effective demand is found in a given short-period situation in both Keynes's and Chick's analyses. Their accounts are far more subtle and detailed than those that have made their way into the textbooks on Keynesian economics (even Ackley (1961) and *Economic Activity*), which are more Hawtrey-like, using unintended changes in inventories rather than unexpected prices as the initiating signals.

The essay for Tony Thirlwall (Chapter 5) concerns the theoretical and econometric specification of the demand for imports in macroeconomic models. Only Thirlwall (with Charles Kennedy) (1997), Wonnacott (1975) and my colleagues and I at Adelaide related the demand for imports to overall expenditure rather than to income. I set out the reasons for this specification and suggested an interpretation for the differences in predicted demands for imports from the two specifications away from the point of effective demand. I then argue that the income specification is after all the correct one but not for the reasons usually given, quoting from T. S. Eliot's *Murder in the Cathedral* (1935) to emphasise the point. The argument rests on the two different concepts of aggregate demand to be found in *The General Theory* but not, alas, in the textbooks that followed it.

The essay for Ingrid Rima's volume (Chapter 6; Harcourt (2007a)), contains a critique of the major mainstream approaches to macroeconomics of the past 30 years and more, followed by the argument that Marx, Keynes and Michal Kalecki would have made far more sense of what has happened over that period (and before and after). Especially is this so for the years since 2008, the events of which occurred after the essay was written and published.

Amiya Bagchi and I have been friends from the early 1960s; Peter Nolan has been a wonderful colleague and friend during my past 28 years at Jesus and he is also a long standing friend of Amiya's. So it was great to combine with Peter in the chapter for Amiya's *Festschrift* (Chapter 8). We tested the inferences of two outstanding political economists, one, Kurt Rothschild, still going strong in his 90s[4], the other, Stephen Hymer, who tragically died when he was only 40, of what would be the most important role of large multinational corporations in the modern world. Peter has a large data set on these companies. We used their experiences recorded there to test the predictions of the two political economists. Rothschild's predictions from his 1947 *Economic Journal* classic were closer to the actual outcome than Hymer's prediction (1976, originally made in his Ph.D dissertation at MIT in 1960), that monopolies rather than large oligopolies would emerge.

In between the chapter for Ingrid Rima and the one for Amiya Bagchi is a short essay (Chapter 7) I wrote to celebrate 20 years of publication of the independent and progressive journal, *The Economic and Labour Relations Review*, from the School of Economics at the University of New South Wales. It is optimistically titled 'The Rise and, Hopefully, the Fall of Economic Neo-Liberalism in Theory and Practice'. Please read on.

Following the essays on post-Keynesian economics are two review articles (Chapters 9 and 10). I have always enjoyed having the space which writing a review article gives the reviewer to discuss the major themes in an author's book, hopefully setting them in context as well. Here I reprint my evaluation (Harcourt (2009b)), of Luigi Pasinetti's recent book (2007), which brings together over 50 years of original theorising by its author. He uses his distinction between truths that hold independently of institutions and those that are institutionally specific, to explain why he thinks that the revolution which Keynes started is yet to be accomplished. He argues that his distinction is the crucial base on which the fulfilled revolution could and should be built. Luigi and I first met in 1956 as Ph.D students at Cambridge, and we both taught there in the 1960s. He went back to Italy in the 1970s, and I returned to Cambridge in the 1980s, having also spent part of the 1970s there. So I also comment in the article on Luigi's take on what has and has not happened there and why.

The other review article (Harcourt (2011)), concerns the collected writings of a great Indian sage, A. K. Dasgupta, Patel (ed.) (2009). I first met Dasgupta in 1963 through our mutual friend, Joan Robinson, when he was Visiting Commonwealth Fellow at Gonville and Caius College in Cambridge. We remained in touch either in person or by letter until his death in 1992. His contributions cover the whole span of economics and political economy, from the history of our subject, always his starting point, through theory to applied work and policy in both developing and developed economies. The three volumes have been edited lovingly and expertly by his daughter, Alaknanda Patel, and two of the volumes are introduced by his son, Partha Dasgupta and his son-in-law, the late I. G. Patel, respectively. The clarity of A. K. Dasgupta's thought and the humanity of his philosophy shine through the pages of the volumes, making them an extraordinarily valuable collection of essays, not least for a world now faced with the effects of climate change and global warming, not to mention disquieting, rising levels of social and political unrest. Dasgupta always had an unconstrained admiration for Gandhi, and it is sad that his last major project on the economics of Gandhi never came to fruition.

I have included two survey articles, one co-authored with Prue Kerr, my long-time collaborator, both written in the past decade (Chapters 11 and 12). They are concerned with the characteristics of Cambridge economics in its greatest and most influential days – when they clearly were either distinct from those of other approaches and/or made the running for others to follow. Alas, those days are now long gone. The present decision makers in the Faculty are determined to make the Faculty a replica of the leading schools in the USA, so forgetting the roles for differentiated products, comparative advantage and historical tradition in economic analysis.

In Part VI on Policy, the first essay (Chapter 13; Harcourt (2007c)), revisits themes I set out in 1992 in the Second Donald Horne Address, 'Markets, Madness and a Middle Way', reprinted in Harcourt (1995). I first try to spell out the systemic effects of the Howard government legislation on enterprise bargaining and the extreme philosophy of 'let managers manage' in a deregulated environment. The backdrop to the analysis is the Kalecki–Russell–Salter 'vision' of how economies actually work.

I then examine the so-called coming pension crisis, reminding readers that all the sophistication in the world in designing ingenious saving schemes will come to nought unless public and private investment is simultaneously increased in order to create the overall saving from which saving may flow into these separate channels. I also discuss some of the intricacies of implementing monetary policy in the light of Hyman Minsky's fundamental analysis of the relationship between the financing of firms and the real rhythms of the economy.

The next essay (Chapter 14), 'Finance, Speculation and Stability: Post-Keynesian Policies for Modern Capitalism', was published in the *Festschrift* for Philip Arestis edited by Giuseppe Fontana, John McCombie and Malcolm Sawyer (2010a). It continues these and other themes, setting out package deals of policies for modern capitalism. When the recent crisis started and there were renewed (they never really ever went away) Jeremiah-like cries of deficit-size fetishism, I asked my audiences the following question: what would be wrong with having government expenditure on green friendly infrastructure, more teacher training, more Ph.D and post doctoral grants and so on, all financed by writing cheques on central banks, and doing so until economies had moved much closer to full employment? Then, I argued, something akin to balanced budget multipliers could be allowed to take over. No one could find any objections to this, and I subsequently discovered that such a proposal emanated many years before from Milton Friedman. So that is alright then.

I have continued to write intellectual biographical essays and tributes, much more often as I approach 80 because so many of my former colleagues and friends have died (not passed on). In Part VII I reprint tributes to my great friend from Ph.D years and on, Tom Asimakopulos; my teacher and Tom's and my friend, Keith Frearson; that great stalward of down-to-earth economics, Brian Reddaway; (with Ajit Singh) Sukhamoy Chakravarty, probably the most learned person I have ever met; one of the most original English theorists, David Champernowne; and the person I regard as the greatest all round British economist of his generation, Robin Matthews, who died recently in 2010 (Chapters 15 to 20).

Part VIII contains two general essays. The first (Chapter 21) is a draft of the essay which I wrote (with the help of Catherine Walston's superb editing) for the volume celebrating 800 years of Cambridge University in 2008–09 (Peter Pagnamenta (ed.) (2008)). This is coupled with the lecture I gave at the celebration of 100 years of the Economics Tripos at Cambridge in 2003 (Harcourt (2009a)). I named what I considered to be the outstanding volumes or articles of Cambridge economists of each decade (up to the 1970s). I drew on the reviews of the volumes together with my own evaluations. Reprinting these essays reminded me yet again how fortunate I have been to be associated with Cambridge, its economics faculty and its colleges (I belong to four) – and, even more, with its political economy.

None of the essays in either of these volumes could have been written, had it not been for the selfless decision by my family that I should return to Cambridge in September 1982. So I dedicate with heartfelt thanks this volume to Joan, Wendy, Robert, Timothy and Rebecca.

Notes

1. Previous volumes are *The Social Science Imperialists* (1982), *Controversies in Political Economy* (1986), *On Political Economists and Modern Political Economy* (1994a), *Post-Keynesian Essays in Biography* (1993), *Capitalism, Socialism and Post-Keynesianism* (1995), *50 Years a Keynesian and Other Essays* (2001a) and *Selected Essays on Economic Policy* (2001b).
2. I was a University Lecturer and a Fellow of Trinity Hall. As I had been appointed to these posts while I was on leave (1963–64) from Adelaide, I took three years' leave without pay as I felt I had a moral obligation to return to Adelaide.
3. By then the first year course at Adelaide had become *Economic Activity* (1967), co-authored by Peter Karmel, Bob Wallace and myself.
4. Alas, since I first wrote this Kurt has died on 15 November 2010 at the age of '96.

References

Ackley, Gardner (1961), *Macroeconomic Theory.* New York: Macmillan.

Arestis, Philip, John McCombie and Roger Vickerman (eds) (2006), *Growth and Economic Development. Essays in Honour of A.P. Thirlwall.* Cheltenham, UK; Northampton, USA, Edward Elgar.

Arestis, Philip, Meghnad Desai and Sheila Dow (eds) (2002), *Money, Macroeconomics and Keynes. Essays in Honour of Victoria Chick*. London: Routledge.

Chick, Victoria (1983), *Macroeconomics after Keynes. A Reconsideration of The General Theory*. Oxford: Philip Allan Publishers Limited.

Chick, Victoria (1992), *On Money, Method and Keynes. Selected Essays*. Ed. Philip Arestis and Sheila C. Dow. Houndmills, Basingstoke, Hampshire: Macmillan.

DeLong, J. Bradford (2000), 'Review of Robert Skidelsky, *John Maynard Keynes: Fighting for Britain 1937–46*', online book review http://www.j-bradford-delong.net/Econ_Articles/Reviews/Skidelsky3.html

DeLong, J. Bradford (2002), 'Review of Skidelsky's *John Maynard Keynes: Fighting for Britain, 1937–46*', *Journal of Economic Literature* 40, 155–62.

Eliot, T. S. (1935), *Murder in the Cathedral*. London: Faber and Faber.

Fontana, Giuseppe, John McCombie and Malcolm Sawyer (eds) (2010), *Macroeconomics, Finance and Money: Essays in Honour of Philip Arestis*. Houndmills, Basingstoke, Hampshire: Palgrave Macmillan.

Forstater, Mathew, Gary Mongiovi and Steven Pressman (eds) (2007), *Post-Keynesian Macroeconomics: Essays in Honour of Ingrid Rima*. London and New York: Routledge.

Harcourt, G. C. (1969), 'A teaching model of the "Keynesian" system', *Keio Economic Studies*, 6, 23–46, reprinted as 'A post-Keynesian development of the "Keynesian" model', in Nell (ed.) (1980), 551–64 (Essay 3).

Harcourt, G. C. (1982), *The Social Science Imperialists: Selected Essays. G. C. Harcourt*. Ed. Prue Kerr. London: Routledge and Kegan Paul.

Harcourt, G. C. (1986), *Controversies in Political Economy. Selected Essays by G.C. Harcourt*. Ed. O. F. Hamouda. Brighton: Wheatsheaf Books.

Harcourt, G. C. (1992a), *On Political Economists and Modern Political Economy: Selected Essays of G. C. Harcourt*. Edited by Claudio Sardoni, London: Routledge.

Harcourt, G. C. (1992b), 'On Keynes and Chick on Prices in Modern Capitalism', in Arestis, Desai and Dow (eds) (1992), 115–23. (Essay 4).

Harcourt, G. C. (1993), *Post-Keynesian Essays in Biography: Portraits of Twentieth Century Political Economists*. Houndmills, Basingstoke, Hampshire: Macmillan.

Harcourt, G. C. (1995), *Capitalism, Socialism and Post-Keynesianism: Selected Essays of G. C. Harcourt*. Cheltenham, Glos: Edward Elgar.

Harcourt, G. C. (1998), 'Political Economy, Politics and Religion: Intertwined and Indissoluble Passions', *American Economist*, 42, 3–18, reprinted in Michael Szenberg and Lall Ramratten (eds) (2004), *Reflections of Eminent Economists*. Cheltenham, UK, Northampton MA, USA: Edward Elgar. (Essay 2).

Harcourt, G. C. (2000), 'Keith Septimus Frearson 19 September 1922–2 February 2000: A Memoir and a Tribute', *Economic Record*, 76, 297–300. (Essay 16).

Harcourt, G. C. (2001a), *50 Years a Keynesian and Other Essays*. London: Palgrave Macmillan.

Harcourt, G. C. (2001b), *Selected Essays on Economic Policy*, London: Palgrave Macmillan.

Harcourt, G. C. (2001c), 'David Gawen Champernowne, 1912–2000: In Appreciation', *Cambridge Journal of Economics*, 25, 439–42. (Essay 19).

Harcourt, G. C. (2004), 'Reddaway, William Brian (1913–2002)', in Rutherford (ed.) (2004), 998–1003. (Essay 17).

Harcourt, G. C. (2006), 'On Specifying the Demand for Imports in Macroeconomic Models' in Arestis, McCombie and Vickerman (eds) (2006), 60–67. (Essay 5).

Harcourt, G. C. (2007a), 'The Theoretical and Political Importance of Keynes: Or, What Would Marx and Keynes Have Made of the Happenings of the Past 30 Years Or More?' in Forstater, Mongiovi and Pressman (eds) (2007), 56–69. (Essay 6).

Harcourt, G. C. (2007b), 'What Is the Cambridge Approach to Economics?', in Hein and Truger (eds) (2007), 11–30. (Essay 12).

Harcourt, G. C. (2007c), 'Markets, Madness and a Middle Way Revisited', *Economic and Labour Relations Review*, 17, 207, 1–10. (Essay 13).

Harcourt, G. C. (2008), 'The Contributions of Tom Asimakopulos to Post-Keynesian Economics', in Wray and Forstater (eds) (2008), 64–79. (Essay 15).

Harcourt, G. C. (2009a), 'The Rise and, Hopefully, the Fall of Neo-Liberalism in Theory and Practice', *Economic and Labour Relations Review*, 20, 1–6. (Essay 7).

Harcourt, G. C. (2009b), 'A Revolution Yet to Be Accomplished: Reviewing Luigi Pasinetti, *Keynes and the Cambridge Keynesians. A "Revolution in Economics" to Be Accomplished*, Cambridge: Cambridge University Press, 2007', *History of Economic Ideas*, 17, 203–8. (Essay 9).

Harcourt, G. C. (2009c), 'Geoff Harcourt on Cambridge Economics First Century', *Cambridge Economics Alumni Newsletter*, Autumn, 2009, 4–6. (Essay 22).

Harcourt, G. C. (2010a), 'Finance, Speculation and Stability: Post-Keynesian Policies for Modern Capitalism', in Fontana, McCombie and Sawyer (eds) (2010), 237–49. (Essay 14).

Harcourt, G. C. (2010b), 'Robin Matthews: A Tribute', *Royal Economic Society Newsletter*, October, 2010, 17–18. (Essay 20).

Harcourt, G. C. (2011), 'The Collected Writings of An Indian Sage: Reviewing Alaknanda Patel (ed.), *The Collected Works of A. K. Dasgupta*, 3 Vols, New Delhi: Oxford University Press, 2009', *Economica*. (Essay 10).

Harcourt, G. C. (2012), *The Making of a Post-Keynesian Economist: Cambridge Harvest. Selected Essays of G.C. Harcourt*. Houndsmills, Basingstoke, Hants: Palgrave Macmillan.

Harcourt, G. C., P. H. Karmel and R. H. Wallace (1967), *Economic Activity*. Cambridge: Cambridge University Press.

Harcourt, G. C. and Prue Kerr (2003), 'Keynes and the Cambridge School', in Samuels, Biddle and Davis (eds) (2003), 343–59. (Essay 11).

Harcourt, G. C. and P. H. Nolan (2009), 'Price Theory and Multinational Oligopoly: Kurt Rothschild and Stephen Hymer Revisited', in Manaj Kumar Sanyal, Mandira Sanyal and Shahina Amin (eds) (2009), 263–88. (Essay 8).

Harcourt, G. C. and Ajit Singh (1991), 'Sukhamoy Chakravarty, 26 July 1934 – 22 August 1990', *Cambridge Journal of Economics*, 15, 1–3. (Essay 18).

Harcourt, G. C. and Sean Turnell (2005), 'On Skidelsky's Keynes', *Economic and Political Weekly*, XI, 4931–46. (Essay 1).

Harcourt, G. C. and Catherine Walston (2008), 'Economics: from Moral Science to Game Theory', in Pagnamenta (ed.) (2008), 168–71. (Essay 21).

Hein, Eckhard and Achim Truger (eds) (2007), *Money, Distribution and Economic Policy: Alternatives to Orthodox Macroeconomics*. Cheltenham, UK; Northampton, USA: Edward Elgar.

Hymer, S. (1976), *The International Operations of National Firms: A Study of Foreign Direct Investment*. Cambridge, MA: The MIT Press.

Keynes, J. M. (1919), *The Economic Consequences of the Peace*, London: Macmillan. C.W., vol II, 1971.

Keynes, J. M. (1936), *The General Theory of Employment, Interest and Money*, London: Macmillan. C. W., vol VII, 1973.

Mantoux, Étienne (1945; 1952), *The Carthaginian Peace or the Economic Consequences of Mr Keynes*, with an introduction by R. C. K. Enson and a Foreword by Paul Mantoux. New York: Charles Scribner's Sons.

Nell, E. J. (ec.) (1980), *Growth, Profits and Property: Essays in the Revival of Political Economy*. Cambridge: Cambridge University Press.

Pagnamenta, Peter (ed) (2008) *The University of Cambridge: An 800th Anniversary Portrait*. London: Third Millenium.

Pasinetti, L. L. (2007), *Keynes and the Cambridge Keynesians: A 'Revolution in Economics' to Be Accomplished*. Cambridge: Cambridge University Press.

Rothschild, K. W. (1947), 'Price Theory and Oligopoly', *Economic Journal*, 57, 299–320.

Rutherford, Donald (ed.) (2004), *The Biographical Dictionary of British Economists, Volume 2, K–Z*. Bristol: Thoemmes Continuum.

Samuels, Warren J., Jeff E. Biddle and John B. Davis (eds) (2003), *A Companion to the History of Economic Thought*, Malden, USA, Oxford, UK: Blackwell Publishing.

Sanyal, Manoj Kumar, Mandira Sanyal and Shahina Amin (eds) (2009), *Post-Reform in Asia: Essays for Amiya Kumar Bagchi*. Hyderabad, India: Orient Blackswan Private Limited.

Skidelsky, Robert (1983), *John Maynard Keynes, Volume One: Hopes Betrayed 1883–1920*. London: Macmillan.

Skidelsky, Robert (1992), *John Maynard Keynes, Volume Two: The Economist as Saviour, 1920–37*. London: Macmillan.

Skidelsky, Robert (2000), *John Maynard Keynes, Volume Three: Fighting for Britain 1937–46*. London: Macmillan.

Szenberg, Michael (ed.) (1992), *Eminent Economists: Their Life Philosophies*. Cambridge: Cambridge University Press.

Szenberg, Michal and Lall Ramratten (eds) (2004), *Reflections of Eminent Economists*. Cheltenham UK; Northampton, MA, USA: Edward Elgar.

Thirlwall, A. P. (1997), *Macroeconomic Issues from a Keynesian Perspective. Selected Essays of A. P. Thirlwall. Volume Two*. Cheltemham UK; Northampton, MA, USA: Edward Elgar.

Turnell, Sean (1999), *Monetary Reformers, Amateur Idealists and Keynesian Crusaders. Australian Economists' International Advocacy, 1925–1950*, unpublished Ph.D thesis, Macquarie University.

Wonnacott, P. (1975), *Macroeconomics*. London: Irwin.

Wray, Randall and Mathew Forstater (eds) (2008), *Keynes and Macroeconomics after 70 Years. Critical Assessments of The General Theory*. Cheltenham, UK; Northampton, MA, USA: Edward Elgar.

Part I
Title Essay

1
On Skidelsky's Keynes (2005)*

with Sean Turnell

I

With the publication of the third volume of his life of John Maynard Keynes, Robert Skidelsky has brought to fruition probably the greatest biography of the twentieth century, certainly the greatest biography of an economist.[†] We agree with Bradford De Long's judgment: 'as a whole, [it] is the finest biography of an economist that I have ever read, or that I expect ever to read' (De Long, 2002, 155). Skidelsky's fundamental aim in the three volumes is to reclaim Keynes for history and this he has done. In this review of the three volumes, Skidelsky (1983, 1992, 2000), though, we concentrate on Keynes, the economist, in particular, on the nature and extent of his contributions to economic theory and practice, how he did economics and what we may learn from this.

To do so is not to ignore Skidelsky's masterly account of Keynes as a person – the development of his character, values, attitudes, sense of well-being, personal confidence and balance over his far-too-short a life in calendar terms. (In terms of intellectual output, it is a cliché to say that he packed far more into his short life than even the most gifted and quick-thinking of his contemporaries or successors could ever have hoped to aspire to.) Skidelsky's brilliant account of Keynes's personality at each stage of his life lays the bases and illuminates the reasons for the changes in Keynes's views and for the specific characteristics of Keynes's contributions over his life time.

Keynes emerges from Skidelsky's skilled portraits as an extraordinarily complex person, much more extreme Jekyll and Hyde than most of us.

---

* Originally published in *Economic and Political Weekly*, vol. 40, 19 November 2005, pp. 4931–46.

Keynes himself was conscious of one of Skidelsky's shrewdest insights. Skidelsky was asked whether he would have liked Keynes; he answered that it would depend upon whether Keynes would have liked him ('yes, enormously, had he liked me', Skidelsky, 18 December 2000). Keynes was painfully aware of the negative effect that aspects of his personality could have on people. He divided his friends (and others) into those who thought he was physically ugly and those who did not. (Keynes thought he was. In a letter (27 April 1905) to Arthur Hobhouse, his first real love, he wrote that he had 'a clever head, a weak character, an affectionate disposition, and a repulsive appearance', Skidelsky 1983, 131.) For a seemingly supremely confident person, Skidelsky shows that Keynes often felt most insecure, that he was intensely sensitive, not least, of course, when his closest friends turned on him at various times in his life: for example, when Duncan Grant left Lytton Strachey for Keynes in 1908 (unsurprisingly, it was Strachey who most turned against him)and, especially, during World War I when he only finally redeemed himself in their eyes by writing *The Economic Consequences of the Peace*, Keynes (1919); and this, despite valiant efforts to help his friends in practical ways when they were under threat for their conscientious objection views during the war.

Keynes could be both incredibly rude in discussion and argument and extraordinarily kind (he had a capacity for loyal, affectionate and practical friendship). He was invariably kind and supportive to students, turning their half-sensible thoughts at his formidable Political Economy Club into brilliant insights and following their careers with sympathy and practical support at key junctures. He practised old-fashioned loyalties – to his parents, his school (Eton) and his college (King's). He was bisexual, almost exclusively gay until he married Lydia Lopokova in 1925 (giving fresh meaning to Mary Paley Marshall's remark that it was the best thing Maynard ever did). Sometimes his relationships were casual and callous; but when they were serious, there was deep commitment, generous gifts and continuous correspondence when they were separated. Indeed his group made letter writing an art form. No doubt they had one eye on posterity, but they also genuinely believed in articulating completely honest and deeply felt emotions to loved ones, as well as delighting in often exaggerated gossip for the amusement of their readers. The Keynes's marriage was an exceptionally happy one, not least because they made each other laugh, a firm foundation of any marriage. It is our belief that this happy marriage played a crucial, even central role in releasing the creative original energy that resulted in the writing of *The General Theory*, not least by transforming Keynes's own feelings of well-being and contentment, allowing him to come more comfortably to terms with the complex traits that made up his personality.

Keynes could be gross, crude, coarse, he had a Rabelaisian wit, an obsessive curiosity about sexual matters, and he often lacked refinement.[1] He could be a show-off and a know-all. This emanated from his remarkably quick and piercing mind, his ability to 'gut' books in a few hours (not that this did not show now and then) and an insatiable curiosity about all manner of things. Keynes had the class and racial prejudices of his time, expressed in distasteful, often disgraceful terms to modern eyes and ears, yet rarely acted upon in his actual relationships. For at his core he was a deeply serious person, still a Victorian as well as an Edwardian, seeking for a philosophy by which to live in both private and public life.

This he was to get from G. E. Moore's *Principia Ethica* (1903) to which he was introduced six months after he became an Apostle.[2] Skidelsky argues that it was 'the most important book in [Keynes's] life' (Skidelsky, 1983, 119). Moore posed a conundrum: 'was it possible both to be good and do good?' (He suspected not). We argue, on the basis of Skidelsky's narrative and other evidence, that Keynes's own life provides a resounding 'yes' to the query.[3] Up to the writing of *The Economic Consequences* (this is discussed at the end of Volume 1), Keynes was a wonderfully clever but often a flip and not overly serious person even though he had developed a philosophy based on Moore's arguments in which transparent friendship combined with loyalty and honesty were the principal 'goods'. Moreover, Skidelsky (1983, 117) argues, 'After 1903 the partition of his life into a private and public sphere became more obvious': 'Philosophy, aesthetics, friendship' in the first, 'political and practical affairs' in the other. The former was his greater priority and 'there was little flow of feeling from one to the other.' His experiences during the First World War matured him and made him fully serious (but no less witty and possessed of an enormous zest for life combined with a huge number of activities). Finally, as we argued, marriage took him to a higher plane, releasing for the rest of his life (and despite his appalling illnesses, from his first heart attack in 1937 on) the energies of a truly creative original thinker/genius.

II

Keynes's first degree was in mathematics. In 1905 he was classed as Twelfth Wrangler, a respectable but rather disappointing result (for JNK but not JMK who had aimed for exactly that result). He stayed on at King's for a fourth year, initially undecided as to whether he should concentrate on moral philosophy or economics. As it turned out he only ever had eight weeks formal instruction in economics, in the Michaelmas Term of 1905 when he wrote essays for Alfred Marshall. The rest he learnt on the job.[4] The first economics book that he read was Jevons's *Theory of Political Economy* (1871; 1970). Keynes thought Jevons to be 'one of *the* minds of the century' (quoted by Skidelsky, 1983, 151, emphasis in original), the author of 'the first modern book in econom-ics – [the author of which] chiselled in stone where Marshall knits in wool' (Keynes, 1933; *C.W.*, vol. X, 1972, 131). He also read Marshall's two privately printed monographs on domestic and international val-ues, Cournot, Edgeworth and, of course, the *Principles*. Keynes wrote to Lytton Strachey (15 December 1905): 'I find economics increasingly satisfactory, and I think I am rather good at it. I want to manage a railway or organise a Trust or at least swindle the investing public...so easy and fascinating to master the principle of these things' (Skidelsky, 1983, 165). Marshall wanted him to take the Economics Tripos and as late as May 1906 was telling him that with a little revision he could get a First in Part II; but Keynes had decided by then to take the Civil Service Examinations.

In the event he came second to Otto Neimeyer, who scored 3917/6000 to Keynes's 3498/6000, and received his worst mark in economics (256/600). Neimeyer went to the Treasury and Keynes had to be content with the India Office where he won golden opinions from his contem-poraries and superiors, despite his relatively short stay and the fact that he spent much of his working hours writing his dissertation for King's. Though he was to write the admired *Indian Currency and Finance* (1913), and to serve on the Royal Commission on Indian Currency and Finance (1913) and even to start editing the *Economic Journal* (in October 1911), he was not an original economist (or even primarily an economist) until the 1920s. By this we mean that he applied what he had learnt from Marshall and the approach of the Cambridge school generally but did not feel he had to amend it in any major way to make his case. For him the quantity theory of money and free trade were twin planks of an orthodoxy he supported and applied. '... Keynes expounded the quan-tity theory with all the fervour of the true believer.' So, even though we know now that 'the history of the Keynesian revolution is largely the story of Keynes's escape from the quantity theory', there was little hint of that escape before the First World War (Skidelsky, 1983, 204).

We must take issue with Skidelsky (1983, 214) who argues that Marshall's version of the quantity theory was a short-period ('short run') proposition. Surely it was a long-period proposition reflecting the heart of the *Principles*, Book V, the long-period theory of normal prices and quantities in competitive equilibrium. When adapted to the requirements of the quantity theory the market-clearing properties of each and every market defined T (Y in the Cambridge version) as the long-period Say's Law position of the economy, V(or k) was given by history and institutional developments, and M by the monetary authorities so that P was the only unknown variable in the long period. Or, at least, even if this were not always so Keynes certainly thought it was, as is witnessed to by the passage containing his best known remarks about mortality in the long run and the 'too easy, too useless a task' economists (read Marshall) set themselves by concentrating on the causes of the 'flat' ocean 'when the storm is long past' (Keynes, 1923; *C.W.*, vol. IV, 1971, 65).

Keynes's first intellectual love was philosophy and his chosen topic within it was probability, on which he worked for many years, first for his Fellowship dissertation at King's (it took him two goes to get it) and then more intermittently up to its publication in 1921 as *A Treatise on Probability*. The failure to get elected to a Fellowship at King's in March 1908 was his first major intellectual set back (Skidelsky (1983, 184) judges it 'the worst academic blow Maynard ever suffered'). Marshall softened the blow by getting Keynes back to Cambridge as a lecturer in the relatively new Economics Tripos (it started in 1903), paid for by Marshall, then Pigou (who succeeded Marshall in the Chair of Political Economy on 30 May 1908). The salary was £100 a year, supplemented in Keynes's case (there were two such posts, Walter Layton getting the other) by a further £100 from John Neville Keynes. On his twenty-fourth birthday, 5 June 1908, Keynes resigned from the India Office. He had written to his father in April that, if he accepted the post 'nothing would suit [him] better' – [although he] should have at once begin to learn a little economics [he] should have more time for rewriting [his] dissertation, with which [his] mind is much absorbed though not [his] time' (Skidelsky, 1983, 184–85).

Skidelsky (1983, 152) finds the key to Keynes's approach to probability in an early essay (23 January 1904), 'Ethics in relation to conduct'. The essay arose from Keynes's reactions to Moore's philosophy, in particular, on how to frame rules of conduct which would be consistent with alternative good states of mind, the ultimate objective. Though Keynes always remained a Moorite, he was never ever exclusively so. Moore thought it virtually impossible both to be good and to do good. Moreover, because of uncertainty, to follow accepted rules of morality was the best we could do and this would moreover bring the best results (Skidelsky, 1983, 152). Keynes wanted to go further, by showing we could make a relative probability judgment without having the knowledge Moore said we should have before our decisions could be rational. For Keynes, 'a statement of probability always has reference to the available evidence and cannot be refuted or confirmed by subsequent events' (Skidelsky, 1983, 153). We must make the best estimate of results in the current circumstances.

Keynes's dissertation developed the ideas of the paper read to the Apostles in January 1904. He set out to create a 'new kind of logic' applicable to 'doubtful argument and uncertain conclusions' which nevertheless may be rational and objective. An important insight was that we recognise that objectively evidence can be *real* yet not conclusive. He argued that we need not be troubled – much – that probability in the strict sense is indefinable since this is also true of many of our most necessary and fundamental ideas. Skidelsky (1983, 183–84) highlights the boldness of Keynes's claim for his ideas – that probability should be considered as the *general theory* of logic with deductive logic the special case which applied to cases of certainty. The parallel with Keynes's claim for his other *General Theory* is, of course, noted by Skidelsky.

Just as Moore was a crucial influence on Keynes's ethics and subsequent conduct, Edmund Burke has strong claims to being 'Keynes's political hero', so that Keynes's life, (Skidelsky, 1983, 157) argues, was to be balanced between two sets of moral claims. 'His duty as an individual was to achieve good states of mind for himself and for those he was directly concerned with; his duty as a citizen was to help to achieve a happy state of affairs for society.' He thought the two claims were logically independent of one another 'and attached greater priority to the first...except when he thought the state was in danger' (Skidelsky, 1983, 157).[5]

III

Recent research finds three elements from Keynes's theory of probability and his philosophical musings which are most relevant for his economics. A key theme is Keynes's argument that in certain disciplines, of which economics is one, the whole may be more than the sum of the parts. Keynes's realisation of this, that overall systems could have lives of their own, that the behaviour of parts (or even atoms) could be constrained by overall relationships would increasingly influence his subsequent work in economics.[6] A typical statement by Keynes on this is to be found in his essay on Edgeworth: 'Mathematical Psychics has not...fulfilled its early promise...The atomic hypothesis which has worked so splendidly in physics breaks down in psychics. We are faced at every turn with the problems of discreteness, of discontinuity – the whole is not equal to the sum of the parts' (Keynes, 1933; *C.W.*, vol. X, 1972, 262).

Secondly, Keynes's systematic pondering on the principles of reasonable or sensible (or, in some instances, not sensible) behaviour in an uncertain environment which started with his work on probability, runs all though the analysis in *The General Theory* itself. Here Marshall as well as Keynes's earlier self were key influences. Thirdly, Keynes's philosophical reasoning discerned many different yet appropriate languages for the analysis of different situations and areas. In economics there is a spectrum of languages running all the way from intuition and poetry through lawyer-type arguments to formal logic and mathematics. All have a rightful place depending upon the issues, or the aspects of issues being discussed. All are consistent with arguments being possible and knowledge being acquired: 'if logic investigates the general principles of valid thought, the study of arguments to which it is rational to attach *some* weight, is as much a part of it as the study of those which are demonstrative' (Keynes, 1921; *C.W.*, vol. VIII, 1973, 3, emphasis in original). Skidelsky's researches provide ample evidence for these generalisations which were to be of much greater importance in Keynes's writings in the 1920s and 1930s and especially when the ideas of *The General Theory* were being developed.

IV

The last major episode of Volume I is concerned with Keynes's role in the First World War, what he did as an economist at the Treasury and at Versailles, his ambivalence about the war and his deep unhappiness about the attitude of his Bloomsbury friends to him as a result. As we know, the episode culminated in his resignation from the Treasury and the writing of *The Economic Consequences of the Peace* (1919), which not only marked his arrival at full moral and intellectual maturity but also made him famous nationally and internationally. The book itself was a passionate, humanitarian application of basically Marshallian orthodoxy to the questions of what implementing reparations in accordance with what the French wanted and Lloyd George (until too late) and Woodrow Wilson were hoodwinked into accepting, would do to the delicate institutions and tacit agreements which underlay the social, political and economic processes of the European economy.

Étienne Mantoux (who was killed just before the defeat of Nazi Germany) wrote a critique of the main arguments of Mr. Keynes's book from the point of view of the analysis in Lord Keynes's *General Theory*. It was published after his death with the title *The Carthaginian Peace or the Economic Consequences of Mr. Keynes* (1945; 1952).

Skidelsky (397–400) thinks that Keynes's book emerges relatively unscathed from Mantoux's critique but this is one of very few of his judgments we do not share. Mantoux was a patriotic Frenchman who died fighting for his country. He was fiercely defensive of its interests but he was also a man of deep intelligence, charm and obvious compassion, with which traits was allied a large fund of common sense. Keynes was, as his *Times* obituarist wrote, a very great Englishman, but he was also a creature of his time, of his class and of his friendships, so that his sympathies were more, it has to be said, with the Germans than with the French. Perhaps this affected his judgment at the time – Mantoux was too polite and decent to say so. But, most importantly, it was the theoretical hindsight provided first and foremost by Keynes himself which allowed Mantoux to make such a strong critique of the early Keynes while at the same time yielding to no one in his admiration of the insights and innovations of the later Keynes.

Keynes's book resulted from passionate but humane anger – anger at folly and injustice as he saw it. To write it he marshalled not only his acute understanding of the received economic theory of the time but also his own sense of orders of magnitude, of the different lengths of time of nevertheless closely interrelated economic processes, in order to make a persuasive economic case against the effects of the provisions of the Treaty. He allied this with withering attacks on the key personalities involved and a sustained attack on what he saw as the political aims of the principal participants both in their own countries and abroad. He also analysed the constraints of *Realpolitik* as they – and he – saw them.

The book played a significant role in the decision of the US Senate not to ratify the Treaty of Versailles and so helped to send the United States in an isolationist direction. Keynes himself had hoped to make Germany the bulwark which kept the United States out of Europe, for like most of his contemporaries in the United Kingdom of that time, he did not like the shift in financial power from London to New York which was then occurring. As the book articulated eloquently and passionately what many others were thinking then, it had a major impact on public and professional, as well as political, opinion in the United Kingdom. It may even be seen, perhaps, as one of the sources of the subsequent policy of appeasement. (Keynes himself was not an appeaser, though he did feel that the *economic* policies of Nazi Germany could be shown to be complementary to the ideas and diagnosis of *The General Theory*.)

The Economic Consequences of the Peace therefore had a direct and very considerable purchase on public affairs in the years following its publication and, more than three-quarters of a century after its first appearance, continues to exercise a powerful influence on our understanding of some of the key turning points in twentieth-century history. The idea that the victorious Allies imposed on Germany conditions which could only lead to economic collapse was, of course, Keynes's, and has been taken up by historians of almost all political persuasions. Germany's economy did indeed collapse in the 1920s, but Mantoux demonstrates that this was not as a result of the payment of reparations, yet historians continue to cite Versailles as the cause of that economic collapse and so, indirectly, of Hitler's subsequent rise to power. Keynes's brief, brilliant polemic colours the way in which numerous historians, and the public at large, see the unfolding of events in Germany in the decades between Versailles and the outbreak of the Second World War. Mantoux's book therefore, is not simply a critique of Keynes's famous work but a stimulus to question the received wisdom's interpretation of the unfolding of events in Germany between the two wars.

Étienne Mantoux's book has not led us to revise our general judgment of Keynes's specific motives and the changes that occurred in his character, but it does make us question the soundness of the theoretical and empirical aspects of Keynes's arguments.[7]

The irony, of course, is that, as Mantoux stresses, the theoretical arguments against Mr. Keynes of *The Economic Consequences of the Peace* are those of Lord Keynes of *The General Theory*.[8] Keynes based his arguments on an implicit assumption of the full employment of resources so that vast structural changes both in Germany and in the countries receiving reparations would have been needed to make their imposition effective. Keynes judged them, on the basis of his sense of the orders of magnitude, to be impossible, economically as well as politically. Mantoux shows in great detail that on both these fronts Keynes was wrong. If we start with the model of *The General Theory*, and especially from a situation of unemployed resources, we know that we may have our cake and eat it too, both in the giving and receiving countries. This is not to say that the practical and political details were not difficult, only that they were not insuperable. Mantoux shows by detailed historical examples that more than was contemplated in the Treaty and its associated reparations was in fact accomplished by Nazi Germany in peace time and in the early years of the Second World War.

It is a tragedy that neither of these two fine, intelligent, admirable human beings lived through the early decades of the new peace. For their combined wisdom might have served to create a more lasting set of institutions with which to fulfil their own now agreed and agreeable ideals. Skidelsky (1983, 402) eloquently concludes his first volume: 'The prospect of civilisation briefly opened up by Moore's *Principia Ethica* had receded over the horizon. The rest of Keynes's life was spent in trying to bring it back into sight.'

V

Volume II, 'the economist as saviour', is a rich tapestry woven around the central core of the publication of *A Treatise on Probability* in 1921, and the making of *A Tract on Monetary Reform* (1923), *A Treatise on Money* (1930) and *The General Theory* (1936). Skidelsky skilfully relates Keynes's extraordinarily varied activities to the changing political, social and economic situations over the period 1920 to 1937. His aim is to provide a detailed narrative of 'the reshaping of [Keynes's] life purpose, his metamorphosis from aesthete, philosopher and administrator into world saviour' (Skidelsky, 1992, *xv*). The word 'saviour' is significant. Keynes more and more came to feel that his generation was a lucky one in that though they repudiated Christian beliefs, they were grounded in Christian moral values, unlike the generation that followed them, Bloomsbury's children, to whom Keynes read 'My early beliefs' in 1938 (the essay itself was published only after Keynes's death).[9]

In the 1920s and the beginning of the 1930s, Keynes was much involved in politics, both in the revival of the Liberal Party (he split from Asquith, a most painful personal process, to champion the return of Lloyd George) and government commissions and bodies, e.g. the Macmillan Committee and the Economic Advisory Council. The aim of both his theoretical and academic writings of the 1920s and of his journalism, often through the *Nation*, but also daily newspapers, was to influence government policy on a number of issues: the appropriate monetary policy with which to tackle inflation and deflation, the return to the Gold Standard at pre-First-World-War-parity in 1925, the case for public works expenditure in the second half of the 1920s. In the 1930s, following the eclipse of the Liberal Party in the 1929 and 1931 elections, Keynes was centred more on Cambridge and Tilton. He collaborated with, on the whole, a different, more academic set of colleagues – the members of the Cambridge 'Circus' (Richard Kahn, Austin and Joan Robinson, James Meade, Piero Sraffa) and Roy Harrod in Oxford. Increasingly, he fell out with Dennis Robertson to whom he had been most close in the development of new ideas in the 1920s, Hubert Henderson who left academia for journalism and then the civil service, and, intellectually, his old friend and rival Ralph Hawtrey on theory and policy (Hawtrey was in effect the first professional economist at the Treasury).

Keynes's tactics as a speculator in the 1920s were akin to those of a Hicksian 'snatcher' (Hicks 1954; 1983). Keynes speculated on the futures markets and the forward exchanges (the latter is the background to one of his most insightful and difficult pieces of theoretical writing, the chapter on the forward exchanges in *A Tract*, 1923, ch. 3) – and ended up a loser.

He became a Hicksian 'sticker' in the 1930s (select a small enough portfolio of shares in companies, the doings of which you could reasonably expect to be able to monitor and master and then, by and large, stick to them). He became a very rich man, mainly because of the revival of the US stock market in the 1930s.

Skidelsky confirms that Keynes's marriage to Lydia Lopokova was indeed *the* watershed of his personal and intellectual life. It is no accident that the writing of *The General Theory* coincided with Keynes's inspiration (and money) behind the setting up of the Arts Theatre in Cambridge, partly to allow Lydia to act, partly as a selfless gift to the City of Cambridge. The Arts Theatre opened the day before *The General Theory* was published on 4 February 1936: 'two projects, linked by a common feeling, converging at a single moment in time' (Skidelsky, 1992, 536).

Keynes saw his role as one of providing a middle way between untrammelled *laissez-faire* conditions, on the one hand, and the centrally planned economies of Communist and Fascist societies, on the other. His object was to save capitalism from itself; he wanted to restore expectations of stability and progress in a world cut adrift, to make possible a society where his philosophy combining private morality with appropriate public activities could be realised. The artist, the scientist and the scholar could thrive, their potential being realisable because of the base provided by the exuberance of the capitalist business person and the sheer productivity of capitalism. Such a social system did not necessarily have to be associated with completely democratic institutions. Keynes was not averse to indirect rule by benevolent philosopher kings or even by benevolent despots. Nevertheless, as Skidelsky argues, overall Keynes's 'genius was to have developed an analysis of economic disorder which justified forms of state intervention compatible with traditional liberal values...the last of the great English liberals' (Skidelsky, 1992, *xv*).

Keynes had some influence on the involved bright young who read economics and went to his Political Economy Club at Cambridge in the 1930s and who were drawn to Marxism and Communism.[10] It has to be said that Keynes never really understood Marx yet explicitly despised him[11] even though, as Claudio Sardoni (1987) has shown, when Marx and Keynes examined the same issues, they usually came up with the same answers, adjectives excepted. This is hardly surprising, since along with Michal Kalecki and, it could be argued, Joseph Schumpeter, they are the deepest interpreters of the processes at work in nineteenth and twentieth-century capitalism.

As Keynes's faith in the efficacy of monetary policy faltered, especially in a deep sustained slump, so he changed his theoretical interest from examining the trade/credit cycle in a dynamic framework, especially in *A Tract* and *A Treatise on Money*, and concentrating on the roles of prices and the rate of interest, to trying to explain sustained unemployment within a more static framework and giving more weight to fiscal and regional policy. The transition required a complete transformation of the Marshallian/Pigovian framework in which he had been brought up to the analysis of a monetary production economy where an environment of inescapable uncertainty led to a continuing fight between inaction associated with the desire to hoard and action associated with enterprise. Both were by-products of the unlovely but necessary (and instinctive) love of money. (Keynes was much influenced by the new Freudian ideas brought to the United Kingdom by his friends in Bloomsbury, especially James Strachey.) The key variables now became total levels of output, income (and their composition) and employment, though the money rate of interest and the general price level also still had major roles to play in the story.

VI

Keynes's theory as opposed to his policy proposals in the 1920s was set firmly within the Marshallian/Pigovian tradition. In *A Tract* the overall framework was that of the quantity theory of money (this is the major reason why some modern Chicago economists regard it as Keynes's best book). Not only is Keynes explicit about this – failure to accept the quantity theory is conclusive evidence of ignorance and stupidity combined, for 'the theory is fundamental ... correspondence with fact not open to question' (Keynes, 1923; *C.W.*, vol. IV, 1971, 61) – but there is also evidence from pupils at his lectures before the first world war that his exposition of the theory was 'the best complete concise outline which [they] knew of'.[12] But Keynes recognised not only, as his teachers had, that it was a long-period proposition but also that monetary policy should be directed at the increasing fluctuations in V (or k) in the short run in order to avoid or subdue the excesses of inflation or deflation. Keynes already accepted deflation as the greater evil (apart from hyper-inflations). The chosen instrument was the rate of interest controlled by the Central Banks of the United Kingdom and the USA. The object was to reduce the amplitude of the fluctuations in the general price level (and, thus, output and employment) around their long-period equilibrium values in which in competitive conditions the real wage cleared the labour market and the natural rate of interest equated the desire to save (in the sense of present consumption foregone for future consumption yet to come) with the desire to invest (consumption foregone technically converted into future consumption yet to come), so determining the composition of total output associated with the market-clearing level of employment.

Keynes had in mind an open economy and for policy stressed that the claims of internal balance (as we would say now) should have top priority, that external balance, or at least the external price level, should no longer be the dominant caller of the tune because this too often required falling price levels and depressed levels of overall activity. The tendency for natural forces (as Milton Friedman still calls them) to dominate the workings of the real economy and the need for monetary factors to be made consistent with them was accepted. But increasingly over the 1920s and especially after the publication of *A Tract*, Keynes recognised the presence of increasing rigidities in both labour and product markets – so much so that by the second half of the 1920s Keynes was actively involved in the Liberal Party enquiries and the production of their Yellow Books concerning the situation and structure of the UK's traditional industries, e.g. textiles, mining, the relationship between industrial structure and the State and the emergence of imperfectly competitive and oligopolistic characteristics. So to say that when he was writing *The General Theory*, he was ignorant of these microeconomic considerations, vividly caught in the folklore of Gerald Shove's crack that 'Maynard never did take the 20 minutes necessary to understand the theory of value', is far from the truth. (It is true that Keynes would draw diametrically opposed inferences about the impact of rigidities on the working of the system in *The General Theory.*) In any event, for his purposes of analysing the workings of the economy as a whole, he did not consider these considerations to be of central importance for the core arguments he was making – an insight noted by Skidelsky as well as by Paul Davidson, Jan Kregel and Nina Shapiro.[13] Skidelsky describes in graphic detail Keynes's activities in the second half of the 1920s but does not perhaps make clear enough the links between them and the construction of the theoretical core of *The General Theory.*

Considerations of internal and external balance came to a head in the mid 1920s when the decision to return to the Gold Standard at pre-war parity was taken. Keynes and his principal ally, Reginald McKenna, lost the battle with the Treasury and the Bank of England and the forces of tradition and conservatism that they represented, the power and interests of the City of London which, as ever, deluded itself that what was optimum for it was also in the national interest. 'Fixed exchanges and sound money...were necessary for economic progress' (Skidelsky, 1992, 188). The basic instinct of Winston Churchill, who was then Chancellor of the Exchequer, was with Keynes. After reading an article by Keynes in the *Nation* in February 1935, he wrote a memo, 'dictated from his bed', to Otto Niemeyer: 'I would rather see Finance less proud and Industry more content' (Skidelsky, 1992, 198). In the end though Churchill's lack of expertise led him against his better judgment to side with the Treasury and the Bank of England, a decision he always regretted. Losing this battle and seeing some of his predictions come true in the General Strike of 1926, that the required lower money-wage level could only be achieved by rising unemployment accompanied by industrial strife, reinforced Keynes's decision, taken in 1924 soon after the publication of *A Tract* in 1923, to write a major work on money which became *A Treatise on Money.* He wished to provide what Marshall had proposed to do in the later volumes of the *Principles* which were never properly written or, indeed, written at all.

VII

The quantity theory remained the principal framework of the theoretical sections of *A Treatise on Money,* and Marshall's method in the *Principles,* the principal box of tools. Keynes's main collaborator at this time was Dennis Robertson – in some respects Keynes had it that Robertson was ahead of him in innovative thinking though both acknowledged that what they both were doing was very much joint work. The title of the book that Robertson published in 1926 – *Banking Policy and the Price*

Level: An Essay in the Theory of the Trade Cycle – highlights the emphasis of their approach. Ralph Hawtrey (though he is not thanked in the preface yet Hubert Henderson is) was also an important influence and critic. He thought the bank rate was the key policy instrument and working capital stocks, its principal target, while Keynes and Robertson more and more came to argue that the long-term rate of interest was the key and its impact on investment in fixed capital, the main target. They all agreed that the term structure of interest rates and the interrelatedness between interest rates also had to be analysed.

Conceptually Marshall still dominated the theoretical structure. Long-period normal competitive equilibrium was the centre of gravitation of the system (in the old classical sense of the concept, see Harcourt 1981; 1982). The happenings of each short period, first to prices and then as a consequence and in following short periods to short-period output and employment, were analysed as stations on the way to the long-period cross.[14] To do this Keynes introduced his 'fundamental equations' which are ways of expressing *within the quantity theory framework* the ingredients which make up the sectoral price levels of available (consumption) and unavailable (investment) goods, as well as providing an expression for the general price level itself. The components of the equations are associated in turn with Keynes's unusual, non-conventional definition of saving as the difference between long-period normal incomes and current consumption expenditures and its link through the conventional definition of investment expenditure to short-period windfall gains or losses. The windfalls signal to the entrepreneurs in which direction to change their outputs and offers of employment in the next short period. Skidelsky engagingly points out the Judaic/Christian and Greek myths associated with these processes, to wit, the widow's cruse and the Danaides' jars, respectively.[15]

It should be stressed that Keynes thought and Skidelsky confirms that the quantity theory identities applied to both short-period and long-period situations, even though, as Patinkin pointed out in 1976, Keynes sometimes wrote as if the identities were more than just identities. More significant is Richard Kahn's point (Kahn, 1975), that the fundamental equations could be given an independent interpretation as descriptions of price formation without *any* need to mention the quantity of money – again, with hindsight, a crucial insight into the possibility of a revolutionary break with the tradition associated with the quantity theory. This aspect of the break is made explicit in the opening pages of chapter 21 of *The General Theory*, 'The theory of prices' (Keynes, 1936; *C.W.*, vol. VII, 1973, 292–94).[16] It also led to the postwar distinction between demand–pull and cost–push inflationary pressures – mark-ups stretched or shrunk because of changes in demand, prices pushed up or brought down because of autonomous changes in the levels of money-wages.

Increasingly, the distinction between those who saved and why and those who invested became crucial and explicit. This was to sow the seeds of an eventual parting of the ways between Robertson and Keynes, one which was never subsequently to be completely overcome. Keynes did make a significant step towards a reconciliation when in 1937 he recognised the existence of the finance motive as a further motive for demanding money (in the form of bank credit) and explicitly distinguished between finance, saving and investment in the process of accumulation (see Keynes, *C.W.*, vol. XIV, 1973b, 201–23).[17] Robertson could justifiably claim that he had always recognised the role of the finance motive and the part that the banks played in meeting its demand. Keynes could just as legitimately say that Robertson emphasised the new flows of finance, investment and saving but virtually ignored the role of existing stocks of financial assets in setting their prices and hence the pattern of interest rates at any moment of time, a point that Kaldor concentrated on in his greatest theoretical paper (Kaldor, 1939). Again Skidelsky gives us in riveting detail the evidence for this narrative but does not spell out the connections as explicitly as he could have.

Skidelsky does emphasise the key parts of *A Treatise on Money* which are relevant for the making of *The General Theory*, in particular, the banana plantation parable, the increasing emphasis on expectations in determining expenditure decisions and the significance of distinguishing between saving and investment. All these strands come together in the banana plantation parable (Keynes, 1930; *C.W.*, vol. V, 1971, 158–60) – the change in planned saving induced by the evangelist to the society in which investment is constructing new banana plantations and consumption is eating bananas, leads to windfall losses associated with the fall in prices of bananas. This in turn induces falls in production and incomes, and a rise in unemployment, thus creating a downward deflationary and contractionary spiral which continues until either the population starves to death – or there is an *ad hoc* change in behaviour with regard to either saving or investment which arbitrarily brings the process to a halt. What is missing (apart from any recognition by Keynes of the Pigou effect) is, of course, any sense of an endogenous multiplier process to bring the downward spiral to a halt at a lower but equilibrium level or rest state of output, employment and prices. This was also missing from 'Can Lloyd George do it?', the pamphlet written by Hubert Henderson and Keynes in 1929 as 'Keynes's main defence of the Liberal programme' (Skidelsky, 1992, 303) and published in May 1929. This omission was not made good until Kahn, Meade and Jens Warming had explicitly set out an expression for the multiplier and the equality of planned saving and investment took on a new, vital role in determining income and employment rather than the normal price levels (overall and sectorally) in the sense of Marshall at full, stock and flow, Marshallian long-period equilibrium as in *A Treatise on Money*.

The book was therefore associated with the analysis of the credit and trade cycle, fluctuations around the long-period equilibrium position and with the dynamic processes which brought the economy to this equilibrium as well as with an account of its characteristics (and those of the short-period situations in which the economy would find itself over the course of the cycle). In *A Treatise on Money* the Cambridge version of the natural rate of interest still ruled the roost so that if the value(s) of nominal money rate(s) of interest was (were) not consistent with it, cumulative changes in prices (and quantities but they were not supposed to be analysed in much detail in a treatise on money[18]) would occur.

The natural rate of interest was the price that cleared the market for real investment and real saving, the real factors of productivity and thrift, caught up in Irving Fisher's marginal rate of return over cost and marginal rate of time preference respectively, the rates at which present consumption goods could be technically and psychologically trans-formed into future consumption goods. These (in Marshallian form) were the lasting loves of Robertson and one of the basic reasons why he stuck tenaciously to the loanable funds theory of the rate of interest.

The narrative is set out fully and absorbingly by Skidelsky and its development is related clearly to Keynes's other activities, for example, his work for the Liberal Party, his evidence to the Macmillan Committee (Skidelsky gratefully draws on Peter Clarke's magisterial account of this and the making of *A Treatise on Money*, Clarke 1988) and other government bodies. Skidelsky emphasises the end product – the attempt to create effective monetary policy through the rate of interest and, as Keynes's faith in it as the unaided way out of a deep prolonged slump such as the UK experienced in the 1920s, the creation of effective fiscal policy through tax remission and public works expenditure. He reproduces some of Keynes's most eloquent pleas for the latter and his exposure of the policy of leaving people idle on the dole when so much could be done for the social infrastructure of then contemporary Britain.

The *simpliste* Treasury view was that there was only a given volume of saving available at any one time so that saving used for public works expenditure meant so much less for the private sector's accumulation. Whatever were the good intentions of those proposing such expenditure, the result was doomed to failure. The sophisticated Treasury view was that the private sector was efficient, that the public sector was inefficient in its use of resources, so that an increase in government capital formation was, by definition, a less efficient use of the community's resources. Moreover, it could have such an adverse effect on the confidence of private investors that overall activity would be reduced and unemployment rise even further.

The apparatus of *A Treatise on Money* was not the appropriate framework in which to tackle answers to these objections. Keynes quickly realised that as well as being 'artistically ... a failure',[19] much of the theoretical content and the tradition to which it belonged were failures too, that a complete reconstruction of the arguments, if not necessarily the method, was needed (Keynes always remained Marshallian in method. One of Robertson's most astute observations paraphrased by Skidelsky (1992, *xxi*), was that Keynes's mind was like 'a powerful search light, moving from object to object, ignoring the interconnections of the whole'.) The stage was now set for the climax in the volume's core, the creation of *The General Theory*.

VIII

Though *A Treatise on Money* was grounded in method and emphasis on an analysis of the credit cycle, yet it was still limited in scope by the belief that a treatise on money was primarily about prices[20] and their control, that it was barred from an in-depth exploration of fluctuations in short-period production and employment because of the constraint imposed by the monetary, real dichotomy, see n. 18 above. We know, of course, that Keynes was unfaithful to himself, not only in his book but even more in his journalism and his activities with public bodies. Nevertheless, the constraint still continued to bite. It was only when he came to make *The General Theory* and to pose the issue as the explanation of a deep sustained slump and thus of the determinants of income and employment, so moving away from the more dynamic analysis of movements over the cycle of *A Treatise on Money*, that he finally escaped from the dichotomy and also Pigou's approach, which was grounded in it.[21] Skidelsky discusses Pigou's procedure of starting with a simplified model of the real economy, especially of the labour market, ignoring monetary matters. The latter were only allowed in later as complications by the application of the method of successive approximation.

That the real still continued to dominate outcomes even then is not unlike Marx's argument that the sphere of production is the fundamental source of the economy's behaviour and that while activities in the sphere of distribution and exchange bring in complications, they are nevertheless dominated by the prior (logical) conditions and relationships set out in the sphere of production, the subject matter of Volume I of *Capital*.[22]

When presented with the arguments of his younger colleagues about *A Treatise on Money* and his lectures on it, especially the assumption that output was given in the short period so that all reactions had initially to occur through price changes, Keynes responded to Joan Robinson more in sorrow than in anger in April 1932. (It had been Austin Robinson who highlighted the puzzle associated with the widow's cruse and the Danaid jar. The fallacy of the widow's cruse *when there was unemployment* was that if business people increase consumption when profits rise, output could increase without any need for prices to rise at all.) Joan had set out this criticism in the draft of an article she wrote in 1931 but which was not published until early 1933. 'You are a little hard on me [wrote Keynes]...only at one particular point [had he] assumed constant output...[he had made] this absolutely clear...one must be allowed at a particular stage of [an] argument to make simplifying assumptions' (Keynes, *C.W.*, vol. XIII, 1973a, 270). Nevertheless, it was only when Keynes made the short period in a macroeconomic, economy-wide sense his focus, abandoned dynamics partly because of this and partly because of his inability to find a representative time unit appropriate for such an analysis,[23] and recognised that real and monetary factors must be intermingled from the start of the analysis, that the full realisation of the extent of his revolution and approach became clear. Skidelsky tells this story very well, drawing on the *Collected Writings* and his own independent excursions into Keynes's papers, Tom Rymes's notes of a representative student at Keynes's lectures 1932 to 1935, Rymes (1989), and Keynes's papers and discussions in the USA in the first half of the 1930s. More and more the (relatively) closed economy nature of the US economy came to influence the model(s) Keynes was setting up. It is often forgotten that before and after *The General Theory*, though Keynes was the compleat Englishman and always had England's best interests at the forefront of his mind (heart) and analysis, yet the setting of his discussions was almost always an international one. This is true, too, of Keynes's stand on whether the quantity of money is an endogenous or exogenous variable. A plausible case can be made that Keynes was always an endogenous money person. Opinions to the contrary are over-influenced by the dominance of *The General Theory* in people's knowledge of Keynes and by not realising that *for his purposes there*, it was sensible to take the supply of money as a 'given', not exogenous, only that its determination was put to one side because of the stage of the economic process from which it was most suitable to start analysis of his central, new issue (see Dow 1997).[24]

Skidelsky's narrative is faithful to events as they occurred with careful discussions of events and the realisation of the significance of key discoveries and advances. He never loses sight of the wood in his careful and entertaining examination of the trees. Readers coming to his account with little or no prior knowledge of why *The General Theory* was so significant, both as a break with the past and as a major insight into the present, will go away with a clear idea of its momentous importance and impact at the time it was written. Indeed, we venture to say, this is also so now because the anti-Keynes backlash of the last 30 years or so has run its course and been proved by events to be the aberration rather than Keynes, as claimed by his opponents. Not that Skidelsky is uncritical of both Keynes and the Keynesians, nor that he does not acknowledge the sometimes powerful arguments of their critics. Nevertheless we think it fair to say that the essence of Keynes's insights deserve to survive and if not dominate yet be of great help in the future development of theory and policy in the much changed situations from when Keynes originally wrote.

IX

What are the major shifts that Skidelsky identifies before he discusses the reactions to *The General Theory* by reviewers and interpreters and critics, especially of course, Harrod, Hicks and Meade, and the start of the rise of *IS/LM* as the way of 'absorbing' Keynes's message? That the shifts themselves are, most and mostly, post-Keynesian in spirit is witnessed to by Skidelsky highlighting Keynes's emphasis on the effects of an environment of inescapable uncertainty on economic decision making and institutions, especially the importance of establishing conventions and norms which nevertheless in certain circumstances prove fragile. Skidelsky may perhaps have put a little too much emphasis on the early chapters on the labour market and the two classical postulates which were, of course, at the forefront of Keynes's mind as he developed his arguments. Nevertheless, we think this emphasis is slightly out of focus because Skidelsky himself was then much concerned about the roles of labour markets and trade unions in economies trying to sustain full employment and faced with irresponsible trade union behaviour which helped to sustain or, even more, accelerate inflationary processes.

Keynes, of course, used the labour market analysis because it tied in with his criticism of Pigou's 1933 book which he took to be the most explicit statement of the classical system he had in mind to criticise. Prior to Pigou's book he had had to create the classical system by the process of rational reconstruction. This was to be found in the key role played by cooperative, neutral and entrepreneur economy models in his lectures (the drafts of which turned up as part of the contents of the laundry basket at Tilton, see *C.W.*, vol. XXIX, 1979, 76–102). Their disappearance from *The General Theory* itself Lorie Tarshis (see, for example, Tarshis 1989) always thought was a grave intellectual and tactical mistake which muddled the discussion of Say's Law and of how the intervention of money distanced the entrepreneur economy from the first two in subtle and ingenious ways. Keynes himself in *The General Theory* (and subsequently, when writing to Harrod, see *C.W.*, vol. XIV, 1973b, 85) thought that the explanation of how the point of effective demand is determined at the intersection of the aggregate demand and aggregate supply schedules was *the* great leap forward (and the restoration of aggregate demand in 'the theory of the demand and supply for output as a whole' after many years absence was the vital first step in making such a leap). From this follows all the subsequent analysis of the components of aggregate demand and their determinants, of aggregate supply (again, its treatment was too skimpy when seen with the hindsight of tactical retrospective), of the determination of the rate of interest and the role of money, of the effects of dropping the provisional assumption of a given money-wage (again, it was a tactical mistake to have assumed it given for 18 chapters), and, finally, of the determination of the general price level in non-quantity theory of money terms. (The last arose from his own inclination and Kahn's long-established scepticism concerning the quantity theory as a causal relationship in the operation of the economy.)

When we come to the end of Skidelsky's account of the making of *The General Theory*, of the contents of the book, we can see in stark relief the contrasts of the finished product with that of the starting places in *A Tract* and *A Treatise on Money*. First, there is no tendency to full employment in either the short or long period (by the 1940s Keynes was doubting whether the long period had any operational significance or content for the issues he was examining in *The General Theory*), that involuntary unemployment is a definite possibility. Secondly, the classical dichotomy could not be defended as holding in either the short or the long period.[25] Thirdly, investment leads and saving responds, a proposition not made completely convincingly by Keynes because of a muddle in his own mind concerning the equality of the two by definition, and the equality as an equilibrium condition, a corollary of aggregate demand equalling aggregate supply at the point of effective demand. Skidelsky identifies this muddle and its cause. Fourthly, the money rate of interest now rules the roost and Keynes's version of the natural rate – his marginal efficiency of capital (investment), better thought of as the expected rate of profit – has to measure up to it (in the old story, the direction was reversed). Fifthly, the rate of interest is primarily a monetary phenomenon,[26] as it is closely related to the workings of the money market, not that for saving and investment. Sixthly, the general price level is determined by the prices of the variable factors and their short-period productivity (with qualitatively inessential modifications for imperfectly competitive market structures, should – when – they occur), and not by M and V. Seventhly, and perhaps the most fundamental factor behind all the arguments to establish the principal characteristics of the system, the overwhelming importance of expectations, especially long-term expectation and their determination and impact on all important economic decisions and relationships in the environment of inescapable uncertainty.

X

One thing that is played down in Skidelsky's account (this is exemplified by the absence of any discussion of Jan Kregel's classic 1976 paper on modelling under uncertainty in Keynes and the post-Keynesians – it is neither in the text nor in the bibliography) is the significance of Keynes's three models of different degrees of complexity in his explanations of different aspects and issues of the same real world he is analysing. This is not to say that Skidelsky fails to emphasise the crucial difference between short-term expectations and their determination and role, and long-term expectations and theirs, only that he does not make explicit the various kinds of argument, the degree of abstraction adopted, as Keynes moved from establishing the existence of the point of effective demand to considering the process by which it could be found if not immediately established and, finally, to his most sophisticated model, using the method of shifting equilibrium to analyse movements over time, embracing an adaptation of the classical concept of centres of gravitation, see Harcourt (1981; 1982).[27] By not referring to Kregel's article and so not commenting on Kregel's interpretation of how Keynes set about tackling analysis of uncertain situations, Skidelsky missed the chance to put forward a definitive view of whether *IS/LM* may be found in *The General Theory* and is it true to Keynes's way of presenting his new ideas at one level of abstraction? Skidelsky's discussion (1992, 622–24) of Hicks's 'little apparatus' is neat and useful. What we would like to have seen was more discussion of why not only Hicks but also Harrod, Meade, Brian Reddaway and David Champernowne, for example, all found *IS/LM* in *The General Theory*. Our own view is that it is there (see Keynes 1936; *C.W.*, vol. VII, 1973, 173), that in a very limited, but within those limits, useful way, it does capture a key portion of Keynes's story; and that Donald Moggridge (1976, 171–74) has written the best account of *IS/LM*'s strengths, weaknesses and limitations in the appendix to his Modern Masters book on Keynes, an account which confirms our interpretation of p.173 above.[28] Moreover, as Peter Kriesler and John Nevile point out in their splendid paper, '*IS-LM* and macroeconomics after Keynes' (2002), though the articles of Hicks, Harrod, Meade, Champernowne and Reddaway share much the same set of equations, Reddaway used the term 'mutual determination'. This 'does not necessarily imply simultaneous determination' (Kriesler and Nevile, 2002, 107) and therefore indicates the Marshallian (rather than Walrasian) setting within which Keynes always worked.

If we use Keynes's most abstract model in which short-term expectations and long-term expectations are assumed to be independent of one another, and short-term expectations are assumed to be realised immediately, *IS/LM* shows clearly the existence of an underemployment, short-period, equilibrium rest state with its accompanying levels of Y, N, i and P. We illustrate this in two simple diagrams (which were originally set out by Richard Goodwin, no mean Keynesian himself, see Harcourt 1993, 108 for the strange story of Goodwin's contribution). We take as given the money-wage level and the stock of nominal money for the short period we are examining, we ignore (for simplicity only) the impact of a different price level on the position of the *IS* curve but not on the *LM* curve. It follows that for every conceivable general price level, there is a different *LM* curve (the lower is the price level, the further to the right is the *LM* curve corresponding to it). So instead of the 'little apparatus' determining a unique set of (real) Y, i values (Hicks had money income on his horizontal axis), we have a family, one for each value of P; see Figure 1.1 where $P_1 > P_2 > P_3$.

We transfer this last relationship to Figure 1.2, where P is measured on the vertical axis and Y on the horizontal axis, as the downward sloping curve $P_{(IS/LM)}$. The upward sloping curve P_{MC} is derived from

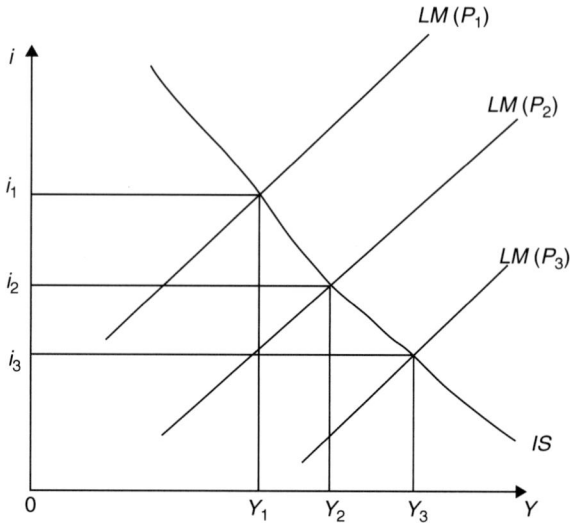

Figure 1.1   A family of equilibrium values of Y and i for different values of P

the aggregate supply function, assuming competitive market structures so that $P = MC$, where MC is the aggregate marginal cost of
production of each level of Y, so that P_{MC} shows the price level associated with each level of Y. The intersection of the two curves is at
the equilibrium price level (P_2) (and Y_2). Picking out the LM curve in
Figure 1.1 corresponding to P_2 allows the equilibrium rate of interest i_2 to be found. So we have *The General Theory* in a nutshell, an
account that is consistent with Keynes's argument on p. 173, provided that all the *cet pars* itemised by Keynes go through together.
Once we allow for feedbacks we leave the world of *IS/LM* and enter
that of Keynes's more and most realistic model of reality, that of
shifting equilibrium.

As a slight digression (yet certainly relevant) we refer to a disagreement between Hawtrey and Keynes. Hawtrey always argued that the
immediate impact of a shock, an unexpected change in demand, for
example, was on quantity through an unintended change in the stocks
of inventories, and any price effects would only come later. Keynes, by
contrast, by using a combination of Marshall's market and short-period
analysis, had the immediate impact affect prices – with given stock supplies, the prices would quickly change to clear the market 'day' of the
stocks. The resulting new and initially unexpected prices so set would

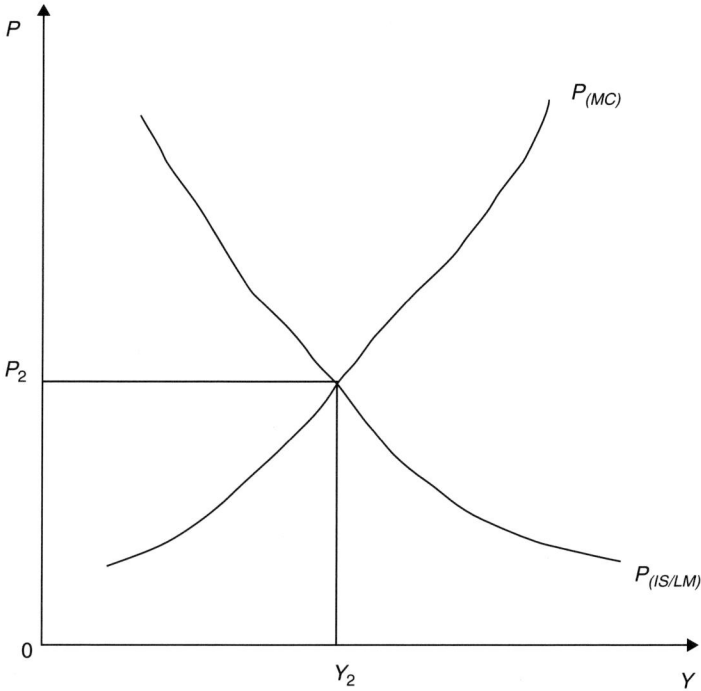

Figure 1.2 Determining the general price level

then lead to new expected prices and to movements along short-period marginal cost and supply curves as entrepreneurs implemented the levels of output and employment which were associated with marginal costs equal to the new expected prices. Skidelsky has done us a signal service by highlighting this point of disagreement and its implications, not least of which was Hawtrey's discovery of the multiplier, only for him to reject it ever afterwards!, see Skidelsky 1992, 444–46. The disagreement arose in their discussions of *A Treatise on Money* but the issue remains relevant for the later volume.

Skidelsky also points out the significance of Keynes's new theory of the rate of interest and why the articles which followed immediately on publication of *The General Theory* concentrated so much on it. For, everything else given, the rate of interest determined by the demand for and supply of money led to the level of investment which in turn via the multiplier led to the equilibrium level of income and employment (and all else that went with them). In a very clear sense then

Keynes saw the rate of interest as the central key to his system even though he was by then pretty sceptical of monetary policy unaided being able to keep a capitalist economy in a stable satisfactory state (or rescue it from a deep sustained slump). Robertson, with his longer term view about the roles of productivity and thrift in ensuring rising standards of living and his almost obsessive respect for Marshall and the past (a stand not much dissimilar to ours on Keynes and his followers), was unwilling to have a theory which so completely seemed to rule out productivity and thrift. Some modern commentators find that the last 30 years or so of developments in macroeconomics in which rational expectations, utility-maximising agents and the long-term neutrality of money have become the norm, affirm the correctness of Robertson's stance rather than Keynes's. All we can say is that if they really think that approach allows us to illuminate the world better than one based on the subtle and, sometimes, not so subtle intuitions of Keynes (and Kalecki and Marx), we can only despair of the judgment and common sense of our profession. Certainly such a view is not one supported by the ample evidence presented in Volume II of Skidelsky's superb biography.

XI

On 16 May 1937 Keynes suffered a major heart attack which greatly reduced his effectiveness (that is to say, he was now only the equivalent of three ordinary mortals) until the Second World War started. While recovering in hospital, 'a sanatorium for the wealthy', Ruthin Castle in Wales, Julian Bell, the elder son of Vanessa and Clive Bell, was killed in the Spanish Civil War. We reprint the letter which Keynes wrote to Vanessa on 29 June 1937 (it ends the narrative of Volume II) because the letter illustrates so vividly, appropriately, the depths of sympathy and kindness in Keynes's close friendships and his uncanny ability quickly to draft exactly the right words of comfort and concern.

My Dearest Nessa,

A line of sympathy and love from both of us on the loss of your dear and beautiful boy with his pure and honourable feelings. It was fated that he should make his protest, as he was entitled to do, with his life, and one can say nothing.

With love and affection,
Maynard

XII

In the final volume of his trilogy, Skidelsky tells us that his objective has been to rescue Keynes from the economists and to place him 'in the world of history where he properly belongs' (2000a, *xxii*).[29] A clarion (if somewhat tongue in cheek) declaration in the turf wars over the 'ownership' of Keynes, it is reminiscent of Kaldor's (1982, 2) claim that 'Keynes was an economic adviser, first and foremost; he was a theoretical economist and the creator of a new intellectual system second.' Of course, the likelihood for success of such a 'rescue', especially from a discipline likely to be protective of one of its few recognisable stars, might be in doubt.[30] Nevertheless, what there can be *no* doubt about is that, in Volume III of this monumental biography, Skidelsky establishes Keynes's place in history – proper intellectual domicile or not.

For it is in history, in the realms of policy and practical affairs, that the immense scholarship of Skidelsky's three volumes is most obviously apparent. There should be no surprise at this. As Skidelsky told *The Economist* upon the release of Volume III, his biography of Keynes was written 'by an economically literate historian, not by a historically literate economist' (Skidelsky, 2000b). Previous reviewers of Skidelsky's volumes, including those with reservations over issues of economic theory contained within them, have been in no doubt about their worth as intellectual, and other, history (see, for example, Presley, 1984, Heilbroner, 1986, Eatwell, 1994, Pollard, 1994, Laidler, 2002, amongst the many).

Keynes's role as policy maker and adviser forms the core narrative of Volume III, and Skidelsky's portrayal of this historic role is the primary concern of the following pages. The specific policy episodes chosen for examination are not, however, the most obvious or even necessarily the most important. There is, of course, an enormous literature devoted to the study of Keynes and practical affairs, and it is not the purpose of this review article to replicate them. The episodes chosen, rather, are those for which Skidelsky's biography is especially enlightening, those that tend to be overlooked, but for which the scale of Skidelsky's work offers new insights, or simply those aspects of Keynes's policy work that the authors of this review article think are especially interesting or relevant to present debates.

XIII

The 1920s and 1930s were the years of Keynes's most public policy advocacy, but it was the Second World War that ushered in his most important policy *work*. A bold claim perhaps, but one that would be hard to refute in the light of the evidence assembled by Skidelsky in Volume III of the biography. In its opening paragraphs, Skidelsky tells us that in 'his narrower, and subordinate sphere, Keynes rivalled Churchill. He was, in fact, the Churchill of war finance and post war financial planning' (2000a, *xv*). This was despite the fact that Keynes held no official position during the war, remaining throughout 'an unpaid, part-time adviser to the Chancellor of the Exchequer' (2000a, *xv*). To foreigners, Keynes was not only the *de facto* Chancellor of the Exchequer, but 'President of the Board of Trade as well' (2000a, *xv*). Keynes's influence was based on personal and intellectual authority, but it was no less real for this.

Skidelsky tells us that he had wanted the original subtitle of Volume III to be 'The Economist as Prince', to juxtapose Keynes the theorist, with Keynes the statesman of the war years (2000a, *xv*). But when it appeared (in the UK) in October 2000, the volume did not bear this subtitle. Instead, the more pugilistic 'Fighting for Britain' was substituted. Meanwhile, by the time Volume III was published in the United States a year later, yet another change had been made – 'Fighting for Freedom' graces the covers of the American edition. Behind all of this lay a tale, and some controversy besides.

Skidelsky chose 'Fighting for Britain' because to label otherwise would hide Keynes's contribution to Britain's survival in the Second World War – a survival that was more precarious than is often supposed. The story is 'above all else, about Keynes's patriotism' (2000a, *xv*). Churchill's war was against the totalitarian powers. Keynes's war was in the provision of the wherewithal for this, but it was also 'to preserve Britain as a Great Power against the United States' (2000a, *xv*). It did not end in victory. In helping to defeat the totalitarian powers, 'Britain lost both Empire and Greatness' (2000a, *xv*).

XIV

Skidelsky's account of the rivalry between Britain and the United States has not been well-received by all. Sylvia Nasar (2002) suggests that 'Skidelsky's otherwise nuanced analysis veers into implausibility' on the topic. Bradford De Long, however, has been by far the most vociferous of the critics. Describing Skidelsky's portrayal of British–US relations in parts of Volume III as 'ugly', he alleges,

> Skidelsky appears to have fallen under the influence of a strange and sinister sect of British imperial conservatives who believe that somehow the U.S. during World War II provided aid to Britain on

niggardly terms, terms guaranteed to destroy Britain as a great power (2000).[31]

De Long declares that such an analysis of British–US economic relations during the war is 'total nonsense' – nonsense, moreover, that '[a] ny economist would know'. Yet, 'Skidelsky seems to believe it.' How to account for this? For De Long, it is quite simple – 'the source of the problem lies in the fact that Robert Skidelsky is not an economist.' This was not, according to De Long, a problem for the first two volumes. Volume I, he says, was mostly about Keynes 'as a developing intellectual', while Volume II was mostly concerned with Keynes 'as politician, trying to influence events by analyses based on the standard monetarist (sic) toolkit of a Cambridge economist between the wars'. Since the largest portion of Volume II is devoted to the theoretical issues surrounding the genesis, construction and aftermath of the revolutionary *General Theory*, the latter claim is surprising to say the least.

In the Preface to the American Edition of Volume III, Skidelsky defends his theme against De Long's attack. Injecting a degree of international relations 'realism' into the debate, Skidelsky reminds us that 'national interests do not disappear just because the cause is noble' (2001, *xiii*). It was, 'as natural for the United States to use her wartime financial leverage to weaken Britain as a financial and commercial rival as it was for the British to try to minimise or evade the strings attached to American help' (2001, *xiii*).

So what is to be made of this contretemps? First, if Skidelsky is not an economist, then neither is De Long an insightful historian of the period. A most revealing example of this is De Long's citation of one of Churchill's speeches as evidence that Britain's war aims did *not* encompass (*pace* Skidelsky) the maintenance of the financial and commercial strength of the British Empire after the war. The speech cited – a famously stirring speech delivered in May 1940 – is worth quoting in part to illustrate how wrong De Long is on this issue:

> You ask, what is our policy? I say it is to wage war by land, sea and air... You ask, what is our aim?...It is victory. Victory at all costs. Victory in spite of all terrors. Victory, however long and hard the road may be, for without victory there is no survival...*No survival for the British Empire, no survival for all that the British Empire has stood for*...[32]

De Long's conclusion from this, that 'Britain fought to defeat a tyranny, not to preserve an empire', would no doubt surprise a Prime Minister who also famously cautioned that he had not become 'the King's First

Minister in order to preside over the liquidation of the British Empire'.[33] Compounding it all is a further observation on the question of imperial preservation, in which De Long states that 'any economist would know that greatness does not lie in numbers of battleships or large foreign exchange reserves'. But this is precisely the point – it was not economists who were in charge of US–Anglo relations during the Second World War. As Woods observes (1990, 8), the Anglo–American dialogue during the Second World War was 'a complex mixture of bureaucratic conflict, conventional politics, transatlantic alliances, national characteristics, mutual images, and circumstances'. Through this glass darkly, however, perceptions of national interest shone through. With respect to US–Anglo relations in the Second World War, this meant that

> Britain received enough aid to enable it to survive and to play a role in the war against the Axis, but not enough to preserve its overseas investments and markets, to maintain its military outposts, or to participate in a system of multilateral commerce (Woods, 1990, 7).

De Long is also a poor reader of his personal subject, for he seems to assume that the issue of conflict in Anglo–American relations is Skidelsky's invention (or that of this 'strange and sinister sect'), and was not something that exercised Keynes. He could hardly be more wrong. Keynes greatly cared about the maintenance of British power, especially the power to act independently of the United States. It is why he found the loan negotiations so fraught since his primary objective in them was 'the retention of enough assets to leave us capable of independent action' (Skidelsky, 2000a, xx). In this same context Keynes even minuted on one occasion that 'America must not be allowed to pick out the eyes of the British Empire' (Skidelsky, 2000a, 98). Skidelsky also reveals (2000a, 92) that earlier in the war 'Keynes was enraged by the anti-imperialist diatribes of his *New Republic* editor, Bruce Bliven, and stopped writing for the journal.'

Skidelsky expected a strong reaction to his story of less than complete harmony between the principal allies of World War Two for two reasons. First, the story 'shatters the myth of the united front against evil' (2001, *xiii–xiv*). Secondly, and generalising very broadly, 'because Americans tend to believe that their nation is uniquely idealistic, and therefore exempt from calculation of self-interest' (2001, *xiv*). Both issues are tendentious – the first because such a myth was surely vanquished many decades ago, in popular discourse as much as in academic revisionism – the second because, while provocative, it is a theory that is not really capable of objective analysis. The differences between Skidelsky and De Long on these issues are reflective, rather, of a clash of national narratives over the Second World War – a clash that is, if anything, intensifying with the passing of years. Sometimes lost in the rhetoric, however, are the substantive issues behind these narratives.

XV

In the context of Skidelsky's biography and Keynes's efforts during World War Two, the greatest substantive issue in US–Anglo relations concerned the 'consideration' the United States expected from Britain for 'Lend-Lease'. This ended in the famous Anglo-American loan that was the subject of Keynes's 'last battle' which, as is movingly described in Volume III, finally killed him. Keynes was Britain's 'envoy extraordinary' over Lend-Lease, and it meant he made four hazardous voyages to the United States during the war, and two after it. In a reminder to readers that communications during the war years were not as they are now, Skidelsky takes the opportunity to point out how this also greatly increased the power and autonomy of envoys such as Keynes:

> Keynes's position as plenipotentiary at large was powerfully reinforced by the slowness and erratic nature of communications between Washington and London....With cipher facilities at the Embassy [in Washington] heavily overburdened, even telegrams of instructions took days to reach Keynes...All this gave Keynes considerable latitude in framing his own proposals...London had little choice but to trust him and hope that the thunderbolts he was forging would not turn into boomerangs (2000a, 119).

The negotiations over the Anglo-American loan are the climax of Volume III. Skidelsky points out that for Keynes it was a matter of *justice* that Britain's spending in the United States for war materials be written off via a grant, rather than being cause for a loan. These expenditures were a 'moral debt' owed to Britain, whose financial sacrifices in a common cause Keynes asserted were 'incomparably greater than those of any other of the United Nations' (2000a, 322). Skidelsky's three volumes enable us to see, however, that Keynes's fight for what he perceived as justice on such matters was not confined to the case of Britain in World War Two. As Skidelsky notes in Volume II in relation to outstanding debts from the *First* World War;

> Keynes had consistently advocated cancellation of inter-Allied debts. He did not consider them moral obligations since they were incurred in a *common cause* (1992, 124, emphasis added).

Skidelsky is not shy in any of the volumes to detail Keynes's faults, but nowhere are these made more apparent than during the loan negotiations. According to Skidelsky, 'Keynes could never understand that American and British interests were not identical, attributing differences to deficiencies in the American political system, and thus over relying on logic and eloquence to overcome them' (2000a, 117). Other shortcomings had been in place from the time of Keynes's first visit to the United States (also on Treasury business) in 1917 during which, according to a contemporary, he had made a 'terrible impression for his rudeness'.[34] Twenty-five years and innumerable negotiations later, Skidelsky tells us that Keynes; was 'not patient'; was 'prone to exasperated outbursts'; 'his great intelligence led him to overcomplicate an argument'; his 'tendency to score points off opponents hampered him as a negotiator'; 'he suffered from an incurable tendency to tell Americans how they ought to be running the country' (2000a, 110). Exhausted and ill by the time of the climax of negotiations in 1946, Keynes was probably not the right person to convince a still ever-insecure United States that the old empire was not about to 'pull a fast one on them' (2000a, 110).

XVI

Apart from the negotiations over Lend-Lease, Keynes's Second World War career was dominated by his efforts to recreate, and reform, the international monetary system. These efforts reached their purest intellectual form in his famous proposal for an 'International Clearing Union' (ICU). Through this device, Keynes believed it would be safe for Britain and other debtor countries to accept multilateral payments, and to begin the process of dismantling the trade and other barriers erected between the wars. Skidelsky argues that the original ICU paper (together with an accompanying one on buffer stocks) 'were the most important he ever wrote in terms of their direct influence on events' (2000a, 205).

Skidelsky is surely correct in his assessment of the importance of the ICU in Keynes's policy work.[35] On this subject Skidelsky's biography outshines all of the others, and many specialty works besides. Above all, Skidelsky uniquely manages to capture the boldness and excitement of the ICU. Of course, we already had Harrod's famously rapt, if somewhat self-centred recollection, Harrod (1951, 525–585). Skidelsky recounts Harrod, but generously casts the net more broadly around Keynes's contemporaries. He cites James Meade, for whom the ICU was 'the only real hope of a generous and spacious economic collaboration after the war';

Lionel Robbins, who thought it 'a real release of fresh air in this surcharged and stale atmosphere'; and, most evocatively, Denis Robertson, who wrote to Keynes he not only read his proposal with 'great excitement' but 'with a growing hope that the spirit of Burke and Adam Smith is on earth again' (2000a, 219).

Encouraged by the scope allowed by three volumes, Skidelsky establishes the longevity of international monetary matters in Keynes's thought. Emerging in numerous 'Keynes Plans' throughout his public life, international monetary reform was first broached by Keynes in *Indian Currency and Finance* in 1913. This proposed an international system in which one or two money centres remained on gold, with all other countries on a gold-exchange standard. As Skidelsky notes (1983, 275), even this far back the eventual elimination of gold and the belief that 'Britain was the natural energiser, and centre, of a reformed monetary order' were constants in Keynes's thoughts. A very similar proposal, albeit with the maintenance of internal price stability in the money centres to the fore, was central to *A Tract on Monetary Reform* published in 1923.

What Skidelsky refers to as Keynes's first 'ideal' international monetary system emerges in *A Treatise on Money*. In *A Treatise*, something not dissimilar to the ICU is proposed – including the prime objective that no country should have to deflate because of a shortage of gold. In order to achieve this, a 'supernational' bank would be established which would issue its own currency (unusually prosaically for Keynes, simply called 'Supernational Bank Money' [SBM]). SBM would count, along with gold, as the reserves of the world's central banks. SBM would be lent to countries with temporary balance of payments problems and its volume varied more generally – via open market operations by the supernational bank – in order to stabilise its value against a basket of commodities. Gold clearly retained a role in this system, but not a liquidity-limiting one. Skidelsky notes that for Keynes this was essentially for appearances sake, 'so as not to divide the "forces of intelligence and goodwill"'. Keynes otherwise maintained his belief that gold was ' "a furtive Freudian cloak" for infantile anality' (Skidelsky, 1992, 154).

The system described in *A Treatise* re-emerges (in a slightly modified form) in *The Means to Prosperity,* but it was not until the Second World War, and the ICU, that any of Keynes's schemes came close to implementation. How close is a debate that takes up many of the pages of Volume III for, of course, Keynes's ICU was not the only proposal on the table.

As is well known, the ICU was opposed by the superficially similar 'Stabilisation Fund' (SF) proposal of the US State Department. Devised by Harry Dexter White, an enormously controversial figure both then and now, the SF was a much more orthodox animal than the ICU.[36] The SF reflected US interests as the world's largest creditor country, just as the ICU was motivated by Britain's debtor status. Skidelsky does a masterful job in contrasting the ICU and SF. As with his coverage of Anglo-American relations generally during the war, however, Skidelsky's approach has not pleased all. The principal protagonist again has been Bradford De Long.

De Long (2000 and 2002) maintains that Skidelsky overstates the differences between the ICU and the SF. Further, Skidelsky's presentation of the battle between Keynes and White (2000a, 239), as 'one of the grand political duels of the Second World War, though it was largely buried in financial minutiae' is, according to De Long, 'a gross misrepresentation'. From the viewpoint of an *economist* he tells us, one is struck not by the differences between the ICU and the SF, 'but by their extraordinary similarities' (De Long 2002, 159).

De Long, however, is wrong. As Skidelsky makes clear throughout the 150 or so pages in Volume III concerned with the monetary plans (and what is also abundantly clear from the source documents), the ICU and the SF were different devices that reflected their different purposes. These were not merely technical, but fundamental differences – a cleavage that is clear from the broadest survey of the issues. The ICU, for example, was based on what Keynes labelled the 'banking principle' – liquidity was *created* via overdrafts available to each country that depended not on their reserve holdings, but the volume of their trade. The SF too made loans, but only out of subscribed capital. The ICU also placed the onus of adjustment for balance of payments difficulties on *creditor* as well as debtor countries, which was an objective long sought by Keynes. The SF placed *no* sanction on creditors. Under the ICU, the foreign exchange market would be replaced by transactions channelled through its accounts (conducted in its own currency, finally named by Keynes 'bancor') via country's central banks. The SF, by contrast, encouraged the emergence of foreign exchange markets. In an effort to eliminate gold as the primary reserve asset the ICU allowed only one-way convertibility – of gold into bancor, but not bancor into gold. Finally though fixed in each, exchange rates were much more rigid in the SF (where a change required approval from the SF governing body) than in the ICU. There are countless other differences, but the above are sufficient to denote *profoundly* different principles, ideas and institutions. Keynes summed it up best when he observed that, in its fundamentals, the SF was 'not much more than a version of the gold standard' (*C.W.*, vol. *XXV* 1980, 160).

XVII

Keynes's first task in the Second World War was to devise ways of securing domestic finance for the war effort – specifically, a means by which resources could be diverted from consumption and into the production of armaments. His ideas to this end, outlined in a series of newspaper articles collected as *How To Pay for the War*, were, in Skidelsky's view, some of the most important he ever wrote.

According to Skidelsky, *How To Pay for the War* is an immensely significant work in the Keynes opus which has hitherto been underestimated.[37] Three issues, he argues, especially stand out from it. The first of these is that it demonstrates, through the application of the principles of *The General Theory* to policy, that Keynes was very much the 'impresario' of his own revolution. Since, however, it argued for policies of restriction, it left many of Keynes's followers behind and to Keynes himself being labelled, Skidelsky tells us, as 'anti-Keynesian' (2000a, *xix*). While this interpretation must be seen in the light of other attempts throughout the biography to 'liberate' Keynes from 'Keynesians', Skidelsky nevertheless demonstrates that *How to Pay for the War* did lead to a rapprochement between Keynes and pillars of orthodoxy such as Treasury and the Bank of England. It also led to a warming of relations between Keynes and Hayek – the latter writing to Keynes following the publication of *How to Pay for the War* that '[i]t is reassuring to note that we agree so completely on the economics of scarcity, even if we differ on when it applies' (2000a, *xix*).

The second critical issue to emerge from *How To Pay for the War* relates, according to Skidelsky, to Keynes's attitude to inflation, and the flexibility of his new theoretical apparatus in dealing with it. Aiming to dispel the (once) widely held notion that Keynes was a dove on inflation, Skidelsky traces the evolution of *How To Pay for the War* in Keynes's writings in the two years leading into the Second World War – writings in which he voiced concerns for what we would now call an 'overheating' British economy. *How to Pay for the War* adapted the economics of a less than fully employed economy into one that was not only able to deal with a situation of excess demand, but also to channel it in socially desirable ways.

The third issue that Skidelsky chooses to highlight from *How To Pay for the War* relates to the element of liberalism that underlay Keynes's approach to wartime policy. According to Skidelsky, *How to Pay for the War* presented an alternative to 'totalitarian' methods – rationing, price controls, physical planning – in favour of an approach that essentially rationed *income*, but otherwise left the price mechanism in place (2000a, *xx*). Whilst only certain aspects of *How to Pay for the War* were adopted by the British Government (forced saving notably), Skidelsky writes that the episode is important for understanding Keynes's view that prices were 'the essential element of freedom in the economic system, however restricted their scope might have to be' (2000a, 67).

XVIII

Keynes influenced policy-making at the highest levels for over forty years. His success on this front, Skidelsky concludes, came largely because of his powers of persuasion. Commenting upon Keynes's defence of the Bretton Woods agreement in the House of Lords in 1946, one of the last and greatest of Keynes's public speeches, Skidelsky observes that '[p]erhaps it is in the realm of rhetoric that his true greatness lies' (Skidelsky, 2000, 448). Keynes himself famously wrote that a 'master economist' required a number of skills 'not often found together'. The master economist had to be 'mathematician, historian, statesman, philosopher...' (Keynes, 1972, 173). Keynes had ascribed these abilities to his one time patron Alfred Marshall, but with much greater accuracy he could have been describing himself. According to Skidelsky, as a policy adviser Keynes had '[i]ntellectual sparkle, analytic power, mental and physical vitality, a capacity to shape theory to events, administrative flair, an instinct for compromise, mastery of persuasive language, loyalty to his department' (2000, 158).

In his splendid review of the first two volumes, Pollard (1994, 138) observed that

> economists are not, on the whole, actors upon the historical stage. Even Keynes, who came closer to being one than most, particularly towards the end of his life, was an adviser, not a decision maker. The interest he excites most is intellectual, not heroic.

The great achievement of Skidelsky's monumental biography, now concluded, is that the historical actor and even the decision maker at critical moments, is plain to see. Perhaps we now have an undisputed subtitle for the promised single-volume abridgement of this great work – *John Maynard Keynes: The Economist as Hero.*[38]

Notes

† We thank but in no way implicate Stephanie Blankenburg, Tony Brewer, John Coates, William Coleman, Robert Dixon, Gordon Fletcher, Prue Kerr, Peter Kriesler, Ray Petridis, Claudio Sardoni, Robert Skidelsky and John Smithin for their comments on a draft of the chapter.

1. Sylvia Townsend Warner's reference to 'that English mixture of the genteel and the raffish' (Kermode, 2001, 242) is at least half apt in the case of Keynes.

2. The Apostles were a secret society that met every Saturday evening in Full Term in Cambridge in the Secretary's room, behind locked doors; they were overwhelmingly a self-selecting group from King's and Trinity (College, not Hall). Most Apostles 'were dons: embryonic, actual or manqué'. They exhibited 'great cleverness with great unworldliness' (Skidelsky, 1983, 119), reflecting 'the peculiar English capacity for keeping its upper-class males in a state of petrified adolescence' (Skidelsky, 1983, 120). High minded and immensely serious when they started in 1820, they were concerned with (Skidelsky quotes Henry Sidgwick) 'the pursuit of truth with absolute devotion and unreserve by a group of intimate friends'. A paper would be read and discussed, accompanied by 'the consumption of anchovies on toast..."whales"...and tea or coffee'. (Skidelsky, 1983, 116). By Keynes's time the society also had active homosexual overtones, the presence of which Moore, the original innocent abroad and at home, never twigged.

3. Skidelsky (1983, 125) quotes a perceptive comment by Pigou on Keynes (when as an undergraduate the latter was Secretary of the Cambridge Union) that 'never in his presence shall "good as means" and "good as ends" pass without challenge.' Skidelsky notes that this was the central distinction of Moore's book, referring us to chapter 6.

4. Peter Kriesler (4 May 2003) informs us that in the course of writing his wonderful biography of Alfred Marshall, Groenewegen (1995), Peter Groenewegen formed the view that Keynes had read a great deal more economics as a result of Marshall's influence than Skidelsky documents.

5. John Smithin (26 June 2003) suggests that the link between Burke and Keynes helps to explain Keynes's conservative side.

6. Marx had the same insight. This led a modern Marxist, James Crotty (1980, 23), to discuss the macroeconomic foundations of microeconomics (in the context of evaluating post-Keynesian economics). Twenty years later Frank Hahn, innocent of all that had gone before, now writes on the same theme.

7. We feel sure that this would have been Keynes's response too, had he and Mantoux ever been able to meet and argue out the issues. Robert Skidelsky (18 June 2003), however, does not completely agree. 'Keynes judged the politics of extracting reparations from Germany better than Mantoux, though I agree he was wrong on "capacity", narrowly interpreted...JMK's estimate of German capacity was based on pre-war export figures when Germany was running a full employment economy. (Average unemployment rate in Germany between 1902 and 1914 was 2%.) So it is a moot point whether GT would have much altered what JMK wrote in 1918.'

8. Ohlin could have said much the same about his celebrated exchanges with Keynes over the transfer problem in 1929.

9. Skidelsky (1992, 517) refers to Virginia Woolf's 'fascinating account' of dinner with Keynes and T. S. Elliot in April 1934. Keynes told Elliot 'he would be inclined not to demolish Xty if it were proved that without it morality was impossible.' Keynes told Virginia Woolf '... our generation ... owed a great deal to our fathers' religion ... the young ... Julian ... brought up without it, will never get so much out of life. They're trivial .. We had the best of both worlds ... destroyed Xty and yet had its benefits.'

10. See Skidelsky (1992, 522–23) in which he describes the experience of Michael Straight (who was then a fervent Marxist) at the Club in 1935 when Keynes crushed David Champernowne's paper on Marx. 'Through the influence of Keynes ... loved ... admired, ... [Straight] lost his belief in Marxism'.

11. In his letter (20 August 1942) to Joan Robinson, written after reading her 1942 *Essay on Marxian Economics*, he wrote that he was 'left with the feeling ... that [Marx] had a penetrating and original flair but was a very poor thinker indeed', that even her 'fascinating' and well written book was nevertheless 'an attempt to make sense of what is in fact not sense'. In 1935, at his Political Economy Club, Keynes admitted to having 'read Marx as if it were a detective story, trying to find some clue to an idea in it and never succeeding' (Skidelsky, 1992, 523), quoting Michael Straight's account.

12. Skidelsky (1983, 217), quoting a letter (1 August 1911) from T. T. Williams.

13. That is *not* to say that, once his central message had been absorbed, it is *not* better to model market structures as realistically as possible, given the necessary constraint of simplicity.

14. Keynes claims in the preface that he is proposing 'a novel means of approach to the fundamental problems of monetary theory ... a method which is useful in describing ... the characteristics of static equilibrium ... also those of disequilibrium [so helping] to discover the dynamical laws governing the passage of a monetary system from one position of equilibrium to another' (Keynes, 1930; *C.W.*, vol. VI, 1971, *xvii*). Peter Kriesler (4 May 2003) comments that there is a parallel here between Keynes's position then and the Bastard Keynesians' position later, that is to say, a belief that full employment would rule in the long run but that there was a role for government policy in the short run because the latter 'could stretch for a long time, until all alive today are dead'.

15. 'God ensured that the widow's jar was always full of water however much the prophet Elijah drank from it; by contrast the Danaides of Greek legend had to carry water to the city of Argos in broken jars' (Skidelsky, 1992, 447). Profits were like the widows cruse – however much of them was spent they remained undepleted by raising the prices and profits of other entrepreneurs. Losses by contrast would be cumulative – if entrepreneurs try to save more, 'the cruse becomes a Danaid jar which can never be filled up' (Keynes, 1930; *C.W.*, vol. V, 1971, 125).

16. For a fuller discussion of these issues see Harcourt 1994; 1995, 48–53.

17. Gordon Fletcher (21 March 2003) reminds us that Keynes also made appeals for reconciliation directly to Robertson himself.

18. For example, Keynes wrote to Hawtrey on 28 November 1930 after publication of the volumes (but in reply to Hawtrey's comments on the proofs): 'The question *how much* reduction in output is caused ... is important ... not strictly a monetary problem. [Keynes had] not attempted to deal with it ... [he was]

primarily concerned with what governs *prices*' (Keynes, 1931; *C.W.*, vol. XIII, 1973a, 145, emphasis in original). Again, 'I am not dealing with the complete set of causes which determine the volume of output ... this would have led me an endlessly long journey into the theory of short-period supply and a long way from monetary theory ... [He agreed] that it will probably be difficult in the future to prevent monetary theory and the theory of short-period supply from running together' (Keynes, *C.W.*, vol. XIII, 1973a, 145–46).

19. Keynes told his parents (September 1930) that he had 'changed his mind too much during the course of writing it for it to be a proper unity'.

20. One of Keynes's innovations within the quantity theory framework was to identify explicitly sectoral price levels and to point to different determinants of them. Similarly, he broke down the overall velocity figure into components, each of which was determined by different factors.

21. Robert Skidelsky (18 June 2003) writes that he would emphasise more than we do that *A Treatise on Money* 'was a stylised description of Britain's peculiar problem in the 1920s, whereas *The General Theory* was a stylised account of the collapse of the US economy between 1929–32. The closed economy idea is not specifically derived from the US ... but is that of a world in depression.'

22. The most obvious manifestation of this is the long debate over the years since the publication of Volumes II and III of *Capital* of the significance of the transformation problem and its various solutions, for GCH's own 'solution', see Harcourt and Kerr (2001, 157–72)!

23. Writing to Ohlin in January 1937, Keynes said he had abandoned a method akin to *ex post* and *ex ante* in 1932 'owing to his failure to establish any definite unit of time ... [he] used to speak of the period between expectation and result as 'funnels of process' but [because] ... funnels are all of different lengths and overlap with one another ... at any given time there is no aggregate realised result capable of being compared with some aggregate expectation at some earlier date' (Keynes, *C.W.*, vol. XIV, 1973b, 184–85).

24. John Smithin (26 June 2003) comments that it was *not* sensible for Keynes to do this, that it was a major mistake in that it 'opened the door for real balance effects, etc., and provided an opening for the anti-Keynesian reaction'.

25. Skidelsky corrects the mistake of Volume I by conceding that the quantity theory *is* a long-period theory.

26. Not completely, since the transactions and precautionary demands for money are related to prices and quantities.

27. In the first model, long-term expectations are given and independent of short-term expectations which themselves are assumed to be realised immediately; in the second model, independence is maintained but short-term expectations are not realised immediately; in the third model, failure immediately to achieve short-term expectations feeds back on long-term expectations and changes the underlying centre of gravitation (equilibrium).

28. Skidelsky succinctly catches the essence of all this when he writes (1992, 624) '... the attempt to shift one curve may have unexpected repercussions on the other.'

29. A somewhat truncated version of this section reviewing Volume III is in the *Festschrift* volume in honour of Peter Groenewegen. See Harcourt and Turnell (2004) in Aspromourgas and Lodewijks (eds) (2004), 236–44.

30. There is, in any case, something of a truce in this 'war', with Skidelsky himself as one of the peacemakers. For more on such matters, see Darity (1994). Moreover, we agree with David Vines's superb case, that 'Keynes needed to create the discipline of international macroeconomics, *and he did so...*' (Vines 2003, 339, emphasis in original). We also agree with Vines that while Skidelsky showed vividly *why* Keynes needed to do this, he does not explicitly show *what* the creation is.
31. This quotation is taken from De Long's (still active) website review, first written in December 2000. In the shorter review published in the *Journal of Economic Literature*, 'strange and sinister sect' has been replaced by the more muted 'set of British imperial conservatives' (De Long 2002, 161).
32. Emphasis added. This speech cited by De Long is famous as that which promised 'blood, toil, tears and sweat'. It is reproduced in full in Cannadine (1989).
33. In a speech by Churchill on 10 November 1942, cited in Gilbert (1991, 734).
34. Sir Basil Blackett, the Treasury's representative in the United States during the First World War. Cited by Skidelsky (1983, 342).
35. Just as Vines (2003) is surely correct concerning its importance for Keynes's theoretical contributions.
36. In an appendix labelled 'Harry Dexter White; Guilty and Naïve' (2000a, 256–263), Skidelsky finds for the prosecution regarding the accusation that White was a Soviet spy. Skidelsky speculates that White's belief that power in the postwar world was best shared between the US and the Soviet Union, allowed him to rationalise passing documents to the Soviets as loyalty to his country. It is a rationalisation that Skidelsky rejects. Skidelsky's verdict is disputed effectively in Boughton and Sandilands (2002).
37. Moggridge (1992, 629) writes that *How to Pay for the War* was 'the most sophisticated and successful of Keynes's many campaigns as a publicist'. Relative to Skidelsky, however, he places less importance on it in defining the canon of Keynes's work. For a criticism of what is seen as *undue* stress placed by Skidelsky on *How to Pay for the War*, particularly as an application of *The General Theory*, see Laidler (2002).
38. The title was in fact, Skidelsky (2005), *John Maynard Keynes: 1883–1946: Economist, Philosopher, Statesman*.

References

Arestis, P., Desai, M. and Dow, S. (eds) (2002), *Money, Macroeconomics and Keynes. Essays in Honour of Victoria Chick, Volume One*, London and New York: Routledge.

Aspromourgas, T. and Lodewijks, J. (eds) (2004), *History and Political Economy. Essays in Honour of P. D. Groenewegen*, London and New York: Routledge Taylor and Francis Group.

Boughton, J. and Sandilands, R. J. (2002), 'Politics and the attack on FDR's economists: From the Grand Alliance to the Cold War, *Intelligence and National Security*, 17.

Cannadine, D. (ed.) (1989), *Blood, Toil, Tears and Sweat: The Speeches of Winston Churchill*, Boston: Houghton Mifflin.

Clarke, P. (1988), *The Keynesian Revolution in the Making*, Oxford: Clarendon Press.

Clarke, P. (1994), 'Keynes in history', *History of Political Economy*, 26, 117–135.

Crotty, James R. (1980), 'Post-Keynesian Economic Theory: An Overview and Evaluation', *American Economic Review* (Papers and Proceedings), 70, May, 20–25.

Darity, W. D. (1994), 'Who Owns John Maynard Keynes?', *History of Political Economy*, **26**, 155–164.

De Long, J. B. (2000), ' Review of Robert Skidelsky, *John Maynard Keynes: Fighting for Britain 1937–1946*', online book review, <http://www.j-bradford-delong. net/Econ_Articles/Reviews/skidelsky3.html>.

De Long, J. B. (2002), 'Review of Skidelsky's *John Maynard Keynes: Fighting for Britain*', *Journal of Economic Literature*, 40, 155–62.

Dow, Sheila C. (1997), 'Endogenous Money', in Harcourt and Riach (eds) (1997), vol. 2, 61–78.

Eatwell, J. 1994, 'Citizen *Keynes*', *The American Prospect*, 5, December.

Gilbert, M. (1991), *Churchill: A Life*, London: William Heinemann.

Groenewegen, P. (1995), *A Soaring Eagle: Alfred Marshall 1842–1924*, Aldershot, Hants., UK; Vermont, USA, Edward Elgar Publishing Limited.

Harcourt, G. C. (1981), 'Marshall, Sraffa and Keynes: Incompatible Bedfellows?' *Eastern Economic Journal*, **5**, 39–50, reprinted in Harcourt (1982), 205–21.

Harcourt, G. C. (1982), *The Social Science Imperialists. Selected Essays*, ed. P. Kerr, London: Routledge.

Harcourt, G. C. (1993), *Post-Keynesian Essays in Biography. Portraits of Twentieth-Century Political Economists*, Houndmills, Basingstoke, Hants: Macmillan.

Harcourt, G. C. (1994), 'Kahn and Keynes and the Making of *The General Theory*,' *Cambridge Journal of Economics*, 18, 11–23, reprinted in Harcourt (1995), 47–62.

Harcourt, G. C. (1995), *Capitalism, Socialism and Post-Keynesianism. Selected Essays of G. C. Harcourt*, Aldershot, Hants: Edward Elgar.

Harcourt, G. C. (2001), *50 Years a Keynesian and Other Essays*, Houndmills, Basingstoke, Hants: Palgrave Macmillan.

Harcourt, G. C. and Prue Kerr (2001), 'Karl Marx, 1818–1883' in Harcourt (2001), 157–68.

Harcourt, G. C. and P. A. Riach (eds) (1997), *A 'Second Edition' of The General Theory*, 2 vols, London: Routledge.

Harcourt, G. C. and S. Turnell (2004), 'Some Reflections on Keynes's Policy and the Second World War', in Aspromourgas and Lodewijks (eds) (2004), 236–44.

Harrod, R. F. (1951), *The Life of John Maynard Keynes*, London: Macmillan.

Heilbroner, R. (1986), 'The Man Who Made Us All Keynesians', *The New York Times*, 11 May.

Hicks, J. R. (1954), 'The Process of Imperfect Competition', *Oxford Economic Papers*, 6, 41–54, reprinted as 'Stickers and Snatchers', in Hicks (1983), 163–78.

Hicks, John (1983), *Classics and Moderns. Collected Essays on Economic Theory*, vol. III, Oxford: Basil Blackwell.

Jevons, W. S. (1871; 1970), *The Theory of Political Economy*, Pelican Classics, edited by R.D. Collison Black, Harmondsworth: Penguin Books.

Kahn, R. F. (1975), *On Re-reading Keynes* (Fourth Keynes Lecture in Economics, the British Academy), Oxford: Oxford University Press.

Kaldor, N. (1939), 'Speculation and Economic Stability', *Review of Economic Studies*, 7, 1–27.

Kaldor, N. (1982), 'Keynes as An Economic Adviser', in A. P. Thirlwall (ed.), *Keynes as a Policy Adviser*, London: Macmillan.

Kermode, Frank (2001), *Pleasing Myself. From Beowulf to Philip Roth*, London: Allen Lane, The Penguin Press.

Keynes, J. M. (1913), *Indian Currency and Finance*, London: Macmillan, *C.W.*, vol. I, 1971.

Keynes, J. M. (1919), *The Economic Consequences of the Peace*, London: Macmillan, *C.W.*, vol. II, 1971.

Keynes, J. M. (1921), *A Treatise on Probability*, London: Macmillan, *C.W.*, vol. VIII, 1973.

Keynes, J. M. (1923), *A Tract on Monetary Reform*, London: Macmillan, *C.W.*, vol. IV, 1971.

Keynes, J. M. (1930), *A Treatise on Money*, 2 vols., London: Macmillan, *C.W.*, vol. V, VI, 1971.

Keynes, J. M. (1933), *Essays in Biography*, London: Macmillan, *C.W.*, vol. X, 1972.

Keynes, J. M. (1936), *The General Theory of Employment, Interest and Money*, London: Macmillan, *C.W.*, vol. VII, 1973.

Keynes, J. M. (1973a), *The General Theory and After. Part I: Preparation*, *C.W.*, vol. XIII, London: Macmillan.

Keynes, J. M. (1973b), *The General Theory and After. Part II: Defence and Development*, *C.W.*, vol. XIV, London: Macmillan.

Keynes, J. M. (1979), *The General Theory and After: Supplement*, *C.W.*, vol. XXIX, London: Macmillan.

Keynes, J. M. (1980), *Activities 1940–4*, *C.W.*, vol. XXV, London: Macmillan.

Kregel, J. A. (1976), 'Economic Methodology in the Face of Uncertainty: the Modelling Methods of Keynes and the Post-Keynesians', *Economic Journal*, 86, 209–25.

Kriesler, P. and Nevile, J. (2002), '*IS-LM* and Macroeconomics after Keynes', in Arestis, Desai and Dow (eds) (2002), 103–14.

Laidler, D. (2002), 'Skidelsky's Keynes: a review essay', *European Journal of the History of Economic Thought*, 9, 97–110.

Mantoux, É. (1945; 1952), *The Carthaginian Peace or The Economic Consequences of Mr. Keynes*, with an Introduction by R. C. K. Enson and a Foreword by Paul Mantoux. New York: Charles Scribner's sons.

Moggridge, D. E. (1976), *John Maynard Keynes*, Harmondsworth, Middlesex: Penguin.

Moggridge, D. E. (1992), *Maynard Keynes: An Economist's Biography*, London: Routledge.

Moore, G. E. (1903), *Principia Ethica*, Cambridge: Cambridge University Press.

Nasar, S. (2002), 'John Maynard Keynes: A Man of Action as Well as Ideas', *The New York Times*, 20 January.

Patinkin, D. (1976), *Keynes's Monetary Thought: A Study of Its Development*, Durham NC: Duke University Press.

Pheby, J. (ed.) (1989), *New Directions in Post-Keynesian Economics*, Aldershot: Edward Elgar.

Pigou, A. C. (1933), *The Theory of Unemployment*, London: Macmillan.

Pollard, S. (1994), 'New Light on An Old Master', *Economic Journal*, 104, 138–53.

Presley, J. R. (1984), 'Review of 'John Maynard Keynes, Volume I, Hopes Betrayed'', *Economic Journal*, 94, 411–12.

Robertson, D. H. (1926), *Banking Policy and the Price Level: An Essay in the Theory of the Trade Cycle*, London: P.S. King.

Robinson, J. (1933), 'A Parable of Saving and Investment', *Economica*, 13, 75–84.

Robinson, J. (1942), *An Essay on Marxian Economics*, London: Macmillan, 2nd edn, 1966.

Rymes, T.homas K. (1989), *Keynes's Lectures, 1932–35. Notes of a Representative Student*, Houndmills, Basingstoke, Hants: Macmillan.

Sardoni, C. (1987), *Marx and Keynes on Economic Recession*, Brighton: Wheatsheaf.

Skidelsky, R. (1983), *John Maynard Keynes, Volume One. Hopes Betrayed, 1883–1920*, London: Macmillan.

Skidelsky, R. (1992), *John Maynard Keynes, Volume Two. The Economist as Saviour 1920–1937*, London: Macmillan.

Skidelsky, R. (2000a), *John Maynard Keynes, Volume Three. Fighting for Britain 1937–1946*, London: Macmillan.

Skidelsky, R. (2000b), 'Ideas and the World', *The Economist*, 23 November 2000.

Skidelsky, R. (2001), *John Maynard Keynes, Volume Three: Fighting for Freedom 1937–1946*, (US Edition) New York: Viking Penguin.

Skidelsky, R. (2005), *John Maynard Keynes: 1883–1946: Economist, Philosopher, Statesman*, London: Penguin.

Tarshis, L. (1989), 'Keynes's co-operative economy and the aggregate supply function' in Pheby (ed.) (1989), 35–47.

Vines, D. (2003), 'John Maynard Keynes 1937–1946: The creation of International Macroeconomics', *Economic Journal*, 113, 338–61.

Woods, R. B. (1990), *A Changing of the Guard: Anglo-American Relations, 1941–1946*, Chapel Hill: University of North Carolina Press.

Part II
Autobiographical Essay

2
Political Economy, Politics and Religion: Intertwined and Indissoluble Passions (1998)*

I

When I returned to Cambridge at the end of August 1997 after two terms of leave in my native Australia, I was delighted to find waiting for me a letter from Professor Szenberg asking me to contribute to his ongoing series on the life philosophies of economists.† In recent years I have written a number of essays which circle around this theme. His request gave me the opportunity to bring the various strands together and, it is hoped, into focus.

II

Let me begin at the beginning. I was born in Melbourne, Australia on 27 June 1931 at the height of the Great Depression, the younger of twin sons of Marjorie and Kenneth Harcourt. According to family lore, I was not expected. The doctor had packed his bag after delivering my brother, John, in the double bed of the home in which John still lives, when the midwife alerted the doctor to my presence, a presence he initially was reluctant to accept. Following a breach birth I spent my first minutes with no clothes on, until my grandmother was contacted to bring some spares. This experience may have something to do with my hedonism in later life.

Both my parents were Jewish. At the time when we were born, they were agnostic and assimilationist in religion, right-wing in politics,

---

* Originally published in *American Economist*, vol. 42, Fall, 1998, pp. 3–18.

especially my mother. Both were born in Australia. My father's father[1] probably came from Transylvania (then Romania, now Hungary); his mother came from Poland. My mother's father came from Germany; her mother's parents were English Jews in origin, who had already been in Australia for a generation. They were rather posh and I often say that my mother married my father as she was going down in the world and he was coming up – his parents were itinerant shopkeepers in New South Wales. My father was brought up as an orthodox Jew but what he came to see as the hypocrisy of religious people of all faiths led him to an agnostic position by his twenties. When I was born he was a leather merchant, working with my maternal grandfather. His mother was dead and he was estranged from his father who previously had left his mother and their four children. My mother had little if any religious sense. She viewed religious affiliations as tags to signal where people stood in the pecking order of society – Melbourne in those days was stuffy, snobby and sectarian. She entered us as Church of England (C of E) at our primary and secondary schools. Being C of E was then regarded as highly respectable, even upper class, certainly much above Methodism, probably on a par with Presbyterianism. This ranking system must have stayed with us. I subsequently became a Methodist, my brother a Presbyterian (after I had paved the way, as it were) and, in the last years of her life, my mother also became a Presbyterian. My father resolutely remained an agnostic to the end of his life.

As I said, Melbourne was a sectarian place. The principal fights were between the Roman Catholics, many of whom were of Irish origin, on the one hand, and all manner of Anglicans and Protestants, on the other. Nevertheless, these warring groups cheerfully formed a united front when ganging up on the Jews – thoughtless, British-style, anti-Semitism was very much alive and well when I was young. Indeed, as a child I heard much of it in my own home. I shall never forget the trauma that engulfed me when as a four- or five-year-old – I may even have been younger – I repeated some anti-Semitic sentiments I had heard at home, expecting approval but instead being told sternly by my father that I was a Jew myself. This was a fundamental landmark in my psychological and philosophical development. From then on I was conscious of being an outsider, a feeling that was confirmed during my boyhood by several episodes which were traceable, directly or indirectly, to the prevailing anti-Semitic attitudes (I described some of these in Harcourt, 1960).

At our primary school our Jewishness was the basis for much of the (verbal) bullying and ostracism we received. It was behind the breakup of a close friendship with another boy. Another incident from this period concerns a holiday my brother and I spent in Ballarat with a family we had previously met on a holiday at Torquay, a Victorian seaside holiday town. A son of the family began acting strangely, he seemed embarrassed to have us there. The next-door neighbours had objected to having Jews staying next to them, principally, it seemed, because Jews had no homeland of their own (this was before Israel had been founded), were anyway generally undesirable, mean and money-grubbing and, I suspect, Christ-killers into the bargain. I tried to explain to him that it was not the Jews fault now that, centuries ago, they had been driven out of their original homeland, that, while they were often associated with business and money, often through necessity, they were neither necessarily mean nor money-grubbing. As for the Christ-killing charge, I mentioned the Romans; I hope I also tried to point out the irony expressed in the rhyme:

> How odd of God
> To choose the Jews
> But not so odd
> As those who choose
> A Jewish God
> And scorn the Jews.

I do not think I had much success with him, or with others in later instances.

These experiences heightened my interest in religion, in the existence or not of God, while, at the same time, reinforcing the sceptical attitudes concerning religion and religious persons that I took over uncritically from my father. I went to divinity classes at both my schools and learnt a lot about the Old and New Testaments; indeed, I won the Divinity Prize at least once at my secondary school. (I must say that now I have embarked on a two-year stretch of reading the Bible, courtesy of the Cambridge Bible which rearranges the readings so that they are relatively interesting and the reader is not bogged down in chapter after chapter of 'begats,' I realise that we were given highly selective readings at school, especially of the Old Testament. The portraits of God and the behaviour of his People that I now find emerging are ambivalent, to say the least.)

III

As I mentioned, my parents' political views were conventionally right-wing, on the whole uncritical and, indeed, adulatory in their support of the views of R.G. Menzies and his, inappropriately named, Liberal Party (which was started after the end of World War II. Before that he had been the leader of the United Australia Party (UAP)). Their support partly reflected their bourgeois background – both my grandfathers were business people, albeit my mother's father had a much larger business until he went broke in the late 1930s. My father continued in his own business until he was well into his seventies. It also reflected their desire to belong to the Australian, especially Victorian (state and variety), middle class and its way of life. For over 50 years, they were the only Jews at their golf club, for example. I do not wish to suggest that they were unprincipled or expedient. They were only too aware of what was happening in Europe – some of our relatives were still in Germany – and they took the steps they thought best to protect us.

My father especially had all the old-fashioned virtues in great abundance and his care during his entire eighties of my mother when she had a terrible stroke in 1972 was heroic. He was an honest, selfless, warm, kind and witty person. He could be stubborn and inflexible, and was prone at times to mild depression. But he was much loved and respected by all who knew him. One woman who had known him since she was a small child wrote after his death that it was always a pleasure, never a chore, to drop in to see him in his old age. (He was 96 when he died.) I should also say that the death of our older sister, Robyn, in her fourth year (she was a blue baby) meant that a sense of grief and sadness pervaded our home though our parents rarely spoke of Robyn herself. My mother was efficiently caring and warm hearted, and basically kind. But she was also most insecure, with the result that she had little sense of proper boundaries in relationships with her children, other relatives, or friends. This was a continuing source of friction and ill will. She mellowed after her stroke when she realised, at last, that people really did care about her and were fond of her.

I had tremendous rows with my parents when I was growing up – so what is new? – and especially when I went to university. Ostensibly these were mostly about politics (I quickly became a democratic socialist at university) and religion, but, especially in my mother's case, it was basically about independence and letting go. My father understood that there are two equally important parts to parenting – love and support and guidance when children are young, love and letting go, coupled with a dependable fall-back position, if needed, when children are grown.

The profession of Christian principles combined with anti-Semitic behaviour (and Catholic and/or Protestant bigotry) were the major stumbling blocks in the way of me accepting belief in God and joining a religious group when I was a schoolboy. In the matter of faith as in my then political views, I was a carbon copy of particularly my father's views, even up to my sixth form (university entrance) years. I remember writing an essay on the illegality of coal miners striking (because coal was an essential commodity for us all), clearing the arguments with my father, and getting a very rude shock when it was returned with a low mark because the teacher wrote, correctly, that it was so intolerant and one-sided – the beginning of wisdom indeed!

My politics then were therefore rather like those of Margaret Thatcher – a belief in 'free enterprise' and the supreme importance of competitive markets as institutions, in the businessman as hero coupled with a dislike of trade unions and of their leaders as obstructionist bully boys, usually Communists (in those days Communism and Unionism were regarded as virtually synonymous by my parents and their friends); a suspicion of the role of government and a dislike of public servants – bureaucrats who were lazy, good-for-nothings lacking initiative and manners, wasting 'taxpayers' money' through their actions and by their salaries, purveyors of enormous numbers of useless forms and likely as not Roman Catholics into the bargain. Labor Party politicians were suspect both as citizens and as people, virtually non-Australian and non-British in attitudes, too often of Irish origin and therefore suspect as far as loyalty was concerned. We, though, were extremely patriotic, almost jingoistic, and pro-British (my formative years took in World War II); we were lost in admiration for Winston Churchill (and shocked at the 'injustice' and 'ingratitude' of the British electorate in turning him and the Conservatives out in 1945). All told, it was admiration for a Never-never-Land composed from Noël Coward's wartime films, Vera Lynn songs, together with 'There'll always be an England'. 'Rule Britannia'. 'Land of Hope and Glory,' and 'God Save the King,' all of which we sang and listened to with bursting chests and much emotion: so much so that even today, I cannot watch the Last Night of the Proms without a resurgence of these emotions, though my rational self detests and disowns the sentiments and sentimentality involved.

IV

So we start with a small boy who became increasingly conscious of feeling an outsider, especially at my secondary school where I had the misfortune to be in forms, the form captain of which was the most rabid Jew-baiter at the school. I countered by trying hard at my school work (a risky strategy because being a 'swot' and too friendly with teachers led to accusations of 'greasing,' of 'sucking up') and even more at sport, where the enthusiasm (if not the skills) of my cousin Richard and myself were legendary. At this time – the mid- to late 1940s – I wanted to be a vet (I had always been mad on animals and birds) and so I struggled with natural science subjects at which I was no good at all. I look economics as a 'fill-in' subject but it was not until I left school, having at last passed the dreaded physics (a prerequisite for veterinary science), that I decided to do economics at university and become a secondary school teacher. The latter decision allowed me to get a scholarship to go to university, to save my parents paying for me – 1950 was just before a generous system of Commonwealth Scholarships was introduced.

Going to the University of Melbourne (to do the B.Com. degree) in 1950 was a revelation: it was, as I have often written, a 'paradise on earth' after school. It was possible to be friendly with lecturers (my first mentor was Joe Isaac). Religious intolerance at a personal level (sectarianism still bugged the Labor Party) as opposed to political intolerance – it was near the start of the Cold War – was virtually absent. I revelled in the atmosphere and loved all lectures (except those on commercial law, a subject which I found to be a nightmare). In particular, economic principles and economic geography were most admirable complements (Paul Krugman please note). As I have explained elsewhere, the lectures on economic geography – it was in effect a course on comparative economic systems – were responsible for me quickly becoming a democratic socialist. Especially crucial was the account of the development of Californian oil fields by 'free enterprise' and the consequences of this, the large permanent losses of natural gas and oil. This alerted me to the irrationality of unfettered competitive capitalism. I felt that any vital resources which were meant to serve the needs of both present and future generations should be developed by organisations with suitably long horizons and so I argued for the nationalisation of all such resources. I still believe my basic reasoning to be correct but I accept that I was naïve to expect that politicians and managers of nationalised industries would *necessarily* have longer time horizons and more enlightened attitudes than their counterparts on boards of private enterprises.

I was also shocked by the descriptions of the disparity in incomes and wealth in many different economic systems, which seemed to me unjust and irrational. I put 'unjust' first because my own experiences of intolerance and of the blatant racism against our indigenous people which was widespread in the middle-class circles in which my parents moved (and not *only* there) often filled me with impotent rage. Sometimes this was expressed in slanging matches with my uncle Sam who, though basically a good and kindly man, was also a very prejudiced one. I still experience these powerful emotional feelings. I cannot, for example, reread *The Ragged Trousered Philanthropists* (Tressell, 1914, 1962), nor, especially, listen to Paul Robeson singing 'Joe Hill' without anger, and, often, tears.

Of course, to start economics at university in 1950 was still to be in an environment enthused by the first flush of *The General Theory* and of the successful application of its principles in both the UK and Australia during World War II. The Commerce Faculty at Melbourne was most Cambridge oriented. We were quickly introduced to Keynes himself (*A Tract on Monetary Reform* in the first year. *The General Theory* itself in the second), Marshall, of course, and Pigou's *Economics of Welfare*,[2] Joan Robinson's *Economics of Imperfect Competition*. Sraffa (1926). Maurice Dobb on *Studies in the Development of Capitalism and Political Economy and Capitalism* (one of my favourite books), and Richard Kahn on the multiplier. In addition, we had Kaldor on the equilibrium of the firm and imperfect competition generally (also the trade cycle), Chamberlin and Triffin, Kalecki on the macroeconomic theory of distribution. Boulding's *Economic Analysis*, Hicks on *Value and Capital*, Hayek on *The Pure Theory of Capital*, Samuelson on *The Foundations* and Wicksteed's *Common Sense*. All this was heady stuff for someone who was amazed to find himself at university, let alone doing well at his subject.[3]

In my third year I took history of economic thought as one of my two specialisations for the third and fourth honours years (my other specialisation was mathematical economics). HET entailed reading many of the greats in the original. The exception for me was Marx – after reading 100 or so pages of Vol. I of *Capital* of which I could make neither head nor tail – I am basically a simple soul – I turned with relief to Paul Sweezy's *Theory of Economic Development* for enlightenment. It was not until I had three brilliant scholars of Marx as research students in the 1970s and 1980s – Prue Kerr, Allen Oakley and Claudio Sardoni – that I was able to make sense of Marx himself.[4] I also browsed long and read widely and haphazardly in the library of the University of Melbourne. Of the many journal articles I read, the single most influential one was Kurt Rothschild's classic, 'Price Theory and Oligopoly' (1947). These experiences provided much of the base on which I erected the structure of economic theory I have used ever since.

With this foundation in economics was allied, very early on, my democratic socialist beliefs. I used then to be much more gung-ho about nationalisation, especially of the financial sector and of essential (for present and future generations) industries such as steel and coal than I am now. But overriding all was the need to create a fair distribution of income and wealth and especially to avoid absolute (and relative) poverty amongst the disabled, the disadvantaged and an inevitable hard core of the inadequate. Of course, then, we took for granted the commitment of governments of all shades of opinion to full employment, regarding achieving it as a necessary characteristic of a just and equitable society (not to mention one claiming to be civilised). Though I was familiar with accounts of the price mechanism and its workings – I had read a lot of Hayek's work on this as well as on capital theory – I was also convinced that the typical market structure in advanced capitalist economies was an oligopolistic one, not a competitive one, so that the blueprints of people such as James Meade and Abba Lerner did not seem to me to be practical, idealistic and appealing though they otherwise were. (Meade idolised Keynes but I do not think they ever saw eye to eye on the efficacy of the price system and competition, and especially on the place in the pecking order of priorities which free trade should take in an ideal world.) Belief in God, any God, took longer to come. It was a prolonged and difficult process.

V

I had no trouble in reconciling the precepts of Christianity with democratic socialist economic principles – indeed, I could not and cannot see how any other conclusion could logically be reached. I was held up by problems of personal faith, and those observed inconsistencies between the practices of many Christians and their professed ideals and beliefs.

Once I convinced myself that, despite my associations with Wesleyanism (my secondary school, Wesley College, and university college, Queen's, were Methodist institutions), I did not need to have a warm feeling somewhere near the pit of my stomach before I could believe, I coupled my democratic socialist beliefs with a decision to regard belief in the Christian God (all Three) as a working hypothesis: let us suppose it to be true and see how we go from there. I took that step in 1953. I still regard it as a correct decision – my working hypothesis has not let me down.

It seemed to me irrational that capitalist institutions should push the exploitation of human selfishness (often called freedom of choice to make it sound better) so far to the front; while simultaneously stunting the development of the Christian (and humanist) virtues of altruism, cooperation, tolerance, compassion, and striving for consensus, not to forget forgiveness. I believe that the only essential difference between socialist humanists and Christian socialists is that the former think that people can bring about desirable reforms by their own unaided efforts. By contrast, Christians believe that it is only by the workings of the Holy Spirit in and through individuals and those individuals in turn working in and through secular and religious groups, that people may be able to achieve what the humanists think people can do unaided. Maybe Philip Wicksteed, a hero from my undergraduate days, put it too strongly: 'If there is no descent of the Holy Spirit there can be no Kingdom of God, in spite of the most perfect and ideal social machinery' (quoted in Steedman, 1994, p. 87). But then, maybe not.[5]

The Holy Spirit works in at least two ways. First, the Holy Spirit removes the intolerable pressures associated with the impossible task of achieving and maintaining personal perfection (think of poor Wittgenstein). This was a preoccupation of Evangelicals in Melbourne during my youth, to my mind, a perverse and unhealthy obsession with gazing at their own navels. Second, the Holy Spirit helps believers to work vigorously and with some chance of success, or at least optimism, within the social and political institutions of their societies. I explicitly rejected the view that religion is related to individual but not to group or social behaviour. I was never under any illusion as to the chances of complete success. That a cause or course of action is right and just does not guarantee that it will succeed. But I do believe that to strive for the Kingdom of God on earth is both correct and feasible for committed democratic Christian socialists even if I am also bound to accept that a just and equitable society is unlikely ever to be fully realised. At one stage on the way I was tempted to become a Roman Catholic but a crucial sermon in which the preacher set out the characteristics of the Roman Catholic. Evangelical and Protestant versions of Christianity led me inexorably towards the last. So I was baptised in 1953 in Queen's College Chapel just before I joined the Australian Labor Party (ALP) (a lagged relationship, my political beliefs having been formed by mid-1950) and when I took up my first lecturing post in Adelaide in 1958. I began to call myself the only Jewish Methodist in that fair city.[6]

VI

So, by the time I graduated in April 1954, I had formulated a working political and religious philosophy/hypothesis and an embryo's, perhaps even an infant's approach to economics from which to proceed. My main interests in economics had also been formed:[7] there were six: first, the links between the behaviour of firms and systemic perform- ance, as illuminated by Keynes's great work, over the trade cycle and beyond – this was the topic of my undergraduate dissertation in 1953. In it I tried to put the arguments of Rothschild's paper on the war- like behaviour of the decision makers in oligopolistic firms who desired secure as much as maximum profits into the framework of *The General Theory*. My aim was to examine a particular issue: Keynes's argument that 'financial prudence,' whereby firms wrote off the book values of their durable assets well ahead of the need to replace them, was a con- tractionary force in the economy as a whole. I conjectured that this might not be so in a world of Rothschild's oligopolists acting according to Clausewitz's *Principles of War*. I looked at the reserve policies of a number of Australian companies over the years of the 1930s depression by examining their profit and loss accounts and balance sheets and constructing their funds statement, in order to see whether any of my inferences were confirmed by their experiences. The overall verdict was the Scottish one of 'not proven'.

Second, a fascination with theories of the trade cycle generally. In my second year as an undergraduate I read the two volumes of Schumpeter's *Business Cycles* (and spelt his name without a 'c' all through an essay I wrote on the trade cycle in the United Kingdom in the nineteenth cen- tury). In our honours years we had lectures on Hicks's *Trade Cycle* and read Kaldor and Swan's review articles of it. A desire to understand the nature of cyclical growth in capitalist economies has remained with me ever since.

Third, the beginning of a lasting love for the analytical history of our subject, as well as an insatiable curiosity about the main players over the years in economics – I read Harrod's life of Keynes in 1951. This gave me an abiding taste for intellectual biography (which was not con- fined either to biographies of economists or, eventually, only to reading what others wrote). Since the early 1970s I have written essays in intel- lectual biography myself. Intellectual biography allows us to begin to see the link between the historical settings of its subjects – their class, their racial, religious and philosophical backgrounds – and the issues of the day on which they write or have written. By analysing these intertwinings, we may hope to understand better their contributions, to recognise both the achievements and limitations of the particular forms which their analyses take and, it is hoped, to be inspired to carry on from where they left off.

Fourth, a desire to understand and do mathematical as well as theoretical economics (they were not explicitly split then as they are now). This has been a continuous source of frustration, for my desire greatly outran my proficiency. I am a poor mathematician and I have only rarely found collaborators who are mathematically gifted (the exceptions are Jorge Araujo and Mohammed Dore).[8] This had not been for lack of trying. For example, my own favourite theoretical paper is the two-sector model of employment and income distribution in the short period which I published in 1965. I wrote it while on leave from Adelaide in Cambridge in 1963–64. It was meant to be the first of a series of papers I wanted to write on these themes: I asked the young Jim Mirlees and, when he said 'no,' the even younger Joe Stiglitz, to collaborate with me on the extensions. Joe lasted a week, a long time in the intellectual life of J. S., before he too said 'no'. So the sequels have never been written by me – Jorge Araujo built on my base in parts of his PhD dissertation. My use of mathematics in articles peaked in 1968 in a paper on investment-decision rules, investment incentives and the choice of technique, though I continue to use simple mathematics and, especially, simple diagrams now and then. My views on mathematics as a good servant but bad master are to be found in an essay in a 1995 selection of my essays.

Fifth, a desire to contribute to down-to-earth, realistic and humane policy based on theoretical developments and applied work. I have done this both through journals and through many years as a backroom boy in the Australian Labor Party where my most important contribution was as the economist on the late 1970s National Commission of Enquiry into the Party's poor performances in the second half of the 1970s. There, I wrote the first draft of the economic policy discussion paper, drawing together the most progressive strands of thinking of people in the Party and of its supporters in the profession at the time. I like to think that it had some influence on the policies of the Party when it was returned to power in the early 1980s; for an independent, rather depressing assessment, see Battin (1996, pp. 103–6).

Sixth, capital theory and distribution theory generally. As I said, I read a lot of Hayek's work when an undergraduate and, of course, the capital bits of *Value and Capital*, as well as Boulding and Schumpeter's writings. But it was going to Cambridge in 1955 which first brought my interest in these issues into sharp focus. My years as a PhD student coincided with Joan Robinson's lectures on what became *The Accumulation of Capital* in 1956. This was another watershed in my development, for it provided, more comprehensively than ever before, the framework within which I have worked. If there is anything original in my PhD dissertation (apart from the empirical work), it is the coupling of the pricing models of Russell Mathews and John Grant, and Trevor Swan, with Joan Robinson's macroeconomic model, in an attempt to analyse the implications of historical cost accounting procedures for measuring incomes for dividend and taxation purposes and for setting prices in a period of inflation. Kaldor (who had been my first supervisor before he went on leave and I went to Ronald Henderson) was then working on his models of distribution and growth and Meade (who succeeded Robertson in 1957 in the Chair of Political Economy) had begun his work on growth theory.

VII

When I took up my first lecturing post at Adelaide in March 1958, I had a number of strokes of good fortune. First, dominating all else, I met Eric Russell for the first time. He became my mentor as well as greatest friend; his influence on me as an economist and as a university person was massive (see Harcourt, 1977a, 1977b). Second, I was able to work directly with John Grant and Russell Mathews as I wrote my PhD dissertation virtually from scratch (I quickly jettisoned all but one chapter of the very rough first draft I brought with me). Third, Peter Karmel, our Head of Department, asked me to review Wilfred Salter's 1960 classic for the *Economic Record;* doing so greatly expanded my understanding of the microeconomic and macroeconomic processes associated with technical progress, and their links to economic policy.[9]

Fourth, Karmel asked me to take over the first year macro course (it was called 'Outlay'); it was essentially an introduction to the economics of Keynes in an Australian setting. The lectures, first given by Karmel, then by me, and subsequently by Bob Wallace, my greatest friend from Melbourne days who was then at Adelaide, were the basis of my first book, *Economic Activity* (1967) (it was written jointly with the other two givers of the lectures).

Fifth, Harold Lydall, Karmel's successor in the Adelaide Chair (Karmel had asked me to take over the Outlay course from him because he had been appointed the foundation vice-chancellor of the new Flinders University of South Australia) asked me to work with him on a puzzle that he had found in some arithmetical examples. The values of the accounting rates of profit he had calculated did not tally with the corresponding values of the economic rates of profit (internal rates of return). This led me to formulate the analysis that became 'The Accountant in a Golden Age' (1965a). The principal reason for the discrepancies between the two measures has to do with the difference in the ways in which accountants and economists respectively calculate depreciation allowances.

VIII

When I returned to Cambridge in August 1963, the burst of productivity that ensued, first in the year of study leave from Adelaide and then during my time as a university lecturer in economics and politics and Fellow of Trinity Hall,[10] had its main source in the experiences of the preceding years in Adelaide. Trying to understand Sraffa's *Production of Commodities by Means of Commodities* (1960) in tandem with Vincent Massaro led me back to undergraduate studies of Ricardo and Marx, at first through a glass darkly but now. I hope, more clearly. While in Adelaide, I had given lectures on Kaldor's postwar contributions to the theory of distribution and growth. This resulted in an article (1963) which criticised aspects of his theory. With my interest in the theory of the firm, especially pricing policies, it was natural to ask what were the pricing policies of Kaldor's businesspeople, or rather, what would they have to be in his theory of distribution if the economy was constrained to be at full employment in *both* the short period and the long period, a proviso which was emerging explicitly in his writings on growth and technical progress in the late 1950s. As I have often remarked, hearing Solow's 1963 Marshall Lectures on a mythical creature called 'Joan' and another called 'Nicky', stimulated me to cease being negative, to accentuate the positive, by developing the two-sector model to which I referred above, in which the ideas of Keynes, Kahn, Kaldor, Kalecki, Joan Robinson, Salter, Solow and Sraffa's recent contributions all came together.

At much the same time. Robin Matthews asked me to review for the *Economic Journal* Minhas's 1963 book on the CES production function and factor reversals in international trade. Writing the review (Harcourt, 1964), in which I combined insights from Salter with those I was obtaining from writing 'The Accountant in a Golden Age,' led eventually to my one excursion into the *Review of Economic Studies* (see Harcourt, 1966), a paper which has often been misunderstood. For example, one referee of the *Review* thought it a woefully inadequate exercise in discovering biases in econometric procedures and Bob Solow in his chapter in my *Festschrift* volumes called it an 'atypical paper' (for me), attributing to me when writing it a subtlety of mind which I could never claim, then or now. I thought its purpose was pretty straightforward, that it was an ironic paper designed to answer the question: suppose we grant the neoclassicals everything except their abstraction in early aggregate production function exercises from the existence of vintages: then, will the methods used in the initial work on CES production functions allow unbiased estimates to be made of the values of a key parameter, the elasticity of substitution of capital for labour of the Salter 'best-practice' isoquant? I tried to show by using a series of, I hoped, plausible growth scenarios with vintages, that large and unpredictable biases emerge.

While I was not explicitly conscious of it, I was in fact moving into a post-Keynesian mode of reasoning when at this time I wrote a number of papers on the choice of technique, investment-decision rules and investment-incentive schemes. For in them I contrasted the results obtained from models which came straight from the world as it was, i.e., I used the actual decision-making rules of businesspeople, with those obtained by standard economic theory. Subsequently, Kaldor was to provide a pithy description of this procedure, not least because he was an outstanding pioneer of its design and use, and of the limitations of standard economic theory, in the first chapter of *Economics without Equilibrium* (1985).[11]

IX

I now come to the two single most important events of my political/academic life. The time is the early to mid-1960s. The wider political background of that time for me was a growing realisation of the immorality of the war in Vietnam and of Australia's disgraceful role in it as one of the US's few 'respectable' allies, a role adopted in order to secure political positions at home and some ill-defined, long-term insurance policies abroad. The details of the background to the war itself were provided for me by Martin Bernal and Ajit Singh in particular. The Faculty at Cambridge and its visitors were, like most other communities then, torn in two: they were either doves or hawks, especially in the early 1960s. For example, in 1963–64. Ken Arrow was a dove, Bob Solow was still a hawk and many of the Faculty were too. But by the end of 1966, when I left for Australia there had been a marked increase in the number of doves, including Solow, who courageously spoke out for his changed position.

I had been a member of the ALP since 1954, President of my local sub branch in the late 1950s and early 1960s and also active in penal reform as Secretary of the Howard League for Penal Reform (SA Branch).

But I was very much a political animal operating within normal channels. This changed when I came home, scandalised by the war and Australia's role in it, including the immoral conscription by birthday ballots of 18-year-old males. I was soon radicalised by the emerging student and anti-war movements of which I immediately became a part in 1967 – a founding member of the Executive Committee of the Campaign for Peace in Vietnam in South Australia and subsequently, for two spells, its chairman (as it was called in those less 'politically correct' days).

The two most intellectually important influences on me articulating my new position on direct action and involvement were Noam Chomsky's essay 'The Responsibility of Intellectuals' (1967) and Hugh Stretton's *The Political Sciences* (1969); the practical influences were the day-to-day experiences of helping to organise a protest movement. My economic analysis started to change as well; not only was my personality intruding more into my writing, but also, as I no longer accepted that ideology and analysis could be separated, I made the former explicit in my writings and my teaching, especially by the end of the 1960s.

As to direct action itself, I thought it was justified if the cause itself was really fundamental and all other avenues had been tried seriously and found wanting. Of course, 'favored nation treatment' could not be claimed for those taking direct action, especially university professors with tenure, though fairness of treatment by police and courts alike when the law was broken could be. That is to say, all the legal consequences of breaking the law had to be accepted but the person involved did not have to accept being bashed up by police, or false accusations – set-ups – such as happened then, especially in the early days of the anti-war protests when the protesters were a small and much-reviled minority whose views were generally unacceptable to the population at large.

I have described elsewhere (see Sardoni, 1992, pp. 5–6) my experiences of those years and those of Joan and the children, now four (Rebecca, our fourth child, was born – when else? – on 10 May 1968, the day the French riots started), with the attendant death threats, potential and, on one occasion, an actual attempt, and so on. Here I want briefly to describe the events which were to change my academic life.[12]

In August 1968 I heard a mysterious rumour that Mark Perlman, the founding editor, wanted me to do a 'Hahn and Matthews' on capital theory for the newly formed *Journal of Economic Literature* (Harcourt, 1969). Sure enough, Perlman arrived in Adelaide to ask me to do just this – evidently, the person he initially commissioned had pulled out and Perlman was left in Australia with a new journal to edit and no author for the survey article of the second issue.

Following a day's 'hard sell,' I said 'yes'. I partially separated from the anti-war movement (with my comrades' blessing), closed a door which was usually open and wrote the first draft in four months. Having to do so wonderfully concentrated the mind, for while I was aware of the issues in a vague, general way. I did not fully understand them, especially the details of the reswitching and capital-reversing debates. Reading the literature more closely. I wrote 'A Child's Guide to the Double-Switching Debate' as the first of five working papers, each on a different aspect and issue, because I found that this was the only way to avoid being overwhelmed by the massive volume of literature to be surveyed. I sent the first paper to about 30 friends ranging from Joan Robinson to Bob Solow and Jim Mirrlees. The favourable feedback emboldened me to keep on and the first draft of the survey was duly sent to Perlman in time for him to have it refereed.

The then economics editor of Cambridge University Press saw the working papers and asked me to write the book of the survey. It would never have been written had I not been invited by Masao Fukuoka to spend three months at Keio University in Tokyo on a Leverhulme Exchange Fellowship. I describe in the Preface (p. ix) of Harcourt (1972) how I lived the selfish life of a scholar and wrote the first draft in two months. There were two main themes: the critique of the conceptual basis of price as an index of scarcity in the theory of value and distribution, and the methodological critique emanating from Joan Robinson of the error of using differences to analyse changes, which became her dominant critique of neoclassical economics. I think she went too far in playing down the first theme – the conceptual basis of an approach *is* a legitimate target for criticism – but was spot on with her insistence on the second critique, one with which Hicks increasingly was to agree and which Kaldor always stressed. His 1984 Raffaele Mattioli Lectures (which were only published in 1996) are replete with examples of analysis which avoids the error, and one of his first papers (1934) already contained the seeds of doubt. Moreover, the best mainstreamers – e.g., Ken Arrow, Franklin Fisher, Frank Hahn – were simultaneously developing path-dependent models.

I wrote a number of commissioned papers on these issues in those years. In one of them, Harcourt (1975; 1982), I began to draw out some policy implications of the capital theory controversies and the post-Keynesian approach more generally. When I returned to Australia in 1973 after a year's leave at Clare Hall in Cambridge, inflation was soon to take off in a major way and the Golden Age of capitalism came to its end. Australia was about to go through an (unintelligent) Thatcherite experiment several years before Thatcher came to power in the UK as the Fraser government from 1975 on cumulatively introduced monetarist policies combined with an ugly confrontationist approach between government, capital and labour. Eric Russell, Barry Hughes, Philip Bentley and I, in support of Ralph Willis, who subsequently became Treasurer in the Keating ALP government, but who was then a lone voice crying in the ALP wilderness, started to develop a package deal for ridding the system (slowly) of inflation while trying to maintain high levels of employment and external balance. This appealed to my continuing interest in policy constrained by *Realpolitik*. With Australia's history and tradition of centralised wage fixing through the Arbitration Commission (sadly – and unwisely – now abandoned),[13] this involved arguing for, amongst other things, indexation combined with restraint on the rate of increase of money wages. My thinking at the time is most fully to be found in the 1982 John Curtin Memorial Lecture, 'Making Socialism in Your Own Country'.

In essence, it involved redistribution through the public sector as the *quid pro quo* to wage-earning groups for accepting incomes policies directed at limiting the rate of increase of money incomes, using the traditional Australian institutions of indexation and the Arbitration Commission. Fiscal and monetary measures were to be directed towards the level of activity, the rate of growth and the post-tax distribution of income. Nationalisation of certain key industries including financial intermediaries was put back on the agenda for discussion and I sat on the fence concerning the tariff, i.e. leave it much as it is and concentrate on export promotion. (The act in my professional life I most regret in retrospect is that I publicly supported, as did most other Australian economists at the time (no excuse, of course), the cut in tariffs by the Whitlam ALP government in the early 1970s. Both the economic reasoning and the timing were wrong.) I opted for a fixed exchange rate, with the proviso that in an economy like Australia's, a change might have to be contemplated from time to time.

X

The final major trauma in my life (to date, and apart from four brushes with death between September 1992 and September 1994) occurred when I was near 50. I – we, for it was a joint family decision, an extraordinarily selfless one by Joan, the children, my father and Joan's parents,

I hope a not too selfish one by me – decided to return to Cambridge to try to document the approach and contributions of Joan Robinson and her circle, to see if there was a coherence in their version of the Cambridge tradition, something worthwhile to try to preserve by telling its and their intellectual histories. I would not have done this had I not believed, passionately, that there was. I still do; if anything, even more so. Of course, I had other reasons as well, that I was too old to play Australian Rules Football (I retired when I was 47), that the cricket club was making me play on matting and I wanted to get back on turf. Life cannot be real and earnest all the time, or, at least, our reaction to it should not be. I am not by nature an overly solemn person and I believe it is tactically sensible (even wise) often to speak true words in the form of jests.

If ever the unfolding of events served to reinforce the need for what I have been trying to do, it is the happenings of the past 20–25 years or so. A great irony of our times is that Marx and Keynes would have had no trouble in explaining their characteristics in terms of their approaches and their theories (suitably modified and updated, of course) – the shift in the balance of economic, social and political power from labour to capital, the emergence of sustained mass unemployment in many advanced economies, the destruction of capacity so that Marxian unemployment has now been added to deliberately induced Keynesian unemployment, the shameful growth of inequality in income and wealth, the smashing of labour unions and the social protection of wage-earners generally in order to create cowed and quiescent workforces, the re-emergence of homelessness and poverty, and, most fundamental as the main cause of instability, the dominance of industrial and commercial capital by domestic and global finance capital. In stark contrast, the mainstream now uses a Fisherian, sometimes even a normative Ramsey representative agent model of lifetime utility maximisation (with all other major real-world institutions and players in society acting merely as *its* agents) to discuss these same characteristics and events: with the result that the concerned young are leaving economics in droves for the more relevant and satisfying social sciences, or even prefer to be hired prize fighters, by choosing to do business studies and to go to business schools instead of economics departments 'proper'.[14]

Even so, I still find it disquieting that so little interest has been shown in mainstream classrooms in the concepts of 'capital' and 'profit,' not only when the capital theory controversies were raging alongside the anti-war movements and student revolts generally but also now, when the events I described above dominate our everyday experience.

As to my major project, sadly, virtually all the major figures have now died, starting with Joan Robinson and Piero Sraffa in 1983, ending – to date – with Austin Robinson in June 1993 and James Meade in December 1995. As I nearly joined them myself, I am rather lagging in getting it altogether in book form. But there are now well over 30 separate essays which provide the essential background to the project and so I do not entirely despair of getting it finished before I call it a day. When I retire in September 1998, I shall be able to spend more time in King's Modern Archives where most of the papers of these economists are housed. While I shall draw mostly on what is in the public domain – I am not a fan of the modern 'tell it all' biography – I do think it necessary to provide evidence on what was going on behind the scenes when their articles and books were being written.[15]

XI

I must confess to having been side-tracked on occasions and in different directions. Since 1992 I have returned to policy on a large canvas, following the invitation to give the Second Donald Horne Address in Melbourne in February 1992, on 'Markets, Madness and a Middle Way'. It spawned further papers, one on macroeconomic policy for Australia in the 1990s (1993; 1995). another on 'A "Modest Proposal" for Taming the Speculators and Putting the World on Course to Prosperity' (1994; 1995). In 1997 I published a paper on economic policy, accumulation and productivity and gave the Seventh Colin Clark Memorial Lecture on 'Economic Theory and Economic Policy: Two Views' (Harcourt, 1997b).

The other major 'side-track' was collaborating with Peter Riach on *A 'Second Edition of The General Theory* (1997). Peter had a bright idea based on the well-known fact that composers have often died before they could finish certain works which others then took up and completed. Keynes had thought of writing at least 'footnotes' to *The General Theory* soon after it was published, but his severe heart attack in 1937 and then World War II and his death in early 1946 prevented him from doing so. Peter's project, which he asked me to join, was to ask a number of Keynes scholars, ranging from Golden Oldies to the up-and-coming, each to write an essay of 6000 words or so on, first, what they thought, based on whatever evidence there was in the *Collected Writings* and other sources, Keynes might have written and, second, why and what they have done on particular aspects of *The General Theory* in the postwar years. It is a most opportune time to have done this, for Keynes is surely rising again from the grave. The book was published in two volumes by Routledge in January 1997, just over 60 years on from the publication of *The General Theory*. (Some of the contributors write, in the first sections of their essays, 'as J. M. Keynes'.) The second volume contains an overview (by James Tobin), essays on extensions and new developments since *The General Theory* was first published, and essays on predecessors and successors. Riach and I wrote a long introduction setting the chapters in context and, between us and the contributors, we accumulated a 50-page bibliography.

XII

I mentioned above my continuing interest in policy questions. Increasingly, as a result principally of the influence of Richard Goodwin, Kaldor, Kalecki and Joan Robinson on my thinking, I have come to realise that the efficacy of single and package deal policy proposals depends vitally on whether individual markets and systems as a whole are best characterised as equilibrating mechanisms, at least as long-term tendencies, or as cumulative causation processes. As I also think that the latter underlie the operations of most major markets and systems, the policy recommendations that I have made explicitly reflect this link. These considerations have especially affected what I have proposed for dealing with the harmful systemic effects of speculation in the markets for foreign exchange, financial assets and property. The same realisation also lies behind my arguments over the years (I first learnt of these from Eric Russell) for tailor-made, permanent incomes policies based on the adjustment of nominal incomes for effective productivity (at least as the starting point). Finally, following the arguments of Keynes and Kalecki in particular, and, more recently, Paul Davidson, I have argued for the recreation of institutions which, while modified for new economic conditions and a changed political environment, nevertheless have the same ultimate rationale as those which came out of Bretton Woods: to wit, to offset the inbuilt contractionary forces in the operation of the world economy. There is also a need for a re-examination of buffer stock schemes for internationally traded primary products, both to protect the real incomes of their producers in the developing countries and to eliminate the potential in the unstable prices of these products for setting off chains of inflation (or deflation) in substantial areas of the world economy as a whole.

XIII

I want to conclude by highlighting three fundamental things. First, though I have only mentioned my students in passing, I want to stress that I regard teaching undergraduates and supervising research students as the most responsible and rewarding tasks university teachers are privileged to have. The achievements and the friendships of students, past and present, are amongst the greatest pleasures and satisfactions of this life.

Second, it may fairly be asked: are my Christian democratic socialist flames still burning as brightly now as when first lit in the early 1950s? The answer is 'yes'. While the going was tough in the 1970s and late 1980s, recent events, e.g., the publication of *Reclaiming the Ground* (Bryant, 1993), the election of, first, John Smith and then Tony Blair as leader of the British Labour Party, the accompanying return to basics (in a non-Majorite manner) cheered me up no end, as have the elections (and re-elections) in Australia of ALP governments in the 1980s and early 1990s, for all their faults and limitations. (Most annoyingly, just as the UK returned a Labour government (1 May 1997), Australia was in its second year of an extremely unpleasant, narrow, ruthless, little-minded conservative government, laughingly called a coalition of the Liberal and National Parties.) Moreover, I am experiencing a sense of *déjà vu* as the Blair Labour government (January 1998) seems to be making many of the mistakes that the Whitlam, Hawke and Keating Labor governments did – do they *never* learn?[16] Of course, the agendas have changed; the proposals are now more modest, more basic – jobs, homes, schools, hospitals, trains, the environment(!) – than in those heady days immediately after World War II. But they still make up a worthwhile agenda for the creation of just and equitable societies, for middle ways which are tailor-made for each country's history, sociological structure and inherited institutions. And they ought to be supported as more and more citizens recoil from the excesses and horrors of both command and market, free-for-all, economies.[17] I hope to play some role in securing these aims.

In a comment on a draft of the essay, Giles Slinger noted that only one of the six aspects of economics cited on pp. 68–70 above – policy proposals – seemed 'to be clearly connected to my religious beliefs'. He asked whether my beliefs had altered '*the way* [I would] have done economics otherwise?' I think the answer is 'no' though I am sure my beliefs affected what I found most vital in economics itself and how I approached our subject. Omar Hamouda once asked me to record what

I thought the purpose of political economy is. Perhaps my answer then (Harcourt, 1986) may help to answer Giles[18] now. Evidently I said that the purpose is: to make the world a better place for ordinary men and women, to produce a more just and equitable society. In order to do that, you have to understand how particular societies work and where the pockets of power are, and how you can either alter those or work within them and produce desirable results for ordinary people, not just for the people who have the power. I see economics as very much a moral as well as a social science and very much a handmaiden to progressive thought. It is really the study of the processes whereby surpluses are created in economies, how they are extracted, who gets them and what they do with them. All economies have created surpluses in one way or another. Capitalism does it in a particular way and that is the process in which I am most interested because I live in capitalist economies. At the same time, I would like to help to create a society where the surplus is extracted and used in a way quite different from that of a capitalist society.

Third, and most fundamentally, I have been blessed with an exceptionally happy marriage and family life. So I end this account of my life philosophy by expressing my thanks to Joan, to our four children, Wendy, Robert, Tim and Rebecca, to Claudio and Jo and to our *numero uno* grandchild, Caterina, for their unstinting love and support.[19]

Notes

† I thank most sincerely but in no way implicate Stephanie Blankenburg, Jeremy Butterfield, Philip Gaudoin, Joan Harcourt, Rebecca Harcourt, Robert Harcourt, Tim Harcourt, Wendy Harcourt, Prue Kerr, Suzanne Konzelmann, Julie McKay, Peter Nolan, Terry Roopnoraine, Bob Rowthorn, Claudio Sardoni, Giles Slinger and Hugh Stretton for their comments on a draft of the essay. I also thank the editor for his positive response and support.

1. Israel Harkowitz. In the 1920s, my father and his brother, Sam, changed the family name to Harcourt a fine old Norman name, as I tell everyone!
2. Because we also read Graaf and Little, I was soon disillusioned with welfare economics.
3. I had been overshadowed by the brilliance of my twin at our schools. Moreover, as was common in those days, we 'jumped' classes, so that we were soon over a year younger than the average age in our class, a handicap for me intellectually and for both of us socially, especially when you consider the extra baggage we had to carry anyway.
4. So I am rather proud of having written, with Prue, the entry on Marx in Malcolm Warner's Encyclopaedia for managers – all managers need and want to know of Karl: see Harcourt and Kerr (1996)!

5. In a wonderfully perceptive comment. Hugh Stretton (7 March 1998) describes his ' "agnostic" working hypothesis [as] a humanism [related to] something in our human nature – much influenced but not created by our upbringing – [which] allows us to figure out our individual versions of *both* the Theory of Moral Sentiments *and* the Wealth of Nations, and the better and worse relations that we may conduct between them' (emphasis in original).

6. Now that the Methodists have ceased to exist in Australia (they have been absorbed into the Uniting Church), it is only in the UK that I may refer to myself as a Jewish Methodist Democratic Christian Socialist; it is always good for a laugh.

7. The prelude to the most fundamental event of my life had also occurred – on the day John and I graduated (he in dentistry), Joan Bartrop (who graduated on the same day in Arts) and I announced our engagement. We had met in our respective final years (1953) at the University of Melbourne, we had an idyllic courtship, and in December 1953 I proposed in the kitchen of her aunt and uncle's house while we were baby-sitting their two children. The proposal was accepted in early 1954. We married in July 1955, just before leaving for Cambridge where I was to do a PhD at King's.

8. After the paper which Dore and I wrote was published in *Economic Letters* in 1986. I received a letter from a Norwegian economist. He said that up till then he had admired my economics and my mathematics. He then pointed out in great detail the awful hash I had made of both in the paper. Since Dore had done the math (they were beyond me: I had merely conjectured the economic approach we might take and Dore most kindly made me a joint author), I asked Bob Rowthorn to adjudicate. He said we were all wrong!

9. I have just finished (January 1998) reviewing Bob Solow's Arrow Lectures on learning from learning by doing and examining a dissertation on evolutionary economics and the role of technical progress in evolutionary processes. In the policy papers which I wrote in 1996 and 1997 I coupled the insights of Salter and Kalecki in a discussion of attaining and then sustaining full employment without inflation. In all these pursuits. Salter's influence remains as fresh and as illuminating as when I first wrote about *Productivity and Technical Change*.

10. These appointments were completely unexpected – I no more thought of having a post at Cambridge, then probably the outstanding centre for economics in the world, than of flying to the moon (indeed the latter was more on the cards at the time). Because I was on leave from Adelaide when I was offered the posts, I decided to take them for three years only, on unpaid leave from Adelaide, because I felt I had a moral responsibility to return there.

11. *Economics without Equilibrium* arose from the first Okun Memorial Lectures at Yale. Okun was a person very much after Kaldor's heart (mine, too), both because of his methods and his rationale for doing economics.

12. Perhaps I could add that in the anti-war activities. I tried to follow the practices of a liberal academic and a Christian. That is to say, I tried to present arguments and critiques fully and fairly rather than as one-sided advocacy, and I tried to remember the essential humanity of those to whom I was

opposed, no matter how angry and distressed I was about what they were doing and supporting.

13. Tim Harcourt reminded me that the Industrial Relations Commission (formerly the Arbitration Commission) is still the institution whereby an annual safety net for low-paid wage-earners who cannot bargain collectively is maintained.

14. I was delighted to find that Paul Samuelson (1997, p. 6) in his ninth decade is so far off the mainstream regression line as to describe the American economy now as having two outstanding characteristics: it is 'a ruthless economy' with a 'cowed workforce'. Karl, that you should have lived to see this day!

15. By the time Joan and I left Cambridge on 30 July 2010 I had with Prue Kerr published an intellectual biography of Joan and Prue and I had edited much background evidence and material. See for example, Harcourt and Kerr (2009), Kerr with Harcourt (eds) (2002), Harcourt (2006).

16. Tim Harcourt thinks I have been too hard on the Hawke and Keating ALP governments. He reminded me that on social issues, they had a creditable record as they did with regard to employment for much of the 1980s. It was their uncertain handling of powerful business and media moguls (always a fiendishly difficult task for Labor politicians and governments), together with the over-enjoyment of the trappings of power (this was especially true of some members of the Whitlam government) that I had in mind.

17. In a wonderfully supportive and wise letter (17 March 1998), Hugh Stretton cited Christopher Hills's *The Experience of Defeat*, 'about the retrospective reflections of the English revolutionary leaders who survived the Restoration'. He asked me 'to recall that the whole of the Leveller program was in force within a couple of centuries...,' so that, today we may hope that even a 'cumulative causation on the Right track' may come to an end, be reversed.

18. Giles also wanted me to be more explicit about when, where and why I had done various things, written certain articles and books. May I refer him (and others) to a companion piece to the present essay, my chapter in Volume IV of Arnold Heertje's series. *The Makers of Modern Economics* (Harcourt, 1998)?

19. To which in October 2010 I may now add Emma-Claire and Yun Shi as grandchildren.

References

Arestis, Philip, Gabriel Palma and Malcolm Sawyer (eds) (1997a), *Capital Controversy, Post-Keynesian Economics and the History of Economics: Essays in Honour of Geoff Harcourt. Volume One*, London: Routledge.

Arestis, Philip, Gabriel Palma and Malcolm Sawyer (eds) (1997b), *Markets, Unemployment and Economic Policy: Essays in Honour of Geoff Harcourt. Volume Two*. London: Routledge.

Battin, Tim (1996), *Abandoning Keynes: Australia's Capital Mistake*, Basingstoke: Palgrave Macmillan.

Brennan, H. Geoffrey and A. M. C. Waterman (eds) (1994), *Economics and Religion: Are They Distinct?* Boston, Dordrecht and London: Kluwer Academic Publishers.

Bryant, Christopher (ed.) (1993), *Reclaiming the Ground: Christianity and Socialism,* London: Hodder and Stoughton.

Chomsky, N. (1967), 'The Responsibility of Intellectuals', in T. Roszak (ed.), *The Dissenting Academy,* New York: Pantheon Books, 1967, 254–98.

Dore M. H. I. and G. C. Harcourt (1986), 'A Note on the Taxation of Exhaustible Resources under Oligopoly', *Economic Letters,* 21, 81–84.

Harcourt, G. C. (1960), 'The Early Verdict', *Nation,* 3 December, reprinted in K. S. Inglis (ed.) (1989), *Nation. The Life of an Independent Journal of Opinion 1958–1972,* Melbourne: Melbourne University Press, 45–46.

Harcourt, G. C. (1963), 'A Critique of Mr Kaldor's Model of Income Distribution and Economic Growth', *Australian Economic Papers,* 2, 20–36.

Harcourt, G. C. (1964), 'Review of Minhas (1963)', *Economic Journal,* 74, 443–45.

Harcourt, G. C. (1965a), 'The Accountant in a Golden Age', *Oxford Economic Papers* (n.s.), 17, 66–80.

Harcourt, G.C. (1965b), 'A Two-Sector Model of the Distribution of Income and the Level of Employment in the Short Run,' *Economic Record,* 41, 103–17.

Harcourt, G. C. (1966), 'Biases in Empirical Estimates of the Elasticities of Substitution of C.E.S. Production Functions', *Review of Economic Studies,* 33, 227–33.

Harcourt, G. C. (1969), 'Some Cambridge Controversies in the Theory of Capital', *Journal of Economic Literature,* 7, 369–405.

Harcourt, G. C. (1972), *Some Cambridge Controversies in the Theory of Capital,* Cambridge: Cambridge University Press.

Harcourt, G. C. (1975), *Theoretical Controversy and Social Significance: An Evaluation of the Cambridge Controversies,* Edward Shann Memorial Lecture, University of Western Australia Press.

Harcourt, G. C. (1977a), 'Eric Russell, 1921–77: A Memoir,' *Economic Record,* 53, 467–74.

Harcourt, G. C. (ed.) (1977b), 'Eric Russell, 1921–77: A Great Australian Political Economist', the 1977 Newcastle Lecture in Political Economy. Reprinted in Sardoni (ed.) (1992), 344–56.

Harcourt, G. C. (1982), *The Social Science Imperialists. Selected Essays. G.C. Harcourt,* Prue Kerr (ed.), London: Routledge and Kegan Paul.

Harcourt, G. C. (1986), *Controversies in Political Economy: Selected Essays of G.C. Harcourt,* O. F. Hamouda (ed.), Brighton: Wheatsheaf Books.

Harcourt, G. C. (1992), 'Markets, Madness and a Middle Way', *The Second Annual Donald Horne Address,* Melbourne: Monash University, also published in *Australian Quarterly,* 64, 1–17.

Harcourt, G. C. (1993), 'Macroeconomic Policy for Australia in the 1990s', *Economic and Labour Relations Review,* 4, 167–75.

Harcourt, G. C. (1994), 'Taming Speculators and Putting the World on Course to Prosperity: a "Modest Proposal" ' *Economic and Political Weekly,* 29, 2490–92.

Harcourt, G. C. (1995), *Capitalism, Socialism and Post-Keynesianism: Selected Essays of G.C. Harcourt,* Cheltenham: Edward Elgar.

Harcourt, G. C. (1997a), 'Economic Policy, Accumulation and Productivity', in Michie and Grieve Smith (eds) (1997), 194–204.

Harcourt, G. C. (1997b), 'Economic Theory and Economic Policy: Two Views' (The Seventh Colin Clark Memorial Lecture 1997), *Economic Analysis and Policy,* 27, 113–30.

Harcourt, G. C. (1998), ' "Horses for Courses." The Making of a Post-Keynesian Economist,' in Arnold Heertje (ed.), *The Makers of Modern Economics*, Vol. IV, Cheltenham: Edward Elgar.

Harcourt, G. C. (2006), *The Structure of Post-Keynesian Economics: The Core Constitution of the Pioneers*, Cambridge: Cambridge University Press.

Harcourt, G. C. and P. Kerr (1996), 'Marx Karl Heinrich (1818–83),' in Warner (ed.) (1996), 3388–95.

Harcourt, G. C. and P. Kerr (2009), *Joan Robinson*, Houndmills, Basingstoke, Hants.: Palgrave Macmillan.

Harcourt, G. C. and P. A. Riach (eds) (1997), *A 'Second Edition' of The General Theory*, 2 vols, London: Routledge.

Kaldor, N. (1985), *Economics without Equilibrium*, Armonk, NY: M.E. Sharpe.

Kaldor, N. (1996), *Causes of Growth and Stagnation in the World Economy*, Cambridge: Cambridge University Press.

Kerr, P. (ed.), with the collaboration of G. C. Harcourt (2002), *Joan Robinson: Critical Assessment of Leading Economists*, 5 vols, London: Routledge.

Michie, Jonathan and John Grieve Smith (eds) (1997), *Employment and Economic Performance. Jobs, Inflation and Growth*, Oxford: Oxford University Press.

Minhas, B. S. (1963), *An International Comparison of Factor Costs and Factor Use*, Amsterdam: North-Holland.

Robinson, Joan (1956), *The Accumulation of Capital*, London: Macmillan.

Rothschild, K. W. (1947), 'Price Theory and Oligopoly,' *Economic Journal*, 57, 299–320.

Salter, W. E. G. (1960), *Productivity and Technical Change*, Cambridge: Cambridge University Press, 2nd edn, 1966.

Samuelson, Paul A. (1997), 'Wherein do the European and American Models Differ?' Address delivered at the Bank of Italy, 2 October.

Sardoni, Claudio (ed.) (1992), *On Political Economists and Modern Political Economy: Selected Essays of G.C. Harcourt*, London: Routledge.

Solow, Robert M. (1997), 'Thoughts Inspired by Reading An Atypical Paper by Harcourt', in Arestis et al. (eds) (1997a), 419–24.

Sraffa, Piero (1926), 'The Laws of Returns under Competitive Conditions', *Economic Journal*, 36, 535–50.

Sraffa, Piero (1960), *Production of Commodities by Means of Commodities. Prelude to a Critique of Economic Theory*, Cambridge: Cambridge University Press.

Steedman, Ian (1994), 'Wicksteed: Economist and Prophet', in Brennan and Waterman (eds) (1994), 77–101.

Stretton, Hugh (1969), *The Political Sciences: General Principles of Selection in Social Science and History*, London: Routledge.

Tressell, Robert (1914, 1962), *The Ragged Trousered Philanthropists*, New York: Monthly Review Press.

Warner, Malcolm (ed.) (1996), *International Encyclopedia of Business and Management*, London: Routledge.

Part III
Post-Keynesian Theory

3
A Teaching Model of the 'Keynesian' System (1969)*

Introduction

1 The purpose of these notes is to outline for teaching purposes a version of the 'Keynesian' model of income-determination in the short period.[†] A feature of the model is that it can handle with very simple algebra the interrelations between the money, goods and labour markets, oligopolistic pricing behaviour and the different consumption behaviour of profit-receivers and wage-earners. The two key expressions are those for the short-run, equilibrium levels of real output and the rate of interest. The model is, if you like, 'Ackley in Algebra'[1] (although the treatment of the price level and the production function differs from Ackley's). The preference for the use of algebra rather than geometry arises from the view that the 'quadrant' approach can mislead students, who may settle for mechanical drill; it may confuse them about the applicability of their results and geometry does not always bring out clearly the limitations of the methodology used. These dangers are more easily avoided, it is believed, when algebra is used.

2 The analysis is essentially comparative statics: – first, the derivation of the *equilibrium* values of real income and the rate of interest from the underlying behavioural relationships and equilibrium conditions, and secondly, comparisons of *differences*, that is, of new equilibrium values with either the old (preceding) ones or with what they would have been in the 'otherwise' situation, when the values of the variables and/or the forms of the relationships are changed. Nothing is said, formally about the process of getting from one equilibrium position to another, or whether the economy will actually do so, and any statement about

---

* Originally published in *Keio Economic Studies*, vol. 6, no. 2 (1969), pp. 23–46.

changes as opposed to *differences* requires an act of faith (which is common to all believers but is not always made explicit). That comparative statics results are so applied to process situations is not stressed enough in the text books.

3 The analysis is short period: the aim is to find the equilibrium values of output and the rate of interest in a period of calendar time of, say, three to six months. The capital stock is given and constant, and prices and money wages are assumed to be decided and *held* for this period of time (see below, paras 3.1 and 3.2).

4 The argument is presented in a number of stages. First, only the goods and money markets are considered. The money market contains two assets – the stock of money (exogenously determined) and bonds. Using a one-commodity, closed two-sector model, and with all relationships assumed to be *linear* functions, the basic expressions for the short-run, equilibrium levels of real output and the rate of interest are obtained. Secondly, a three-asset money market is included to allow a discussion of the Radcliffe Committee, Gurley and Shaw model.[2] The analysis is then extended by introducing the labour market and the short-run aggregate production function, price-making and the price level, and different consumption behaviour by wage-earners and profit-receivers. This allows a discussion of the impacts of different price levels and different distributions of real income on the equilibrium values.

The simplest case: goods and money markets

The equilibrium conditions

1.1 The equilibrium condition in the goods market is that plans and actuality coincide, *i.e.*, that aggregate planned (and actual) spending match actual output (or, *ex ante* and *ex post* investment equal *ex ante* and *ex post* saving). The equilibrium condition in the money market is that the demand for money equals the supply of money, *i.e.*, that the rate of interest settles at a level where people are content to hold the exogenously given stock of money.

The basic relationships

1.2 (i) *The goods market*
     (a) The consumption function
     This is the usual relationship in *real* terms,

(1.1) $$C = \bar{A} + cY_p = \bar{A} + cY,$$

$$(\text{as } Y = Y_p)$$

where

    C = consumption expenditure;
    $\bar{A}$ = autonomous item in the consumption function;
    c = aggregate mpc.;

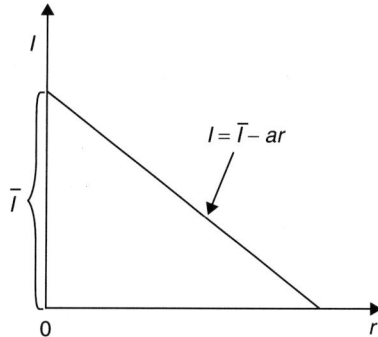

and

    Y = real income (and Y_p = real personal disposable income).

1.3 (b) The investment function

Planned investment expenditure in real terms, following Keynes and taking as given the state of short-term and long-term expectations, is regarded as a simple, decreasing function of the rate of interest. *i.e.*,

(1.2) $I = \bar{I} - ar,$

where
    $\bar{I}$ = planned investment expenditure per period;
    a = the slope of the line, *i.e.*, the *absolute* responsiveness of planned investment expenditure to changes in the rate of interest;
    r = rate of interest;
and
    I = the level of investment expenditure when $r = 0$, which could, perhaps, be regarded as autonomous investment expenditure *in a very special sense.*
The two functions are shown in Figures. 3.1 and 3.2.

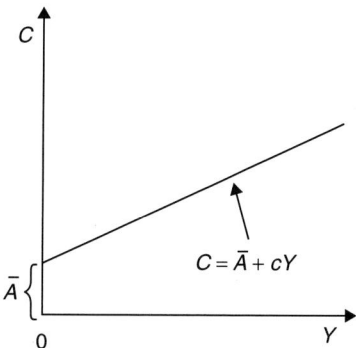

Figure 3.1 The consumption function   *Figure 3.2* The investment function

1.4 Because I is related to r, the aggregate demand schedule – the sum of planned consumption and investment spending – and the equilibrium level of output cannot be determined until the rate of interest is known. And, as will be shown below, the rate of interest cannot be determined until the level of output is known. The two key equilibrium values therefore have to be determined *simultaneously, i.e.*, they are those values of the level of output and the rate of interest which, together, are consistent with (satisfy) the equilibrium conditions in both markets.

1.5 (ii) *The money market*

(a) The demand for active balances
This relationship is the demand for money to satisfy the transactions motive. It is regarded as a simple proportional function of the level of activity (measured in real terms in the present simple case but, in general, in money terms, see below, para 3.9).

(1.3) $M_1 = lY,$

where
M_1 = the demand for active balances;
l = a constant reflecting the public's present spending habits and other transaction motives.

(b) The demand for idle balances
1.6 This is the Keynesian liquidity preference function: the demand for money to satisfy the speculative motive. It is a function of the rate of interest and reflects peoples' uncertainty *now* about the *future* level of the rate of interest. It has two features; first, the function is downward sloping and interest-elastic. Secondly, it is perfectly elastic at a minimum positive rate of interest – the 'liquidity trap' level.

1.7 The liquidity preference function may be drawn as a curve with a vertical stretch at the 'liquidity trap' level of the rate of interest, r^* (see Figure 3.3).[3] This curve may be approximated by two straight lines (the dotted lines in Figure 3.3). They are, respectively, a vertical line at $r = r^*$, of which only the section *above A* has economic meaning, and the line BC, of which *only* the section AC has economic meaning. The equation of the line BC is:

(1.4) $M_2 = M^* - br,$

where
M_2 = the demand for idle balances;
b = the slope of the line, *i.e.*, the *absolute* responsiveness of the demand for idle balances to changes in the rate of interest;

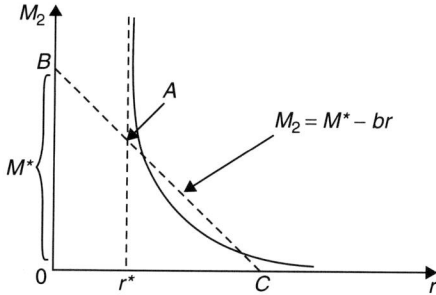

Figure 3.3 The liquidity preference function

and
 M^* = vertical intercept on the M_2 axis, which has no economic meaning.
(c) The supply of money

(1.5) $M = \bar{M}$,

where
 $\bar{M}$ = the exogenously given stock of money.

The equilibrium values

1.8 The equilibrium values of Y and r may be obtained from the two equilibrium conditions.

The goods market condition

$$Y = E(=C(Y) + I(r))$$

i.e.,

(1.6) $\begin{aligned} Y &= \bar{A} + cY + \bar{I} - ar \\ &= \frac{\bar{A} + \bar{I} - ar}{1 - c}, \end{aligned}$

where
 E = aggregate demand.
 (Expression (1.6), when written as: $r = \dfrac{\bar{A} + \bar{I}}{a} - \left(\dfrac{1-c}{a}\right)Y$, is the Hicks-Hansen *IS* schedule.)

The money market condition

$$\bar{M} = M_1(Y) + M_2(r)$$

i.e.,

(1.7) $\bar{M} = lY + M^* - br.$

1.9 Expression (1.7) may be solved for r to give:

(1.8) $r = \dfrac{lY + M^* - \bar{M}}{b} \left(= \dfrac{M^* - \bar{M}}{b} + \dfrac{l}{b} Y \right)$

(This is the Hicks-Hansen *LM* schedule.)
Substituting (1.8) in (1.6), the expression for the equilibrium level of real income is obtained, *viz.*,

(1.9) $Y = \dfrac{\bar{A} + \bar{I} - \dfrac{a}{b}(M^* - \bar{M})}{1 - c + \dfrac{a}{b}l}.$

Finally, by substituting (1.9) in (1.8), and rearranging terms, the corresponding expression for the equilibrium value of the rate of interest is obtained:

(1.10) $r = \dfrac{l(\bar{A} + \bar{I}) + (M^* - \bar{M})(1 - c)}{b\left(1 - c + \dfrac{a}{b}l\right)}$

(provided $r > r^*$).
(The values implied by (1.9) and (1.10) correspond to the values of Y and r associated with the intersections of the *IS* (1.6) and *LM* (1.8) schedules.)[4]

1.10 It should be noticed that the value of r, so obtained, must be greater than r^*. If it is not, the 'liquidity trap' level of the rate of interest prevails, idle balances will absorb whatever cash remains after the needs of active balances have been met, *i.e.*, idle balances are purely residual, and the level of activity will be determined by the consumption function and the level of investment expenditure associated with the 'liquidity trap' level of the rate of interest. The money market therefore has no impact (other than this) on the goods market, and the equilibrium level of real income is obtained from the goods market equilibrium condition, $Y = E$, alone.

Thus

$Y = E = \bar{A} + cY + \bar{I} - ar^*$

i.e.,

(1.9a)[5] $Y = \dfrac{\bar{A} + \bar{I} - ar^*}{1 - c}.$

That $r = r^*$ is, of course, a very important possibility which should not be lost sight of. For the remainder of these notes, though, it will be assumed that the value of r in equation (1.10) exceeds r^* and that the value of Y in equation (1.9) is greater than $\dfrac{br^* + \bar{M} - M^*}{l}$, the value of Y at which $r = r^*$ in (1.8), but is less than the full employment level of real output.[6]

1.11 Equation (1.9) contains elements which are familiar from the simple goods market model of income-determination, namely, the autonomous items of expenditure, $\bar{A}$ and $\bar{I}$, and $\dfrac{1}{1-c}$, the expression for the simple multiplier. That (1.9) reduces to $Y = \dfrac{\bar{A} + \bar{I}}{1-c}$ may be seen by supposing that the quantity of money is such that the equilibrium level of income is $\dfrac{\bar{A} + \bar{I}}{1-c}$ and that the equilibrium rate of interest, *if it could be established*, is zero. The required value of the stock of money may be found by solving for $\bar{M}$ in

(1.10b)
$$\frac{\bar{A} + \bar{I} - \dfrac{a}{b}(M^* - \bar{M})}{1 - c + \dfrac{a}{b}l} = \frac{\bar{A} + \bar{I}}{1 - c}$$

i.e.,

$$\bar{M} = l\left(\frac{\bar{A} + \bar{I}}{1 - c}\right) + M^*.$$

With this value of the stock of money, $Y = \dfrac{\bar{A} + \bar{I}}{1-c}$ and only a zero value of r is consistent with money market equilibrium. Thus

$$\bar{M} = M_1 + M_2;$$

i.e.,

$$l\left(\frac{A + \bar{I}}{1 - c}\right) + M^* = l\left(\frac{\bar{A} + \bar{I}}{1 - c}\right) + M^* - br,$$

which is only true when $r = 0$.

1.12 So much for special casery. In the general case, the multiplier, which is now $\left(\dfrac{1}{1 - c + (a/b)l}\right)$, is seen to be reduced in value, relative to the simple case of $\dfrac{1}{1-c}$, by elements which determine the absorption into active balances as activity rises. These elements are, respectively, the (absolute) responsiveness of planned investment spending to changes in r (*i.e.*, a), the (absolute) responsiveness of the demand for idle balances to changes in r (*i.e.*, b), and the public's habits with regard to active balances (*i.e.*, l). If a is small, so that planned investment expenditure is *little* affected by a given change in r, if b is large, so that the demand for idle balances is *greatly* affected by a given change in r, and if the public economises greatly in the use of active balances, so that l is small, the monetary factors have little impact on the flow of induced spending and the value of the multiplier will be close to the simple value.

1.13 The multiplicand, $\bar{A} + \bar{I} - \dfrac{a}{b}(M^{\star} - \bar{M})$, also has monetary factors in it. $M^{\star}$ may be regarded as the shift factor of the liquidity preference function – the greater is its value, the greater will be the cash demanded for idle balances at any *given* rate of interest and, *cet par*, the lower will be the level of economic activity associated with any given money stock. Given the value of $M^{\star}$, the magnitude of its impact depends on the *relative* values of a and b. Similarly, the greater is the quantity of money, the higher will be the level of planned investment spending and therefore the greater will be the level of economic activity. The impact of a given quantity of money on the level of economic activity through the multiplicand also depends on the value of a/b.

1.14 The value of the equilibrium rate of interest will be greater, the larger are the values of $\bar{A}$, and $\bar{I}$ and $M^{\star}$, and smaller, the larger is the value of $\bar{M}$. The impact of $M^{\star}$ perhaps needs explaining (the other results are clear intuitively). The larger is the value of $M^{\star}$, the larger is the demand for idle balances at any *given* rate of interest. Therefore it is to be expected that the higher is the value of $M^{\star}$, the higher will be the equilibrium value of r and the lower will be the equilibrium value of Y.

1.15 The impact of different values of l, a and b on the equilibrium value of r is ambiguous (this is not always true of their impact on the equilibrium value of Y). The different values give rise to conflicting effects on the demand for money and the level of activity. For example, a fall in the value of l means that, *per unit of real output*, active balances are economised on and so r would tend to fall. On the other hand, a tendency for r to fall will stimulate a rise in activity which will offset the initial fall in r. Which effect predominates depends on the values of other coefficients and autonomous items.[7]

1.16 This section is concluded by setting out the impact of unit increases in $\bar{I}$, $\bar{A}$, $M^{\star}$ and $\bar{M}$ respectively, on the equilibrium levels of real income and the rate of interest (see Table 3.1). The signs of the resulting changes are also shown.

2 The Radcliffe Committee, Gurley and Shaw model

2.1 So far a strictly 'Keynesian' analysis has been presented. In this section some post-'Keynesian' developments associated with the Radcliffe Committee and the works of Gurley and Shaw are introduced.[8] The essential point of these developments is that businessmen and consumers demand 'liquidity' rather than money alone in order to satisfy the transactions and speculative motives. The money market must therefore be regarded as containing at least three assets – money, near-money and bonds, where near-money is short-term assets such as treasury bills and other assets which are traded on the short-term money market.

2.2 As a result of the existence of near-money, *shifts* in the functions of the demands for active and idle balances become important determinants of the levels of activity and the rate of interest in the short run. If planned spending rises, it is argued that economies will be made in the use of active balances, so that the demand for active balances will not rise *proportionately* with (money) income. Therefore I cannot be regarded as a constant. Moreover, the liquidity preference schedule may move to the left as well; people may prefer to hold near-money rather than bonds as activity rises because the capital loss is smaller and can be avoided altogether by holding the assets for only a short period of time.[9]

Table 3.1 Impact of unit change in the simplest case

Unit change in	$\bar{I}$	$\bar{A}$	M^*	$\bar{M}$
Resulting change in				
Y	$\dfrac{1}{1-c+\dfrac{a}{b}l}$	As for $\bar{I}$	$-\dfrac{\dfrac{a}{b}}{1-c+\dfrac{a}{b}l}$	$\dfrac{\dfrac{a}{b}}{1-c+\dfrac{a}{b}l}$
r	$\dfrac{1}{b\left(1-c+\dfrac{a}{b}l\right)}$	As for $\bar{I}$	$\dfrac{1-c}{b\left(1-c+\dfrac{a}{b}l\right)}$	$\dfrac{1-c}{b\left(1-c+\dfrac{a}{b}l\right)}$

2.3 These effects are fitted easily into the model presented in Section 1 by making l and M^* *variables* which are functions of the levels of autonomous planned expenditures, $\bar{A}$ and $\bar{I}$. ($\bar{A}$ and $\bar{I}$ are the parameters of the consumption and investment functions which determine their respective positions; changes in $\bar{A}$ and $\bar{I}$ cause the functions to shift.) Thus,

(2.1) $\qquad l = \bar{l} - j\left(\bar{A} + \bar{I}\right)$

and

(2.2) $\qquad M^* = \bar{M}^* - k\left(\bar{A} - \bar{I}\right).$

Writing (2.1) and (2.2) in this form allows the demand for active balances to increase less than proportionately when income rises and produces the leftward shift in the liquidity preference schedule.

2.4 The expressions for the equilibrium values of Y and r now become:

(2.3) $\qquad Y = \dfrac{(\bar{A} + \bar{I}) - \dfrac{a}{b}(\bar{M}^* - k(\bar{A} + \bar{I}) - \bar{M})}{1 - c + \dfrac{a}{b}(\bar{l} - j(\bar{A} + \bar{I}))}$

and

(2.4) $\qquad r = \dfrac{\{\bar{l} - j(\bar{A} + \bar{I})\}\{\bar{A} + \bar{I}\} + \{\bar{M}^* - k(\bar{I} + \bar{A}) - \bar{M}\}(1 - c)}{b\left[1 - c + \dfrac{a}{b}(\bar{l} - j(\bar{A} + \bar{I}))\right]}$

2.5 It can be seen that (2.3) and (2.4) reduce to (1.9) and (1.10), respectively, if l and M^* are constants rather than variables. Now suppose that values of $\bar{l}$, $\bar{M}$, j and k, are chosen such that for *given* initial values of $\bar{A}$ and $\bar{I}$, the values of Y and r implied by (2.3) and (2.4) are the *same* as those implied by (1.9) and (1.10) respectively. Then it is clear that a rise in $\bar{A}$ and/or $\bar{I}$ will have a greater impact on the equilibrium value of Y in the Radcliffe Committee, Gurley and Shaw model than in the 'pure' 'Keynesian' case. It can also be shown that while the value of r in the 'Keynesian' case rises when $\bar{A}$ and/or $\bar{I}$ are increased, it may *fall* in the Radcliffe Committee, Gurley and Shaw case; and, even if it rises, it certainly will not rise by as much as in the 'Keynesian' case.[10] It is results of this nature which have lead to suspicion of 'pure' monetary policy and concentration, instead, on the importance of overall liquidity.

2.6 It should be added that this is as far as this particular form of analysis can go. $[M^* - k(\bar{A} + \bar{I})]$ and $[\bar{l} - j(\bar{A} + \bar{I})]$ are *not* reversible functions. The economies in the use of active (and idle) balances once learnt, are not forgotten. This model therefore can be used only to make the point that the rise in activity is likely to be greater, following a rise in autonomous expenditure, and the change in the rate of interest is likely to be less, than would be predicted by the simple 'Keynesian' model with a two-asset money market.

3 The complex case – goods, money and labour markets, the distribution of income and the price level

3.1 In this section the labour market and the price level are considered as well as the goods and money markets; the short-run aggregate production function and the different values of the mpc's of wage-earners and profit-receivers, respectively, are introduced. No (short-run) equilibrium condition is assumed in the labour market, *i.e.*, it is assumed that equilibrium in both the money and the goods markets *in the short run* is consistent with the existence of involuntary unemployment. It is also assumed that the money-wage rate is given for the period of the analysis, *i.e.*, that money wage bargains are remade period by period (and are influenced by factors such as the current level of unemployment, and changes in prices and (national) productivity) but are held for the period concerned.

3.2 Similarly, prices are assumed to be constant for the period concerned but to change from period to period due to changes in capacity, labour productivity, expected sales and the money-wage rate. A very simple form of oligopolistic pricing is assumed, namely, that firms mark up their average wage costs by a percentage mark up,[11] the value of which is determined by existing capacity and expected sales. It could be argued that the greater is the existing level of capacity, the smaller will be the mark-up; and the greater is the level of expected sales, the higher will be the mark-up. Constant rather than diminishing returns to labour are assumed in the short run. These simple assumptions are more in accord with empirical findings concerning pricing and production behaviour in manufacturing industry[12] than the usual ones of flexible prices, perfect competition in the goods market, and diminishing marginal productivity of labour in the short run. All relevant quantities, unless the contrary is stated, are measured in terms of base period prices (indicated by the subscript *b*).

The labour market and money wages

3.3 The demand for labour may be written as:

(3.1) $\qquad N = \alpha Y,$

where

> N = employment per period;
> α = labour requirement per unit of output (the inverse of labour productivity).

and

> Y = real output,

i.e., the demand for labour is simply a derived demand from the goods market determined by expected sales and the short-run aggregate production function. The money wage equation is:

(3.2) $\qquad w = \bar{w},$

where

> w = money wage

and

> $\bar{w}$ = *current* value.

The price level

3.4 The current price of a unit of aggregate real output (P_t) is:

(3.3) $\qquad P_t = \dfrac{\bar{w}N}{Y}(1 + \bar{v})$

$\qquad\qquad\quad = \alpha\bar{w}(1 + \bar{v}),$

where

> $\bar{v}$ = the percentage mark-up.

The price in base period (P_b) is:

(3.3a) $\qquad P_b = \alpha_b\bar{w}_b(1 + \bar{v}_b) \equiv 1$

as P_b is the numeraire. α_b is likely to be greater and $\bar{w}_b$ is likely to be less than its current counterpart, but $\bar{v}_b$ may be $\geqslant \bar{v}_t$.)

The goods market

(a) The consumption function

3.5 To obtain an expression for the consumption function, it is necessary, first, to look at the national accounts of any period. GNI in terms of *current* prices is:

(3.4) $Y_m \equiv W + P,$

where
  W = total wages,
  P = total profits,
and
  Y_m = money GNI.
Now

(3.5) $Y_m \equiv \overline{w}N + \overline{v}\ \overline{w}N \equiv \overline{w}\alpha Y + \overline{v}\ \overline{w}\alpha Y \equiv \alpha\overline{w}Y\left(1 + \overline{v}\right).$

It follows that output *in base period prices, i.e.,* in real terms, is:

(3.6) $Y \equiv Y_m \dfrac{P_b}{P_t} \equiv \alpha\overline{w}Y(1 + \overline{v})\dfrac{P_b}{P_t}.$

3.6 It can be seen from (3.5) and (3.6) that the higher is the money-wage rate, the greater is the money value of wages and profits associated with a given level of real output, but that their *real* values are unchanged because money wages, profits and prices all rise by the *same* proportion; *i.e.,* if $\overline{w}_2 > \overline{w}_1$, $\alpha\overline{w}_2 Y(1+\overline{v}) > \alpha\overline{w}_1 Y(1+\overline{v})$ $\left(\text{by}\ \left\{\dfrac{\overline{w}_2}{\overline{w}_1}-1\right\}\right)$, but $\alpha\overline{w}_2 Y(1+\overline{v})\dfrac{P_b}{P_{t_2}} = \alpha\overline{w}_1 Y(1+\overline{v})\dfrac{P_b}{P_{t_1}}.$ On the other hand, the higher is the value of $\overline{v}$, the higher is the value of total money profits, total money wages remain unchanged, but total *real* wages are less (and total real profits are correspondingly greater). (The rise in money profits is $\left(\dfrac{\overline{v}_2}{\overline{v}_1}-1\right)$ and the rise in prices is $\left(\dfrac{1+\overline{v}_2}{1+\overline{v}_1}-1\right)$, which is $< \left(\dfrac{\overline{v}_2}{\overline{v}_1}-1\right)$.) That is to say, there is a shift in the distribution of any given level of real income to profit-receivers.

3.7 The consumption function in terms of current prices may be written as:

(3.7)
$$C_m = \overline{A}_{w,p}\dfrac{P_t}{P_b} + c_w\alpha\overline{w}Y + c_p\overline{v}\alpha\overline{w}Y$$
$$= \overline{A}_{w,p}\dfrac{P_t}{P_b} + (c_w + \overline{v}c_p)\alpha\overline{w}Y,$$

where
  $\overline{A}_{w,p}$ = autonomous spending on consumption goods (assumed to be fixed in *real* terms) by wage-earners and profit-receivers combined,

  c_w = mpc of wage-earners;

c_p = mpc of profit-receivers;

and

$c_p < c_w$.

In real terms, *i.e.*, (3.5) is deflated by $\dfrac{P_b}{P_t}$,

$$(3.8) \qquad C = \bar{A}_{w,p} + (c_w + \bar{v}c_p)a\bar{w}\frac{P_b}{P_t}Y.$$

It should be noted that the higher is the value of P_t, the greater is the share of real profits in any given level of real income; therefore because $c_p < c_w$ the *lower* is the level of planned consumption spending in real terms associated with this level of real income.[13]

(b) The investment function

3.8 This is written as before as, for simplicity, planned investment demands are assumed not to be affected by the price level.

$$(3.9) \qquad I = \bar{I} - ar.$$

The money market

(a) Demand for active balances

3.9 For obvious reasons, money held in *active* balances will be related to the *current* money value of any given level of real output. The M_1 function is therefore written:

$$(3.10) \qquad M_1 = l\frac{P_t}{P_b}Y$$

((3.10) should be compared with (1.3) above.)

(b) Demand for idle balances

3.10 Keynes probably would have argued that the demand for idle balances was unaffected by the price level, *i.e.*, that people demand, at any given rate of interest, a certain amount of money for speculative purposes which is not, however, fixed in real terms. That is to say, a 'money illusion' is present. If Keynes's view is adopted, the M_2 function may be written as before (*i.e.*, as $M_2 = M^* - br$, for $r > r^*$ (1.4)).

3.11 However, if it is believed that people do not suffer from 'money illusion,' *i.e.*, that they demand, at a given rate of interest, a constant amount of money in *real* terms, this effect may be allowed for easily by writing the M_2 function (for $r > r^*$) as:

$$(3.11) \qquad M_2 = \frac{P_t}{P_b}(M^* - br).$$

The higher is P_t, the greater is the demand for money to hold in idle balances at any given value of r. In what follows, (3.11) is used rather than (1.4); but 'money illusion' easily can be introduced by removing $\dfrac{P_t}{P_b}$ from all money terms.

(c) Supply of money

3.12 The supply of money equation is written as before (see (1.5) above):

(3.12) $\qquad M = \bar{M}.$

Equilibrium values of Y and r

3.13 Proceeding as before by imposing the equilibrium conditions in the money and goods markets, the following expressions may be obtained:

(1) Equilibrium rate of interest (first step)

(3.13) $\qquad r = \dfrac{lY + M^* - \dfrac{P_b}{P_t}\bar{M}}{b}.$

(2) Equilibrium level of real income

(3.14) $\qquad Y = \dfrac{\bar{A}_{w,p} + \bar{I} - \dfrac{a}{b}\left(M^* - \dfrac{P_b}{P_t}\bar{M}\right)}{1 - \alpha\bar{w}\dfrac{P_b}{P_t}(c_w + \bar{v}c_p) + \dfrac{a}{b}l}.$

(3) Equilibrium rate of interest (second step)

(3.15) $\qquad r = \dfrac{l(\bar{A}_{w,p} + \bar{I}) + \left(M^* - \dfrac{P_b}{P_t}\bar{M}\right)\left(1 - \alpha\bar{w}\dfrac{P_b}{P_t}(c_w + \bar{v}c_p)\right)}{b\left(1 - \alpha\bar{w}\dfrac{P_b}{P_t}(c_w + \bar{v}c_p) + \dfrac{a}{b}l\right)}.$

3.14 It should be noted immediately that (3.13), (3.14) and (3.15) reduce to (1.8), (1.9) and (1.10) respectively, if $\dfrac{P_t}{P_b} = 1$ (or if the price level is ignored), $c_p = c_w = c$, and $\bar{A}_{w,p} = \bar{A}$. Whenever these conditions do not hold, the new expressions allow the impacts of the price level, different mpc's and the distribution of income on the level of activity and the rate of interest to be analysed. (The Radcliffe Committee, Gurley and Shaw modifications could also be easily introduced.)

3.15 With the new expressions it is possible to answer such (limited) questions as what will be the impact of a lower level of the money wage on the *equilibrium* values of real output and the rate of interest? What will be the impact of a higher mark-up on the two equilibrium values? Notice again that these are not equivalent to asking: will a wage cut or a rise in the markup *in fact* raise (or lower) the level of economic activity (though the answer to the second rather than the first of these questions is more likely to be approximated to if the results of the equilibrium comparisons are used).

A lower money wage

3.16 The lower is the level of the money wage, the higher will be the equilibrium level of Y and the lower will be the equilibrium value of r.

Examining, first, (3.14), it can be seen that the *positive* term, $\dfrac{a}{b}\dfrac{P_b}{P_t}\bar{M}$, in the numerator will be higher, the lower is the value of $\bar{w}$. This is the only term affected by a change in the value of $\bar{w}$, and it *raises* the value of Y. (At first sight, $a\bar{w}\dfrac{P_b}{P_t}(c_w + \bar{v}c_p)$ appears to be affected as well; however, any change in $\bar{w}$ is exactly matched by one of the same amount in P_t, so that the expression as a whole is not affected. This is as it should be, since, with the present assumptions, (see para 3.6) the distribution of income is not affected by a change in the value of $\bar{w}$.)

3.17 Now examine (3.15), and remember that conflicting factors are at work. On the one hand, the lower is the price level, the lower is the demand for money to satisfy the transactions demand per unit of *real output* and to satisfy the demand for idle balances at a given rate of interest. These two factors imply a lower rate of interest. On the other hand, the higher is the level of activity, the greater is the proportion of a given stock of money which will go into active balances, and, therefore, the higher will be the rate of interest. It appears, though, that the first two factors outweigh the third, for the only term affected, $-\dfrac{P_b}{P_t}\bar{M}\left(1 - a\bar{w}\dfrac{P_b}{P_t}(c_w + \bar{v}c_p)\right)$ in the numerator, is greater, the smaller is the value of $\bar{w}$, with the result that the equilibrium rate of interest is less, the smaller is the value of the money wage rate.

A higher percentage mark-up

3.18 The higher is the value of the mark-up, the lower is the equilibrium value of real output (beware of monopolists!). The equilibrium value of the rate of interest, however, can be either higher or lower, depending upon the actual values of the conflicting factors at work.

3.19 That the first result is so can be seen by examining (3.14). The value of the positive term, $\dfrac{a}{b}\dfrac{P_b}{P_t}\bar{M}$, in the numerator, is reduced and the value of the negative term $a\bar{w}\dfrac{P_b}{P_t}(c_w + c_p)$, in the denominator is also reduced – both of which reduce the value of Y.

3.20 The lower equilibrium level of activity would, other things being equal, imply a fall in the equilibrium rate of interest. On the other hand, the higher price level raises the demand for active balances per unit of real output and the demand for idle balances at any given level of the rate of interest. These effects are all reflected in (3.15) but the outcome is, in general, indeterminate.

3.21 For completeness, the impacts of unit increases in $\bar{I}$, $\bar{A}_{w,p}$, M^* and $\bar{M}$ on the equilibrium values of Y and r are set out in Table 3.2.

4

4.1 The models presented in these notes can be used to answer questions other than those explicitly mentioned. The questions can refer to short period puzzles or period by period problems. In the latter case, the model in Section 3 is especially suited to analysis of the period by period link between money wages, prices, and investment decisions.[14] It is also possible to bring in the rest of the world and government sectors, though, of course, this adds to the complexity of the results. Finally, the present approach makes a convenient link between the simple model of income-determination in the goods market and the capital-stock adjustment models of the trade cycle presented, for example, in R. C. O. Matthews' book on the trade cycle and H. R. Hudson's 1957 article.[15]

Table 3.2 Impact of unit change in the complex case

Unit change in	$\bar{I},\bar{A}_{w,p}$	M^*	$\bar{M}$
Resulting change in Y	$\dfrac{1}{1-a\bar{w}\dfrac{P_b}{P_t}(c_w+\bar{v}c_p)+\dfrac{a}{b}l}$	$\dfrac{\dfrac{a}{b}}{1-a\bar{w}\dfrac{P_b}{P_t}(c_w+\bar{v}c_p)+\dfrac{a}{b}l}$	$\dfrac{\dfrac{a}{b}\dfrac{P_b}{P_t}}{1-a\bar{w}\dfrac{P_b}{P_t}(c_w+\bar{v}c_p)+\dfrac{a}{b}l}$
r	$\dfrac{l}{b\left[1-a\bar{w}\dfrac{P_b}{P_t}(c_w+\bar{v}c_p)+\dfrac{a}{b}l\right]}$	$\dfrac{1-a\bar{w}\dfrac{P_b}{P_t}(c_w+\bar{v}c_p)}{b\left[1-a\bar{w}\dfrac{P_b}{P_t}(c_w+\bar{v}c_p)+\dfrac{a}{b}l\right]}$	$\dfrac{\dfrac{P_b}{P_t}\left[1-a\bar{w}\dfrac{P_b}{P_t}(c_w+\bar{v}c_p)\right]}{b\left[1-a\bar{w}\dfrac{P_b}{P_t}(c_w+vc_p)+\dfrac{a}{b}l\right]}$

Appendix 1

A1.1 In this appendix the following question is asked: in the simple goods market model, an increase in investment expenditure of $\Delta \bar{I}$ results in an increase in the equilibrium level of income of $\Delta Y = \Delta \bar{I} \left\{ \dfrac{1}{1-c} \right\}$; what *simultaneous* increase in the quantity of money would be necessary in the present model in order that a *horizontal* shift in the investment demand schedule of $\Delta \bar{I}$ will result in an increase in the equilibrium level of Y of $\Delta \bar{I} \left\{ \dfrac{1}{1-c} \right\}$? In answering this, it is also shown that the resulting change in the equilibrium level of interest is zero (as is intuitively obvious).

A1.2 If there is no change in $\bar{M}$, a horizontal shift in the investment demand function of $\Delta \bar{I}$ will result in a rise in the equilibrium level of Y of $\Delta I \left\{ \dfrac{1}{1-c+(a/b)l} \right\}$. (The corresponding change in the equilibrium level of r will be $\dfrac{l}{b} \left\{ \dfrac{\Delta \bar{I}}{1-c+(a/b)l} \right\}$ (see (1.10) in the text). However, the *desired* change in Y is $\Delta \bar{I} \left\{ \dfrac{1}{1-c} \right\}$ and so the shortfall of equilibrium Y is:

$$(A1.1) \qquad \Delta \bar{I} \left\{ \frac{1}{1-c} - \frac{1}{1-c+\dfrac{a}{b}l} \right\} = \frac{\Delta \bar{I} \dfrac{a}{b} l}{(1-c)\left(1-c+\dfrac{a}{b}l\right)}.$$

A1.3 A unit change in the stock of money has an impact on the equilibrium value of Y of $\left\{ \dfrac{a/b}{1-c+(a/b)l} \right\}$ (see (1.9) in the text). Therefore, the value of the desired increase in the money supply, $\Delta \bar{M}$, may be found by solving for $\Delta \bar{M}$ in:

$$\frac{\Delta \bar{I} \dfrac{a}{b} l}{(1-c)\left(1-c+\dfrac{a}{b}l\right)} = \frac{\Delta \bar{M} \dfrac{a}{b}}{1-c+\dfrac{a}{b}l}$$

i.e.,

$$(A1.2) \qquad \Delta \bar{M} = \frac{l \Delta \bar{I}}{1-c}.$$

That a simultaneous shift in the investment demand schedule of $\Delta\bar{I}$ and a rise in $\bar{M}$ of $\left\{\dfrac{l\Delta\bar{I}}{1-c}\right\}$ does change the value of Y by $\left[\dfrac{\Delta\bar{I}}{1-c}\right]$ can be checked by putting these values in equation (1.9) and finding the increase in Y relative to the original value. That $\Delta r = 0$ may be seen by examining (1.10); the only changes which occur, as between the old and the new levels of Y and r, are:

$$\frac{l}{b}\left\{\frac{\Delta\bar{I}}{1-c+\dfrac{a}{b}l}\right\} - \frac{\Delta\bar{M}}{b}\left\{\frac{1-c}{1-c+\dfrac{a}{b}l}\right\}$$

$$= \frac{l}{b}\left\{\frac{\Delta\bar{I}}{1-c+\dfrac{a}{b}l}\right\} - \left\{\frac{(l\Delta\bar{I})}{b(1-c)}\right\}\left\{\frac{1-c}{1-c+\dfrac{a}{b}l}\right\}$$

$$= 0 .$$

Appendix 2: a linear version of the Hudson model of the trade cycle

A2.1 In this appendix it is shown how the model of section 1 can be extended easily to make a linear version of Hudson's model of the trade cycle. The extensions are two: investment is made a function of the level of real output and the capital stock as well as of the rate of interest; and the period to period changes in the capital stock are taken into account.

Goods market equilibrium

A2.2 The equilibrium condition in the goods market in the short run is still that *ex ante* $S = ex\ ante\ I$. However, I is now a function of the level of real output and the existing capital stock (K) as well as of the rate of interest. For simplicity, S remains a function of income only (Hudson makes S a function of r as well, but this does not alter the analysis in any essential way). At low levels of Y (less than $\bar{Y}$), the marginal propensity to save, ($s = 1 - c$), is assumed to be greater than the marginal propensity to invest (a_1). At high levels, the opposite result is assumed, i.e., $s < a_3$. Thus

(A2.1) $\qquad S = -\bar{A} + (1-c)Y = -\bar{A} + sY$

and, for $Y \leq \bar{Y}$,

(A2.2a) $\qquad I = \bar{I} - ar + a_1 Y - a_2 K, \quad (a_2 < s).$

For $Y \geq \bar{Y}$,

(A2.2b) $\qquad I = \bar{I} - ar + a_1 \bar{Y} + a_3 \left(Y - \bar{Y}\right) - a_2 K, \quad (a_3 > s).$

A2.3 In any short period (as defined by a *given* value of K) and for all values of Y, there are, therefore, unique values of r which are consistent with the equilibrium in the goods market. The *IS* schedule is obtained by imposing the goods market equilibrium condition to obtain
(i) for $Y \leq \bar{Y}$,

(A2.3a) $\qquad r = \dfrac{\bar{I} + \bar{A} - a_2 K}{a} - \left(\dfrac{s - a_1}{a}\right) Y$

(ii) for $Y \geq \bar{Y}$,

(A2.3b) $\qquad r = \dfrac{\bar{I} + \bar{A} - (a_3 - a_1)\bar{Y} - a_2 K}{a} + \left(\dfrac{a_3 - s}{a}\right) Y.$

The *IS* schedule therefore contains two sections, one downward-sloping, the other, upward-sloping (see Figure 3.5).

Money market equilibrium

A2.4 A given money supply, $\bar{M}$, is assumed (but the analysis can be modified easily to include a flexible money supply, say $M = \bar{M} + b_1(Y - Y^*)$

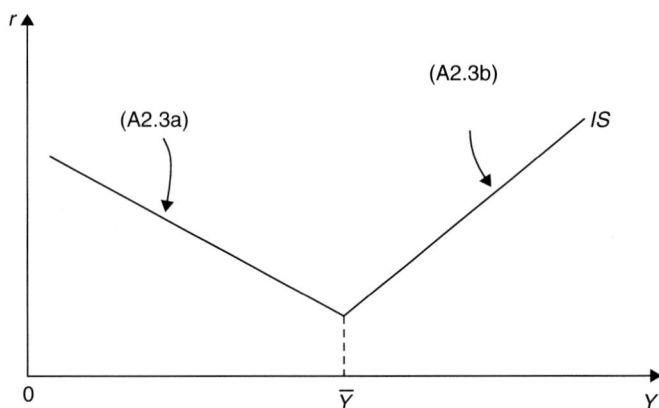

Figure 3.5   The *IS* schedule

where $Y* = \dfrac{br* + \bar{M} - M*}{l}$ and $b_1 < l$, see below). The equilibrium condition implies that:

(A2.4) $\qquad\qquad r = \dfrac{M* - \bar{M}}{b} + \dfrac{l}{b}\,Y$

for $r \geq r*$ and $Y \geq \dfrac{br* + \bar{M} - M*}{l}\,(= Y*)(> \bar{Y})$.

For $Y \leq Y*$,

(A2.4a) $\qquad\qquad r = r*.$

At $Y = \dfrac{\bar{M}}{l}$,

(A2.4b) $\qquad\qquad r = \dfrac{M*}{b}$

and Y cannot exceed $\bar{M}/l$, no matter how high is the value of r.
The LM schedule therefore has three sections (see Figure 3.6).[16]

Full equilibrium in the short period

A2.5 Next, the LM and IS schedules are put together. There are, in general, two possible stable equilibrium positions (A and C) and one

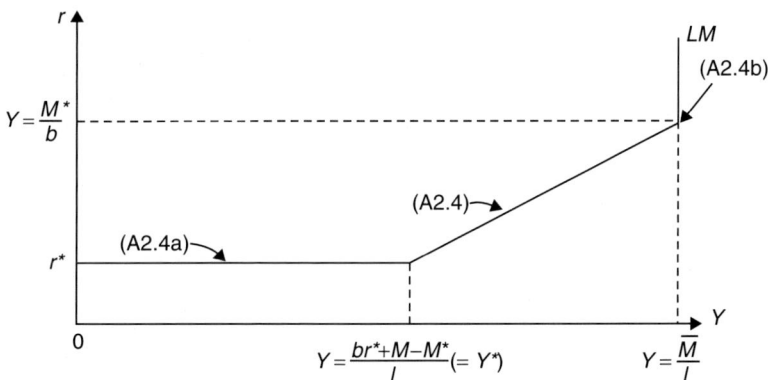

Figure 3.6 The LM schedule

unstable one (*B*) (see Figure 3.7). At *A*, which is the intersection of (A2.3a) with (A2.4a),

(A2.5a)
$$Y = \frac{\bar{I} + \bar{A} - a_2 K - ar^*}{s - a_1}.$$

[Notice that (A2.5a) is the simple goods market solution, *i.e.*, (1.9a) of the text, if a_1 and $a_2 K$ are ignored.]

A2.6. At *C* (the (A2.3b), (A2.4) intersection),

(A2.5b)
$$Y = \frac{\dfrac{\bar{I} + \bar{A} - (a_3 - a_1)Y - a_2 K}{a} - \dfrac{M^* - \bar{M}}{b}}{\dfrac{l}{b} - \dfrac{a_3 - s}{a}}$$

IS is less steep than *LM* at *C*, which implies that $\dfrac{l}{b} > \dfrac{a_3 - s}{a}$ which implies in turn that the numerator of (A2.5b) is positive, for *Y must* be positive.

[(A2.5b) may also be written as:

(A2.5c)
$$Y = \frac{\bar{I} + \bar{A} - (a_3 - a_1)\bar{Y} - a_2 K - \dfrac{a}{b}(M^* - \bar{M})}{1 - c - a_3 + \dfrac{a}{b}l}$$

which becomes the goods and money market solution, *i.e.*, (1.9) of the text if a_1, a_3, $\bar{Y}$ and $a_2 K$ are ignored.][17]

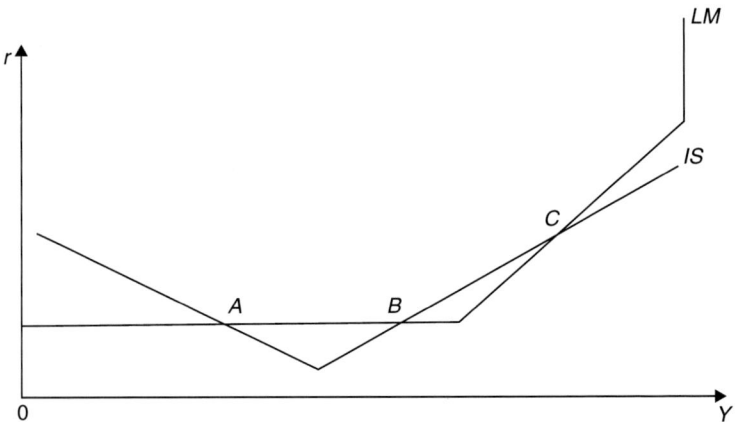

Figure 3.8   Possible equilibrium values of *r* and *Y*

The cycle

A2.7 Suppose the story is started in a slump, *i.e.*, at *A*. Assume that realised investment per period [as given by (A2.5a) and (A2.2a)] is *less* than depreciation. *K* will fall from period to period and the *IS* curve will *rise* (because *I* is greater, *cet par*, the lower is the value of *K*) until *A* and *B* coincide. The economy will then expand to the boom position, *C*. At *C*, it may be supposed that gross capital formation is greater than depreciation; the *IS* curve therefore falls from period to period until *C* and *B* coincide, and the economy returns to *A*.

A2.8 Hudson adds a number of refinements to this basic analysis which will not be discussed here. The main purpose of this appendix has been to show how this dynamic theory of economic fluctuations can be linked on simply to the comparative statics analysis of the Keynesian system.

Post script (2011)

In the essay I wrongly used 'period' and 'run' interchangeably. 'Period' is a theoretical concept; 'run' is an actual historical episode.

Secondly, it would be more correct to write 'mutual determination', not 'simultaneous determination'.

Thirdly, it would be more correct to refer to the given stock of *M* rather than it being exogenous.

Notes

† I am most grateful to Denzo Kamiya for suggesting a considerable improvement to the form of the M_2 function and to Tatsuro Ichiishi for working out the implications of this for the analysis. The paper is dedicated to the 1967 Economics III A Class of the University of Adelaide who acted as the unwilling guinea pigs on whom the ideas of the paper were tried out, and who, though they protested vigorously via wall posters, nevertheless refrained from actual violence to the person of the author (except on the football field). 'Keynesian' is, of necessity, in quotes in the title following the publication of Axel Leijonhufvud's *On Keynesian Economics and the Economics of Keynes* (London: Oxford University Press, 1968).

1. Gardner Ackley, *Macroeconomic Theory*, (New York: Macmillan, 1961).
2. *Report* of the Committee on the Working of the Monetary System (London: 1959); J. G. Gurley and E. G. Shaw, *Money in a Theory of Finance* (Washington, DC: The Brookings Institution, 1960).
3. Usually the rate of interest is measured on the vertical axis and the demand for money is measured on the horizontal axis; this follows the Marshallian

tradition of putting dependent and independent variables on their respectively 'wrong' axes. By reversing this procedure in order to follow the usual mathematical convention I am trying to do for the liquidity preference function what Professor Knight failed to do for supply and demand curves.

4.

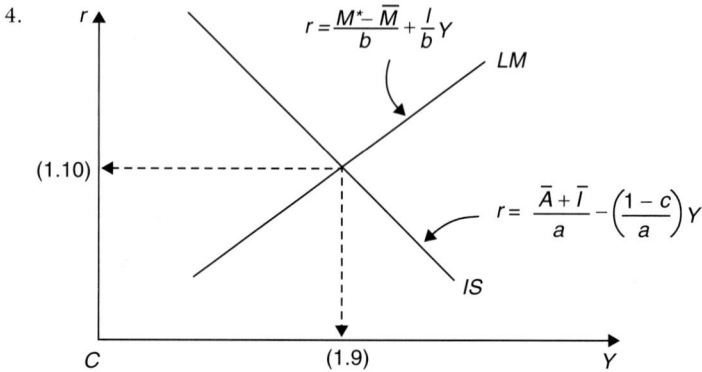

Figure 3.4   Short-period equilibrium

5. It is assumed that $\bar{M} \geq lY = l\left\{\dfrac{\bar{A} + \bar{I} - ar^*}{1 - c}\right\}$.

6. At $Y \gtrless \dfrac{br^* + \bar{M} - M^*}{l}(= Y^*)$, the amount of money available for idle balances is $\leq M^* - br^*$, the demand for money for idle balances at the intersection of (1.4b) with the vertical line at $r = r^*$. Thus when $Y > Y^*$, r must be greater than r^* so that cash is released from idle balances to finance the higher level of active balances.

7. If (1.10) is partially differentiated with respect to l, whether
   $$\frac{\delta r}{\delta l} \gtrless 0 \text{ depends upon whether } (\bar{A} + \bar{I}) \gtrless \frac{a}{b}(M^* - \bar{M}).$$
   It is not obvious which of these conditions is most likely to be met.

8. An excellent account of the implications of these developments for the 'Keynesian' model is to be found in Laurence S. Ritter, 'The Role of Money in the Keynesian System', in M. G. Mueller (ed.), *Readings in Macroeconomics* (New York: Holt, Rinehart and Winston, 1966). The analysis of this section is an algebraic presentation of Ritter's arguments.

9. See Lawrence S. Ritter (1966), p. 167.

10. To show this, partially differentiate (1.10) and (2.4) with respect to $(\bar{A} + \bar{I})$. For (1.10),

   (2.1a) $\dfrac{\delta r}{\delta(\bar{A} + \bar{I})} = \dfrac{l}{b\left(1 - c + \dfrac{a}{b}l\right)}.$

For (2.4)

$$\left\{1-c+\frac{a}{b}(\bar{I}-j(\bar{A}+\bar{I}))\right\}\{\bar{I}-2j(\bar{A}+\bar{I})-(1-c)k\}$$

(2.2a)

$$\frac{\delta r}{\delta(\bar{A}+\bar{I})}=\frac{+\left(\frac{a}{b}j\right)\{(\bar{I}-j(\bar{A}+\bar{I}))(\bar{A}+\bar{I})+(1-c)(\bar{M}^{*}-k(\bar{A}+\bar{I})-\bar{M})\}}{b\left\{1-c+\frac{a}{b}(\bar{I}-j(\bar{A}+\bar{I}))\right\}^{2}}$$

(2.2a) may be written as

$$\frac{\bar{I}-2j(\bar{A}+\bar{I})-(1-c)k}{b\left[1-c+\frac{a}{b}(\bar{I}-j(\bar{A}+\bar{I}))\right]}$$

(2.2b)

$$+\frac{\left(\frac{a}{b}j\right)[\{\bar{I}-j(\bar{A}+\bar{I})\}\{\bar{A}+\bar{I}\}+(1-c)\{\bar{M}^{*}-k(\bar{A}+\bar{I})-\bar{M}\}]}{b\left\{1-c+\frac{a}{b}(\bar{I}-j(\bar{A}+\bar{I}))\right\}^{2}}$$

The first part of the expression is <(2.1a) and, for some reasonable values of
k, *et al.*, may be <0; the second part of the expression, while almost certainly
>0, is *small* in relation to the first part.

11. Strictly speaking, it is their average *direct* costs which *firms* mark-up. But, for
the *economy* as a whole, raw material costs cancel out and it is *as if* overall
average wage costs were marked-up.

12. See, for example, R. R. Neild, *Pricing and Employment in The Trade Cycle*
(London: Cambridge University Press, 1964).

13. From (3.3) and (3.8) we obtain:

$$C = \bar{A}_{w,p} + \frac{c_w + \bar{v}c_p}{1 + \bar{v}}P_b Y$$

(3.8a)

$$\frac{c_w + \bar{v}c_p}{1 + \bar{v}} \equiv \frac{1}{1 + \bar{v}}c_w + \frac{\bar{v}}{1 + \bar{v}}c_p ,$$

where the 'weights', $\dfrac{1}{1+\bar{v}}$ and $\dfrac{\bar{v}}{1+\bar{v}}$, are the respective shares of wages

and profits in a unit of output, and $\dfrac{c_w + \bar{v}c_p}{1 + \bar{v}}P_b$ is the overall mpc. It is obvi-

ous that, when $\bar{v}$ rises, the first 'weight' declines and the second rises; thus,
because $c_p < c_w$, the overall mpc declines.

14. The forms that these links might take have been discussed in the author's
paper, 'A Two-Sector Model of the Distribution of Income and the Level of
Employment in the Short Run', *Economic Record*, 41, 1965, 163–17.

15. R. C. O. Matthews, *The Trade Cycle* (Cambridge: Cambridge University Press,
1959); H. R. Hudson, 'A Model of the Trade Cycle' *Economic Record*, 333, 1957,
375–89. A linear version of Hudson's model is presented in Appendix 2.

16. With a flexible money supply for $Y \le Y^*$,

(A2.i) $M = \bar{M}$ and $r = r^*$

For $Y \ge Y^*$,

(A2.ii) $M = \bar{M} + b_1(Y - Y^*)$ and $r = \dfrac{M^* - \bar{M} + b_1 Y^*}{b} + \left\{\dfrac{1 - b_1}{b}\right\} Y$

The *LM* schedule therefore has two sections only (see Figure 3.7) and the upward-sloping section has a flatter slope than its counterpart for a constant money supply.

The value of Y^* depends on the value of $\bar{M}$. If the value of $\bar{M}$ with a flexible money supply differs from its value with a constant money supply, the *LM* schedule starts to rise at a lower (higher) level of Y, according to whether the value for the flexible supply is less than (greater than) the value for the constant supply. (The former case is shown in Figure 3.7)

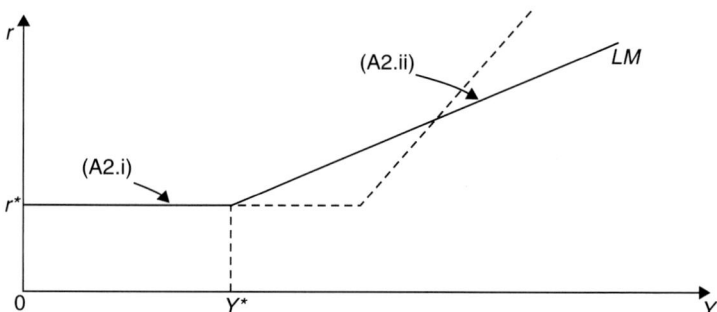

Figure 3.7   The *LM* schedule with a flexible money supply

17. The corresponding condition with a flexible money supply is:

(A2.iii) $Y = \dfrac{\dfrac{\bar{I} + \bar{A} - (a_3 - a_1)\bar{Y} - a_2 K}{a} - \dfrac{M^* - \bar{M} + b_1 Y^*}{b}}{\dfrac{1 - b_1}{b} - \dfrac{a_3 - s}{a}}.$

4
On Keynes and Chick on Prices in Modern Capitalism (2002)*

David Champernowne once told me that to introduce prices into a macroeconomic model requires that you choose the simplest possible model of pricing which still retained a link with reality, with real world practice.[1] Only then could you hope to avoid the whole model becoming too complicated for you to be able to understand what was going on. I thought of this advice, by which I was most struck at the time and have remembered ever since, when I started to think about the present chapter on Keynes and Chick on prices in modern capitalism for Vicky's *Festschrift*.

May I pay a tribute to Vicky herself? The more I read what she writes on Keynes, money and the operation of modern capitalism, the more struck I am by her deep understanding, wisdom and brilliant economic intuition. Not for Vicky the quickly written technical piece – have model, will travel – in order to build up a c.v. Instead, she thinks deeply about fundamentals and then shares her thought processes and her findings with us rather in the manner of John Hicks (always one of her favourites). Moreover, Vicky's writings grow out of and are, first and foremost, integral to her teaching. Not only she is a gifted economist, she is also that rare person, especially nowadays, a devoted and gifted teacher, from whom we other teachers have much to learn. Most of all, Vicky is a loyal, loving and caring friend. It is a privilege to contribute to this collection of essays in her honour.

Before *A Treatise on Money* and *The General Theory*, Keynes, as we know, was a critical quantity theory of money person in his discussions of the general price level and inflation and deflation, and a Marshallian, pure

* Originally publihsed as chapter 12 of Philip Arestis, Meghnad Desai and Sheila Dow (eds), *Money, Macroeconomics and Keynes: Essays in Honour of Victoria Chick, Volume One* (London, Routledge, 2002), pp. 115–23.

and simple, in his understanding of the formation of relative prices in general, and individual prices in firms and industries in particular. Thus, he declared himself to be a quantity theory person in *A Tract*, taking acceptance or not of it to be the litmus paper test of whether or not the person concerned was an economist (and intelligent) (Keynes 1923 [1971a]: 61). Of course, he gave cheek to his teacher Alfred Marshall concerning the long run and 'the too easy, too useless a task (p. 65) which the long-period version of the theory set. And he directed his then recommendations on monetary policy mainly towards reducing the amplitude of fluctuations in the short-period velocity of circulation in order to achieve and sustain as stable a general level of prices as possible.

In Keynes's biographical essay of Marshall (Keynes 1933 [1972]: 161–231), he described very clearly how Marshall tried to tackle time by using his three-period – market, short, long – analysis with its lock-up and subsequent release of different variables from the *ceteris paribus* pound. This time period analysis was used by Keynes in his analysis of sectoral price formation – the fundamental equations of *A Treatise on Money*. There, he analysed sectoral price formation, short period by short period, with quantities given each period but changing between them in response to prices set and profits (windfalls) made or not made. He told a story of convergence, short period by short period, on the Marshallian long-period, stock and flow, equilibrium position at which Marshall's form of the quantity theory and Keynes's new equations for prices coincided. (Convergence was required to occur either because of a shock to the system which look it away from its long-period equilibrium position, or because a new equilibrium had come into being as a result of changes in the underlying fundamental determinants of the position – tastes or techniques or endowments.)

For Keynes this was still quantity theory. But for Richard Kahn, who had always been sceptical of the quantity theory *as a causal process*, the fundamental equations were relations which brought into play cost–push and demand–pull factors, as we would say now, without need for the quantity of money and its velocity to be mentioned at all. This was a significant insight that Keynes absorbed when writing *The General Theory* (see his statement at the beginning of chapter 21 where his emancipation from the traditional quantity theory is virtually complete).[2] Moreover, after *The General Theory* was published, he was beginning to question whether long-period analysis and especially the concept of long-period equilibrium had any part at all to play in economy-wide descriptive analysis.[3] This viewpoint has been lost sight of in modern macroeconomic analysis but it was a characteristic of the writings of those closest to Keynes either in person and/or in spirit, for example, Joan Robinson, Tom Asimakopulos, Richard Goodwin, and it was a characteristic reached independently, as ever, by Michal Kalecki and Josef Steindl.

Many scholars have been puzzled about why Keynes, when developing his new theory, took so little notice of the prior 'revolution' in the theory of value associated, especially in Cambridge, with Piero Sraffa, Richard Kahn, Austin and Joan Robinson and Gerald Shove. (There was also, of course. Edward Chamberlin in the other Cambridge but I doubt if his version impinged much on Keynes's consciousness.) When taxed on this, Keynes expressed himself perplexed as to its relevance *for his purposes*, see, for example, his reply to Ohlin in April 1937 about Joan Robinson reading the proofs and 'not discovering any connection' (Keynes 1937 [1973b]: 190). Not that Keynes was unappreciative of the writings of Kahn and Joan Robinson (let alone those of Piero Sraffa. Austin and Shove), it was just that he did not accept their particular relevance for his own context, in which Champernowne's maxim to which I referred above may have played a part. (I do not mean that Champernowne explicitly put it to Keynes, only that they applied the same methodological principle.) After all, Keynes did put in the appropriate provisos about imperfect competition when stating the two classical postulates in chapter 2 of *The General Theory* (pp. 5–6), but wrote as though they were but minor modifications, of no essential importance for his central argument and results. Similarly, when he responded to the findings of Michal Kalecki (1938), John Dunlop (1938) and Lorie Tarshis (1939b) in the late 1930s, he pointed out that accepting non-freely competitive pricing helped the *policy* applications of the new theory in that expansion from a slump without inflationary worries was now a greater possibility (Keynes 1939 [1973a, appendix 3], pp. 394–412).

Be that as it may, Keynes used Marshallian competitive analysis in his new macroeconomic context in order to derive the aggregate supply curve and the aggregate proceeds, which needed a model of prices, of the function. By Marshallian competitive analysis I mean free competition in a realistic setting of actual firms of a viable size and an environment characterised by uncertainty in which all major economic decisions have to be made. The modern literature associated, for example, with Martin Weitzman's 1982 *Economic Journal* paper whereby involuntary unemployment is argued to be impossible with modern perfect competition, would have seemed to Keynes (and I suspect to Vicky as well) as silly-cleverness of a most extreme form. (It is argued that if people were sacked, they could borrow freely on a perfect capital market at a given rate of interest and because of complete divisibility, could set up a minute, one-person firm selling a product for which it is a price-taker.)

When Keynes told his story of the role of prices in the determination of the point of effective demand, he chose those ingredients that most easily allowed plausible aggregation of individual decisions. In effect, he asked: What is it reasonable to expect a business person in an uncertain, competitive environment to know when making daily or weekly production and employment decisions? Here the assumption of price-taking implied that the *expected* price for the product of the industry in which the firm operated was currently known, implicitly determined by the interaction of appropriate short-period supply and demand curves. On the basis of this, which provides the information for what the price is expected *to be*, and from knowledge of existing short-period marginal cost curves (user cost is a complication with which Keynes and others after him, for example, Lorie Tarshis, James Tobin and Christopher Torr, have grappled), the decisions on production and employment could be made. It fitted in with the assumption that what motivated business people was the desire to maximise short-period *expected* profits.

Since it is reasonable to assume that the behaviour was representative (there is a further puzzle to be dealt with in the capital goods trades), aggregate supply and aggregate demand could be determined. Whether individual expectations about prices were correct or not would be determined by the overall outcome of all these individual actions – here the so-called impersonal forces of the market were supposed to do their thing in determining actual prices. If, overall, prices turned out to be different than what was expected, there is an implication in Keynes's argument that, with reasonable behavioural assumptions, people would so respond to non-realisation as to move the economy itself closer to the point of effective demand where aggregate demand and supply matched and expectations were fulfilled.

In telling this story, both Keynes and Vicky distinguished between two versions or, rather, two concepts of aggregate demand. The first related to what is in the minds of business people themselves – what *they* expect their prices and sales to be. It is the role of the onlooking (macro) economist to add these up and relate the resulting totals to the corresponding values of production and employment. The other concept, which alone seems to have made it to the textbooks, short-circuits the actual decision makers in firms and shows what levels of planned expenditure on consumption and capital goods may be expected (planned) *in a given situation* to be associated with each possible level of production and employment. Here the Keynesian consumption function (with its *mpc* < 1) makes an explicit entrance along with, as a first approximation, a given level of overall *planned* investment expenditure.

In Keynes's story it is the non-realisation of the expected prices of individual products which sets in motion the groping process, the changes in production and employment initiated by individual business people, which takes the economy eventually to the point of effective demand. There is a crucial assumption that the immediate non-realisation of short-term expectations does not affect – feed back on – long-term expectations so that planned investment and the consumption function remain stable while the convergent process occurs. This is the second of Keynes's three models of reality that Kregel identified for us in 1976.

With this assumption, the convergence process is a simple one and follows logically. If prices turn out to be greater than expected – we could think of actual prices being those which clear the given stock of supplies on Marshall's market day – short-period flow production is adjusted upwards as individual producers move up short-period marginal cost curves to the new points of marginal cost equals expected price which maximise short-period expected profits.[4] Because the *mpc* is less than unity, supplies will increase more than demands and the point of effective demand will be reached, or, at least, the economy will be brought closer to it. A similar story may be told if prices turn out to be less than expected, so that aggregate supply is momentarily outrunning aggregate demand (version 2). In Keynes's story there is no place for unintended changes in inventories (because prices do the task of unintended changes in inventories in a fixed-price model), with the consequence that planned investment expenditure, including planned changes in stocks, is achieved. Nevertheless, the market signals that ensue are stabilising.

In a fixed-price model, in which business people have in mind expected sales at given unchanging prices, the non-realisation of expectations shows itself in unexpected, unintended changes in inventories (or lengthening or shortening queues if the products concerned are not available in stock). If these are interpreted as a misreading of what sales are and the immediate non-realisation of *planned* changes in inventories is not allowed to affect current investment plans, the accompanying induced changes in output and employment again bring the economy closer to the point of effective demand. In this case it is obvious that, because changes in supply are greater than changes in demand because the *mpc* is less than unity, convergence is occurring. As this case may be interpreted as either one of price-setting behaviour by individual firms or price-following of a leader by some firms, or both, it shows clearly *why* Keynes did not think the degree of competition mattered for his purposes. It was taken 'as given' though not constant – 'merely that, in this ... context, [Keynes was] not considering or taking into account the effects and consequences of changes in [it]' (Keynes 1936 [1973a]: 245). In the modern developments of imperfect competition and Keynesian theory, in which many participants argue that only imperfectly competitive market structures allow Keynes-type results to occur, I sometimes think this simple but profound point is overlooked – but see Nina Shapiro (1997) for an exception and Robin Marris (1997) for a typical counter-argument.

It is true that, though Keynes had marvellous intuition about the nature of interrelated economic processes, each of a different length, in *The General Theory* as opposed to *A Treatise on Money*, he despaired of finding a common or determinate time unit to which all of them could be reduced. So he settled for setting out his crucial ideas in *The General Theory* in terms of establishing existence as we would say now – the factors responsible for the point of effective demand. He told us after the book was published (he had Ralph Hawtrey's responses especially in mind) that he wished he had made his exposition more clear cut, concentrating on these fundamental issues and then discussing the process of achievement of unemployment equilibrium, including discussing whether the factors responsible for the fundamental process of groping by entrepreneurs for the rest state were or were not interrelated with those responsible for the point of effective demand itself and whether there was or was not feedback from one to the other.[5]

As far as prices are concerned in this context, what Keynes needed to establish was that *at any moment of time* individual business people could reasonably be expected to have in mind what price would be expected for his or her product for the relevant production time period. Then, in Keynes's exposition, knowledge of their respective marginal cost curves would allow them to decide on output and employment. At the level of the firm, the known marginal cost included their estimates of user cost, even though user costs net out in the aggregate; so that their prices and the overall price level (and expected changes in both) were influenced by user cost and the important factors involved in its determination. Provided this was a reasonable assumption about what was possible in reality, aggregation to obtain Keynes's aggregate supply and demand functions and ultimately to determine the general price level should be possible in principle, as it should be also if the same approach is taken to non-Marshallian free competition.

This argument may also bear on the disagreement between Tom Asimakopulos and Joan Robinson on the nature of the short period and, in particular, on its length in macroeconomic analysis. Asimakopulos

(1988: 195–97) thought it had to be finite – a definite stretch of time – not a point, 'the position at a moment of time', Robinson (1978: 13), as Joan Robinson was ultimately to insist. I think I see what Joan had in mind. In particular, it does allow us to avoid the puzzle with Tom Asimakopulos's approach of how to handle different short periods of different firms and industries which have to be abstracted from, rather artificially and arbitrarily, in order to coherently aggregate to the economy as a whole.

Keynes himself never systematically investigated this aspect of the analysis. Some post-Keynesian economists, especially Tom Asimakopulos, have investigated in great, precise detail, the nature of these aggregations, see, for example, Asimakopulos (1988, ch. 5). A classic paper on the same issues is Tarshis's chapter in the *Festschrift* for Tibor Scitovsky, Boskin (1979), on the aggregate supply function and both Marris (1991, 1997) and Solow (1998) have recently written about it. It is, moreover, in Lorie Tarshis's unpublished Ph.D. dissertation (1939a) that we find one of the fullest discussions of the role of user cost in the determination of prices at the level of the firm, industry and economy, as well as an extremely subtle discussion of different planning time periods and their corresponding marginal costs.

I think the arguments above reflect the common-sense meaning of Champernowne's remark. The principal point I want to make here is that Keynes's intuition about the irrelevance of market structure and the exact nature of price setting for his immediate purposes was spot on.

I hope I am right in saying that when I read Vicky on these issues, I detect that her approach and judgement are the same as those I claim to have detected in Keynes. It is true that she takes the analysis of the time periods associated with various interrelated economic processes, including those related to price setting, much further than Keynes did. As with Keynes she is insistent that we have to analyse the role of money and its accompanying institutions right from the start, that the real and monetary aspects of the economy cannot be separated in either the short or the long period. When it comes to a discussion of the determination of the prices of financial assets and the roles which they play in the determination of overall employment, as well as her own original insights, she also draws on Keynes and his astute pupil Hugh Townshend for inspiration (see Chick 1987). Her findings on these issues affect her discussion of the determination of the prices of capital goods (new and second hand), just as similar matters affected the discussion on the same issues by another of her mentors, Hy Minsky.

This is principally because, as with the setting of prices of financial assets, we are dealing with markets where existing stocks as well as new flows have a major impact on prices, as do speculative expectations about the future course of prices by both producers and purchasers. Indeed, stocks usually dominate flows in the process. In the case of durable capital goods there are two major factors – the demand for the services of existing capital goods and the relative importance of these for the determination of the prices of the new flow production of them. The feedback from the determination of the prices of financial assets, where some of the latter are associated with the original creation of the stocks of durable goods, affects the demand for their services and their valuation overall. But there is also a role for the conditions of production and the prices of the services of the variable factors, especially labour services, in determining the supply prices of capital goods. This analysis is common ground for Keynes, Vicky and Paul Davidson.

Vicky is also very careful to make explicit the two concepts of aggregate demand which we mentioned above and to discuss their different but indispensable roles. Once it has been granted that Keynes was escaping from the economic theory of certainty, the first concept of aggregate demand, the summation of business people's expectations about prices and sales in a given situation, is especially crucial. For while it is necessary to move onto the second concept in order to determine the point of effective demand, the move would not be possible unless there had been the prior account of how production, income and employment came to be created in the first place.[6] And, as we have seen, this account must be accompanied by some account of price setting and what prices are doing in the process. For this affects both the point of effective demand and what happens if it is not found first time around, as it were. It is on these issues, in which the determination of output and employment has top priority yet prices too have an indispensable role, that Vicky, as ever, has written clearly and decisively (see, for example, Chick 1983).

Notes

1. I am most grateful to Stephanie Blankenburg, Prue Kerr and the editors for their comments on a draft of the chapter.
2. 'So long as economists are concerned with ... the theory of value, they ... teach that prices are governed by supply and demand ... in particular, changes in marginal cost and the elasticity of short-period supply [play] a prominent part. But when they pass ... to the theory of money and prices, we hear no more of these homely but intelligible concepts and move into a world where prices are governed by the quantity of money, by its income-velocity, by the velocity of circulation relatively to the volume of transactions, by hoarding, by forced saving, by inflation and deflation *et hoc genus omne* ... One of the

objects of the foregoing chapters has been to...bring the theory of prices as a whole back to close contact with the theory of value' (Keynes 1936 [1973a]: 292–93).

3. 'I should, I think, be prepared to argue that, in a world ruled by uncertainty with an uncertain future linked to an actual present, a final position of equilibrium, such as one deals with in static economics, does not properly exist' (Keynes 1936b [1979]: 222). Incidentally on the previous page (221), Keynes gives some credence to my pedantic insistence that we should distinguish between runs (actual history) and periods (analytical devices in which the economist controls what changes and what does not). He wrote (to Hubert Henderson, 28 May 1936): '... the above deals with what happens in the long run, i.e. after the lapse of a considerable period of time rather than in the long period in a technical sense'.

4. I once had a brawl with Don Patinkin about all this. He wanted to expunge from p. 25 of *The General Theory*, the assumption of maximisation of short-period expected profits as the motivating force behind the behaviour of business people. I used Lorie Tarshis's arguments from his classic 1979 paper on the aggregate supply function to argue, I hope persuasively, against literary vandalism, see Harcourt (1977: 567–68).

5. '[I]f I were writing the book again I should begin by setting forth my theory on the assumption that short-period expectations were always fulfilled; and then have a subsequent chapter showing what difference it makes when short-period expectations are disappointed' (Keynes 1937 [1973b]: 181). 'The main point is to distinguish the forces determining the position of equilibrium from the technique of trial and error by means of which the entrepreneur discovers what the position is' (Keynes 1937 [1973b]: 182).

6. Joan Robinson once told me that the following, which arises from the distinction between the two concepts of aggregate demand, was 'a very subtle point'! In Australia we write the aggregate demand for imports as a function of aggregate demand, not aggregate income. The argument is that in a given situation, business people will demand those imports needed for the production they plan to match their expected sales. In the short period the amount of imports per unit of output needed to match sales is pretty much a given. This implies that aggregate import demand is a function of the first concept of aggregate demand – what sales are expected to be – not the second – what will be demanded overall at each level of demand and income. At the point of effective demand, the amount of imports will be the same as that which would be predicted by relating the demand for them to *either* concept of aggregate demand. But away from the equilibrium position, the predictions differ. If we assume that prices are given, the differences between the two predictions correspond to the import contents of the *unintended* changes in inventories associated with the corresponding excess demand or supply situations. (My second thoughts on the validity of this argument are to be found in Chapter 5.)

References

Asimakopulos, A. (1988). *Investment, Employment and Income Distribution.* Cambridge and Oxford: Polity Press in association with Basil Blackwell.

Boskin, M. J. (ed.) (1979). *Economics and Human Welfare: Essays in Honour of Tibor Scitovsky*. New York: Academic Press.

Chick, V. (1983). *Macroeconomics after Keynes: A Reconsideration of The General Theory*. Oxford: Philip Allan.

Chick, V. (1987). 'Townshend, Hugh (1890–1974)', in Eatwell, Milgate and Newman (eds), Vol. 4, 1987, 662.

Dunlop, J. T. (1938). 'The Movement of Real and Money Wage Rates', *Economic Journal*, 48, 413–34.

Eatwell, J., Milgate, M. and Newman, P. (eds) (1987). *The New Palgrave. A Dictionary of Economics*, Vol. 4, Q to Z. London: New York and Tokyo: Macmillan.

Harcourt, G. C. (1977). 'Review of Don Patinkin, *Keynes' Monetary Thought: A Study of Its Development*. North Carolina: Duke University Press, 1976', *Economic Record*, 53, 565–69.

Harcourt, G. C. and Riach, P. A. (eds) (1997). *A 'Second Edition' of The General Theory*, Vol. 1. London: Routledge.

Kalecki, M. (1938). 'The Determinants of Distribution of the National Income', *Econometrica*, 6, 97–112.

Keynes, J. M. (1923 [1971a]). *A Tract on Monetary Reform, C. W.*, Vol. IV. London: Macmillan.

Keynes, J. M. (1930 [1971b]). *A Treatise on Money, 2 vols, C. W.*, Vols V, VI. London: Macmillan.

Keynes, J. M. (1933 [1972]). *Essays in Biography, C. W.*, Vol. X. London: Macmillan.

Keynes, J. M. (1936 [1973a]). *The General Theory of Employment, Interest and Money, C. W.*, Vol. VII. London: Macmillan.

Keynes, J. M. (1937 [1973b]). *The General Theory and After, Part II, Defence and Development, C. W.*, Vol. XIV. London: Macmillan.

Keynes, J. M. (1979). *The General Theory and After, A Supplement, C. W.*, Vol. XXIX. London: Macmillan and Cambridge: Cambridge University Press.

Kregel, J. A. (1976). 'Economic Methodology in the Face of Uncertainty: The Modelling Methods of Keynes and the Post-Keynesians', *Economic Journal*, 86, 209–25.

Marris, R. (1991). *Reconstructing Keynesian Economics with Imperfect Competition*. Aldershot, Hants.: Edward Elgar.

Marris, R. (1997). 'Yes, Mrs Robinson! *The General Theory* and Imperfect Competition', in Harcourt and Riach (eds), Vol. 1 (1997: 52–82).

Robinson, J. (1978). 'Keynes and Ricardo', *Journal of Post Keynesian Economics*, 1, 12–18.

Shapiro, N. (1997). 'Imperfect Competition and Keynes', in Harcourt and Riach (eds), Vol. 1 (1997: 83–92).

Solow, R. M. (1998). *Monopolistic Competition and Macroeconomic Theory*. Cambridge: Cambridge University Press.

Tarshis, L. (1939a). 'The Determinants of Labour Income', Unpublished Ph.D. dissertation. Cambridge: Cambridge University Library.

Tarshis, L. (1939b). 'Changes in Real and Money Wages', *Economic Journal*, 49, 150–54.

Tarshis, L. (1979). 'The Aggregate Supply Function in Keynes's *General Theory*', in Boskin (1979: 361–92).

Weitzman, M. L. (1982). 'Increasing Returns and the Foundations of Unemployment Theory', *Economic Journal*, 92, 787–804.

5
On Specifying the Demand for Imports in Macroeconomic Models (2006)*

When I wrote a book note for the *Economic Journal* in 1998 on Volume 2 of Tony Thirlwall's splendid *Selected Essays. Macroeconomic Issues From a Keynesian Perspective* (1997), I said:

> With Tony Thirlwall what you see is what you get. He has strong views, well thought out and stuck to, he is lucid, humane and persuasive to those who have eyes to see and ears to hear – not many of us left, unfortunately. He is proud to be called, and to call himself, 'an unreconstructed Keynesian'. He is; he is also an original and innovative economist who, within a broadly Keynesian framework, has with his papers illuminated our understanding of some of the most pressing modern issues.

Of course, the content, scope and depth of Tony's essays should have warranted a review, preferably a review article, but such is the technocratic and Philistine character of our age and profession that an appraisal of his contributions in the public domain is almost invisible, confined, as it is, to a short book note only available on the web. (Book notes are no longer published in the journal itself.)

In one of his essays on 'the input-output formulation of the foreign trade multiplier', Tony points out that together with himself only Wonnacott (1975) and Harcourt, Karmel and Wallace (1967) treat the demand for imports in macroeconomic analysis as a function of Gross

* Originally published in Philip Arestis, John McCombie and Roger Vickerman (eds), *Growth and Economic Development: Essays in Honour of A. P. Thirlwell*, Cheltenham, UK and Northampton, MA: Edward Elgar Publishing, pp. 60–67.

Expenditure (that is to say, gross of expenditure on imports) rather than of National Income. Even then, Wonnacott and Harcourt, Karmel and Wallace barely scratch the surface of such a treatment. By contrast, in Tony's essay (written with the late Charles Kennedy), their treatment is allied with an analysis of the movements of imports through the input-output structure of the economy.

These considerations prompted this essay for Tony's volume, to which I feel privileged and proud to contribute. I want to investigate some more the *raison d'être* for treating imports as a function of expenditure rather than income and also refer to the links between Keynesian macroeconomic national accounting concepts and categories, and the production interdependent models of Leontief and Sraffa.

I first wrote on the second topic when I was working on the first draft of a chapter on the national accounts in *Economic Activity* (chapter 2). At much the same time I was also working with Vincent Massaro on Piero Sraffa's 1960 classic, *Production of Commodities by Means of Commodities*, especially on Sraffa's ingenious device of sub-systems, see Harcourt and Massaro (1964). It was through these two (non-trivial) pursuits that I obtained at least a glimpse of the nature of the complex relationships between the respective systems of Keynes and Sraffa, so deftly and deeply developed by Tony and Charles Kennedy in their essay. But first I want to investigate the implications of making imports a function of expenditure and try to develop a simple quantitative estimate of the bias introduced into macroeconomic models by making imports a function of income. I then question both procedures in the light of Keynes's two concepts of the aggregate demand function in *The General Theory* – see pp. 24, 25, 29, 30. I hope these musings, albeit incomplete and inconclusive, will nevertheless be of interest to Tony, who has that indispensable characteristic of the really great economist, to wit, to know when perhaps definite answers may not be given to important questions in economics, a lesson I learnt very early on from my greatest Australian mentor, Eric Russell. Incidentally, it was Eric who led the way on the Australian scene in making imports a function of expenditure.

Why is it the most common practice to make the demand for imports a function of income rather than expenditure? I suppose the most convincing rationale must be that imports, like saving and taxation, are all leakages from the flows of expenditure, production and income that need to be offset by injections of investment, government and export expenditures in order to establish the short-period equilibrium flow of national income, production and expenditure. Moreover, saving and taxation are self-evidently leakages from the received income of the community. Therefore, in modelling an open economy with a government sector and deriving an expression for the full multiplier at work, symmetry requires that the three marginal propensities reflecting the three leakages be added together in the multiplier formulation: $1/(s + t + m)$. However, while this reasoning seems valid for saving and taxation, is it obviously so for imports as well? No, because imports are demanded in any short period, when techniques of production, relative prices and exchange rates may be taken as given, in order to make production possible in response to anticipated (or even known) sales. Therefore, the level of final expenditure on commodities associated with consumption, investment, government, and export categories of expenditure seems the obvious place to go to in order to find what sectoral and total demand for imports are likely to be in any given short-period situation. Of course, the bulk of activity takes place in firms that produce intermediate goods, not final goods, and so we must conceive of demands being passed down the line, as it were, in the interdependent production processes that characterise the structure of modern economies. This is implied in the simple Keynesian constructions of the models in, say, *Economic Activity* where total imports are made a simple proportional function of total gross expenditure. As a simplification, no distinction is made between the import requirements associated with the production of the different categories of commodities. It is acknowledged, of course, that there may well be more imports required per unit of production, of, say, consumption, investment or even export commodities than those associated with much government expenditure, for example. This is regarded as a complication to be brought in later once the essential principles have been understood and the analysis worked through. Furthermore, by making imports a function of expenditure, the import requirements in production needed to match autonomous expenditures are explicitly taken into account in the formula for the open economy multiplier.

Suppose then that we accept that expenditure is the principal determinant of import requirements, that it signals what imports will be needed in any given short-period situation to produce the commodities to match expenditure. Does it make any essential difference to the ultimate answers that we give for the determination of levels of production and income whether we have used expenditure or income as the determinants of import demand?

The answer is that at *short-period equilibrium* there is no difference. At equilibrium aggregate demand equals aggregate supply (and total planned injections are equal to total induced leakages), so we must get the same overall answer. (We have to make allowance for the fact that the marginal propensity to spend on imports from expenditure has a different numerical value to the marginal propensity to import from income, because income by definition is always less than expenditure; but one is reducible to equivalence with the other in order to determine the same overall demand for imports.) This is clear in Figure 5.1, which is based on the diagrams in chapter 12 of *Economic Activity*.

On the vertical axis we measure expenditure (E) and income (Y), on the horizontal axis, Y, all in real terms. We take $\bar{I}$, $\bar{G}$, and $\bar{X}$ to be autonomous and C to be a function of Personal Disposable Income (Y_d), $C = C(Y_d)$, with changes in C induced by changes in Y_d. (There is an autonomous term in the consumption function and in the short period a unique relationship between Y_d and Y so that C may be related in a derived way to Y.) m is the marginal propensity to spend on imports and so *domestic* expenditure is $(1 - m)(E)$, where $E = C(Y_d) + \bar{I} + \bar{G} + \bar{X}$.

The difference between the two lines is the expenditure on imports at each level of income. Not only is the 45° line a reference point, it may also be interpreted as an aggregate supply (and demand) line, plotting expected demand for *domestic* production against domestic production

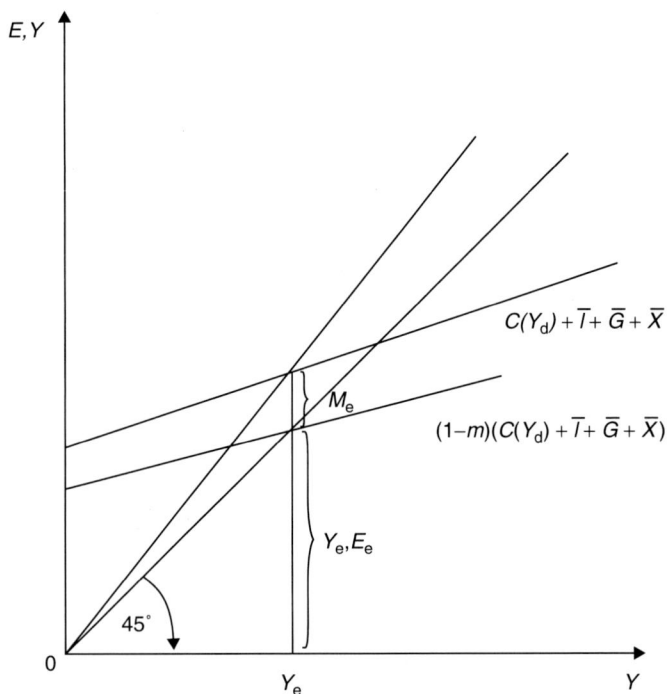

Figure 5.1   Short-period equilibrium in an open economy with a government

itself. (All the microeconomic activities in different market structures go on behind the line, as it were, as individual businesspeople react to expected prices, as in Keynes's *General Theory*, or to expected sales, when we have more realistic imperfectly competitive, monopolistic competitive and oligopolistic structures, and decide on short-period production and employment, creating the incomes that lead to consumption spending, saving and tax payments.) Then for each level of domestic demand and production to be possible in the short period, there must be accompanying inputs of imports. This is shown by the straight line starting at the origin and situated *above* the 45° line by the amount of imports needed, determined by the marginal propensity to import associated with each level of, and change in, Y. At the equilibrium level of Y, OY_e, which is determined by the intersection of $(1 - m)(E)$ with the 45° line, *both* methods of estimating the demand for imports give the same answer, *QED*!

Away from the equilibrium level, though, the answers differ. The demand for imports is estimated to be greater by the expenditure method (M_E) than by the income method (M_Y) to the *left* of the equilibrium intersection points, and to be less, to the right of the intersection, see Figure 5.2.

Is it possible to say anything more quantitative about this discrepancy? We know that in a very simple model, if we suppose prices to be given and constant in the short period, then to the left of the intersection of the aggregate demand function with the aggregate supply function (as we have defined them), we have an unintended run-down of stocks (or a failure to add to them as much as planned) because aggregate demand exceeds aggregate supply (planned investment exceeds planned saving); to the right of the intersection, we have an unintended build-up of stocks because of the excess supply situations which characterise these positions. Then, a moment's reflection suggests (when I told Joan Robinson this she said it was a *very* subtle point) that the difference in the demand for imports predicted by the two methods is equal to *the import components of the unintended changes in stocks occurring*. To the left of the equilibrium point, if we accept for the moment that the expenditure method is the correct way to specify the demand for imports, the income method results in an *underestimate* of the total demand for imports by these amounts; to the right of the equilibrium point, it results in an overestimate. So perhaps this simple result could be taken as a starting point for actual estimates of total imports in given periods of actual time, if it is accepted that the economy is rarely if ever to be found at its short-period equilibrium level. Elsewhere (see Harcourt 1981; 1982), I have argued that the short-period equilibrium level is a sort of centre of gravitation, a sometimes justified short cut for viewing actual national income and expenditure figures as though they were identical with the levels corresponding to their centres of gravitation; in which case no bias would need to be estimated.

Until I started to think about this essay for Tony's volume, I must admit I thought that where we have now reached was the end of the matter. Now I am not so sure. The reason why is as follows: as we mentioned earlier, there are two different concepts of the aggregate demand function in *The General Theory*, only one of which has on the whole survived in later writings by Keynes himself and others, and in the textbooks. The first, which I think is more fundamental, is the summation of what businesspeople think the sales of their products will be in any given short period. It is these expectations which guide their production planning, employment offers and, I now want to argue, *their orders for imports*. Some businesspeople will produce only to order and will know exactly what employment to offer and imports to buy. Others, whether they sell final goods or supply intermediate goods, have to anticipate what their sales will be and therefore what production to

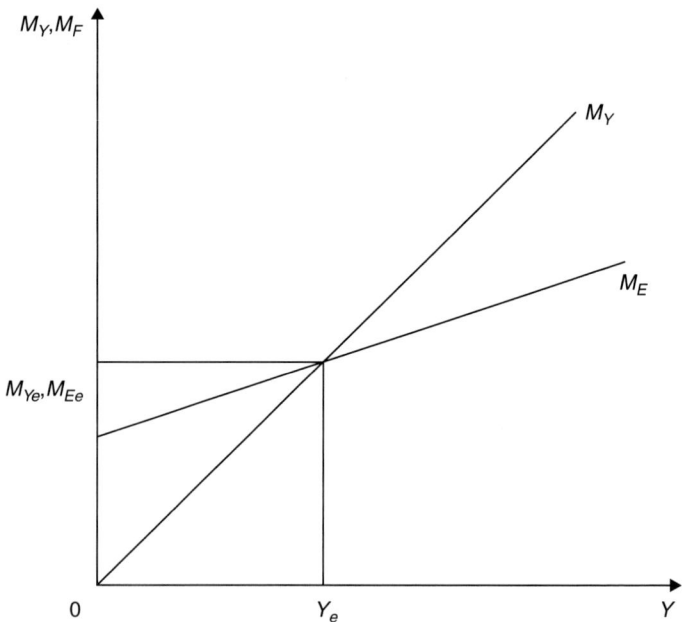

Figure 5.2 Demands for imports by the expenditure and income methods

plan, employment to offer and imports to buy. Keynes put it like this (he ignored imports, of course).

> ... in a given situation of technique, resources and factor cost per unit of employment, the amount of employment, both in each individual firm and industry and in the aggregate, depends on the amount of proceeds which the entrepreneurs expect to receive from the corresponding output ... let D be the proceeds which entrepreneurs expect to receive from the employment of N men, the relationship between D and N being written $D = f(N)$, which is called the *aggregate demand function*. (1936; *C.W.*, vol VII, 1973, 24–25, emphasis in original)

If we suppose that included in these decisions are sales to stock in their own businesses, then the total of *all* these expectations of sales by business people must be *exactly* equal to the production being planned and implemented and therefore the total income that is created (it would be irrational for them to produce either more or less). Hence the 45° line is both a reference point *and* the aggregate demand (and supply) function. It is the aggregate supply function because, remembering our assumptions, it corresponds with Keynes's definition:

> ... the aggregate supply price of the output of a given amount of employment is the expectation of proceeds which would just make it worth the while of the entrepreneurs to give that employment ... Let Z be the aggregate supply price of the output from employing N men, the relationship between Z and N being written $Z = \varphi(N)$, which can be called the *aggregate supply function'*. (1936; *C.W.*, vol. VII, 1973, 24–25, emphasis in original)

Of course, whether the individual and total expectations are realised or not depends upon the subsequent reactions of the income receivers with regard to their spending on consumption goods as indicated by the aggregate consumption function, which is a major component of the second concept of the aggregate demand function in *The General Theory*, that is to say, the sum of planned expenditures on all final goods, either related to income levels or autonomously in the simple case here for $\bar{I}$, $\bar{G}$ and $\bar{X}$. This interpretation is implied in Keynes's summing up of his theory on pp. 28–32, especially in (3) and (5), p. 29:

> (3) The amount of labour N which the entrepreneurs decide to employ depends on the sum (D) of *two* quantities, namely D_1, the amount

which the community is expected to spend on consumption, and D_2, the amount which it is expected to devote to new investment ...

[...]

(5) Hence the volume of employment in equilibrium depends on (i) the aggregate supply function, φ, (ii) the propensity to consume, χ, and (iii) the volume of investment, D_2 the essence of the General Theory of Employment'. (emphasis in original)

The latter form of the aggregate demand function does not in principle have to be known by individual businesspeople who, of course, are mainly interested in what their specific prices and/or sales will be. But it is known to us, the all-seeing macroeconomists, looking at the economy as a whole. And it is for this reason, as well as others, that import demands were related to expenditure in the models of the three sets of authors mentioned above.

But were they correct to do so? Probably not, because if the argument above concerning the first concept of the aggregate demand function is correct, then the *initiation* of production, employment and demand for imports must come from the combined (but uncoordinated) actions of all the businesspeople in the community. In which case, the demand for imports will be related to points on the 45° line, not to points on the expenditure relationship which is derived from the second concept (onto which Keynes quickly moved). So the more common method of estimating the demand for imports by making it a function of income will give the right answer, though up until now, says he modestly, exposing former treason, for the wrong reason.[1] Moreover, there will be no reason to correct for biases in the estimates of the demand for imports, as was suggested above, because income, *whether equilibrium or not*, is the relevant major determinant of such demand in the short period.

I shall be the first to cheer if Tony shows that I am now wrong and that he and Kennedy, in a much more detailed and persuasive way, and the other authors were right all the time. So, over to you, Tony, and many congratulations on your splendid contributions as a wise, unreconstructed Keynesian!

Note

1. 'The last temptation is the greatest treason:
   To do the right deed for the wrong reason.'

Eliot (1935), 44.

References

Eliot, T. S. (1935), *Murder in the Cathedral*, London: Faber and Faber.

Harcourt, G. C. (1981), 'Marshall, Sraffa and Keynes: Incompatible Bedfellows?' *Eastern Economic Journal*, 5, 39–50. Reprinted in Harcourt (1982).

Harcourt, G. C. (1982), *The Social Science Imperialists: Selected Essays*, ed. by Prue Kerr, London: Routledge and Kegan Paul. Reprinted in the Routledge Library Editions series in 2003.

Harcourt, G. C. and Vincent G. Massaro (1964), 'A Note on Mr Sraffa's Sub-Systems', *Economic Journal*, 74, 715–22.

Harcourt, G. C., P. H. Karmel and R. H. Wallace (1967), *Economic Activity*, Cambridge: Cambridge University Press.

Keynes, J. M. (1936), *The General Theory of Employment, Interest and Money*, London: Macmillan, *C.W.*, vol. VII, 1973.

Sraffa, P. (1960), *Production of Commodities by Means of Commodities: Prelude to a Critique of Economic Theory*, Cambridge: Cambridge University Press.

Thirlwall A. P. (1997), *Macroeconomic Issues from a Keynesian Perspective. Selected Essays of A.P. Thirlwall. Volume Two*, Cheltenham, UK and Northampton, MA, USA: Edward Elgar.

Wonnacott, P. (1975), *Macroeconomics*, London: Irwin.

6
The Theoretical and Political Importance of the Economics of Keynes: Or, What Would Marx and Keynes Have Made of the Happenings of the Past 30 Years and More? (2009)*

Introduction

I start with two propositions: first, that Maynard Keynes and Karl Marx, were they still with us, would have made far more sense of the happenings of modern capitalism of the past 30 to 40 years than do the more modern approaches to macroeconomics of the same period; and, second, that Keynes would have sat down and tried again to save capitalism from itself.[†] (Marx may have rubbed his hands and hoped that its demise, so often predicted by him and his followers, was at last on hand – but I would not bet on this.) It may surprise you that I couple Keynes and Marx together, but I would argue – the evidence is supplied in a fine book by Claudio Sardoni (1987) – that when Marx and Keynes examined the same issues in the capitalist process, they came up with much the same answers. Perhaps, on further reflection, this should not be surprising, for along with Michal Kalecki and Joseph

* Originally published in Mathew Forstater, Gary Mongiovi and Steven Pressman (eds), *Post Keynesian Macroeconomics: Essays in Honour of Ingrid Rima*, London and New York: Routledge, 2007, pp. 56–69.

Schumpeter (said by Joan Robinson to have been Marx with the adjectives changed), they have made the deepest, most insightful analyses of the laws of motion of capitalist society in our profession.[1]

Modern macro and its limitations

I shall say more about their analyses below. First, let me clear out of the way why I think the modern approaches are less than satisfactory: they employ *either* representative agent models, *or* Frank Ramsey's benevolent dictator model, *or* an emphasis on certain imperfections in the workings of capitalist institutions, such as are to be found in New Keynesian models – sticky wages and prices, imperfectly competitive market structures, asymmetrical information, and the like.

Modeling the economy as a representative agent rules out by assumption one of the fundamental insights of Keynes (and Marx), to wit, the fallacy of composition, that what may be true of the individual taken in isolation is not necessarily true of all individuals taken together. This implies that when looking at the macroeconomic processes at work in capitalism, we cannot presume that the whole is but the sum of the parts. Indeed it is not. We have, therefore, to consider the macroeconomic foundations of microeconomics as James Crotty (1980), citing Marx, told us long ago, and on which Frank Hahn, innocent of all this, is now working. Wynne Godley also has been working most innovatively on this theme for many years. Moreover, that great and wise Keynesian, Lorie Tarshis, regarded the use of the representative agent as the greatest heresy of modern macroeconomics and explained why in Tarshis (1980); see also Harcourt (1995; 2001a).

As for Ramsey's benevolent dictator model, a re-read (or a read for the first time) of his classic 1928 article 'A Mathematical Theory of Saving', together with his own scathing assessment of it,[2] ought to show how fanciful it is to argue that, in a completely different setting, it could illuminate what has been happening in actual interrelated modern economies in recent decades or, in fact, any decades. As for the New Keynesians, while it is possible to applaud many of their policy conclusions and make common cause with them on them (a plea I first made in a 1980 paper that was not published until 1996; see Harcourt, 1996–97; 2001a), I submit that their policies do not always follow logically from their theories. By basing their results on imperfections, they imply that if the latter were not there in the first place, or were to be removed, all would be well. But as Marx and then Keynes argued, freely competitive capitalism with power diffused equally between all individual decision makers and those affected by such decisions, especially wage-earners, so that, in effect, no one individual has any power, still would not work in an optimal manner. In particular, it would not necessarily provide full employment of labour and capital either in the short or the long period, so that booms and depressions, inflations and deflations, and, in certain circumstances, deep crises could still be the order of the day. An especially astute argument for an aspect of this set of arguments is to be found in Nina Shapiro's 1997 paper, 'Imperfect Competition and Keynes'.[3] She argues plausibly that an economy characterised by freely competitive market structures would have cycles of greater amplitudes and higher average levels of unemployment over time than one characterised by imperfectly competitive market structures. This insight is shared both by her contemporaries, for example, Paul Davidson and Jan Kregel, and by distinguished predecessors like Austin Robinson, who always lamented the relative lack of interest by Keynesians in the early post-war years in the systemic effects of market structures, regional experiences and requirements, and the like, Miehal Kalecki, whose review of *The General Theory*[4] forcefully makes this point in his usual lucid and succinct way, and John Kenneth Galbraith in his greatest classic, *The New Industrial State* (1967). All these economists, together with Marx and Keynes, were analysing how key decisions made in an environment of inescapable uncertainty impact on systemic behaviour.

The thrust of Austin Robinson's, Galbraith's, and Shapiro's argument is that anything that reduces the impact of uncertainty on firms' decisions on the production, employment, and, most importantly, accumulation[5] is likely to result in more satisfactory and stable systemic behaviour. Especially is it likely to beget a higher rate of accumulation on average and so a greater chance of absorbing (offsetting) the level of saving associated, if not with full employment levels of income, at least with high levels, certainly higher levels than would occur in a system characterised by the Marshallian freely competitive structures that Keynes used most of the time in *The General Theory* itself.

Though the New Keynesians have mounted vigorous and, to my mind, telling counterattacks on the New Classical Macroeconomics within the latter's own framework (see, for example, Hahn and Solow, 1995), they have not themselves completely escaped from the clutches of what Joan Robinson (1964) once aptly dubbed 'Pre-Keynesian Theory after Keynes'. It is true that they have routed the extreme idea associated with the beginning of the use of the hypothesis of rational expectations by the New Classical macroeconomists that the world may be analysed *as if* perfect competition and perfect foresight reigned so that the Arrow–Debreu model could be used as the base on which to erect theory and policy. And it is also true that the rational expectations hypothesis, when it is uncoupled from the Lucas vertical aggregate supply curve, is just a hypothesis deserving to be tested. Indeed, if it were found not to be inconsistent with the facts, and if the world is correctly illuminated by Keynes's model, coupling them together would serve to reinforce policies of intervention, for then thinking alone could make it so, as it were. Yet, having cheered all this, there are still so many remnants of what Keynes dubbed classical economics present in the New Keynesian approach as to make it logically unacceptable as the appropriate model or even 'vision' for starting an analysis of the modern world: that is to say, a world in which foreign exchanges have been floated, sometimes dirtily, often freely, financial markets have been deregulated, credit has been made 'available to all,' capital controls have been removed in many economies, labour markets have been made flexible (a euphemism for making the sack effective again by re-creating the reserve army of labour after the full employment years of the long boom as the Marxists have it or Golden Age of capitalism as the Left Keynesians dubbed it), international trade has been liberalised at least in some directions, often at the expense of the South and to the benefit of the North, and technical advances have reduced the length of the short run in financial and other markets to hours rather than weeks or months. For it is not obvious that the equilibrating mechanisms of supply and demand (even if associated with path dependence) with their underlying theme of harmony, balance, and voluntary choice are universally the appropriate tools to use.[6] So let us reiterate the essential lessons that Keynes taught us.

Essence of Keynes

I briefly sketch what I have come to believe is the essence of Keynes's new position, *as he saw it* himself in 1936 and 1937, the culmination of his journey from *A Tract on Monetary Reform* (1923) through *A Treatise on Money* (1930) to *The General Theory*[7] I do not give chapter and verse for what I have to say; it is based on my reading over many years of *The General Theory* and Keynes's other books, the *Collected Writings* (1971–79), and much secondary literature, especially in recent years Robert Skidelsky's superb three-volume biography of Keynes (Skidelsky, 1983, 1992, 2000).

The essential characteristics of the Marshallian system as Keynes viewed it was, first, the domination of the long period and, second, a strict distinction between the real and the money. In the real system, supposing there to be free competition, the object of the analysis was to determine long-period normal equilibrium prices and quantities, using partial equilibrium supply and demand analysis (but showing in an appendix that the same principles apply in a general equilibrium system, to wit, that equilibrium prices were, as we say now, market-clearing). The analysis was as applicable to the markets for the services of productive factors as it was to the markets for commodities. As for the process of accumulation, there was a supply of real saving, consumption foregone, associated with maximising expected utility choices between present and future consumption, with the rate of exchange reflecting time preference at the margin: and a demand for saving, investment, in which the technical possibilities of transforming present consumption into future consumption at the margin were the key concepts. The price which cleared this market and set the composition of the national income between consumption and saving/investment was the natural rate of interest, a real concept.

The general equilibrium version would have as a corollary the Say's Law level of long-period overall output, itself a 'simple' summation of the individual quantities of commodities (and employment) associated with the long-period market-clearing prices of individual markets. So what determined overall employment (and *zero, non*-voluntary, unemployment) was not an interesting *theoretical* question, if it were ever even to be asked: only simple summation was required.

When we come to the discussion of the determinants of the general price level – so far only relative prices and quantities have been discussed, neither money nor money prices played any significant analytical role – the quantity theory of money tautology could easily be turned into a theory. For if M was determined by the monetary authorities, V was given by institutions and historical customs and T was interpreted as the total of transactions associated with the Say's Law long-period equilibrium position. P remained the only unknown. Moreover, if V and T were given, changing M would, at least as a long-period tendency, change P in the same proportion. (Keynes would have expressed all this in terms of the Marshallian/Cambridge version of the quantity theory but the story is essentially the same.) Money, therefore, was only a veil in the long period.

The object of volume II of an ideal *Principles of Economics* was to set out this basic theory, analyse the causes of fluctuations around the long-period position (the trade or business cycle), and design institutions which either allowed the economy to return as quickly as possible to the equilibrium position after a shock, or to move as painlessly as possible to a new equilibrium position if the basic real determinants of it – tastes, endowments, techniques of production – themselves changed. The essential task of the monetary authorities was to ensure that the money rate of interest was consistent with the underlying natural rate of interest which, like saving, ruled the roost in the process of accumulation. This, in the crudest, simplest form, was the system on which Keynes was brought up, as he came to see it.

Because of the real/monetary dichotomy, and because he was writing on money, Keynes felt inhibited about spending time on the intricate happenings to output and employment in the short period and over the cycle – 'the intricate theory of the economics of the short period'. Nevertheless, in *A Tract* he recognised them and especially the evils of unemployment and deflation – hence he cheeked Marshall about our mortality in the long run – but, *analytically*, he was looking for institutions and their behaviour which would give price stability and allow the economy to settle at its long-period Say's Law position. In *A Treatise on Money* he presented the famous banana plantation parable but he was unable analytically to stop the downward spiral of activity and prices until either the inhabitants had starved to death or there was an *ad hoc* change in their accumulation behaviour (Keynes, 1930, pp. 158–60). The endogenous process and its end had to wait for the publication of Kahn's multiplier article in 1931 which also contained 'Mr. Meade's Relation' – the derivation of the value of the multiplier by concentrating on the leakage into saving.

In *The General Theory*, Keynes (1936) replaced the old system by a radically new, indeed revolutionary, system. As a Marshallian his basic tools were demand and supply functions, now aggregate ones. His emphasis was on the short period in its own right, suitably adapted for analysis of the economy overall. (This had been the emphasis, too, in Kahn's 1929 Fellowship dissertation on *The Economics of the Short Period*, though Kahn's analysis was microeconomic.) The dichotomy between the real and the money disappeared in both the short period and the long period (which Keynes ultimately ceased to believe to be a coherent concept in macroeconomics). Money and other financial assets and monetary institutions entered the analysis from the start (institutions were only sketched relatively to the rich analysis in *A Treatise on Money*, a deliberate choice by Keynes). Aggregate planned expenditures drove the system which operated in an environment of inescapable uncertainty. The latter had inescapable consequences for vital decisions, especially regarding investment expenditures and the holding of money and other financial assets. Investment dominated and saving responded through the consumption function. The consumption function was, of course, the relationship between aggregate disposable income and the distribution of income between the classes, on the one hand, and planned consumption expenditure, on the other. Keynes intimately related it to the (income) multiplier through the marginal propensity to consume. The amount saved (but not the form in which it was held) was treated as a residual. Investment was determined by expected profitability, on the one hand, and the money rate of interest, representing the alternative ways of holding funds (and their availability and cost), on the other. Subsequently, in 1937, finance, especially through the banking system and the stock exchange, was also to play a vital role as, *cet. par.*, the ultimate constraint on investment expenditure. The money rate of interest therefore ruled the roost and the expected rate of profit (the marginal efficiency of capital, the counterpart to the natural rate of interest in the old system) had to measure up to it. The money rate of interest was depicted as the price which cleared the money market by equating the demand for money with its supply, not as the (real) price which equalised desired saving and investment.

The rest state in both the short period and the long period could be associated with involuntary unemployment – people willing to work in existing conditions but with the level of aggregate demand such as there not to be sufficient demand for their services. Nor was there any effective way for them to signal that it would be profitable to employ them; indeed, there would be no profitable way to employ them unless there were to be a rise (or an expected rise) in real expenditures. Up to full employment, the outcome in the labour market depended on what happened in the commodity market. The quantity theory was replaced as an explanation of the general price level by old-fashioned Marshallian short-period competitive pricing, suitably (or perhaps not) adapted to the economy as a whole. There were therefore at least three 180-degree turns between the old and the new: investment dominated saving, the commodity market dominated the labour market and the money rate of interest dominated the expected rate of profit. The forces which would make planned accumulation even on average absorb full employment saving were unreliable and weak, not to be relied on even as tendencies. Moreover, the general price level was determined by factors other than the quantity of money.

Keynes's post-*General Theory* developments

The new system was the base on which Keynes would build his theory of inflation in *How to Pay for the War* (1940) and his policy proposals for the international world order in the post-war period. In a superb review article on the third volume of Skidelsky's biography of Keynes

(Skidelsky, 2000), David Vines (2003) makes a convincing case for the proposition that Keynes provided the conceptual basis for modern international macroeconomic theory. Of course this is not to be found explicitly in *The General Theory* itself. That book was mainly concerned with a closed economy model in order to highlight the central theoretical propositions and insights of the new theory. Nor did Keynes analyse the trade cycle or long-term growth issues systematically in *The General Theory*, and some of his *obita dicta* asides look rather strange now.

For most of *The General Theory* Keynes was content to discuss existence and stability propositions in the short period, focusing especially on the factors that were responsible for the point of effective demand at which aggregate demand and aggregate supply, and planned investment and planned saving (more generally, injections into and leakages from the expenditure-production-income circuit) were equalised. (He said later that if he were to write the book again he would have been more careful to separate out the fundamental factors responsible for the existence of the point of effective demand from the other set responsible for stability and reaching the point through a groping process by business people. He thought that Ralph Hawtrey had confused the two. See Keynes, *CW*, XIV, 181–82.)

In his starkest model, one designed not so much to describe the world as it is, but to bring out most simply what was at stake, he assumed, as Jan Kregel (1976) has told us, that short-term expectations concerning immediate prices, sales, costs, *et al.* were always realised and were independent of long-term expectations concerning their future courses, the ingredients most relevant for investment decisions, so that planned investment could provisionally be taken as a given and the point of effective demand established immediately. In his most sophisticated model of (the same) reality, the independence of the two sets of expectations was scrapped, the point of effective demand was not realised immediately and indeed it changed over time as the model of shifting equilibrium came into play. This last apparatus is in rudimentary form the starting point for the development of growth theory by Richard Kahn and Joan Robinson, Nicky Kaldor and Luigi Pasinetti, and the models of cyclical growth developed by Kalecki (independently) and Richard Goodwin.

Both Marx and Keynes recognised that when financial capital was not moving in tandem with industrial and commercial capital (Marx would and Keynes would not have put it this way), malfunctions and sometimes crises were likely to occur. Keynes set out his ideas on this in, for example, the key chapter 12 of *The General Theory* on the operation and non-operation of the stock exchange and its relationship to real accumulation and activity generally. Another key step was in his 1937 (Keynes, 1937a and 1937b) papers on the rate of interest and the finance motive, which discuss how the banking system in particular holds the key to the realisation of investment plans, taking as given the state of long-term expectations. The stock exchange also has a key role because the repayment of the bank loans used to finance the setting up of investment projects, the start of the process of accumulation, depends upon the firms concerned being able subsequently to place new issues of shares and debentures at satisfactory prices. (The demand for the new issues comes, in part at least, from the placement of the new saving created by the new investment.) The point is that finance and saving are sharply separated by their roles and place – timing – in the process of accumulation.

These ideas were subsequently developed by Hyman Minsky in particular, writing under the rubric of his financial instability hypothesis. Minsky spelled out ideas, perhaps more implicit than explicit in the writings of Keynes and Dennis Robertson, suggesting that the natural, probably inescapable, cyclical movements on the real side of the economy can be amplified both upwards and downwards by events in the financial aspects of the economic process. Minsky stressed the feedbacks associated with the disparities between expected cash flows and actual or realised cash flows in the accumulation/production process, and emphasised how non-realisation acts on confidence and expectations, stoking the boom in its early stages, accelerating the downturn and deepening and prolonging the subsequent recession or depression.[8]

Marx and Keynes's insights applied to the monetarist episode

As well as pointing out the implications of disparities in the progress of finance capital in relation to commercial and industrial capital, Marx's analysis of the inherent contradictions in capitalism are of immediate relevance for our purposes in this chapter. Unlike Keynes, Marx made a clear distinction between happenings in the sphere of production, on the one hand, and happenings in the sphere of distribution and exchange, on the other. As far as the possibility of and limits to accumulation are concerned, it is conditions in the sphere of production – the length and intensity of the working day, the state of the class war between capital and labour, employer and employee – that ultimately determine the size of the potential surplus created for the realisation of profits and for future accumulation. Whether this potential is realised or not, though, depends upon happenings in the other sphere of distribution and exchange. It is here that Keynes, Kalecki, and developments based on their contributions come into play: the combination of the theories of investment and of the distribution of income determined by the expanded version of the theory of effective demand decides how much of the potential surplus is realised in actual profits and accumulation (see, for example, Harris, 1978).

These ideas help to explain one of the paradoxes of recent decades. Monetarism has rightly been called by the late Thomas Balogh (1982) 'the incomes policy of Karl Marx'. Ostensibly, the theory was meant to justify policies designed to rid the system of inflationary tendencies. In fact, it was associated with the attempt to swing the balance of economic, social, and political power back from labour to capital. (The reverse swing had occurred cumulatively in many advanced capitalist economies during the years of the long boom.) The means to this end was the re-creation of the reserve army of labour, so making the sack an effective weapon again and creating cowed and quiescent workforces and greater potential surpluses for national and, increasingly, international capital accumulation.

What was not realised was that the emergence of heavy and sustained unemployment, ostensibly to push short-run rates of unemployment above so-called natural rates and then let them converge on natural rates where inflation could be sustained at steady rates and accelerating rates of inflation would be things of the past, would simultaneously have such an adverse effect on what Keynes called the 'animal spirits' of business people, the ultimate determinants of rates of accumulation. Hence we have had decades in many economies in which inflation has been drastically reduced yet accumulation has been sluggish, certainly well below the levels needed to offset full-employment saving and below the levels achieved during the long boom itself. In those countries where this had *not* occurred, despised Keynesian policies have continued to be used, sometimes unintelligent ones such as those implemented, for example, during the last six years of Ronald Reagan's Presidency in the USA and now by President Bush the Second.

Since attaining full employment by the use of fiscal policies was no longer on the agenda in the former countries and monetary policies were mainly directed at general price levels and exchange rates, contractionary forces were widely prevalent in these countries, as the politicians and their advisors waited (or claimed to be waiting) in vain while the impersonal forces of competitive markets allied with monetarist rules allowed the economics to seek and find their natural rates.

'Visions' and policies

It is fair to say that Keynes never completely threw off the vision of the working of economies in terms of an equilibrium framework. He did, of course, argue that government intervention was needed to help attain a satisfactory full employment equilibrium (internal balance) in each economy. This was an essential step towards equilibrium associated with external balance in the international system and the possibility then to take advantage of the classical principles of free trade on which he had been brought up.[9] The proposals he put forward at Bretton Woods were designed to provide the institutions and the liquidity that would make all this possible. That the Americans, principally through Harry Dexter White, won out on both the institutions and the provision of liquidity adopted for the post-war period was a tragedy; for this ensured that the Bretton Woods system contained within it the seeds of its own eventual destruction from its very inception. (How Marx would have laughed!)

One of the major changes in vision since Keynes's death about how markets, economies, even whole systems work, associated with Keynes's followers, especially Kaldor and Joan Robinson, is the concept of cumulative causation. The concept has its origins in Adam Smith (what has not?) and was brought into prominence in the modern era by Allyn Young (1928), Kaldor's teacher at the LSE, and subsequently championed by Kaldor and independently by Gunar Myrdal. The way I illustrate the essential idea of the concept for my students is through the analogy of a wolf pack (I am not a zoologist so I may be completely wrong about how wolves behave; but as I am an economist, at least *I* think so, let us assume I am right). There are two major views on the workings of markets, economies, whole systems. The dominant one is that akin to a wolf pack running along. If one or more wolves get ahead or fall behind, powerful forces come into play which return them to the pack. (The parallels with the existence of an equilibrium that is stable, and that the forces responsible for existence are independent of those responsible for stability are, I hope, obvious.) The other view has the forces acting on the wolves who get ahead or fall behind make them get further and further ahead or fall further and further behind, at least for long periods of time. This view captures the notion of virtuous or vicious processes of cumulative causation. Which view is 'correct' makes a drastic difference to our understanding of the world and how specific policies are perceived, recommended and evaluated.

I illustrate with an example, the case for freely floating exchange rates. A classic paper arguing for them is by Milton Friedman (1953). Underlying his argument is the first wolf pack analogy, that in a competitive setting there exists a set of long-period stable equilibrium exchange rates that quickly would be found and then kept more or less in place by a free float. In this setting the systemic effects of speculation would be beneficial, for speculators with their superior knowledge, intelligence, and information would help the system to reach the equilibrium pattern more quickly than in their absence and then sustain it there.

But suppose that the second wolf pack analogy is the correct or at least more correct description of how foreign-exchange markets work. Then there is no set of stable equilibrium exchange rates 'out there' waiting to be found and now a float combined with speculative activity will be systemically harmful, accelerating the movements in both directions of exchange rates away from one another and also of systems, at least for long periods of time. I submit that the second scenario is more akin to what has happened over much of recent decades, and provides a rationale for various schemes suggested to curb the action of speculators. (My own suggestions may be found in Harcourt (1994; 1995; 2001b). I had generalised the Tobin tax proposal without, I must confess, being aware at the time of its existence!)

It is not only in markets characterised by processes of cumulative causation processes that speculation may be systemically harmful. Any market in which stocks dominate flows and expectations about the behaviour of other participants in the market dominate the more usual economic factors – preferences, costs of production – in the setting of prices may experience periods when speculation is harmful.[10] An obvious example is the stock exchange. On this we may recall Keynes's famous description in chapter 12 of *The General Theory* of what may happen when 'enterprise becomes a bubble on a whirlpool of speculation' (Keynes, 1936, p. 159).

A post-Keynesian solution to Kalecki's dilemma?

Let me close with another example of how Keynes and Keynesian/ Kaleckian/Marxian ideas are still relevant for both our understanding and policy-making. The ideas I present now are based on Kalecki's famous 1943 paper 'Political Aspects of Full Employment' and the writings of my two greatest Australian mentors, the late Erie Russell (Meade and Russell, 1957; Russell, 1965) and the late Wilfred Salter (1960), both devoted Keynesians; see Harcourt (1997; 2001b) for the arguments and references.

Kalecki set out graphically the vital difference between the political economy of getting to full employment after a deep slump, when all classes are in favour of this, the wage-earners in order to get jobs, business people in order to receive higher profits, the government in order to reduce the risk of serious social unrest, on the one hand, and the political economy of sustaining full employment, on the other hand. In conditions of sustained full employment, as I argued above, there is a cumulative shift of economic, social, and political power from capital to labour. The capitalist class, indeed conservative elements generally, get more and more uneasy about the emerging situation. An environment is created in which, for example, monetarist ideas will be well received, and more than one economist will be prepared to be a hired prize fighter in support of those ideas as guides to government (and central bank) actions.

Is there an answer to this, on the face of it, inescapable dilemma in our sorts of economies? Keynes and his followers recognised that attaining and then maintaining full employment would carry with it cumulatively rising inflationary pressures associated with rising money-wage demands. It is no accident that Joan Robinson always said that, from 1936 on, 'Incomes Policy' was her middle name, a perceptive insight no doubt reinforced by having an actual middle name of Violet. Russell and Salter recognised this dilemma and argued in Australia for a full-employment policy that included an incomes policy implemented through our centralised wage-fixing body (then the Australian Arbitration Commission). In broad outline, at a starting point, money incomes were to be adjusted periodically for changes in prices and in *overall* productivity. Not only is this adjustment equitable, it is also efficient.

It is equitable because at the level of the economy as a whole, capital and labour are complements and the impact of their combined activity on overall productivity ought to be reflected in changes in the *real* incomes of all citizens. It is efficient because with full employment, such an overall policy discourages low productivity, often declining industries whose time has passed and encourages high productivity, often expanding industries whose time has come. The result is a regime with higher increases in overall productivity than would occur otherwise, certainly than would occur in a regime characterised by so-called flexible labour markets, such as are the UK's and the USA's pride and joy. There would be therefore an agreeable *quid pro quo* for money income restraint in the form of rising real incomes, so providing a possible solution to Kalecki's dilemma. There are, of course, all sorts of qualifications and modifications and exceptions to the starting rule – I discuss these in the article referred to above. Here I wanted to set out the core argument as starkly as possible.

Conclusion

In conclusion, I want to say that Keynes and his ideas are still alive and well; that subsequent developments by others complement agreeably his own revolutionary contributions; and that people of goodwill who wish to see established just and equitable societies worldwide have in these ideas an essential starting point.

Notes

† A lecture originally given at the conference on 'Keynes and After,' held at the Faculty of Economies and Business Administration, University of Iceland, Reykjavik, on 10 October 2003. I thank the organizers for allowing me to publish it as a chapter in this volume. I am most grateful to the editors of the book for their helpful comments on a draft of the chapter. I would also like to pay tribute to Ingrid Rima for many years of friendship, support, and inspiration.

1. Marx's views on socialism are another matter altogether; see Harcourt and Kerr (2001).
2. In a letter to Keynes (28 June 1928) when he submitted the article to the *Economic Journal*, he wrote: 'Of course the whole thing is a waste of time.' It had distracted him from 'a book on logic ... [because] it [was] much easier to concentrate on than philosophy and the difficulties that arise rather [obsessed him].'
3. Fairness demands that I refer the reader to Robin Marris's paper, 'Yes, Mrs. Robinson! *The General Theory* and Imperfect Competition' that immediately precedes Shapiro's paper in Harcourt and Riach (eds), vol. 1 (1997). Marris argues that Keynes-type results only go through with imperfectly competitive microeconomic foundations.
4. Kalecki's review, though published in Polish in 1936, was not available in full in English until 1982; see Targetti and Kinder-Hass (1982).
5. The firm is the most fundamental unit of analysis in Keynes's macroeconomics, a point emphasised repeatedly by Tarshis, one of Keynes's most devoted pupils and disciples; see Harcourt (1995; 2001a).
6. Steven Pressman (9 November 2004) chides me for being 'a little harsh on New Keynesian economics and a bit unfair to them. First, in part, New Keynesian economics was an attempt to beat rational expectations at its own game. This can explain some of the 'pre-[Keynesian]' side to it that [I] object

to'. I thought I had said that when citing Hahn and Solow (1995) above. Second, he reminds me that 'there are many strands of New Keynesian economics that are more Keynesian or Post Keynesian than neoclassical.' He cites Joe Stiglitz's work (with Weiss) on 'credit rationing,' for example (Stiglitz and Weiss, 1981). But Stiglitz's ideas were anticipated by Kalecki in 1937 with his principle of increasing risk, an acknowledgement that Stiglitz only made towards the end of his series of articles on the issue. So, having rethought as asked, I'm really not *that* repentant!

7. Perhaps we should start from *A Treatise on Probability* (1921) and *The Economic Consequences of the Peace* (1919) as important insights from them are to be found in his later views and theories.

8. For some policy implications of Minsky's insights, see Harcourt (2001a, ch. 15).

9. Skidelsky (1992, p. xv) called him 'the last of the great English liberals'.

10. The seminal and classic paper on this is Kaldor (1939).

References

Balogh. T. (1982) *The Irrelevance of Conventional Economics* (London: Weidenfeld & Nicholson).

Crotty. J. R. (1980) 'Post-Keynesian Theory: An Overview and Evaluation'. *American Economic Review*, 70, pp. 20–25.

Friedman, M. (1953) 'The Case for Flexible Exchange Rates', in *Essays in Positive Economics* (Chicago: University of Chicago Press).

Galbraith. J. K. (1967) *The New Industrial State* (Boston: Houghton Mifflin).

Hahn. F. and Solow, R. (1995) *A Critical Essay on Modern Macroeconomic Theory* (Oxford: Blackwell).

Harcourt, G. C. (1994) 'A 'Modest Proposal' for Taming Speculators and Putting the World on Course to Prosperity'. *Economic and Political Weekly*, 29, pp. 2490–92: reprinted in Harcourt (2001b).

Harcourt, G. C. (1995) 'Lorie Tarshis, 1911–1993: An Appreciation', *Economic Journal*, 105, pp. 1244–55; reprinted in Harcourt (2001a).

Harcourt, G. C. (1996–97) 'Critiques and Alternatives: Reflections on Some Recent (and Not So Recent) Controversies,' *Journal of Post Keynesian Economics*, 19, pp. 171–70: reprinted with an Addendum in Harcourt (2001a).

Harcourt, G. C. (1997) 'Pay Policy, Accumulation and Productivity,' *Economic and Labour Relations Review*, 8, pp. 78–89; reprinted in Harcourt (2001b).

Harcourt, G. C. (2001a) *50 Years a Keynesian and Other Essays* (Houndmills, Hants.: Palgrave Macmillan).

Harcourt, G. C. (2001b) *Selected Essays on Economic Policy* (Houndmills, Hants.: Palgrave).

Harcourt, G. C. and Kerr, P. (2001) 'Karl Marx, 1818–83', in Harcourt (2001a).

Harcourt, G. C. and Riach, P.A. (eds) (1997) *A 'Second Edition' of The General Theory*. 2 vols (London: Routledge).

Harris, D. J. (1978) *Capital Accumulation and Income Distribution* (Stanford: Stanford University Press).

Kahn, R. F. (1929) *The Economics of the Short Period* (London: Macmillan, 1989).

Kahn, R. F. (1931) 'The Relation of Home Investment to Unemployment', *Economic Journal*, 41, pp. 173–98.

Kaldor, N. (1939) 'Speculation and economic stability', *Review of Economic Studies*, 7, pp. 1–27; reprinted in Kaldor (1960).

Kaldor, N. (1960) *Essays on Economic Stability and Growth* (London: Duckworth).

Kalecki, M. (1937) 'Principle of Increasing Risk', *Economica*, 16, pp. 440–46.

Kalecki, M. (1943) 'Political Aspects of Full Employment', *Political Quarterly*, 14, pp. 322–31.

Keynes, J. M. (1919) *The Economic Consequences of the Peace* (London: Macmillan).

Keynes, J. M. (1921) *A Treatise on Probability* (London: Macmillan).

Keynes, J. M. (1923) *A Tract on Monetary Reform* (London: Macmillan).

Keynes, J. M. (1930) *A Treatise on Money*, 2 vols (London: Macmillan).

Keynes, J. M. (1936) *The General Theory of Employment, Interest and Money* (London: Macmillan).

Keynes, J. M. (1937a) 'Alternative Theories of the Rate of Interest', *Economic Journal*, 47, pp. 241–52; reprinted in *CW*, XIV.

Keynes, J. M. (1937b) 'The "Ex-Ante" Theory of the Rate of Interest', *Economic Journal*, 47, pp. 663–69; reprinted in *CW*, XIV.

Keynes, J. M. (1940) *How to Pay for the War* (London: Macmillan); reprinted in *CW*, XXV.

Keynes, J. M. (1971–79) *The Collected Writings of John Maynard Keynes*, Vols I–XXIX (London: Macmillan); cited here as *CW* followed by volume number.

Kregel, J. A. (1976) 'Economic Methodology in the Face of Uncertainty: The Modelling Methods of Keynes and the Post-Keynesians', *Economic Journal*, 86, pp. 209–25.

Marris, R. L. (1997) 'Yes, Mrs. Robinson! *The General Theory* and Imperfect Competition', in Harcourt and Riach (eds) (1997), vol. 1.

Meade, J. E. and Russell, E. A. (1957) 'Wage Rates, the Cost of Living and the Balance of Payments', *Economic Record*, 33, pp. 23–28.

Ramsey, F. (1928) 'A Mathematical Theory of Saving', *Economic Journal*, 38, pp. 543–59.

Robinson, J. (1964) 'Pre-Keynesian Theory after Keynes', *Australian Economic Papers*, 3, pp. 25–35.

Russell, E. A. (1965) 'Wages Policy in Australia', *Australian Economic Papers*, 4, pp. 1–26.

Salter, W. E. G. (1960) *Productivity and Technical Change* (Cambridge: Cambridge University Press).

Sardoni. C. (1987) *Marx and Keynes on Economic Recession* (Brighton: Wheatsheaf).

Shapiro. N. (1997) 'Imperfect Competition and Keynes', in Harcourt and Riach (eds) (1997), vol. 1.

Skidelsky, R. (1983) *John Maynard Keynes, Volume One. Hopes Betrayed, 1883–1920* (London: Macmillan).

Skidelsky, R. (1992) *John Maynard Keynes, Volume Two. The Economist as Saviour. 1920–1937* (London: Macmillan).

Skidelsky, R. (2000) *John Maynard Keynes, Volume Three. Fighting for Britain, 1937–1946* (London: Macmillan).

Stiglitz, J. E. and Weiss, A. (1981) 'Credit Rationing in Markets with Imperfect Competition', *American Economic Review*, 71, pp. 393–410.

Targetti, F. and Kinda-Hass, B. (1982) 'Kalecki's Review of Keynes' *General Theory*,' *Australian Economic Papers*, 21, pp. 244–60; Kalecki's review, 'Some Remarks on Keynes' Theory', is pp. 245–53.

Tarshis, L. (1980) 'Post-Keynesian Economics: A Promise that Bounced?' *American Economic Review*, 70 (May), pp. 10–14.

Vines, D. (2003) 'John Maynard Keynes 1937–46: The Creation of International Macroeconomics', *Economic Journal*, 118, pp. F338–F361.

Young, A. (1928) 'Increasing Returns and Economic Progress', *Economic Journal*, 38, pp. 527–42.

7
The Rise and, Hopefully, the Fall of Economic Neo-Liberalism in Theory and Practice (2009)*

I count it a great privilege to contribute the opening essay to this issue of *The Economic and Labour Relations Review*, which is celebrating its first 20 years. Over that time, the journal has been an outlet for independent and outspoken, often unfashionable views, upholding traditions steeped in the thoughts of Michal Kalecki and Maynard Keynes, and some of Australia's wisest economists. (Even Karl Marx gets a mention.) I am most grateful to the editors for asking me to be their opening bat.

Since the 1970s, we have seen the rise to dominance in theory and policy of what Joan Robinson (1964) aptly dubbed 'Pre-Keynesian theory after Keynes'. In the economics profession, these phenomena have been especially associated with the writings of Milton Friedman, Friedrich von Hayek and Robert Lucas, Jnr. They have spawned many surrogates in the USA, the UK, Continental Europe, Latin America, parts of Asia and, sadly, in the Antipodes as well. In the political sphere, President Reagan, Mrs. (as she then was) Thatcher and, in Australia, first, Bill Hayden and then Malcolm Fraser were instrumental in implementing monetarist policies and, more widely, backing deregulation of financial markets, freely floating exchange rates, lowering tariff barriers, and the removal of domestic and international capital controls. Nor did Bob Hawke, Paul Keating and their successors in the ALP avoid the virus. An era of international capitalism, red in tooth and claw, was ushered in. Ruthless swashbuckling capitalists (industrial, commercial and financial) combined with cowed and quiescent workforces often arising from

* Originally published in *Economic and Labour Relations Review*, vol. 20, December 2009, pp. 1–6.

labour markets euphemistically described as flexible, came increasingly to dominate economic and social life.

Commitment to full employment was downgraded or dropped altogether. (I have mentioned before the infamous meeting at Melbourne University in the late 1970s of eight or so Australian professors of economics, called by the late Heinz Arndt, in order to do just this in Australia.) On the surface, control of inflation through monetary policy became the dominant policy. Worship of the free market as *the* institution for all seasons and activities became the modern equivalent of the Golden Calf; Moses, the Law and the prophets (read Keynes and Kalecki) were argued to be discredited; they were despised or, at best, neglected.

Why did all this happen? There are many interrelated causes and events, intellectual, political and social. At the level of theory, a major factor in my view was the tragedy that post-war generations of students of economics, especially in the USA, were brought up on Paul Samuelson's (and Alvin Hansen's) textbook versions of Keynesian economics instead of on Lorie Tarshis's textbook, *The Elements of Economics: An Introduction to the Theory of Price and Employment* (1947).

Lorie's book was the first in the USA to contain an account of the economics of Keynes: about 250 pages which were true to Keynes's lectures when Keynes was writing *The General Theory* (Lorie, then an affiliated student at Trinity College, Cambridge, attended these lectures of Keynes in the early to mid-1930s). Lorie's account was true also to *The General Theory* itself. In particular, the central core of Keynes's analysis was presented in terms of Keynes's aggregate demand and supply analysis.

Lorie's book was cruelly done (almost) to death by right-wing forces led by Merwin K. Hart and, later, William Buckley, Jnr. so that many departments that had initially proposed to set it as the text got cold feet and reneged.[1] While the first edition of Samuelson's textbook (1948) still received the tail end of the right-wing backlash, it did not prevent his textbook from dominating economics courses for the next 30 years and more.

Had Lorie's book been the base on which the teaching of Keynes's ideas was erected, the stagflation episode of the 1970s could not have been said to have discredited Keynes's system. For an imported cost-price shock (or an autonomous rise in money wages) could have been shown to have so affected the position of Keynes's aggregate supply function that, *cet. par*, both the general price level would have been raised, and the levels of activity and employment reduced. The former rise could have precipitated a price-wage (and a wage-wage) spiral to go with the rise in unemployment. Nor could the Phillips Curve have been regarded as an integral part of Keynes's system (Friedman's so-called Keynesian missing equation). Indeed, as we know from Keynes's critique of Jan Tinbergen's econometric work on investment expenditure in the 1930s, the very idea of a dependable long-run relationship, lasting over long periods of time, which could be used as the basis for policy proposals, was thoroughly alien to Keynes's thought (and, I suspect, to Bill Phillips's also) (Harcourt 2001: 183–87).

The subsequent attempts to derive Keynes-type results within a Walrasian framework – by Don Patinkin and early Bob Clower, for example – led attention away from Keynes's own essentially Marshallian approach to economic theory and policy and made possible the rise of the neoclassical synthesis which still receives some space in textbooks even today. (Clower and Axel Leijonhufvud, to their great credit, changed tack to think again in a Marshallian context and, as a result, have written fine papers which interpret and expand deeply Keynes's ideas.) But also in the wake of Friedman's and especially Lucas's influence, we find modern macroeconomics done more and more in terms of representative agent models of the economy, or by an inappropriate application of Frank Ramsey's benevolent dictator model, or through real business cycle 'analysis', or through so-called New Keynesianism. In the last, microeconomic theories of the reasons for 'imperfections' existing in goods and labour markets are used to derive systemic results which are argued to look Keynes-like. In the process, the fallacy of composition and Keynes's stress that the whole is often more than the sum of the parts, have been removed by assumption from analysis (in the first three approaches) and inadequately tackled, if at all, in the fourth. Moreover, in the fourth approach, there is the quite unKeynes implication that the removal of imperfections could make economies function in socially optimum ways. The final irony is that the dominant model that is used in graduate courses to discuss monetary matters and policy logically cannot find a role for money and its characteristics within its formal construction, as Colin Rogers in a number of devastating critical papers has shown us (Rogers 2006).

Of course, there were more than purely intellectual (or even academic scribbling) reasons for what has happened. In the years of the Long Boom (as the Marxists dubbed it) or Golden Age of Capitalism (more the left-Keynesian description) from the 1950s to the early 1970s, major social and political as well as economic events were occurring. Their combined effect was to aid cumulatively the rise to dominance of the anti-Keynesian intellectual forces itemised above. There was growing hostility to 'big government' and stroppy labour behaviour, uncannily reminiscent of the events which Kalecki predicted in his remarkable

1943 article, 'Political aspects of full employment'. There, he analysed the great differences between, on the one hand, the political economy of getting back to full employment after a deep slump, and, on the other, the political economy of sustaining full employment, what I like to call the Kaleckian dilemma. Thus, Kalecki wrote of the second situation:

> The *maintenance* of full employment would cause social and political changes which would give a new impetus to the opposition of the business leaders [to full employment]. Indeed, under a regime of permanent full employment, the sack would cease to flag its role as a disciplinary measure. The social position of the boss would be undermined and the self-assurance and class-consciousness of the working class would grow. Strikes for wage increases and improvements in conditions of work would create political tension...true...profits would be higher under a regime of full employment than they are on average under *laissez-faire*, and even the rise in wage rates resulting from the strong bargaining power of the workers is less likely to reduce profits than to increase prices, and thus affect adversely only...rentier interests. But 'discipline in the factories' and 'political stability' are more appreciated than profits by the business leaders. Their class instinct tells them that lasting full employment is unsound from their point of view, and that unemployment is an integral part of the normal capitalist system. (Kalecki 1943; *C.W.* Vol. I 1990: 351, emphasis in original)

Add on to this the growing unpopularity of the Vietnam War in the USA (especially when it was realised that it could not be won), Australia and New Zealand (the only respectable allies of the Americans in this most immoral war, even more immoral than the recent adventures in Iraq), and in Europe and Asia. The effects of these social movements were compounded by President Johnson's attempt to finance the war without increasing taxes, so that the US economy tended to overheat even prior to the oil price rise shocks which amplified inflationary tendencies. The consequent rise of protest movements and student revolts all round the world associated with the war and much needed reforms in the institutions of higher education, together with civil rights and feminist movements and these other events brought the conservative forces in society to rally around what were previously thought to be the odd ball approaches of Friedman, for example.

In addition, as the new wave of globalisation spread, international capitalism became more and more determined to increase the potential surpluses available for national and international accumulation. This desire fed neatly into support for Monetarist policies, aptly described by the late Tommy Balogh (1982: 77) as 'the incomes policy of Karl Marx'. Friedman's arguments revolved around the concept of the natural rate of unemployment; he argued that away from the natural rate prices would either fall or rise cumulatively, reflecting excess supplies or demands in individual competitive markets. This implied that control of inflation, for example, was to be implemented by aiming at the establishment of the natural rate through monetary policy (short sharp shocks) until it was reached by control of the money supply such that the rate of inflation would now remain constant. This reflected the fact that in the real sector, the pattern of relative prices in both goods and labour markets were market clearing ones (allowing for actual imperfections which created a divergence from the underlying pure Walrasian system that modelled the economy). What this really meant, though, was that contractionary policies were employed to raise levels of unemployment (the reserve army of labour) in order to make the sack an effective weapon again. This would provide the cowed and quiescent labour forces associated with the reversal of the cumulative movement of economic, social and political power to labour from capital which had occurred in the Golden Age of Capitalism, back to capital which could then create a larger potential surplus for profits and accumulation.

If all this is taken to be the ravings of an unreconstructed Marxist (which I am not!), let me remind you that it is basically and independently a paraphrase of arguments in a lecture given by Paul Samuelson at the Bank of Italy in his ninth decade (Samuelson 1997: 6–7; Harcourt 2006: 127). In comparing the different experiences of the (then) present day American and European economies, he stressed 'two main factors ... One: In America we now operate ... the Ruthless Economy. Two: In America we now have a Cowed Labor Force ...'.

What was forgotten (possibly never known) was the existence of a basic contradiction – to wit, that creating larger potential surpluses by these measures, i.e., through high sustained unemployment and sluggish aggregate demand, simultaneously adversely affected the accumulators' 'animal spirits', so that in the event the potential surpluses often failed to be realised. If we examine the performances of many economies in this era, it will be found that, often for long periods, rates of accumulation were sluggish relatively to those achieved in the Golden Age of Capitalism.

Moreover, as finance capital came to dominate industrial and commercial capital, Minsky-type effects emerged. With finance capital out of kilter with the other two, the inescapable growth cycles of capitalist economies had their amplitudes enlarged by the impact of Minsky-type effects. The latter arise from the non-realisation of expected cash flows from investment projects which are needed to back up the extra financial commitments that financed investment and which were already written into the liability sides of balance sheets (Harcourt 2000; 2001). In addition, the cumulative extension of credit to all, while obviously an individual 'good', became more and more a public 'bad' at the systemic level as changes in borrowing and lending rates to consumers, combined with wealth effects, served to make the Keynesian consumption function as unstable and volatile as investment expenditure traditionally was known to be: hence, the enlarged amplitudes of trade cycles and deeper and more prolonged slumps.

Accompanying the rise to dominance of finance capital and the emergence of new sophisticated financial instruments, the workings and effects of which became increasingly hard to understand, were technical advances that shrank the historical length of short runs from months or even years to days or even hours. The steady movement towards an obsession with obtaining maximum short-term results, regardless of their longer term effects both on the decision-makers directly concerned and the industries and economies in which they occurred – that is to say, the rise of what John Hicks (1954; 1983) called snatching behaviour, built more and more potential sources of instability into economic systems. Alfred Marshall's insistence that there are three periods of equal importance in economic analysis – market, short and long periods – was increasingly neglected in actual economic behaviour and decision-making, even if it lingered on, a pale shadow of its former prominence, in academic teaching and research. Behaviour in more and more important markets – the foreign exchange markets, the stock exchanges, the housing markets, for example – came increasingly to resemble the behaviour of casinos. As Maynard Keynes reminded us many moons ago: 'When the capital development of a country becomes a by-product of the activities of a casino, the job is likely to be ill-done' (Keynes 1936; *C.W.* Vol. VII 1973: 159).

Yet policy advisors and academics alike were still urging us to trust the workings of 'freely competitive markets' and arguing that, overall, governments should remain in the background. Bubbles emerged in key markets and now, as we know, the whole box of tricks has been exposed and a major crisis, both financial and real, has emerged. Our pre-Keynesian advisors are unable to tell us either why, or what should be done. Fortunately, common sense has prevailed in many countries and old-fashioned Keynesian and post-Keynesian policies are emerging.

Whether they are of great enough magnitude to succeed remains, alas, to be seen. If they do, the 'hope' in my title will surely be fulfilled and the editors of, and contributors to, *The Economic and Labour Relations Review* should surely be praised for their role in the outcome.

Note

1. See Harcourt (1982: 372–73) for the details of the attack on Lorie's book.

References

Balogh, T. (1982) *The Irrelevance of Conventional Economics*, Weidenfeld & Nicolson, London.

Bellofiore, R. and Ferri, P. (eds) (2000) *Financial Fragility and Investment in the Capitalist Economy: The Economic Legacy of Hyman Minsky*, Edward Elgar, Cheltenham.

Harcourt, G. C. (1982) *The Social Science Imperialists. Selected Essays*. Ed. Prue Kerr, Routledge and Kegan Paul, London.

Harcourt, G. C. (2000) 'Investment expenditure, unrealised expectations and offsetting monetary policies' in Bellofiore and Ferri (eds), pp. 69–75, reprinted in Harcourt (2001), pp. 197–205.

Harcourt, G. C. (2001) *50 Years a Keynesian and Other Essays*, Palgrave Macmillan, Houndmills, Basingstoke, Hampshire.

Harcourt, G. C. (2006) 'Paul Samuelson on Karl Marx: Were the Sacrificed Games of Tennis Worth It?', ch. 8 in Szenberg, Ramrattan and Gottesman (eds) *Samuelsonian Economics and the Twenty-First Century*, Oxford University Press, New York, pp. 127–41.

Hicks, J. R. (1954) 'The Process of Imperfect Competition', *Oxford Economic Papers*, 6, pp. 41–54, reprinted as 'Stickers and Snatchers', ch. 12 of Hicks (1983), pp. 163–78.

Hicks, John (1983) *Classics and Moderns. Collected Essays on Economic Theory*, Vol. III, Basil Blackwell, Oxford.

Kalecki, M. (1943) 'Political aspects of full employment, *Political Quarterly*, 14, pp. 322–31; *C.W.* Vol. I (1990), pp. 347–56.

Keynes, J. M. (1936) *The General Theory of Employment, Interest and Money*, Macmillan, London; *C.W.*, Vol. VII (1973).

Robinson, J. (1964) 'Pre-Keynesian Theory after Keynes', *Australian Economic Papers*, 3, pp. 25–35.

Rogers, C. (2006) 'Doing without Money: A Critical Assessment of Woodford's Analysis', *Cambridge Journal of Economics*, 30, pp. 293–306.

Samuelson, P. A. (1948) *Economics: An Introductory Analysis*. McGraw Hill, New York.

Samuelson, P. A. (1997) 'Wherein Do the European and American Models Differ?' Address delivered at the Bank of Italy, 2 October 1997, No. 320, mimeo.

Szenberg, M., Ramrattan, L. and Gottesman, A. A. (eds) (2006) *Samuelsonian Economics and the Twenty-First Century*, Oxford University Press, New York.

Tarshis, L. (1947) *The Elements of Economics. An Introduction to the Theory of Price and Employment*, Houghton Mifflin, Cambridge, MA.

8
Price Theory and Multinational Oligopoly: Kurt Rothschild and Stephen Hymer Revisited (2009)*

with P. H. Nolan

Introduction

Well over 50 years ago, Kurt Rothschild (1947) published 'Price Theory and Oligopoly' in the *Economic Journal*.[†,1] In it Rothschild appraised the strengths, limitations and weaknesses of the imperfect and monopolistic competition theories, which were then only in their second decade, as illuminators of actual price and other behaviour. Finding them wanting, at least for considerable portions of observed, real world behaviour, especially when oligopolistic structures ruled, and because the then emerging theory of games was as yet unproven, he suggested that economists should turn to another set of principles for enlightenment.

Rothschild noted that in situations where price-setters had considerable discretionary power concerning the prices they set for their products, they also had to take into account the likely reactions of their few, often equally powerful, competitors. He suggested that this conjunction of events led to the creation of twin objectives – a desire for *secure* profits became as important as the desire for *maximum* profits. This modification of the essential aims of oligopolistic firms led him in turn to suggest that Clausewitz's principles of war could be the basis for the most relevant explanation of behaviour in oligopolistic market structures.

Rothschild (1947: 312–19) listed a number of propositions which may be deduced from Clausewitz's writings, about the likely behaviour of oligopolists. They are:

* Originally published in *Post-Reform Development in Asia: Essays for Amiya Kumar Bagchi*, Orient Blackswan, 2009, pp. 263–88.

1. Price rigidity is an essential aspect of 'normal' oligopolistic price strategy (p. 312).
2. Oligopolistic circumstances lead to a multitude of conditions surrounding the quoted price (p. 312).
3. Under oligopoly the price tends to be the outcome of a variety of conflicting tendencies within the firm, all of which have to be taken into account before a full explanation may be arrived at (p. 313).
4. Price wars, though infrequent, are nevertheless a dominant feature of oligopoly. They may be caused by internal or external factors; preparation for them, both aggressive and defensive, leads to measures which are peculiar to oligopoly. The outcome of a successful price war may be either the complete annihilation of a rival's independence or the reduction of the rival's status to that of a price follower (p. 317).[2]
5. The oligopolistic struggle for position and security includes political action of all sorts right up to imperialism. The inclusion of these 'non-economic' elements is essential for a full explanation of oligopoly behaviour and price (p. 319).

When Rothschild wrote, he mainly had in mind the experiences of individual industries in individual economies in the inter-war and post-war years. He drew upon empirical research in the USA and UK for his examples. Multinational firms then were conspicuous by their relative absence. The last thirty years or more have seen the rise of giant international oligopolists overflowing national boundaries, often setting up vertically integrated, multi-product firms with their various operations spanning several countries. Even more than when Rothschild wrote is it impossible with such trends to separate the 'economic from the political' (p. 317) if a 'complete picture' is to be obtained.[3] Later in the chapter we examine recent histories of some of these firms and industries in the light of Rothschild's wise conjectures of 1947.

First, though, we note that the late Stephen Hymer wrote classic books and articles on oligopoly and multi-national firms, starting with his 1960 Ph.D. dissertation at MIT, *The International Operations of National Firms: A Study of Foreign Direct Investment.*[4] Between the submission of his dissertation and his tragically early death at 40 in a car crash in 1974,[5] Hymer not only made his mark on the profession but also, like many others of his generation, became so radicalised in reaction to domestic and world political events in the 1960s that he became a Marxist in his political and economic analysis, making a 'cathartic' public commitment (Pitelis and Sugden 2000: 2). (Hymer had always been a progressive thinker who hated injustice and poverty.) While this change of direction affected his design of political and economic policies and, of course, his analysis of historical episodes, there was nevertheless a continuity in the nature of his predictions about future happenings. It is these which are of central concern for our purposes in this chapter.[6]

One of the first questions Hymer posed was why large firms would prefer to start subsidiaries in other countries rather than concentrate either on exporting to other countries or licensing local firms in other countries. He acknowledged that all three tactics could be followed but argued that the third would come to dominate so that there would be a long-run tendency for a world of multinational monopolies to develop in many of the world's most important industries. In arguing this, Hymer, as Graham (2002: 36) points out, rather overlooked the countervailing power of rival oligopolistic firms at home and subsequently abroad, so that a more likely outcome would be the dynamic evolution of large multinational oligopolies.[7] Nevertheless, Hymer's two major conjectures – a continuing rise in the sizes of multinational firms and in the uneven development associated with their existence whereby some groups within them, usually in the parent company, continuously gain through income and status, while others, usually in the overseas subsidiaries, increasingly lose out both relatively and even absolutely – remain, we believe, intact. We now contrast the views of Rothschild and Hymer, together with those of other non-mainstream economists, who wrote either after Rothschild and/or alongside and after Hymer, with the views of the mainstream. Our discussion occurs under the rubric of global industrial consolidation and the cascade effect, a concept developed by P. H. Nolan.

The theoretical debate

Mainstream view

The 'mainstream', 'neoclassical' view of the competitive process believes that the perfectly competitive model best describes the essence of capitalist competition. Departures from it are viewed as exceptional. In this view, there are limitless opportunities for firms from developing countries to 'catch-up' if they are forced into competition on the free market of the 'global level playing field'. At the heart of the mainstream view is the self-equilibrating mechanism of market competition. It is believed that the basic driver of the capitalist process, competition, ensures that if any firm enjoys super-normal profits rivals will soon enter to bid away those profits and undermine any temporary market dominance that the incumbent enjoys. The neoclassical approach emphasises the importance of competition among small firms as the explanation for the prosperity of the advanced economies. Milton Friedman, for example, believes that there is 'a general bias and tendency to overemphasise the importance of the big versus the small': 'As I have studied economic activities in the United States, I have become increasingly impressed with how wide is the range of problems and industries that can be treated as if it were competitive' (Friedman 1962: 120–23).

Mainstream economists argue that managerial diseconomies of scale set in after firms reach a certain size. The classic expression of this view was contained in Marshall's *Principles of Economics*:

> [H]ere we may read a lesson from the young trees of the forest as they struggle upwards through the benumbing shade of their older rivals. Many succumb on the way, and a few only survive: those few become stronger with every year, they get a larger share of light and air with every increase of their height, and at last in their turn they tower above their neighbours, and seem as though they would grow on for ever and for ever become stronger as they grow. But they do not. One tree will last longer in full vigour and attain a greater size than another; but sooner or later age tells on them all. Though the taller ones have a better access to light and air than their rivals, they gradually lose vitality; and one after another they give place to others, which though of less material strength, have on their side the vigour of youth ... [I]n almost every trade there is a constant rise and fall of large businesses, at any one moment some firms being in the ascending phase and others in the descending. (Marshall 1890; 1920: 315–16)

Most mainstream economists believe that 'mergers mostly fail'.[8] Such studies are usually based on an analysis of short-term returns to shareholders. The explanation that is usually advanced for mergers is the pursuit of power and wealth by CEOs, who are alleged to pursue their own interests at the expense of shareholders.

In recent years, the argument has gained ground that advances in information technology have created the possibility for a radical change in the nature of the firm. Activities that it was formerly rational to carry out within the firm can now be performed by networks of small firms connected by the internet (Castells 2000). This is widely thought to herald the rise of a new form of a 'post-Fordist' economic system based around 'clusters' of small businesses that can both compete and cooperate at different times (Piore and Sabel 1984; Porter 1990). This view appeared to be strongly reinforced by the rapid rise in the extent of outsourcing activities that were formerly carried on within the firm. In Coasian terms (Coase 1988), the very boundaries of the firm have shifted. Many researchers argue that the large corporation is 'hollowing out', and rapidly becoming an 'endangered species': 'While big companies control ever larger flows of cash, they are exerting less and less direct control over business activity. They are, you might say, growing hollow' (Malone and Laubacher 1998: 147).

The spread of global markets has greatly reinforced the belief that 'catch-up' at the level of the firm is the normal path of capitalist development. It is argued that markets have become so vast that it is hard to imagine that any firm or small group of firms could dominate any given sector.

Non-mainstream view

From the earliest stages in the development of modern capitalism, there were economists who believed that capitalism contained an inherent tendency towards industrial concentration. Marx, in *Capital* Vol. 1, argued that there was a 'law of centralisation of capital' or the 'attraction of capital by capital'. The driving force of concentration was competition itself, which pressured firms to cheapen the cost of production by investing ever larger amounts of capital in new means of production and in 'the technological application of science', which in turn creates barriers to entry. In the early 1970s, on the eve of the modern epoch of globalisation, Hymer, as we have seen, visualised the possible outcome of the capitalist process if existing restrictions on merger and acquisition were lifted:

> Suppose giant multinational corporations (say 300 from the US and 200 from Europe and Japan) succeed in establishing themselves as the dominant form of international enterprise and come to control a significant share of industry (especially modern industry) in each country. The world economy will resemble more and more the United States economy, where each of the large corporations tends to spread over the entire continent, and to penetrate almost every nook and cranny. (Hymer 1972)

Marshall's *Principles of Economics* provides numerous reasons to explain 'the advantages that a large business of almost any kind, nearly always has over a small one' (Marshall 1920: 282). These included economies in procurement, transport costs, marketing, branding, distribution, knowledge, human resources, and management (Marshall 1920:

282–84). By contrast, his explanation of 'managerial diseconomies of scale' resorts merely to an analogy ('the trees in the forest') without logic or evidence.

Edith Penrose's path-breaking book, *The Theory of the Growth of the Firm*, addresses directly the issue of possible limits to the growth of the firm. Like Marshall, she identifies a number of potential advantages that can be enjoyed by the large firm (Penrose 1995: 89–92). She considers that the most significant advantages for the large firm are those that she terms 'managerial economies'. Penrose concludes that there are no theoretical limits to the size of the firm:

> We have found nothing to prevent the indefinite expansion of firms as time passes, and clearly if some of the economies of size are economies of expansion, there is no reason to assume that a firm would ever reach a size in which it has taken full advantage of all these economies. (Penrose 1995: 99)

Alfred Chandler has demonstrated the central role of the large, oligopolistic firm in technical progress in the business history of today's high-income countries. That was, in its turn, central to the whole growth dynamic of maodern capitalism. He has shown that the modern industrial enterprise 'played a central role in creating the most technologically advanced, fastest growing industries of their day'. These industries, in turn, were 'the pace-setters of the industrial sector of their economies'. They provided an underlying dynamic in the development of modern industrial capitalism (Chandler 1990: 593). Chandler emphasises the paradox that even as the numer of firms in a given sector shrinks, competition between increasingly powerful firms can intensify. As Chandler and Hikino (1997: 31) observe, 'market share and profits changed constantly, which kept oligopolies from becoming stagnant and monopolistic'.

The succession of studies which purport to show the irrationality of mergers and acquisitions is almost entirely based on the analysis of the consequences for shareholder value in the short term. The much smaller number of studies which analyse the long-term impact of mergers and acquisitions on business survival and growth show a different story (Chandler 1990; Nolan 2001a and 2001b; Boston Consulting Group 2004). They suggest, rather, that well-selected and well-executed mergers and acquisitions that have a clear strategic purpose can increase the business capacity of the firm concerned. They can strengthen the firm's presence in given geographical markets, increase their access to technologies they formerly did not possess, acquire scarce human resources, add valuable brands to their portfolios, and enable long-term savings through economies of scale and scope in procurement, research and development, and marketing.

The evidence: the global business revolution

In the 1990s, many of the constraints on firm growth were removed.[9] Vast regions of the world were opened for competition. Privatisation was enacted across alomost all countires. Cross-border restrictions on mergers and acquisitions were removed from all but a few sectors. China joined the WTO at a time of unprecedented concentration among the world's leading 'system integrators'. However, the depth of this challenge is even deeper than it appears at first sight due to the profound changes taking place through the 'cascade' effect. In addition to intense concentration among 'systems integrators', an explosive process of industrial concentration has taken place at the level of the upper reaches of the global value chain. The invisible changes taking place 'below the water level' of the 'iceberg' of industrial concentration are at least as powerful as those that are more easily visible 'above the water level'.

Systems integrators

The global business revolution witnessed massive asset restructuring, with firms extensively selling off 'non-core businesses' in order to develop their 'core businesses' and upgrade their asset portfolios. The goal for most large firms became the maintenance or establishment of their position as one of the handful of top companies in the global market-place. Although the intensity abated in the wake of the collapse of the late 1990s stock market bubble, the merger and acquisition process has continued at a high level in recent years. An unprecedented degree of industrial concentration has been established among leading firms in sector after sector. By the 1980s, there was already a high degree of industrial concentration within many sectors of the individual high income countries (Pratten 1971; Prais 1981). However, the global business revolution saw for the first time the emergence of widespread industrial concentration across all high income countries, as well as extending deeply into large parts of the developing world.

By the early 2000s, within the high value-added, high technology, and/or strongly branded segments of global markets, which serve mainly the middle and upper income earners who control the bulk of the world's purchasing power, a veritable 'law' had come into play: a handful of giant firms, the 'systems integrators', occupied upwards of 50 per cent of the whole global market.[10] The top two firms accounted for 100 per cent of the entire global market for large commercial aircraft and 70 per cent of the carbonated soft drinks market; the top three firms accounted for over 80 per cent of the gas turbine market and for 70 per cent of the farm equipment market, for over 60 per cent of the mobile phone market, and over 50 per cent of the market for LCD TVs; the top four firms accounted for over 60 per cent of the elevator market; the top five firms accounted for over 80 per cent of the digital camera market; the share of the top six firms accounted for over 70 per cent of the auto industry market and the top ten firms accounted for over 50 per cent of the pharmaceutical market.[11]

Cascade effect

The process of concentration through simultaneous de-merger of non-core businesses and merger of core businesses is cascading across the value chain at high speed. In sector after sector, leading firms, with powerful technologies and marketing capabilities, actively select the most capable among their numerous suppliers, in a form of 'industrial planning', adopting 'aligned suppliers' who can work with them across the world. Thus, across a wide range of activities a 'cascade effect' is at work in which intense pressures developed for first tier suppliers of goods and services to the global giants to themselves merge and acquire, and develop leading global positions. These, in their turn, pass on intense pressure upon their own supplier networks. The result was a fast-developing process of concentration at a global level in numerous industries supplying goods and services to the systems integrators. For example, in the auto industry, there are thirteen giant auto components firms (*Fortune 500*), with revenues of between US\$ 13–41 billion (*Fortune*, 2 August 2004). Each segment of the automobile is dominated by two or three of these giant sub-systems integrators, including complete systems for brakes, transmission, electrical circuits, temperature controls, audio, glass, seats, and exhausts. They dominate the technologies of their respective sector. The world's top 700 companies ranked by research and development (R & D) expenditure include 31 auto components suppliers, all headquartered in the high income countries, with research and development expenditure ranging from US\$ 82 million to US\$ 2.9 billion. The R & D expenditure of the top five auto components firms ranges from US\$ 630 million (ZF) to US\$ 2.9 billion (Robert Bosch) [Department of Trade and Industry (DTI) 2003: 62–64].

Planning and coordination: the external firm

Through the hugely increased planning function undertaken by systems integrators, facilitated by recent developments in information technology, the boundaries of the large corporation have not only 'shifted', so that a wider range of goods and services is procured from outside the firm, but the very boundaries of the firms have become blurred. The core systems integrators across a wide range of sectors have become the coordinators of a vast array of business activity outside the boundaries of the legal entity in terms of ownership. The relationship extends far beyond the purchase price. In order to develop and maintain their competitive advantage, the systems integrators deeply penetrate the value chain both upstream and downstream, becoming closely involved in business activities that range from long-term planning to meticulous control of day-to-day production and delivery schedules. Competitive advantage for the systems integrator requires that it must consider the interests of the whole value chain in order to minimise costs across the whole system.

If we define the firm not by the entity which is the legal owner, but, rather, by the sphere over which conscious coordination of resource allocation takes place, then, far from becoming 'hollowed out' and much smaller in scope, the large firm can be seen to have enormously increased in size during the global business revolution. As the large firm has 'disintegrated', so has the extent of conscious coordination over the surrounding value chain increased. In a wide range of business activities, the organisation of the value chain has developed into a comprehensively planned and coordinated activity. At its centre is the core systems integrator. This firm typically possesses some combination of a number of key attributes. These include the capability to raise finance for large new projects, and the resources necessary to fund a high level of R&D spending to sustain technological leadership, to develop a global brand, to invest in state-of-the-art information technology and to attract the best human resources. Across a wide range of business types, from fast-moving consumer goods (FMCG) to aircraft manufacture, the core systems integrator interacts in the deepest, most intimate fashion with the major segments of the value chain, both upstream and downstream.

Upstream

The relationship of the core systems integrator with the upstream first tier suppliers extends far beyond the price relationship. Increasingly, leading first tier suppliers across a wide range of industries have established long-term 'partner' or 'aligned supplier' relationships with the core systems integrators. There are some key aspects of the intimate relationship between systems integrators and upstream firms. First, leading first tier suppliers plan the location of their plants in relation to the location of the core systems integrator. Secondly, it is increasingly the case that the aligned supplier produces goods within the systems integrator itself. It is common for leading suppliers of specialist services, such as data systems, to physically work within the premises of the systems integrator. Thirdly, leading first tier suppliers plan their R&D in close consultation with the projected needs of the core systems integrator. An increasing part of R&D is contracted out to small and medium-sized firms. This is typically under the close control of the systems integrator. Fourthly, product development is intimately coordinated with the systems integrator. Finally, precise product specifications are instantaneously communicated to the leading suppliers through newly developed information technology. The production and supply schedules of leading first tier suppliers are comprehensively coordinated with the systems integrator to ensure that the required inputs arrive exactly when they are needed and the inventory of the systems integrator is kept to a minimum.

Downstream

Planning by systems integrators extends downstream also. Manufacturers of complex capital goods are increasingly interested in the revenue stream to be derived from maintaining their products over the course of their lifetime. New information technology is increasingly being used to monitor the performance of complex products in use, with continuous feedback to the systems integrator in order to construct optimum servicing schedules. Through this pervasive process, systems integrators deeply penetrate a wide range of firms that use their products. However, penetration of the downstream network of firms is not confined to complex capital goods. Systems integrators in the FMCG sector increasingly coordinate the distribution process with specialist logistics firms in order to minimise distribution costs. They work closely with grocery chains and other selling outlets, such as theme parks, movie theatres, oil companies (petrol stations have become major locations for retailing non-petrol products), and quick-service restaurants, to raise the technical efficiency in the organisation of the selling process. The FMCG systems integrators often have their own experts working within the retail chain.

Employment

A large corporation may have a total procurement bill of several billions of dollars. The procurement could involve purchases from numerous firms that employ a much larger number of full-time equivalent employees 'working for' the systems integrator than are employed within the core firm itself. A leading systems integrator with 100–200,000 employees could easily have the full-time equivalent of a further 400–500,000 employees 'working for' the systems integrator, in the sense that their work is coordinated in important ways by the core firm. In this sense, we may speak of an 'external firm' of coordinated business activity that surrounds the modern global corporation and is coordinated by it.

Competition

From a mainstream perspective, 'greater competition' is equated with a larger number of firms in a given sector. In the non-mainstream view, 'greater competition' is equated with increased intensity of competition between powerful oligopolistic firms. Far from stifling 'competition', powerful oligopolies can produce increasingly intense competition as giant global firms struggle with other such firms, applying greater resources in R&D and marketing, and leveraging greater procurement budgets to lower costs and stimulate technical progress across the supply chain.

Challenges for developing countries

The high income economies (HIE) contain just 15 per cent of the world's total population. Firms headquartered in these countries account for 94 per cent of the companies listed in the *Fortune 500*, which ranks firms by sales revenue (Table 8.1). They account for 96 per cent of the firms in the *Financial Times (FT) 500* list of the world's leading firms, ranked by market capitalisation. They account for almost 100 per cent of the firms included in the list of the world's top 700 firms ranked by expenditure on research and development, which is a critical indicator of the distribution of global business power. There is not a single firm from the low/ middle income economies (L/MIE) in the list of the world's 'top 100 brands' (Sorrell 2004).

The cascade effect: the cases of aerospace and beverages

A single large commercial aircraft costs over $200 million. A single serving of a soft drink or a beer costs only around one dollar. However, as we will see in this section, common processes are at work in both industries through the impact of the 'cascade effect'.

Table 8.1 Dominance of the global big business revolution by firms based in high income countries

High/low/middle income economies	Population (2000)		GNP (a) (2000)		GNP (b) (2000)		Fortune 500 companies© (2003)		FT 500 companies (d) (2003)		Top 700 companies by R&D expenditure (2002/3)	
	billion	%	$b.	%	$b.	%	No.	%	No.	%	No.	%
HIEs	0.903	15	24,828	80	24,781	55	472	94	480	96	697	100
L/MIEs	5.152	85	6,336	20	20,056	45	28*	6	19**	4	3	negl.

Notes: a) at official rate of exchange; b) at PPP dollars; c) ranked by sales revenue; d) ranked by market capitalization.
*China = 14, India = 4, Brazil = 3, Russia = 3, Mexico = 3, Venezuela = 1, Malaysia = 1, Thailand = 1. ** Russia = 7, China = 4 (all floated in Hong Kong), India = 3, Mexico = 3, Brazil = 2.
Sources: Financial Times, 27 May 2004; World Bank. 1998 and 2002. World Development Report 1998, 2002, New York: Oxford university Press. Fortune, 26 July 2004; department of Trade and Industry (dTI). 2003. The uK R & d Score Board 2003. Edinburgh: DTI.

Aerospace

By the late 1960s, the US commercial aeroplane industry had been reduced to just three main producers: Boeing, McDonnell Douglas, and Lockheed.[12] The competitive pressure from Boeing on its rivals was intense. By the mid-1990s, Lockheed had ceased production of the Tristar, and McDonnell Douglas was in deep financial difficulties in its commercial aeroplane division. In 1997 came the path-breaking merger of Boeing and McDonnell Douglas. Following the merger, Boeing accounted for over four-fifths of the world's total commercial aircraft in service. From the 1950s to the 1970s, there were several European companies each manufacturing large jet airliners (by the standards of the time).[13] By the late 1960s it was apparent that none of them was able to compete with Boeing. In 1970, France and Germany decided to join forces to build a family of large commercial aeroplanes that could challenge Boeing's dominance, and preserve a wide array of high technology supplier industries within Europe. They were later joined by Britain and Spain. Without massive support from the respective governments, Airbus could never have become established. By the early 2000s, Airbus had overtaken Boeing in the market for large commercial aircraft. The two companies are now locked in head-to-head duopolistic rivalry. Boeing has staked much of its future on the medium-sized 787 ('Dreamliner'), while Airbus has done the same with the super-large A380. The USSR possessed a highly sophisticated aerospace industry that produced thousands of large jet passenger planes,[14] and with institutional change could have challenged the West's leading companies. Today, the industry is in ruins.

Modern aircraft and engines have become so complex that a major aspect of competitive advantage has become the ability to integrate the whole system of supply to produce the final product. The systems integrators increasingly focus on the coordinating and planning function within the supply chain, rather than direct manufacture. As much as 60–80 per cent of the end-product value of aerospace products is now derived from the external supply network (Murman *et al.* 2002: 18). The systems integrators have made large investments in IT systems, including mergers and acquisitions, in order to coordinate and control the supplier networks tightly with the core design and assembly location. Airbus and Boeing each have chosen a small number of suppliers in each major segment of the aircraft which are designated as 'preferred suppliers' and meet their rigorous technical and business performance criteria. They have actively reorganised the institutional structure of the supply chain in order to reduce the number of suppliers and nurture large-scale sub-systems integrators. This constitutes a form of industrial policy at the level of the systems integrator firm, picking and nurturing 'winners'. They each penetrate deeply into their respective supply chain. Surrounding each of them is a truly 'external firm'.

In order to meet the demands of the systems integrators, the major sub-system and key component suppliers themselves need to invest heavily in R & D, and to expand in order to benefit from cost reduction through economies of scale and scope. A powerful merger movement has taken place at all levels of the supply chain to the systems integrators. Through continuous merging and acquiring 'core businesses' that meet their strategic goals, and through divesting 'non-core businesses' in order to 'upgrade' their asset portfolios, a group of giant sub-systems integrators have established or strengthened their competitive position in businesses covering one or more aircraft sub-systems.

Just three firms, United Technologies, GE and Rolls-Royce, account for the entire global supply of engines for large commercial aircraft. BAe Systems supplies all the wing sets for Airbus planes. Honeywell will supply the core avionics systems for both the A380 and the B787. Goodrich and Snecma will supply the main segments of the landing gear for the A380 and B787. Smiths Industries will supply the control systems for the landing gear of both the A380 and B787, as well as the control systems for the wing flaps on the A380. Rockwell Collins will supply the pilot control systems for the B787 and the navigation sensors for the A380. Scecma and Goodrich together account for three-quarters of the world market for braking systems on large commercial aircraft. Goodrich will provide nacelles and thrust reversers, fuel quantity indicating system, fuel management software and proximity sensing systems for the 787. Michelin, Goodyear and Bridgestone are the only firms capable of supplying tyres for large commercial aircraft. Saint-Gobain is the sole supplier of aircraft glass to Airbus. Alcoa and Alcan account for most of the world's supply of aluminium for aircraft assembly. Each A380 will use around one million Alcoa 'lockbolts'. Even in smaller sub-segments of the aircraft, niche sub-systems integrators dominate the respective segment of the aircraft. For example, Jamco is sole supplier to Boeing for aircraft lavatories, and Labinal will supply the bulk of electrical wiring for both the A380 and B787. Meggitt supplies the fire and smoke detectors for almost all large commercial aircraft. Recaro and B/E Aerospace account for most of the market for seats on large commercial aircraft.

Giant aerospace programmes, such as the A380, Boeing 787, JSF (Joint Strike Fighter) and A400M (military transporter) are likely to stay in production for several decades. Among the hundreds of suppliers to these giant programmes that will form the core of the world's aerospace industry for the coming decades, there is hardly a single supplier at any level in the supply chain from indigenous firms in developing countries. Once the suppliers have been fixed for the respective aircraft, it is difficult for new entrants to displace the established suppliers. A strong 'lock-in' effect operates with 'aligned suppliers' who have developed technologies to meet the specific needs of the systems integrator. They may have a sophisticated understanding of the direction that is needed in technical progress in order to meet the customer's needs. They may also have the benefit of economies of scale achieved over years of supplying a specific programme and have developed invaluable experience in producing the given product over time. They may have developed a relationship of trust with the customer over the long term. In sum, it will be extremely difficult for indigenous firms in developing countries to enter the supply chain of the world's leading systems integrators and compete successfully on the 'global level playing field' with the established members of the supply chain. Consolidation has affected every level of the industry, with even small 'niches' occupied by a small number of focussed, technically sophisticated firms.

Beverages

Since the 1980s, the global beverage industry[15] has witnessed high-speed consolidation. In the carbonated soft drinks sector, just two firms now account for around three-quarters of total global sales. In the broader category of non-alcoholic drinks, just five firms account for over one-half of the global market. The beer industry lags some way behind, but the trend towards consolidation is clear, with emergence of super-large global firms, such as Anheuser-Busch, SAB Miller, and Interbev.[16] The closely related food industry has undergone its own process of consolidation, resulting in the emergence of a group of super-large international firms, such as Nestle, Unilever and Sara Lee. The beverage and food industry are both experiencing intensifying pressure from the emergence of giant retailers, such as Wal-Mart, Metro, Carrefour, and Tesco.[17]

The massive procurement expenditure by the world leading beverage producers on material inputs and services has increased the pressure for consolidation from the higher reaches of the supply chain. In many areas, the 'cascade effect' pressures on the supply chain from the beverage industry are applied simultaneously by the food industry. This 'cascade effect' has stimulated a wave of consolidation in the beverage industry's supply chain. Moreover, as the higher reaches of the supply chain have struggled to meet the global needs of the world's leading beverage companies, the process of consolidation within their ranks has produced further 'cascade' pressure on the supply chain of these firms, as they struggle to lower costs, and achieve the technical progress necessary to meet the fierce demands of the world's leading systems integrators who stand at the centre of their respective supply chains.

The global consumer packaging industry is huge, worth about US$ 300 billion annually. The top ten global packaging firms account for between 40 and 80 per cent of global markets, depending on the sector. The world's leading beverage firms interact closely with the leaders of the packaging industry to work together for ways to meet their needs better through innovations in product and process technologies. Key pressures on the packaging industry have included cost and weight reduction, improved customer safety, increased product life and enhanced appearance. Technical progress has also been achieved through contributions from the primary material suppliers in the aluminium, steel, PET resin industries, as well as in the suppliers of machinery. The world's leading beverage firms have interacted with this process at every step, acting as 'systems integrators' for the overall process of technical progress, and nurturing institutional change so that leading suppliers have sufficient scale to meet the beverage companies' strict requirements.

Over 200 billion beverage cans are consumed annually. Since the late 1980s, the world's metal can industry has rapidly consolidated. Three firms now stand out as the global industry leaders,[18] between them accounting for almost nine-tenths of the combined markets of Europe and North America, and they are rapidly expanding into developing countries. The metal can industry is a major consumer of both aluminium and steel, and places intense pressure on the steel and aluminium industries to achieve technical progress, improve product quality and lower costs. The other major users of primary metals have also consolidated at high speed during the global business revolution, including the automobile, aerospace, construction and household durable goods industries. They also place intense pressure on the steel and aluminium industries, which have experienced intense consolidation. Two firms (Alcoa and Alcan) together produce over two-fifths of global aluminium output (by weight), and an even larger fraction of the aluminium sheet for beverage cans. In the steel industry, recent years have seen a stream of giant mergers. Leading steel firms focus on high value-added, high technology products for global customers, and the world's top ten steel firms now account for close to three-fifths of total global sales revenue from the industry (Nolan and Haichuan 2004).[19]

Glass bottles are still the main form of primary packaging in the beer industry, and, despite its relative decline, the glass bottle remains an important form of packaging for soft drinks, especially in developing countries. Following successive rounds of merger and acquisition in the 1990s, the glass bottle industry has become highly consolidated. The two super-giants of the industry (Owens-Illinois and Saint-Gobain) now account for around two-thirds of global glass bottle production.[20]

PET (plastic) bottles were developed in the late 1960s, and quickly became the most important form of primary packaging in the soft drinks industry, though it still has a less important place in the beer industry. In recent years, the industry has become increasingly concentrated. By 2003, excluding the production by beverage companies for self-consumption, the top four firms accounted for almost two-thirds of the total production of PET bottles in North America and Europe. Much of the technical progress in the PET bottle industry has been achieved by the specialist machine builders, which make two different types of machinery, namely 'pre-forms' and the equipment that 'blows' the pre-forms into their final bottle form. Each of these sectors is dominated by specialist high technology firms. One firm alone (Husky) accounts for around three-quarters of the total global market for high volume PET injection machines, while another specialist firm (Sidel)[21] has a near monopoly on the purchase of advanced blowing equipment by the world's leading beverage companies.

In the supply of beverage filling line equipment, the high value-added, high technology segments of the market supplying the world's leading beverage companies are dominated by just two firms (KHS and Krones), which together account for almost nine-tenths of global sales of high-speed beverage bottling lines. The world's leading beverage companies have bought machines almost exclusively from these two companies because of their high levels of reliability, low operating costs, high speed, more consistent filling height, and low rates of damage to bottles and product. Each of them spends heavily on research and development.

The advertising and communication sector has witnessed intense merger and acquisition activity, alongside the global expansion of their main customers. The world's top ten spenders each spend an average of US\$ 2–3 billion annually. They account for a large share of the revenues of the leading advertising and marketing firms. In addition, the advertising and communication companies face increasingly powerful global media companies, such as Disney, News International, Time Warner, and Viacom, with which they place their products. The advertising and communication industry has become polarised into a small number of immensely powerful firms and a large number of small firms. By 2001, the top four firms in the sector[22] accounted for almost three-fifths of total global advertising revenue.

The world's leading beverage companies are among the largest purchasers of trucks.[23] Their truck fleets are enormous, amounting to hundreds of thousands of trucks for the industry leaders. The world's leading truck manufacturers experience intense pressure from their global customers to lower costs and improve technologies. This intensifies the pressure to increase scale in order to achieve greater volume of procurement and push down costs across their own value chains, including suppliers of truck components (engines, brake systems, tyres, exhaust systems, seats, informatics, and ventilation systems) and materials (steel, aluminium and plastics). Greater scale also enables them to achieve faster technical progress through economies of scope (coordinated technical progress that can be used in different divisions of the company) in order to provide the customer with more reliability, lower fuel costs, greater safety and more effective pollution control. Since the 1980s, industrial concentration in the truck industry has greatly increased. By the late 1990s, the world's top five truck makers accounted for half of total global sales in terms of the number of units sold, but an even higher share of the total market value, as the leading truck companies tended to produce far higher technology vehicles. In 2003 industry leader Daimler-Chrysler's truck division alone had revenues of US$ 36 billion and operating profits of US$ 1.1 billion, and spent US$ 1.3 billion on research and development.

Conclusion

Mainstream, neoclassical economists consider that opening up developing economies to global competition provides broad opportunities for indigenous firms to catch up with firms whose headquarters are in the high-income countries. Their view is based on the belief that the basic tendency of capitalism is competition with strict limits to growth of firm size: they believe that by forcing weak firms to compete with strong ones, the weak can learn from the strong, imitate them and overtake them. In fact, the epoch of the global business revolution since the 1980s has witnessed an unprecedented degree of industrial consolidation and concentration of business power at a global level. The 'commanding heights' of the global business system are almost entirely occupied by firms from high-income countries. This presents a deep challenge for Chinese firms and policy-makers.

The most easily visible part of the structure of industrial concentration are the well-known firms with powerful, globally recognised technologies and/or brands. These constitute the 'systems integrators' or 'organising brains' at the apex of extended value chains. As they have consolidated their leading positions, they have exerted intense pressure across the whole supply chain in order to minimise costs and stimulate technical progress. However, the challenge is even deeper than it at first appears.

This chapter has closely examined the value chains in two sectors with totally different products, aerospace and beverages. It has shown that these two sectors have striking similarities in the way in which the core systems integrators have stimulated a comprehensive transformation of industrial structure across the whole supply chain. At every level there has taken place an intense process of industrial concentration, mainly through merger and acquisition, as firms struggle to meet the strict requirements that are the condition of their participation in the systems integrators' supply chains. This 'cascade effect' has profound implications for the nature of competition. It means that the challenge facing firms from developing countries is far deeper than at first sight appeared to be the case. Not only do they face immense difficulties in catching up with the leading systems integrators, the visible part of the 'iceberg', but they also face immense difficulties in catching up with the powerful firms that now dominate almost every segment of the supply chain, the invisible part of the 'iceberg' that lies hidden from view beneath the 'water'.

At the dawn of the twenty-first century, the reality of the intense industrial concentration among both systems integrators and their entire supply chain, brought about through pressure from the 'cascade effect', presents a comprehensive challenge for both Chinese firms and policy-makers. Finally, we submit that the theories and conjectures of Rothschild and Hymer, together with those of the other non-mainstream authors we discussed above, make far more sense of the empirical findings we have reported than do the corresponding theories and conjectures of the mainstream, ancient and modern.

Notes

† It is a pleasure and a privilege to contribute to the volume of essays in honour of our friend of many years, Amiya Bagchi. We have long admired his scholarly

work and enjoyed his company. It is also a nice touch that the three of us have been or are still, Fellows of Jesus College, Cambridge.

1. It was the single most influential article that G. C. Harcourt read as an undergraduate in Melbourne in the early 1950s; see Harcourt (1999).
2. Nicholas Kaldor's typical market structure in his post-war theorising was oligopoly with a dominant price-setter surrounded by smaller firms that were price-followers; see, for example, Kaldor (1985). Adrian Wood developed this view in his *Theory of Profits*, Wood (1975). See, also, Harcourt and Kenyon (1976)
3. In a footnote on page 318, Rothschild includes a typical topical example: he wondered 'how some of the 'pure' economic theorists would deal with the advertisements now appearing in the press against the nationalisation of certain industries. Are they to be included in selling costs – for advertisements they certainly are – or are they to be neglected because they represent political action?'
4. See Kindleberger (2002) for an assessment of Hymer's contributions and an account of why his dissertation was not published until 1976. (The late Charles Kindleberger supervised Hymer's dissertation, 'One of [his] few claims to fame', Kindleberger (2002)). It was mainly because it lacked squiggles, being written in plain English and was easy to understand. For a comprehensive account of Hymer's principal contributions, see the special issue of *Contributions to Political Economy* in 2002, edited by Pitelis and Sugden.
5. His dissertation was thus published posthumously.
6. In one of the most insightful contributions to the symposium on Hymer's legacy, Graham (2002: 32 in Pitelis and Sugden eds 2002) argues that 'Hymer remained throughout his life a neoclassical in terms of his analytic thinking.' This is not as paradoxical as it may seem at first sight. A good case can be made that *in his economic analysis* Marx also was often at one with later neoclassical reasoning, for example, that a rise in real wages during the upturn and boom would induce capital-using, labour-saving innovations. Of course, for Marx, the systemic outcome of this tendency was not at all the benign result that would be predicted by true neoclassical believers!
7. Graham therefore gives Hymer higher marks for his perceptive, ahead-of-his-time, questions than for some of his specific answers.
8. Meeks (1977) is the classic study of this topic. The view that 'most mergers fail' is parroted remorselessly among mainstream academics of all ideological persuasions.
9. Unless otherwise indicated, the data in this section are from Nolan (2008) and Nolan and Zhang (2004).
10. Even in less well-known sectors, the share of systems integrators has typically become very high. For example, the global market share of the top two firms in the financial information sector stood at 86 per cent, and at 77 per cent in electronic games; the share of the top three firms stood at 71 per cent in legal publishing and at 62 per cent in artificial joints; the share of the top five firms stood at 77 per cent in recorded music; and the share of the top six firms stood at 60 per cent in water management (Nolan and Zhang 2004).
11. In fact, these data understate the true degree of concentration, because many firms focus on specific sub-branches of their sector. For example, within the

pharmaceutical industry, in many therapies, just one or two firms account for almost the entire global market.

12. The issues in Section 3–4 are analysed in more detail in Nolan and Zhang (2004). Due to limitations of space, this section focuses only on commercial aircraft. However, the military aircraft industry has also witnessed intense consolidation during the past decade, with equally profound consequences for the supply chain.

13. These included the UK's de Havilland (Comet), Vickers (VC10), Hawker Siddeley (Trident), and BAC (BAC 111), Germany's VFW (VFW 614), France's Sud Aviation (Caravelle), and the Netherlands' Fokker.

14. Tupolev alone produced almost 2000 Tu-134s and 154s, which placed it roughly on a par with McDonnell Douglas, though far short of Boeing. Antonov and Ilyushin also produced large commercial aircraft.

15. Unless otherwise indicated, data in this section are taken from Nolan and Zhang (2004). For a detailed study of the 'cascade effect' in the global beverage industry see Nolan (forthcoming).

16. In the USA, the top three firms account for around four-fifths of the market. In Japan and Europe, the top two or three firms account for over 70 per cent of the respective markets.

17. There are now more than thirty giant retail groups with annual revenues of more than $10 billion, including seven super-giants with revenues of over $50 billion (*Fortune*, 26 July 2004).

18. These are Ball, Crown and Rexam.

19. The steel industry is often thought to be relatively unconsolidated, as the top ten firms account for 'only' around 27 per cent of global output by weight.

20. Between them they produce more than sixty billion glass bottles annually, that is to say, around ten bottles for each person in the world.

21. In 2003, Tetra Laval, the Swedish/Swiss packaging giant, acquired Sidel. With the weight of Tetra Laval behind it, Sidel will be in an even better position to maintain its leading position in the global PET pre-form blowing industry.

22. WPP, Omnicom, Interpublic, and Publicis.

23. Either directly, or through their 'third party' logistics suppliers. Most beverages are delivered to customers by truck.

References

Boston Consulting Group, 2004. *Growing Through Acquisitions*. Boston: BCG Publishing.

Castells, M. 2000. *The Rise of the Network Society*. Oxford: Blackwells (second edition).

Chandler, A. 1990. *Scale and Scope: The Dynamics of Industrial Capitalism*. Cambridge, MA: Harvard University Press.

Chandler, A. and T. Hikino. 1997. The Large Industrial Enterprise and the Dynamics of Modern Economic Growth. In *Big Business and the Wealth of Nations*, eds A. Chandler, F. Amatori and T. Hikino. Cambridge: Cambridge University Press.

Coase, R. H. 1988. The Nature of the Firm. In *The Firm, the Market and the Law*, ed. R. H. Coase. Chicago: University of Chicago Press.

Department of Trade and Industry (DTI). 2003. *The UK R&D Scoreboard 2003*. Edinburgh: DTI.

Fortune, 26 July and 2 August 2004.

Friedman, M. 1962. *Capitalism and Freedom*. Chicago: University of Chicago Press.

Graham, E. M. 2002. The contributions of Stephen Hymer: One View. In *'Contributions to Political Economy'* Special Issue: 21(27–41) ed. C. N. Pitelis and R. Sugden, 2002.

Harcourt, G. C. 1999. Horses for courses: the making of a post-Keynesian economist. In *The Makers of Modern Economics* IV: 32–69. ed. Arnold Heertje. Cheltenham, UK; Northampton, MA, USA: Edward Elgar.

Harcourt, G. C., and Peter Kenyon. 1976. Pricing and the investment decision, *Kyklos* 29: 449–77.

Hymer, S. 1972. The multinational corporation and the law of uneven development, reprinted in, *International Firms and Modern Imperialism*, ed. H. Radice, 1975. Harmondsworth. Penguin Books.

Hymer, S. 1976. *The International Operations of National Firms: A Study of Foreign Direct Investment*, Cambridge, MA: The MIT Press.

Kaldor, N. 1985. *Economics without Equilibrium: The Okun Memorial Lectures at Yale University*. Cardiff: University College: Cardiff Press.

Kindleberger, C. P. 2002. Stephen Hymer: Life and the political economy of multinational corporate capital. In *Contributions to Political Economy*, ed. C. N. Pitelis, and R. Sugden, 2002. Special Issue: 21: 5–7.

Malone, T. W., and R. L. Laubacher. 1998. The dawn of the e-Lance economy. *Harvard Business Review*. September–October.

Marshall, A. 1920. *Principles of Economics*. London: Macmillan (first published in 1890).

Marx, K. 1867. *Capital*, Vol. 1. New York: International Publishers (1967 edition).

Meeks, G. 1977. *Disappointing Marriage*. Cambridge: Cambridge University Press.

Murman, Earll *et al.* 2002. *Lean Enterprise Value: Insights from MIT's Lean Aerospace Initiative*. New York: Palgrave Macmillan.

Nolan, P. 2001a. *China and the Global Business Revolution*. London: Palgrave Macmillan.

Nolan, P. 2001b. *China and the Global Economy*. London: Palgrave Macmillan.

Nolan, P. (2008). *Coca-Cola and the Transformation of the Chinese Business System*. London: Palgrave Macmillan.

Nolan, P. and Rui Huaichuan. 2004. The Cascade Effect and the Chinese Steel Industry. Mimeo.

Nolan, Peter, and Robert Ash. 1995. China's economy on the eve of reform. *China Quarterly* 144 (December): 980–98.

Nolan, P. and J. Zhang. 2004. Industrial Consolidation, the Cascade Effect and the Challenge of the Global Business Revolution for Developing Countries: The Case of Aerospace and Beverages, paper prepared for Conference on International Competitiveness of China's Industries, Ministry of Commerce, China, Xiamen, September.

Penrose, E. 1995. *The Theory of the Growth of the Firm*. Oxford: Oxford University Press (second edition).

Piore, M., and C.Sabel. 1984. *The Second Industrial Divide: Possibilities for Progress*. New York: Basic Books.

Pitelis, C. N. and R. Sugden eds. 2002. Preface. *Contributions to Political Economy* 21: 1–4. Special Issue.

Porter, M. 1990. *The Competitive Advantage of Nations*. London: Macmillan.

Prais, S. J. 1981. *Productivity and Industrial Structure*. Cambridge: Cambridge University Press.

Pratten, C. 1971. *Economies of Scale in Manufacturing Industry*. Cambridge: Cambridge University Press.

Rothschild, K. W. 1947. Price Theory and Oligopoly. *Economic Journal* 57 (227): 299–320.

Sorrell, M. 2004. The Advertising and Marketing Services Industry: Outlook Good and Getting Better. In WPP, Annual Report.

Wood, A. 1975. *A Theory of Profits*. Cambridge: Cambridge University Press.

Part IV
Review Articles

9

A Revolution Yet to Be Accomplished: Reviewing Luigi Pasinetti, *Keynes and the Cambridge Keynesians: A 'Revolution in Economics' to Be Accomplished* (2009)*

1

Two of Luigi Pasinetti's mentors – Nicholas Kaldor and Richard Goodwin – published major volumes in their seventies.[†] Kaldor's 1985 Raffaele Mattiole Lectures, *Causes of Growth and Stagnation in the Word Economy*, (1996) were given just over one year before his death and seen through the Cambridge University Press by Tony Thirlwall and Ferdinando Targetti; the lectures are, in effect, an account of his legacy to our profession. Goodwin's *magnum opus, The Dynamics of a Capitalist Economy: A Multi-Sectoral Approach* (1987), co-authored with Lionello Punzo, brought together in a grand synthesis, the two major preoccupations of his academic life – aggregative cycle models and production-interdependent models – on which he had been working since the late 1930s. It is a pleasing symmetry then that Pasinetti's volume has also been published in the second half of his eighth decade and that it, too, draws together themes on which the author has been working for a life time.

The volume, begun long before as the Caffè Lectures of 1994, is a remarkable bringing together of the major issues on which he has been working since the 1950s, together with his evaluation of the contributions of Keynes and his close colleagues or followers – Richard Kahn, Joan

---

* Originally published in *History of Economics Ideas*, vol. 17, 2009, pp. 203–8.

Robinson, Nicholas Kaldor, Piero Sraffa and Richard Goodwin.[1] *Keynes and the Cambridge Keynesians* is an original and, devoutly to be hoped, influential path-breaking book. As I have often pointed out (see, for example, Harcourt 2006, 123), Pasinetti is probably the last great system builder of our profession and he is the senior living heir of the post-Keynesian tradition especially associated with what he calls in the book the Cambridge School of Keynesian Economics. The objectives of the book are to put into historical perspective the contributions of this School, to explain why they are a revolution in economics still 'to be accomplished' and to provide explicitly an outline of the framework (which is implicit and often confused in the individual contributions of the members of the School) that will make such an accomplishment possible.

2

To set the context for this review may I point out that Luigi Pasinetti and I have been close friends and sometimes colleagues together in Cambridge since 1956? We first met as Ph.D. students in Cambridge (Pasinetti was at Gonville and Caius, I was at King's). We discussed together Joan Robinson's *magnum opus*, *The Accumulation of Capital* (1956). Pasinetti was way ahead of me in understanding her technical analysis, especially of the choice of techniques in the economy as a whole, Wicksell effects and all that. In the 1960s we were both University Lecturers in the Cambridge Faculty (Pasinetti had a Fellowship at King's, I, at Trinity Hall. I was on leave without pay for three years from the University of Adelaide to allow me to take up the completely unexpected appointments which happened while I was on a year's study leave (1963–64) from Adelaide).

The 1960s was an exciting decade to be in Cambridge. The Faculty members read like a Who's Who (ancient and modern) in modern economics; Frank Hahn and Robin Matthews wrote their famous survey of growth theory (1964); Ken Arrow (who was a visiting fellow at Churchill for 1963–64) and Hahn were writing their definitive text on general equilibrium theory, Arrow and Hahn (1971); Bob Solow gave the 1963–64 Alfred Marshall Lectures on two mythical creatures, 'Joan' and 'Nicky' (only one of the real ones, Joan Robinson, was in Cambridge to hear him); and the Cambridge-Cambridge capital theory controversies came to a head first with the publication of Piero Sraffa's 1960 classic, *Production of Commodities by Means of Commodities*, then in the *QJE* symposium in 1966 following Levhari's failed attempt in 1965 to destroy the economy-wide application of Sraffa's analysis of capital-reversing and reswitching (Pasinetti 1966 was the first to show why Levhari was wrong) and, finally, the 1969, 1970 exchanges between Pasinetti and Solow (1970) over Irving Fisher's concept of the social rate of return on investment. I returned to Australia at the end of 1966 and did not return permanently to Cambridge until 1982. Pasinetti returned permanently to Italy in the mid 1970s as Professor of Economic Analysis at the Università Cattolica del Sacro Cuore in Milan. So we both had much the same number of years teaching at Cambridge but I now outstrip him in total years spent there as I have been there for the 10 years so far of my retirement (which began in 1998). I mention all this in order to indicate the position from which I come when I make judgements in the review which either reinforce or, in some instances modify or put a different slant on Pasinetti's arguments, claims and interpretations.

3

The book is in three parts (books). The first is the revised text of the 1994 Caffe Lectures which formed the basis of a manuscript submitted to Cambridge University Press and for which I was an (enthusiastic) reader. To this in subsequent years he has added (Book 2) insightful and absorbing biographical essays of his mentors/teachers and colleagues at Cambridge – Kahn, Joan Robinson, Kaldor, Sraffa and Goodwin. In Book 3 he sets out his explanation why the Keynesian revolution is still to be accomplished, not least because of mistakes by the Cambridge Keynesians, what form it will take and how more appropriate it will be than mainstream economics for tackling the pressing complex problems that the modern world of interrelated and, on the whole, advanced capitalist nations have produced. Altogether, the volume is a huge undertaking carried out successfully. It reveals deep, prolonged thought, a capacity to handle complex interrelationships in theory and in historical and biographical developments and to integrate them in a satisfying, clear and understandable way. Few modern economists can match Pasinetti's clarity of expression and explanation, especially when he is doing complex, technical analysis.

He finds in Keynes and the Keynesians two major foundations: first, that Keynes in *The General Theory* provided a theory of a monetary production economy in which real and monetary elements were integrated from the start of the analysis. This reflected, he argues, Keynes's desire, perhaps implicit, to stress the production theory of classical political economy rather than the exchange, resource allocation theory of the neoclassicals, including his teacher Alfred Marshall. It must be said, though, that while Keynes used Marshall's supply and demand analysis of value, it was Marshall's insights into the monetary and financial aspects of the economy that held the greatest attraction for, and had the greatest influence on him – even though it was these he was most to discard in *The General Theory*.

Secondly, what has been an explicit characteristic of Pasinetti's work much more than of Keynes and the younger Keynesians, the distinction between economic principles which are independent of institutions and economic principles which are situation-specific and dependent on particular institutions, but which, nevertheless, have the first set of principles underlying them. He argues that this is implicit in Keynes's writings but not perceived at all clearly by Keynes himself. As to the first point, Pasinetti argues that once the industrial revolution started we needed a system of thought based much more on the production and, subsequently, learning aspects of the economy than on the exchange aspects with which is associated the theory of resource allocation. There is a sense in which this reflects the contrast between, on the one hand, volume I of Marx's *Capital* and volumes II and III, on the other. In particular, Marx's analysis of value, surplus value and the source of exploitation in the sphere of production of capitalism logically precedes the schemes of reproduction and the analysis of prices of production and the transformation problem in volumes II and III. The use of the same distinction in a theory of distribution, accumulation and growth is a feature of Donald Harris's writings (1975, 1978) as well as of Joan Robinson's analysis from *The Accumulation of Capital* (1956) on, summarised in her banana diagram in *Essays* (1962, 48). The diagram incorporates the two-sided relationship between accumulation and profitability, with actual accumulation helping to determine the actual rate of profits and the expected rate of profits helping to determine planned rates of accumulation. These are combined with the Keynes-Kalecki theory of effective demand (and the role of differential marginal saving rates), extended to the medium to long period.

Pasinetti's natural system also has similarities with Marx's schemes of expanded reproduction. Both set out the conditions which ensure, period by period, that both aggregate demand and supply and their compositions match. They further have in common that they are not necessarily descriptive of reality, but rather reference points. In Marx's case they serve to show why the conditions are unlikely to be realised in an unregulated competitive capitalist economy except by a fluke, so that instability and sometimes crisis may result. (As Joan Robinson pointed out in 1953, see CEP, vol. IV, 1973, 262–63, Harrod's dynamic theory, and especially his key concept, g_w, is an independent (for Harrod) rediscovery of Marx's volume II.) Again, as with Marx, meeting the conditions does not imply steady growth though it is one possibility (see Sardoni 1981). In Pasinetti's system the conditions are the normative requirements for full employment to be attained and sustained over time.

This suggests one way in which the post-Keynesian emphasis on cumulative causation processes (especially by the later Kaldor) and cyclical growth processes (Goodwin and Kalecki), whereby each short period grows out of preceding ones, with long-period and short-period factors serving to determine between them income, employment, prices, the distribution of income and accumulation of each short period, may be incorporated into the way ahead that Pasinetti sets out in Book 3.

When writing this I was pleased to see that Vivian Walsh (2008, 229), quoting Walsh 2003, 372–73, made a similar evaluation of Pasinetti's contributions (though he stresses Smith's influence rather than Marx's). Walsh wrote:

> ...Pasinetti derives what are arguably the most characteristic concepts of his growth theory explicitly from Smith: the central role of technical innovation occurring unevenly in different sectors, and the method of analysis in terms of vertically integrated sectors...This involves treating the model economy as a set of vertically integrated sectors, in each of which only one final consumption good is produced...Pasinetti's [break] out of the steady state in a manner far beyond traverse...[stimulated] the development of a theory of structural economic dynamics...they also strikingly enrich the demand and consumption side of classicism.

4

It is significant that, in his biographical essays, Pasinetti devotes more space to Sraffa's work and influence than to those of any other of his mentors. Classical economics in the form set out by Sraffa was more congenial than any other exposition to Pasinetti's purpose of grafting Keynesian insights onto his predecessors. This is not to say that his deep understanding of the literature and especially of Ricardo (one of his first articles was on Ricardo's theory of distribution and growth, Pasinetti 1960) were not also influential. But Sraffa's emphasis on production interdependence which Pasinetti has absorbed into his own original theories of vertical integration of labour inputs, the foundations of the theory of structural dynamics, and his learning model are emphasised in his thought and in his way forward.

> Sraffa's *production of commodities by means of commodities* and my own *production of commodities by means of labour* are not only complementary but actually susceptible to being integrated into each other through the analytical device of vertical integration (Pasinetti, 1973), which eventually leads to an interpretation of the pure labour scheme as representing the most essential foundational version of the whole production paradigm. (Pasinetti 2007, 273; emphasis in original)

The one sphere which still seems to be underdeveloped is the key role of money and finance in the overall narrative. Pasinetti takes us part of the way with his ingenious theories of the natural rate of interest and he applauds the writings of Paul Davidson and the late Hy Minsky, and 'the remarkable recent work' by Wynne Godly and Marc Lavoie (2007) in building on 'Keynes's intuitions and elaborations on the typical instability of the financial markets in…monetary production economies' (Pasinetti 2007, 236–37).

5

Finally, I want to comment on what Pasinetti sees not only as the failure of Keynes's revolution yet to be accomplished as an intellectual system but also the failure of Keynes's pupils to establish successors in the Faculty itself. This he attributes partly to political and tactical ineptitude, partly to personality traits that led to great alienation especially from those not in agreement with their approaches. It is true that with the recent retirement of Bob Rowthorn (though of the Keynesians he really only admired Kaldor) and Ajit Singh there is no one amongst their successors with a chair in the Faculty. Nevertheless, at the level of lecturerships many people sympathetic to the Cambridge School of Keynesian Economics were appointed besides Pasinetti himself and me in the 1960s and even 1970s and 1980s. It was the failure to secure appointments at chair level, and to get people like Pasinetti and Goodwin promoted internally to chairs that the succession eventually failed.

Nor was this all due to ineptitude for it has to be remembered that as the original Keynesians aged, there was a huge expansion of universities in the United Kingdom so that many young people in Cambridge went off to chairs elsewhere. Both Pasinetti and Mario Nuti returned to Italy in the 1970s. Moreover, while Brian Reddaway was not a disciple of Richard Kahn or Joan Robinson, he was of Keynes and he had considerable influence on applied work in the Faculty through his Directorship of the Department of Applied Economics (DAE) (1955–70), as had Richard Stone before him and then with Alan Brown leading the DAE growth project. Similarly, though Godley's group in the DAE in the 1980s faced severe unfair criticism, nevertheless they made innovative contributions inspired by Keynes and Kaldor in particular and now come to full fruition in the volume with Lavoie published in 2007. So it was (is) not all doom and gloom. But it must be admitted that those who now control the Faculty and those who put them there, especially Hahn and Matthews, increasingly outmanoeuvred the first generation of Keynesians and Keynesian sympathisers (of course, both Hahn and Matthews are Keynesians too) in the day to day running and staffing of the Faculty.

Notes

† A review essay of Luigi L. Pasinetti, *Keynes and the Cambridge Keynesians: A 'Revolution in Economics' to be Accomplished*, Cambridge, Cambridge University Press, 2007, pp. xxiii–384.

1. Kaldor was neither a pupil nor a colleague of Keynes but he became, especially in the post-war years, the person who in many dimensions most resembled Keynes. Goodwin was Roy Harrod's pupil in Oxford in the 1930s so, indirectly at least, was influenced by Keynes. He came to Cambridge in the 1950s from Harvard and was a colleague of the other people mentioned in the text. He was also an eclectic. Keynes was one of the principal influences on him, together with Marx, Wicksell, Schumpeter and Leontief.

References

Arrow K. J. and Hahn F. H. 1971, *General Competitive Analysis*, San Francisco, Holden-Day; Edinburgh, Oliver and Boyd.

Godley W. and Lavoie M. 2007, *Monetary Economics. An Integrated Approach to Credit, Money, Income, Production and Wealth*. London, Palgrave Macmillan.

Goodwin R. M. and Punzo L. F. 1987, *The Dynamics of a Capitalist Economy: A Multi-sectoral Approach*, Polity in association with Basil Blackwell.

Hahn F. H. and Matthews R. C. O. 1964, 'The theory of economic growth: a survey', *Economic Journal*, 74, 779–902.

Harcourt G. C. 2006, *The Structure of Post-Keynesian Economics. The Core Contributions of the Pioneers*, Cambridge, Cambridge University Press.

Harris D. J. 1975. 'The theory of economic growth: a critique and a reformulation', *American Economic Review, Papers and Proceedings*, 1, 15, 329–37.

Harris D. J. 1978, *Capital Accumulation and Income Distribution*, Stanford, CA, Stanford University Press.

Kaldor N. 1996, *Causes of Growth and Stagnation in the World Economy*, Cambridge, Cambridge University Press.

Levhari D. 1965, 'A nonsubstitution theorem and switching of techniques', *Quarterly Journal of Economics*, 79, 98–105.

Pasinetti L. L. 1960, 'A mathematical formulation of the Ricardian system', *Review of Economic Studies*, 27, 78–98.

Pasinetti L. L. 1966, 'Changes in the rate of profit and switches of techniques', *Quarterly Journal of Economics*, 80, 503–17.

Pasinetti L. L. 1969, 'Switches of technique and the "rate of return" in capital theory', *Economic Journal*, 79, 508–31.

Pasinetti L. L. 1970, 'Again on capital theory and Solow's "rate of return"', *Economic Journal*, 80, 428–31.

Pasinetti L. L. 1973, 'The notion of vertical integration in economic analysis', *Metroeconomica*, 25, 1–29.

Robinson J. 1953, *On Re-reading Marx*, Cambridge Students' Bookshop: repr. in CEP, vol. iv, 1973, 247–68.

Robinson J. 1956, *The Accumulation of Capital*, London, Macmillan.

Robinson J. 1962, *Essays in the Theory of Economic Growth*, London, Macmillan.

Sardoni C. 1981, 'Multisectoral models of balanced growth and the Marxian schemes of reproduction', *Australian Economic Papers*, 20, 383–97.

Solow R. M. 1970, 'On the rate of return: reply to Pasinetti'. *Economic Journal*, 80, 423–28.

Sraffa P. 1960, *Production of Commodities by Means of Commodities. Prelude to a Critique of Economic Theory*, Cambridge, Cambridge University Press.

Walsh V. 2003, 'Sen after Putman', *Review of Political Economy*, 15, 315–94.

Walsh V. 2008, 'Freedom, values and Sen: towards a morally enriched classical economic theory'. *Review of Political Economy*, 20, 199–232.

10

The Collected Writings of an Indian Sage: Reviewing Alaknanda Patel (ed.), *The Collected Works of A. K. Dasgupta*, 3 Vols, 2009 (2012)*

Amiya Kumar Dasgupta (1903–92) was one of India's outstanding economic theorists of the twentieth century, 'undoubtedly the most distinguished economic theorist of his time in India' is the late I. G. Patel's assessment (Vol. III, 1). A.K., as he was usually known, was an extraordinary teacher; he wrote a great amount, amazingly so when we read of the huge amounts of time he gave to his students, to prolonged discussions with friends and colleagues (overlapping sets), as well as corresponding with economists and others all over the world. His collected writings have now been gathered together in the three volumes under review, expertly and lovingly edited by Dasgupta's daughter, Alaknanda Patel, also an economist. She led a devoted team for the task, including her late husband, I. G. Patel, and her brother, Partha Dasgupta, both outstanding economists who knew the work of the older Dasgupta very well indeed.

Partha Dasgupta wrote the Introduction to Volume II, which contains his father's contributions to economic theory, both on specific theoretical issues and broad overviews of classical and modern theories. I. G. Patel wrote the Introduction to Volume III, principally A. K. Dasgupta's writings on policy but also tributes to close friends and mentors, for example, Lionel Robbins, Sachin Chaudhuri and Birendranath Ganguli. All three volumes have a common Preface and the informative, affectionate and moving Biographical Sketch by the editor. In addition, Volume I is fully and insightfully introduced by Dilip Nachane,

---

* Originally published in *Economica*, vol. 79, 2012, pp. 199–206.

'the most thorough scholar of A. K. Dasgupta's economics' (Preface, *xii*). In it are reprinted the first, *The Conception of Surplus in Economic Theory* (1942), and the last, *Epochs of Economic Theory* (1985), of Dasgupta's 10 books. Both books are on the concept of surplus as a unifying concept in an understanding of the development and content of economic theory, but otherwise are poles apart in thrust and interpretation.

Thereby hangs an ironic tale. In 1934 Dasgupta, who was then a young lecturer at Dacca University,[1] pursued his 'daring dream' backed by a university loan to do a Ph.D overseas. Initially he meant to go to Cambridge to study with Piero Sraffa and this had been arranged; but he was so enthralled by Robbins's *Nature and Significance* ... (1932) that he went to the LSE instead. There, he wrote his dissertation, with Robbins as his supervisor, on the concept of surplus principally but, as always, critically, from a neoclassical point of view. The dissertation was the basis for his first book. By the time he came to write *Epochs of Economic Theory* (1985) (which was soon acknowledged as a classic), he had swung round to a viewpoint more consistent with what he would have obtained from Sraffa. The classical concept of surplus becomes the dominant organising concept for an approach to understanding the development of our subject, the writing of theory and the provision of wise policy.

Though Dasgupta always admired and remained a close friend of his teacher, Robbins – his affectionate review article of Robbins's *Autobiography* is reprinted in Volume III – he had far more of Marx and Marshall in his later approaches to theory and policy.[2] Partly this was because he was an Indian patriot who was never tempted permanently to seek glittering prizes abroad. He was passionately interested in the development of pre- and post-Independence India and he felt that the issues that the Classicals and Marx were concerned with – distribution, accumulation, growth – were also those which dominated India's development. (As with the Classicals and Marx, he also wrote on value within this context.) He was attracted to Marshall, not because of his neoclassical strand, but because Marshall drew on Smith and Ricardo in the development of his own thought.[3] Dasgupta wrote some profound papers on Marshall, especially on his theory of international values, on path-dependence in Marshall's period analysis and on whether the Marshallian market period was better illustrated by the market for corn or for fish. Ricardo was pre-eminent amongst the economists Dasgupta admired. He dated the beginnings of economics as a serious science with Ricardo's (and Malthus's and West's) theories of rent in which there was the first systematic analysis of the implications of inescapable scarcity for human wellbeing.

The principal theme of *Epochs* is that it is the times that make the theory required, that long historical time periods are characterised by dominant theoretical structures – the Classical, the Marginalist (he regarded Neoclassical as on the whole a misnomer) and the Keynesian. (He was criticised for stopping here but in the light of recent events, it now looks like he was taking a perceptive long view.) He rejects the idea of advances from error to truth as the end point of economic theory, a view he was more inclined to accept in his Ph.D and first book; he argues that in different periods and situations, earlier theories may be the relevant ones again for aspects of the problems of the current period.

Though he was not an uncritical admirer of Maynard Keynes and argued that Keynes's theory of involuntary unemployment had only a very limited application to understanding India's employment and development problems, I think he would have been sympathetic to Keynes's method. Keynes argued that in a subject such as economics, there is a whole spectrum of languages which are relevant to its issues or aspects of its issues, running all the way from intuition and poetry through lawyer-like arguments to formal logic and mathematics (see Harcourt in Sardoni (ed.) (1992), ch. 11). Indeed, Dasgupta's writings embody this point of view. He is as comfortable with homely examples and empirical judgements of a broad nature, usually backed up by telling orders of magnitude, as he is with formal analysis which, in his case, uses ingeniously simple but pedagogically satisfying diagrams and simple algebra. Moreover, he always placed his theoretical insights within the context of their historical origins, both with respect to authors and situations. For example, when writing about international trade or public finance he was as explicitly aware of Ricardo's and Marshall's and Pigou's contributions as he was of the latest discussions in journals and books. He always stressed, as Amartya Sen (Vol I, 354) comments, 'The benetrating lesson' that there 'was a need to see theory as a discipline on its own – fundamentally distinct from but not unrelated to practice'.

Dasgupta's teaching and writings illuminated generations of Indian economists. Many of his writings were published in *Economic Weekly* (subsequently to become *Economic and Political Weekly (EPW)*, the widely read, influential and respected journal of his closest and greatest friend Sachin Chaudhuri. In its early days the journal was an outlet for many different views and discussions set out in a rigorous manner but within the context of a liberal philosophy as befitted both its founder and his friend. Sadly, this evidently ceased to be the case in the later years of Dasgupta's life (Chaudhuri had died in 1966), finally resulting in his resignation in 1991 from the journal's overseeing body (see Biographical Sketch, *xxxv–xxxvi*).

As ought now to be well known (but is not), Dasgupta independently discovered what in effect is Arthur Lewis's model of development with unlimited supplies of labour Lewis (1954). Dasgupta gave a series of external lectures at the University of Lucknow in 1949 and published the gist of them in an article in *Economic Weekly* in 1954 with the title, 'Keynesian economics and under-developed countries', see Vol. II, 303–11. In his 1994 *Economic Journal* obituary article (reprinted in Vol. I, 346–55), Amartya Sen called this article 'a truly pioneering analysis' (Vol. I, 349).

The author himself did not think his contribution at all original, merely an application of what any person familiar with Ricardo's writings would make. As long as real wages were at a subsistence level, because of unlimited supplies of labour, the Dasgupta–Lewis–Ricardo results followed. In a sequel to the original article published in 1987, Dasgupta quotes from *The General Theory* (10) to show that Keynes concurred with the analysis (see Vol. II, 318 and n 9, 323). (This led Dasgupta to wonder why then Keynes failed to understand Ricardo though he did understand Malthus!) Partha Dasgupta rightly deplores the fact that the textbooks, even those written by Indian economists, still do not refer to the Dasgupta–Lewis model. (I have similar feelings about the failure of textbooks to refer to the Solow–Swan model.)

Both in theory and in policy recommendations, when writing on development, Dasgupta's emphasis was always on the need to accumulate capital *and* create employment, in order to secure rising standards of living and the basis for a sustainable tolerable life for all citizens, especially those least well off. He himself lived an austere life – his family had not been well off and his oldest brother had denied himself partly to make sure the youngest, A. K. Dasgupta, would have the chance to fulfil his potential. Dasgupta thought it behoved the better off – civil servants, the higher echelons in industry and the universities – not to go in for conspicuous consumption. He was opposed to relatively high levels and rates of increase of their wages and salaries, partly because he thought them unnecessary for achieving productivity and efficiency, partly because he did not wish to see incomes paid out of surplus creation wasted on expenditure on imported luxury goods and the domestic manufacture of them. For Dasgupta, the surplus should be devoted to accumulation in the wage goods and capital goods industries and to the provision of social infrastructure. One of his books was *A Theory of Wage Policy* (1976); another was *The Economics of Austerity* (1975). In the last years of his life he was planning a volume on the economics of Gandhi, the one person for whom he had unconstrained admiration. Sadly, he was never to bring this to fruition, a huge loss to the profession and even more to the world, which so desperately needs in these times of global warming and environmental degradation a persuasive blueprint for just and moral development and living. Dasgupta was far too good a liberal to insist that this should be imposed, only that it should be part of informed and intelligent discussion.[4]

Because of these emphases in Dasgupta's thinking, he was a supporter of planning in Indian development. He wrote prolifically on all aspects of planning, periodically taking part in the operations of the Planning Commission itself. Initially he was an enthusiastic supporter but over the years he became increasingly disappointed with the objectives and outcomes of successive plans. However, I do not think he would have been an enthusiastic or uncritical supporter of many aspects of the last two decades and more of Indian economic development.

In his discussions of planning he started from the relationships in Harrod's theory but he also had a deep understanding of the processes of market and production interrelationships which a Walrasian approach was meant to illuminate. Central to his approach are the different requirements that the distinction between Marxian and Keynesian unemployment pose. In this he was at one with Michal Kalecki and Nicholas Kaldor and it is significant that they both have several entries in each of the three name and subject indexes to the volumes.

Dasgupta spent several periods abroad. First were the two years at the LSE for his doctoral research and for the start of his life-long appreciation of Western opera, music and plays, partly guided by Robbins. (He had a similar knowledge and love of their Indian counterparts.) Alaknanda Patel recounts the poignant tale of her father walking around the LSE buildings on the evening before he was to return to India, 'convinced he would never return' (Vol. I, xliii). But, of course, he did, especially when Partha Dasgupta was an LSE Professor and I. G. Patel was its Director. In 1978 he was elected an Honorary Fellow of the LSE, an honour of which he was most proud. He was at the IMF for a three year stint in 1950–53 and in 1963–64 he was Commonwealth Visiting Fellow at Gonville and Caius College, Cambridge. (This was the first time I met him, through our mutual friend, Joan Robinson.) In 1973 he was a Visiting Fellow at the IDS, University of Sussex. Otherwise, he mainly taught at various Indian universities, or directed research institutes, sometimes surrounded by and attracting like-minded souls, sometimes very much on his own as far as his colleagues' interests were concerned. (It is stressed in the accounts of his life that, early on, he was way off the regression line of Indian economists because of his devotion to theory and its development, even though he saw this as intimately connected with the formulation of policy, the overriding interest of most of his early contemporaries.)

The place where he and his wife and children were happiest was Dacca, where he was for 20 years, from 1926 to 1946. Sadly, politics within the Faculty (not partition) brought this idyll to an end, see Biographical Sketch, Vol. I, *xxviii*. At other places, too, local and/or university politics sometimes conspired to make him move, sometimes duty called. Always at the centre of the life of the family was Shanti Dasgupta, his much loved wife, who provided unconstrained support and extraordinary hospitality, not only for the immediate family and nephews, nieces and others but also for all manner of visitors. She was a 'city person' with strong likes and dislikes, allowing 'her instincts and emotions to rule'. Her children 'thought she was happy to keep reason at bay, there was enough from one source!' (Vol. I, *xxvi*). The three volumes are dedicated to her:

> For Ma
> The inspiration behind us all.

Dasgupta himself vigorously affirmed his enormous debt to his help mate, saying that without her he would not have achieved what he did, 'Never, never, never' (Vol I, *xxvi*). In his affectionate review article of Robbins's *Autobiography* he wrote with insight of the not dissimilar role of Lady Robbins in their marriage: '[T]he lovely lines with which the book is dedicated to her are [an] eloquent acknowledgement...of the sweetness and felicity that she provided all [those] years to Robbins' life and activity' (Vol. III, 548).

Dasgupta did not spare himself from his own high critical standards, admitting, for example, that he was not able to join full time the struggle for independence, though as a student he, 'along with thousands of others, stopped attending classes in response to...Gandhi's call for "non-cooperation"' (Vol. I, *xxii-xxiii*). 'He recalled much later, "One of our leaders came from a very poor family, the only son of a widowed mother who had struggled to bring him up. He was a brilliant student and could have had a most distinguished career as a scientist. He gave it all up to join the freedom movement...I did not have that kind of courage"' (Vol. I, *xxiii*). But he was a man of courage and integrity, capable of critical self-knowledge as well as an accurate assessment of his own worth (but never as an own trumpet blower). With Joan Robinson, he was present at the start of the student riots in Paris in May 1968. (His account of this episode is reprinted as 'What I saw in Paris' in Vol. III, 555–57. He supported their aims (if not always their means of achieving them)). He wished that teachers in Indian universities were more supportive of their own students' demands. A. K. Dasgupta was indeed a wise man, a sage, an inspiration to both his own and our present generation. Modern readers will receive enormous insights (and hopefully experience proper humility) by reading these three essential volumes.

Notes

1. Dasgupta graduated with the top First in both the B.A. (Hons.) and M.A. courses at Dacca in the 1920s and became a lecturer even before he had finished his M.A.
2. It is significant that Dasgupta was the only economist asked to contribute to the Centenary celebrations of Marx's *Capital* and Marshall's *Principles*.
3. Partha Dasgupta quotes from some notes his father made about Marshall, that he was 'a marginalist [who] took over the method of analysis – the role of time – from…Smith and Ricardo, giving it a form all his own.…There is accumulation and decumulation in Marshall's short period…Marshall points to a steadily progressive economy. But he does not analyse it [because Marshall's] analytical *technique* [was] a handicap [when reconciling] microeconomic analysis with macro-economy' (Vol. II, 5, emphasis added), as both Roy Harrod and Joan Robinson argued when they tackled the classical problems of distribution and growth in post-Keynesian times. Nor did the older Dasgupta accept (though he admired) modern attempts to solve the problem by building on the capital theory of Edmond Malinvaud and Paul Samuelson (Vol. II, 6).
4. No doubt in it he would have brought in the good case he made for some overlapping similarities in the writings of Marx and Gandhi about the operation of social structures, see Vol. III, 476–77.

References

Dasgupta, A. K. (1942), *The Conception of Surplus in Theoretical Economics*. Calcutta: Dasgupta & Co.

Dasgupta, A. K. (1954), 'Keynesian economics and under-developed countries', *Economic Weekly*, Independence Number, 26 January; *C.W.*, Vol. II, 303–11.

Dasgupta, A. K. (1985), *Epochs of Economic Theory*. Delhi: Oxford University Press.

Dasgupta, A. K. (1987), 'Keynesian economics and under-developed countries again', *Economic and Political Weekly*, 19 September; *C. W.*, Vol. II, 312–24.

Lewis, W. A. (1954), 'Economic development with unlimited supplies of labour', *Manchester School of Economic and Social Studies*, 22, 139–91.

Robbins, Lionel (1932), *An Essay on the Nature and Significance of Economic Science*, London: Macmillan.

Robbins, Lionel (1971), *Autobiography of an Economist*, London: Macmillan.

Sardoni, Claudio (ed.) (1992), *On Political Economists and Modern Political Economy. Selected Essays of G. C. Harcourt*, London and New York: Routledge.

Sen, A. K. (1994), 'Amiya Kumar Dasgupta (1903–1992)', *Economic Journal*, 104, 1147–55; *C.W.*, Vol. 1, 346–55.

Part V
Surveys

11

Keynes and the Cambridge School (2003)*

with Prue Kerr

We start with Maynard Keynes's central ideas.[†] We then discuss the strands that emerged in the work of others, some contemporaries, some followers, some agreeing and extending, others disagreeing and/ or returning to ideas Keynes sloughed off or played down. *The General Theory* is the natural starting point. We trace developments from and reactions to it, especially by people who were associated, at least for part of their working lives, with Cambridge, England. In the concluding paragraphs, we briefly discuss the contributions of those not geographically located in Cambridge who nevertheless worked within the tradition of Keynes and the Cambridge School.

Keynes and the Classics

The General Theory emerged as a reaction to the system of thought, principally associated with Alfred Marshall and A. C. Pigou, on which Keynes was brought up and which he was to subsume, misleadingly, under the rubric of the classical school. Keynes rationally reconstructed the classical system by setting out what, though it could not be found in the writings of any one 'classical' economist, must have been assumed and developed if sense were to be made of their attitudes and claims. (Keynes's procedure could be equally well described as opportunistic.)[1] In its most stark form, the classical system assumes a clear dichotomy between the real and the monetary, with the real the dominant partner, at least in the long period. In a competitive environment there

* Originally published as chapter 22 of Warren J. Samuels, Jeff E. Biddle and John B. Davis (eds), *A Companion to the History of Economic Thought*, Malden, USA, Oxford, UK: Blackwell Publishing, 2003, pp. 343–59.

is a tendency to market-clearing in all markets (including the labour market), again, at least in the long period. This determines the values of equilibrium normal long-period prices and quantities, including those for the services of the factors of production. It also provides the theoretical value of T in Irving Fisher's version of the quantity theory of money (QTM) (Y in Marshall's version) and, together with the assumption of an exogenous value of M and a given value of $V(k)$, makes the general price level (P) proportional to M. The natural rate of interest – a real concept – equilibrates real saving and investment, determining the composition of full-employment Y, itself determined by the full-employment equilibrium value of employment in the labour market. The money rate of interest has to adjust to the real rate which rules the roost.

This is more a Marshallian than a Ricardian view of the world; it assumes Say's Law in a form in which the original classical political economists would never have stated it, as far as full employment of labour (as opposed to capital) is concerned.

This system underlay Keynes's *Tract* and *Treatise on Money*, though Keynes champed at the bit of its constraints, wishing to analyse short-period happenings to production and employment and propose policies appropriate for other than that long run in which we are all dead. Even in *A Treatise on Money*, long-period stock and flow equilibrium and its attainment dominated the core of the analysis. Keynes felt guilty analysing short-period changes in output and employment, but he did allow himself the banana plantation parable, the analysis of which was incomplete because Kahn's multiplier analysis had not yet occurred.

These constraints were virtually completely removed in *The General Theory*. The real-money dichotomy was discarded, money and financial matters entered from the start of the analysis, fully integrated with real happenings. Money, analytically, had all its dimensions – a store of value as well as a medium of exchange and a unit of account. Emphasis moved from the long to the short period. Keynes's predilections in this regard were reinforced by the approach and work of his favourite pupil, now colleague, Richard Kahn, whose King's fellowship dissertation, 'The economics of the short period', made the short period worthy of study in its own right – though, as we shall see, it is not unanimously agreed that *The General Theory* is or should be short period in emphasis. The switch from saving determining investment to investment determining saving, already occurring in Cambridge and elsewhere, became complete in *The General Theory*. The money rate of interest, now the price which equalised the demand for and supply of money, ruled the roost; the *General Theory* version of the natural rate of interest, the *mec* (it should have been the *mei*), had to measure up to it. The heretical concept of an unemployment equilibrium or rest state, the point of effective demand, emerged as the central proposition of *The General Theory*. With Say's Law refuted, QTM no longer explained the general price level. Keynes substituted for it a macroeconomic version of Marshall's short-period supply curve. With marginal-cost pricing usually assumed to occur, there was an upward sloping relationship between activity and the general price level in any given situation. Some of his closest colleagues and co-workers – Roy Harrod, Kahn, Austin and Joan Robinson, Gerald Shove, Piero Sraffa – had helped to develop the then emerging theory of imperfect competition. Keynes noted this but did not think it of central importance for his new, different purposes – he took as given the degree of competition. (Michal Kalecki showed in his review article of *The General Theory* how right Keynes's instinct was. Nevertheless, Kalecki and, subsequently the post-Keynesians, for example, Nicholas Kaldor, Alfred Eichner, G.C. Harcourt and Peter Kenyon, Sydney Weintraub, Adrian Wood, were to make mark-up pricing, replete with a theory of the determination of its size, an integral part of the theories of employment and distribution.) Crucially, Keynes's philosophical views, developed while he was still an undergraduate and most comprehensively expressed in his 1909 King's Fellowship dissertation, *A Treatise on Probability* (subsequently published in 1921), are an integral aspect of the complex analysis of *The General Theory*. We refer to the modern writings on the significance of this in the concluding paragraphs.

We should also mention the sad happening that Keynes's closest collaborator in the development of monetary theory during the 1920s, Dennis Robertson, parted company with him as *The General Theory* emerged. Robertson was shocked by Keynes's disrespect for his elders and betters (read Marshall). He thought the policy implications were dangerous because Keynes's analysis did not capture the rich, inescapable dynamics of the interactions of the real and monetary sectors of industrialised economies. They implied cyclical developments, around which monetary and fiscal measures should attempt to fit like a glove but not try to remove, in order to preserve the potential of long-term rises in productivity and the standard of living generally. The rift was both a personal and professional tragedy. (Gordon Fletcher (2000) contains a superb account of the psychological and intellectual reasons for it.)

Kahn and Joan Robinson were always hostile to the *IS/LM* version of Keynes's system as it came down to the profession and the textbooks, principally through J. R. Hicks's famous 1937 article. They never said why in print but it became clear in the post-war period that they thought it cut out Keynes's emphasis on how an environment of inescapable uncertainty affected how (usually) sensible people did the best they could when making economic decisions. They also thought it impossible to properly set out Keynes's new ideas within the framework of Hicks's adaptation of the Walrasian system. The latter underlay *Value and Capital* (1939), written while Hicks was teaching in Cambridge in the second half of the 1930s (it was conceived when he was at LSE) so that it was the natural framework within which for him to try to understand Keynes's new theory. Keynes, Kahn, Austin and Joan Robinson were always resolutely Marshallian in method, even for macroeconomics. Yet passages in *The General Theory* (see, for example, p. 173) may legitimately be interpreted in terms of *IS/LM*. They show its great limitations as well as the basic insight it gives (see Donald Moggridge 1976, 171–74). The two relationships cannot be taken to be independent of one another; changes in the value of a parameter underlying one may often affect those underlying the other, leading to Keynes's shifting equilibrium model and to the modern analysis of path-dependence (which Kaldor initially set out in 1934!). Several of Keynes's closest allies did *The General Theory* in terms of *IS/LM*, admittedly in algebra or words, not diagrams. Thus Brian Reddaway's review, Harrod's and James Meade's contributions to the session at the Oxford conference at which Hicks presented his paper are so set out. Indeed, Hicks read Harrod's and Meade's papers *before* he wrote his and produced the diagram; (see Warren Young (1987)).

Keynes, Keynesians and the Second World War

Though a group of Keynesians dispute it, see p. 208 below, those closest to Keynes regarded Keynes's core model as set in the short period. He was mostly concerned with the employment-creating effects of investment expenditure and virtually ignored its capacity-creating effects. He analysed the conditions for the establishment of a rest state which could be associated with unemployment in a situation in which the existing stock of capital goods, supplies of skilled and unskilled labour, the quantity of money and the degree of competition were given. He provided a sketchy analysis of the trade cycle in a later chapter and made some asides about prospects for long-term growth (or their lack) but never systematically examined them in *The General Theory* itself. He set out policy proposals for attaining full employment in the short term, starting from a deep slump but, again, only sketched in the difficulties associated with sustaining full employment. (Kalecki (1943) analysed the crucial difference between the political economy of getting to full employment and sustaining it.) In war time, Keynes and his ideas played a major role in getting the British economy through

World War II without major inflationary problems. Keynes illustrated his theory's generality in *How to Pay for the War* (1940). There he introduced the concept of an inflationary gap – aggregate demand in real terms exceeding full-employment aggregate supply – and the steps to be taken to eliminate the gap to avoid rising prices, queues forming and order books lengthening.

During the war two of Keynes's closest associates, Meade and Richard Stone, developed a comprehensive system of national accounts based on the relationships in Keynes's theory to help the war effort by avoiding bottlenecks and shortages. Building on these foundations Stone developed the accounts uniformly and internationally. (He received the Nobel Prize in 1984 for these 'fundamental contributions'. Meade received it in 1977 for his contributions to international economics, also built on Keynesian foundations.) Economic historians, for example, Alan Cairncross, Phyllis Deane, Charles Feinstein and Brian Mitchell, used the Keynesian system and national accounts to reinterpret aspects of the industrial revolution and in the case of Deane, to analyse the problems of developing countries.

Growth and distribution

In the post-war period, Kahn, Joan Robinson and Sraffa, stimulated by Harrod's seminal pre-war and early post-war writings on growth and by the problems of reconstruction and development generally, turned their attention to 'generalising *The General Theory* to the long period'. (They were later joined by Kaldor and then Luigi Pasinetti.) They reached back over the neoclassical interlude of resource allocation and price theory generally to the preoccupations of the classical political economists and Marx with growth, distribution and the role of technical progress, taking in the findings of the Keynesian revolution in the process. Harrod posed two fundamental problems: first, the instability of his warranted rate of growth, g_w – the rate of growth which, if attained, would be sustained because actual outcomes would persuade decision-makers concerning accumulation that they were doing the correct rates of accumulation. If it were not attained, the economy would give out destabilising signals; the actual rate of growth, g, would tend to move further and further away from g_w in either direction depending upon whether $g \gtrless g_w$. The second <INLINE> problem was whether there were forces at work which could bring g_w and g_n together, where g_n, the natural rate of growth, represented the supply potential of the economy associated with the rates of growth of its labour supply in quantity and quality. There was no reason why g_w should equal g_n because g_w was concerned with accumulators achieving their desires, not wage-earners necessarily being fully employed, as they would be on g_n. The Cambridge Keynesian growth theorists addressed these two basic problems. (John Cornwall, much influenced by Kaldor's approach in particular and unwilling to accept Harrod's assumption that g_n was independent of g_w, has over the past 40 years and more, illuminated our understanding of the development of capitalist economies over time by analysing how g_w and g_n feedback into one another; see Harcourt and Medhi Monadjemi (1999).)

To illustrate significant differences in their approaches, we consider those of Kahn and Joan Robinson, on the one hand, and Kaldor, on the other. Both developed macroeconomic theories of distribution. Kaldor called them 'Keynesian' because he found their origins in the passages in *A Treatise on Money* on the widow's cruse and because they incorporated the Keynesian view that investment led and saving responded to it. Kaldor initially argued that in the long period the economy grew at full employment along g_n; the role of the multiplier was to determine the distribution of income between profits and wages, supposing that the marginal propensity to save from profits, s_π, exceeded that from wages, s_w, and money prices were more flexible than money wages in the long period. If the economy were not saving the right amount to allow the provision of the accumulation needed to keep the economy on g_n, the gap between planned investment and saving would so change the distribution of income as prices change more rapidly than money wages, as to bring about an overall saving ratio equal to the required investment ratio in long-period full-employment income. (Kalecki in the 1930s developed a similar theory for the short period but did not require the economy to be at full employment. Saving therefore could be brought to equality with investment by changes in income *and* its distribution, the resulting rest state could be associated with involuntary unemployment. Moreover, Kalecki explicitly linked pricing practices and their determinants in different sectors of the economy to the distribution of income.)

Kahn and Joan Robinson developed their arguments in two stages. First, they examined the properties of Golden Ages, so-called because they were mythical states, never to be realised in reality. Their aim was to make precise certain definitions – profits, capital, saving, investment – and relationships which could only be made so in Golden Ages (or steady states as the neoclassical growth theorists called them) where expectations and actuality always matched. They identified several variants of Golden Age, some with desirable properties, others not,

Bastard Golden Ages, with sustained unemployment of labour. They then attempted to analyse processes occurring in historical time (as opposed to the logical time of Golden Age analysis), never completely successfully. Indeed, towards the end of her life, Joan Robinson sometimes despaired of ever achieving this, though in one of her last papers (co-authored with Amit Bhaduri, 1980), she was less pessimistic than in her nihilistic paper of the same year, originally entitled 'Spring cleaning' (1980; 1985). There she argued we should scrap everything and start anew.

Kaldor though was happy to use steady-state analysis in descriptive analysis of the real world, making sense in explanations of the occurrence of his famous 'stylised facts' – near enough regularities over time to require explanation. He wrote a series of papers in the 1950s and 1960s, starting from his famous 'Alternative theories of distribution' (1955–56). They were both Keynesian and classical because he now introduced a technical progress function relating productivity growth to the rate of take-up through accumulation of the flow of new ideas through time. In the most refined version, investment is specifically related to embodiment at the margin of new ideas and to productivity growth. All incorporate Kaldor's (and, eventually, other Cambridge growth theorists') refusal to accept the neoclassical distinction between movements *along* a given production function (deepening) and movements *of* the production function due to technical progress. Kaldor regarded the distinction as incoherent – new accumulation carried with it, indissolubly, new ways of making products, and, often, new products themselves.

Kaldor's and Joan Robinson's views were not *that* different from the pioneering work of Wilfred Salter on vintages in *Productivity and Technical Change* (1960), except that at any moment of time, the *ex ante* production function of 'best practice' techniques was whittled down to one point endogenously created to meet the needs of the moment (in the light of expectations about the future), while Salter allowed a choice of techniques to occur. Eventually, Kaldor rejected this approach. He ultimately thought that the problems of steady growth arose from the difficulty of keeping the growth of the availability of primary products in line with the growth of the absorptive capacity of the industrial sectors of the world. In his view neither the Keynesian nor the neoclassical models could handle the *complementarity* of an integrated world. A multi-sector model was required to tackle the mutual interdependence of the sectors where the development of each depends upon and is stimulated by the development of others. Different pricing behaviour as between the sectors tended to frustrate the emergence of harmonious interdependence. Kaldor's approach has been developed by his biographer, Tony Thirlwall, often with John McCombie (see, for example, McCombie and Thirlwall (1994)). But we have run ahead of our story.

The Capital Theory critique

Simultaneously with these positive developments of Classical cum Marxian cum Keynesian ideas occurred a critique of the foundations of neoclassical value, growth and distribution theory associated with the so-called Cambridge controversies in the theory of capital. Starting as an attack on the capital variable in the aggregate production function, it developed, especially in the hands of Joan Robinson and Kahn, into a critique of the long-period method – comparisons of long-period positions with different values of a key parameter to analyse processes occurring in actual time. Summed up in Joan Robinson's phrase, 'History versus equilibrium', it is the error of using differences to illuminate the results of changes. Another strand of the critique was precipitated into the public domain by Joan Robinson in 1953–54 (developed long before by Sraffa, it was revealed with the publication of *Production of Commodities* in 1960.) It questioned the robustness of the intuition that prices, including distributive prices, were reliable indexes of scarcity. This intuition was refuted in the 1960s by the capital-reversing and reswitching results. They destroyed the theoretical foundations of the inevitability of a downward-sloping demand curve for capital (outside the domain of one commodity models) and of negative relationships between the rate of profits (r), on the one hand, and capital-output ratios and sustainable levels of consumption per head, on the other. Indeed, the coherence of the concept of a marginal product of capital (outside the one commodity domain) was called into question. The marginal productivity theory of distribution became problematic, for reasons other than those adduced within the neoclassical framework (see Mandler (1999)).

In the 1950s Kahn and Joan Robinson extended Keynes's liquidity preference theory of the rate of interest to take in the stock market, adding equities to bonds as financial assets competing with the holding of money. They built on Keynes's 1937 papers setting out his insight of *A Treatise on Money*, lost sight of in *The General Theory*, that finance, not saving, was the ultimate constraint on the rate of accumulation, provided expected profits were buoyant. (Depressed expected profits obviously bite in a slump, regardless of the state of finance – hence

Keynes's pessimism about an effective role for easier credit terms *on their own* in revival from a slump.) Also associated with these developments were Kaldor's seminal ideas from the late 1930s about the operation of markets where stocks dominate flows and expectations of future price movements on both sides of the market dominate the impact of the usual determinants of prices.

Sraffa's *Production of Commodities*

Sraffa had started long before the 1950s on a critique of the founda-tions of the neoclassical value and distribution theory. The first public inklings of this, as Joan Robinson saw it, was in the 1951 Introduction to the Ricardo volumes edited by Sraffa in collaboration with Maurice Dobb. She was then searching for a satisfactory theory of the origin and size of the rate of profits in her emerging work on growth theory. In the Introduction Sraffa discussed Ricardo's theory, starting with a reconstruction, historical and rational, which involved the use of a corn model to explain Ricardo's early view that the profits of the farmer ruled the roost. This was to be replaced in the *Principles* by a labour embodied theory of profits, an obvious link to Marx but without the concept of exploitation. (Smith and Ricardo recognised the existence of class war and the lack of harmony in the operation of capitalism.) Joan Robinson had been absorbing Marx's messages from the mid-1930s, encouraged first by her friendship with Kalecki and then in order to take her mind off the war.

When *Production of Commodities* was published, a few reviewers sensed Sraffa's twofold purpose – to provide a prelude to a refutation of the conceptual and logical foundations of (neoclassical) economic theory and revive the approach of the classical political economists and Marx to value and distribution theory. The latter was intended to make possible a coherent theory of the laws of motion of capitalist society, already potentially there in Marx's writings, but with errors removed and unfinished business completed. Such were the views of Dobb and Sraffa, Joan Robinson (with reservations) and Kalecki. The core organ-ising concept is the surplus – its creation, extraction, distribution and use. In the book, Sraffa examines production with a surplus in a system of single commodity industries; the determination, first, of r and long-period relative prices when the value of w is given and then of w and prices when the value of r is given; joint production systems in order to analyse fixed capital; land, in order to take in price-determined rent; and the choice of technique to complete the story *and* show the non-robustness of the intuition of price as an index of scarcity in distribution theory. The system of Sraffa's book is a rigorous representation of the structure of the centres of gravitation associated with the natural prices of Smith and Ricardo and the prices of production of Marx.[2] It is not one side of Marshall's demand and supply story of the determination of long-period equilibrium normal prices (it has been so interpreted by even such astute critics as Samuelson and Mandler).

Sraffa's method is seen by Sraffians as the examination of the outcome of persistent forces in establishing centres of gravitation of the economic system. It incorporates the classical political economists' insight that in a competitive environment there is a tendency towards equality of profit rates in all activities; thus a theory of the overall rate of profits to which they tend in value is needed, a macroeconomic theory because it 'could not be otherwise' (Pasinetti, 1962, 277). It provides the basis for the revival of classical theory as well as a prelude to a critique of neoclassical theory. The initial critique was spelt out in the capital theory debates of the 1950s to 1970s (see Harcourt (1972)). Positive aspects of the rehabilitation may be found in, for example, Heinz Kurz and Neri Salvadori's work on long-period production (1995).

Long-period Keynesians

Sraffa, though a close friend of Keynes, was not bowled over by *The General Theory*. (He did defend Keynes's *Treatise on Money* against Friedrich Hayek's attack, in the process using the concept of own rates of interest. Keynes used the concept to play a key role in the crucial, difficult chapter 17 of *The General Theory*. We suspect Sraffa would not have approved because he used the concept in an internal critique of Hayek's system, not to analyse actual economies.) Sraffa's followers embraced Keynes but argued that for his theory to be revolutionary, he must provide (or have provided) a *long-period* theory of effective demand purged of neoclassical left-overs in, for example, the *mec* of his investment theory which, they argue, is vulnerable to the capital theory critique (not so, according to Pasinetti). Murray Milgate (1982) is the most detailed argument for this viewpoint but there are prior articles by, for example, Pierangelo Garegnani, gathered together (including dissent from Joan Robinson) in the 1983 collection edited by John Eatwell and Milgate.

Pasinetti, Goodwin and Kalecki

The most original, ambitious and sustained attempt to marry classical political economy (as revived by Sraffa) and Keynes's insights is found in the writings of Pasinetti, senior heir to the 'pure' post-Keynesian school of economic thought now the founding members are dead. His multi-sectoral growth model, originally developed in his Cambridge Ph.D. dissertation in the 1950s and 1960s and reaching maturity in his 1981 book (and 1993 students' guide), is a *tour de force*. It absorbs Kahn's and Joan Robinson's Golden Age analysis, *The General Theory's* principal insights, Kaldor's growth and distribution theories and Sraffa's analysis of value, distribution and production-interdependent systems. It takes in the principal issues of what Baumol called the magnificent dynamics of classical political economy. A principal distinction stands out: Pasinetti's insistence that we understand the principles of an institution-free system before we take into account the role of institutions and particular historical episodes. Pasinetti illustrated this distinction in his discussion of the principle of effective demand in Keynes's theory (1997).

The method of the long-period Keynesians was never acceptable to Joan Robinson and Kahn, or to Goodwin and Kalecki (who never explicitly engaged with it). Joan Robinson experimented with the long period in a Marshallian sense in the 1930s after *The General Theory's* publication to see whether Keynes's new results went through in this setting. She became increasingly dissatisfied with her findings, in the post-war period, repudiating Marshallian method and concepts as such. Keynes was arguing by the mid 1930s that long-period equilibrium probably had no conceptual basis in his new theory. (He did not go as far as Joan Robinson in spelling out why.) The really innovative developments are associated with Kalecki and Goodwin. (Goodwin supervised Pasinetti's research in its early stages.) They increasingly refuted the notion of the trend and cycle as separable concepts, brought about by non-overlapping determinants. Independently, they developed models of cyclical growth as characteristic of the movement of capitalist economies. The basic idea was put succinctly (as ever) by Kalecki: 'the long-run trend is only a slowly changing component of a chain of short-period situations ... [not an] independent entity' (Kalecki, 1971, 165). Goodwin, too, ultimately married production-interdependence models (as well as Sraffa, Leontief was a mentor at the other Cambridge) with aggregate, Keynes-type cyclical models which also had Marxian ingredients (he was Harrod's pupil at Oxford and Schumpeter's colleague at Harvard) (see, for example, Goodwin and Punzo (1987)). Bhaduri and Joan Robinson (1980) entwined Kalecki and Marx with Sraffa. Sraffa's role was to provide thought experiments at a high level of abstraction, resulting in an acceptable theory of the rate of profits.

Frank Hahn at Cambridge

We have concentrated on the writings of, mostly, those closest to Keynes (or his ideas) as well as being influenced by the classicals and Marx and becoming more and more disillusioned with neoclassical economics. But we also mentioned how others discerned in the *IS/LM* approaches the core of Keynes's system, at least as a starting point and a pedagogical device. Though the developments flowing from this were deplored by the first group, this way of 'doing' Keynes has been most influential in teaching and the development of theory and policy. Some occurred in Cambridge itself. Perhaps the most original is associated with Frank Hahn (in his LSE Ph.D. thesis, published years later in 1972; he came to Cambridge in 1960). Hahn modified the *IS* portion of Hicks's apparatus to take in a macroeconomic theory of distribution in which the marginal propensity to save from profits exceeded that from wages and induced investment levels had to be matched by corresponding voluntary savings. This implied a relationship between income levels and the share of profits. He married this with a supply-side story whereby entrepreneurs, operating in an uncertain environment, could only be persuaded to accumulate at a rate which made the income levels feasible and organise production and employment so as to bring them about if they received certain shares of national income as profits. The intersection of the two relationships was a stable, short-period rest state for income and distribution.

In Cambridge, Hahn collaborated with Robin Matthews to write a survey article on growth theory (1964), the role model for surveys ever afterwards. Matthews also published two books on the trade cycle which were Keynesian in their orientation, one an historical study, the other a wide-ranging text book in the Cambridge Economic Handbooks series. It was full of original ideas. One of the most innovative came from his 1950s study of the saving function and the problem of trend and cycle. He reinterpreted Duesenberry's ratchet effect by relating spending and saving to previous lowest levels of unemployment in booms (rather than highest levels of income) so that the growth in productivity was taken into account. He also wrote on the financial aspects of the Keynesian multiplier working out over time.

After an interlude on general equilibrium theory and giving his name to a process in growth theory, Hahn became a leading critic of Monetarism and the New Classical Macroeconomics of the 1970s on. He was aghast at their policies and even more so at what he regarded as their intellectual dishonesty in claiming that their theoretical analysis of how the economy worked justified their proposed policies. Though he never understood Marx, we think he would have had some sympathy with Thomas Balogh's quip that Monetarism was the incomes policy of Karl Marx. In the 1980s and, with Robert Solow, in the 1990s, he courageously criticised them from within, attempting to provide alternatives which, using modern theoretical methods, came up with Keynes-type results (Hahn and Solow, 1996). But there are none so blind...; we fear their work has been ignored by those they attacked *and* their potential allies, the post-Keynesians.

Stone and Meade in the Post-war Years

Stone, the first Director (1945–55) of the Department of Applied Economics (DAE), developed in collaboration with J. A. C. Brown an eclectic growth model which was nevertheless inspired by Keynes's original ideas. Known as the Cambridge Growth Project, its aim was to design a model which allowed the expenditure and production-interdependence of the British economy to be tracked over the medium to longer term under different scenarios. Its origin was Brown's suggestion that they bring together previous work in the DAE on social accounting, input-output and consumer behaviour to build such a model for the British economy. (The complementarity with Pasinetti's contributions is not fanciful.) David Champernowne (Keynes's pupil when Keynes was writing *The General Theory*) also made fundamental contributions in the post-war period in his own independent way to our understanding of Keynes's theory in the short and long periods, and growth and distribution theory.

We must also document Meade's post-war writings, not only on international trade (in a Keynesian setting) at LSE but also on growth theory when he succeeded Robertson in the Chair of Political Economy in 1957. His growth theory was neoclassical in the Solow/Swan sense but he never forgot his Keynesian credentials. As with Solow and Swan (who never forgot their's either), he assumed that short-period effective demand puzzles had been taken care of by an all-wise government, so that the long-period effects of substitution between the factors of production responding to changes in the prices of their services and the effects of technical progress could be analysed. As a side issue Meade (sometimes with Hahn) clarified some of the issues raised in Pasinetti (1962) on dependence of the long-period rate of profits solely on the saving propensity of a class of pure capitalists and the natural rate of growth. Meade's 1966 note, using superbly as ever geometry, allows the reader/viewer to discover easily the properties of Pasinetti Land and its dual MSM Land, where Harrod-type ideas rule and the capitalist class has ceased to exist. (MS stands for Modigliani and Samuelson who wrote a long paper on the issues, M stands for Meade.) In the 1980s Meade in collaboration with a number of younger colleagues worked on stabilisation policies, incorporating the techniques of control engineering. (Meade was a great supporter of Bill Phillips's pioneering work on these issues with these techniques at LSE in the 1940s, 1950s and after.) Meade's last book, published just before his death in 1995, was concerned with policies directed at the attainment of full employment and a just distribution of income and wealth: a fitting endpoint for a lifetime of service and decency, steeped in Keynes's tradition.

Kaldor and Keynes's mantle

The person at post-war Cambridge who most took on Keynes's mantle was undoubtedly Kaldor. We have referred to his contributions to growth theory in which, initially, the Keynesian influence was strong. But it was within the framework of Keynes's own system that he made the most direct contributions, including an internal critique of details of the system. First, Kaldor could not accept Keynes's microeconomic foundations of, in the main, Marshallian marginal cost pricing. In its place Kaldor put his representative firm/industry model of a price leading and setting oligopolist surrounded by followers. In the 1960s and 1970s he developed aspects of these views, on their own and in macroeconomic settings, providing fertile suggestions for future research. (Wood's 1975 book is the most direct heir.) Kaldor's objections were related to his life-long preoccupation with cumulative causation processes and his appreciation of an all-pervading influence of increasing returns, especially in manufacturing industry, so that he could not accept atomistic competition as a general pricing model (outside primary industries). Secondly, he thought Keynes made a tactical mistake by departing from his otherwise life-long view to treat the money supply in *The General Theory* as exogenous, not endogenous, or at least given (probably what Keynes did). This is a mistaken view of how the banking system and the Central Bank operated. It also proved to be a hostage to fortune as Monetarists grew more and more influential. Kaldor was one of the few UK voices in the wilderness taking them on. He was a pioneer of the view that the money supply is endogenous, that it is overwhelmingly demand which creates the money supply. Here he was joined by James Trevithick who also continued the Keynesian tradition in teaching and in two classic texts on inflation and involuntary unemployment respectively. Like Keynes, Kaldor was active in policy – advising the UK Labour governments in the 1960s and 1970s and international governments too, sometimes with unexpected and startling results.

Other Cambridge contributors in the post-war years

Another Cambridge economist who made seminal contributions in similar areas is Robin Marris. *The Economic Theory of 'Managerial' Capitalism* (1964) is a highly original account of modern firm behaviour, the path-breaking aspects of which are now being fully realised. His 1980s and 1990s writings on imperfectly competitive foundations of the Keynesian system are also strikingly original and controversial – he argues that only these micro foundations allow Keynes's macroeconomic results to go through.

Bob Rowthorn published the seminal paper on conflict inflation in 1977. It is the starting point in the modern literature for discussions of this process, the idea that sustained rates of inflation bring about an uneasy truce between capital and labour. Both fail to achieve completely their aspirations for accumulation and standards of living respectively.

What of Austin Robinson, who worked so closely with Keynes for many years (and whose obituary article of Keynes (1947), is required reading alongside the subsequent biographies – Harrod, Moggridge and Robert Skidelsky's unmatchable three volumes)? Austin was an applied political economist *par excellence*. Armed with his deep and astute understanding of Marshall, Pigou and Keynes and with his wide knowledge of the real world in developed and developing countries, in government service and as an advisor, he devoted much time in the post-war period to development problems. (Austin also stressed what he considered to be a neglected aspect of post-war Keynesian developments, detailed analysis and knowledge of individual firm and industry behaviour, and of regional problems.) In his writings on developing economies he made wise diagnoses and put forward sensible, practical humane policy proposals which took into account the detailed cultural and sociological characteristics of the societies and the aspirations of all their citizens. In these pursuits he was joined by Brian Reddaway, whose writings on development and on the British economy reflect a similar highly intelligent, practical approach. Reddaway succeeded Stone as Director of the DAE in 1955; he did and supervised applied work which was clearly Keynesian inspired in its approach and theoretical structure.

Reddaway (who succeeded Meade in the Chair of Political Economy) was succeeded at the DAE by Wynne Godley. With Frances Cripps, other DAE officers and Robert Neild, Godley brought an amalgam of Marshall and Keynes to his view of how the UK economy works and how to forecast in the short term. He developed a consistent set of flow and stock constraints associated with the interrelationship of real flows and stocks and their financial counterparts. These had their origins in Keynes's theory and the characteristics of Marshall's long period, modified for macroeconomic analysis.

Finally, we mention the highly original approaches of Ajit Singh to development problems, Frank Wilkinson to the understanding of the labour market, and Tony Lawson to methodological and philosophical issues, all of which add considerably to the traditions and achievements of Keynes and the Cambridge School. Singh is a major spokesman for views which are a creditable and decent alternative to those of the so-called Washington consensus on development strategies. Wilkinson has analysed in much detail the functioning of labour markets, both individually and in relation to the economy as a whole. He takes an historical and institutional perspective, and shows great sympathy and understanding for wage-earners and unions. Lawson's writings on critical realism and open systems, vestiges of which he discerns in Keynes's writings, have opened up an international debate on the legitimacy of mainstream theory and econometric practice. The latter assume a closed system. Lawson argues that a discipline such as economics should be concerned with analysis of an open system.

With the retirement and then death of many of the main *dramatis personae*, the Cambridge Faculty has become more and more a clone of leading US schools. The traditions outlined here are still carried on by a besieged minority, mostly centred around the *Cambridge Journal of Economics*. Some still have a foothold in the Faculty; others form a thriving colony in the Judge Institute of Management Studies (now the Judge Business School) or are scattered around in colleges as college, not university, teachers. More optimistically, in centres other than Cambridge, Keynes and the Cambridge tradition are to be found under the wide embracing rubric of post-Keynesianism.

The Cambridge tradition in other centres

We think especially of the writings of the late Athanasios (Tom) Asimakopulos, Avi Cohen, (the late) John and Wendy Cornwall, Omar Hamouda, Marc Lavoie, the late Tom Rymes and, most of all, the late Lorie Tarshis in Canada; the late Keith Frearson, Robert Dixon, Peter

Groenewegen, the essay's authors (when there!), Joseph Helevi, John King, Peter Kriesler, John Nevile, Ray Petrides, Colin Rogers (and his South African country person, Christopher Torr), Trevor Stegman, Michael White and others in Australia; the late George Shackle, Philip Arestis, Victoria Chick, Sheila Dow, Douglas Mair, Peter Reynolds, Peter Riach, Judy Rich, Malcolm Sawyer, Ian Steedman and others in the UK; and of the late Sidney Weintraub, Allin Cottrell, Paul Davidson, Sandy Darity, Amitava Dutt, Gary Dymski, the late Al Eichner, the late John Kenneth Galbraith (and son James), Rick Holt, Jan Kregel, Michael Lawlor, Fred Lee, Stephen Marglin, the late Hyman Minsky, Basil Moore, Edward Nell, Steve Pressman, Roy Rotheim, Nina Shapiro, the late Paul Wells and others in the USA.

In continental Europe, there are strongholds, particularly by those who were influenced by Piero Sraffa, as well as by Keynes. We have mentioned Garegnani and Pasinetti in Italy. We add Maria Cristina Marcuzzo, Alessandro Roncaglia, Neri Salvadori, Claudio Sardoni, Roberto Scazzieri and the late Paolo Sylos-Labini (and many others of course). In Germany, Bertram Schefold is a major Sraffian scholar as were Heinz Kurz and Christian Gehrke (they are now in Austria). There are other major contributors in Austria, especially Michael Landesmann, the late Kurt Rothschild and the late Josef Steindl. In Switzerland Mauro Baranzini has written fine books and essays which especially reflect Pasinetti's approach. Heinrich Bortis's magnificent monograph (1997) is a synthesis of the main strands of thought to be found under the post-Keynesian rubric; it exhibits a humane political philosophy and provides a guide to effective, decent policies. In India, Amit Bhaduri, the late Krishna Bharadwaj and their colleagues, especially at JNU, and the late Sukhamoy Chakravarty at the Delhi School have made major contributions to the tradition. In addition, they applied the approach in their deep understanding of economic and political processes in developing economies. Pervez Tahir in Pakistan critically evaluated Joan Robinson's writings on development in general and China in particular. In Central and Latin America (especially in Brazil) pupils of Davidson, Harcourt, Kalecki and Marglin are making significant contributions broadly within the tradition described in the essay. There is also a thriving Post-Keynesian Society in Japan.

Economics and Philosophy

Most important for our present purposes is the work of the last three decades on the links between Keynes's philosophy and his economics. Many seminal writings on these themes started their lives as Ph.D.

dissertations in Cambridge – Rod O'Donnell, Anna Carabelli, John Coates, Flavio Comim, Jochen Runde, for example. An early, influential volume edited by Lawson and Hashem Pesaran was published in 1988. Subsequently John Davis published a major monograph (1994a), and edited a major volume (1994b) on similar themes.

Three crucial aspects of Keynes's economic writings, especially in *The General Theory* and after, emanate from his philosophical understanding. The first is the realisation that in the operation of an economic system, the whole may be more than the sum of the parts – hence his emphasis on the need in macroeconomic analysis to avoid the fallacy of composition, a lesson largely forgotten as representative agent models have come to dominate modern analysis. The second is that in a discipline such as economics there is a whole spectrum of relevant languages, according to which issues, or aspects of issues, are discussed. It runs from intuition and poetry through lawyer-like arguments to formal logic and mathematics. All have rightful places, none should have a monopoly – truth does not only come in the guise of a mathematical model. The third (derived from Marshall) is that we need to analyse how (usually) sensible people decide in situations of inescapable uncertainty, the one sure constant of all economic life and therefore another 'incontrovertible' proposition of our 'miserable subject' (Keynes to Bertil Ohlin, 29 April 1937, *CW*, vol. XIV, 1973, 190).

Notes

[†] We thank but in no way implicate the editors for their comments. We are indebted to Sheila Dow for allowing us to see a draft of her essay, 'Postwar Heterodox Economics: Post Keynesian'.

1. Michael Ambrosi (2003) shows convincingly that Pigou 1933 has provided the classical system Keynes was seeking.
2. Ajit Sinha (2010) subsequently persuaded me that Sraffa himself may not have seen it this way nor was it necessary for the logic of Sraffa's system in his 1960 book to prevail.

References

Ambrosi, G. M. (2003), *Keynes, Pigou and Cambridge Keynesians: Authenticity and Analytical Perspective in the Keynes-Classics Debate*, Houndmills, Basingstoke, Palgrave Macmillan.

Bhaduri, Amit and Joan Robinson (1980), 'Accumulation and Exploitation: An Analysis in the Tradition of Marx, Sraffa and Kalecki', *Cambridge Journal of Economics*, 4, 103–15.

Bortis, Heinrich (1997), *Institutions, Behaviour and Economic theory. A Contribution to Classical-Keynesian Political Economy*, Cambridge, Cambridge University Press.

Davis, John B. (1994a), *Keynes's Philosophical Development*, Cambridge, Cambridge University Press.

Davis, John B. (ed.) (1994b), *The State of Interpretation of Keynes*, Boston, Kluwer.

Eatwell, John and Murray Milgate (eds) (1983), *Keynes's Economics and the Theory of Value and Distribution*, London, Duckworth.

Fletcher, Gordon (2000), *Understanding Dennis Robertson: The Man and His Work*, Cheltenham, U.K., Northampton, M.A., USA, Edward Elgar.

Goodwin, R. M. and L. F. Punzo (1987), *The Dynamics of a Capitalist Economy: A Multi-sectoral Approach*, Cambridge, Polity Press.

Hahn, F. H. (1972), *The Share of Wages in the National Income*, London, Weidenfeld and Nicolson.

Hahn, F. H. and R. C. O. Matthews (1964), 'The Theory of Economic Growth: a Survey', *Economic Journal*, 74, 779–902.

Hahn, F. H. and R. M. Solow (1996), *A Critical Essay on Modern Macroeconomic Theory*, Oxford, Blackwell.

Harcourt, G. C. (1972), *Some Cambridge Controversies in The Theory of Capital*, Cambridge, Cambridge University Press.

Harcourt, G. C. and M. Monadjemi (1999), 'The Vital Contributions of John Cornwall to Economic Theory and Policy: A Tribute from Two Admiring Friends on the Occasion of His 70th Birthday', in M. Setterfield (ed.), *Growth, Employment and Inflation. Essays in Honour of John Cornwall*, Houndmills, Basingstoke, Hants., Palgrave Macmillan, 10–23.

Harrod, R. F. (1939), 'An Essay in Dynamic Theory', *Economic Journal*, 49, 14–33.

Harrod, R. F. (1948), *Towards a Dynamic Economics*, London, Macmillan.

Hicks, J. R. (1937), 'Mr. Keynes and the "Classics"', *Econometrica*, 5, 147–59.

Hicks, J. R. (1939), *Value and Capital*, Oxford, Clarendon Press.

Kaldor, N. (1955–56), 'Alternative Theories of Distribution', *Review of Economic Studies*, 23, 83–100.

Kalecki, M. (1943), 'Political Aspects of Full Employment', *Political Quarterly*, reprinted in Kalecki (1971), 138–45.

Kalecki, M. (1968), 'Trend and Business Cycles Reconsidered', *Economic Journal*, 78, 263–76, reprinted in Kalecki (1971), 165–83.

Kalecki, M. (1971), *Selected Essays on the Dynamics of the Capitalist Economy 1933–1970*, Cambridge, Cambridge University Press.

Keynes, J. M. (1937a), 'Alternative Theories of the Rate of Interest', *Economic Journal*, 47, reprinted in C.W., vol XIV, 1973, 201–15.

Keynes, J. M. (1937b), 'The "Ex Ante" Theory of the Rate of Interest', *Economic Journal*, 47, reprinted in C.W., vol. XIV, 1973, 215–23.

Keynes, J. M. (1940), *How to Pay for the War*, London, Macmillan, reprinted in C.W., vol. IX, 1972, 367–439.

Keynes, J. M. (1973), *The General Theory and After: Part II Defence and Development*, C.W., vol. XIV, edited by Donald Moggridge, London and Basingstoke, Palgrave Macmillan.

Kurz, Heinz D. and Neri Salvadori (1995), *Theory of Production: A Long-Period Analysis*, Cambridge, Cambridge University Press.

Mandler, M. (1999), *Dilemmas in Economic Theory*, Oxford, Oxford University Press.

Marris, R. L. (1964), *The Economic Theory of 'Managerial' Capitalism*, London, Macmillan.

Meade, J. E. (1966), 'The Outcome of the Pasinetti Process: a Note', *Economic Journal*, 76, 161–65.

Milgate, M. (1982), *Capital and Employment: A Study in Keynes's Economics*, London, Academic Press.

Moggridge, D. E. (1976), *John Maynard Keynes*, Harmondsworth, Middlesex, England, Penguin Books Ltd.

McCombie, J. S. L. and A. P. Thirlwall (1994), *Economic Growth and the Balance-of-Payments Constraint*, Houndmills, Basingstoke, Hants., Palgrave Macmillan.

Pasinetti, L. L. (1962), 'Rate of Profit and Income Distribution in Relation to the Rate of Economic Growth', *Review of Economic Studies*, 29, 267–79.

Pasinetti, L. L. (1981), *Structural Change and Economic Growth*, Cambridge, University Press.

Pasinetti, L. L. (1993), *Structural Economic Dynamics*, Cambridge, Cambridge University Press.

Pasinetti, L. L. (1997), 'The Principle of Effective Demand', in G. C. Harcourt and P. A. Riach (eds), *A 'Second Edition' of The General Theory, Volume I*, London, Routledge, 93–104.

Robinson, E. A. G. (1947), 'John Maynard Keynes 1883–1946', *Economic Journal*, 57, 1–68.

Robinson, Joan (1953–54), 'The Production Function and the Theory of Capital', *Review of Economic Studies*, 21, 81–106.

Robinson, Joan (1980; 1985), 'The Theory of Normal Prices and Reconstruction of Economic Theory', in G. R. Feiwel (ed.), *Issues in Contemporary Macroeconomics and Distribution*, London, Macmillan, 157–65.

Rowthorn, R.E. (1977), 'Conflict, Inflation and Money', *Cambridge Journal of Economics*, 1, 215–39.

Salter, W. E. G. (1960), *Productivity and Technical Change*, Cambridge, Cambridge University Press.

Sinha, Ajit (2010), *Theories of Value from Adam Smith to Piero Sraffa*, New Delhi and Abington, Routledge.

Sraffa, Piero (1951), 'Introduction' to *The Works and Correspondence of David Ricardo, Volume I, On the Principles of Political Economy and Taxation*, ed. Piero Sraffa with the collaboration of M. H. Dobb, Cambridge, Cambridge University Press, xiii–lxii.

Sraffa, Piero (1960), *Production of Commodities by Means of Commodities. Prelude to a Critique of Economic Theory*, Cambridge, Cambridge University Press.

Wood, A. (1975), *A Theory of Profits*, Cambridge, Cambridge University Press.

Young, Warren (1987), *Interpreting Mr. Keynes*, Cambridge, Polity Press.

12
What Is the Cambridge Approach to Economics? (2007)*

Introduction

I take the Cambridge approach to economics to mean the approaches of the great days of the Faculty of Economics and Politics in Cambridge (it is now, significantly, the Faculty of Economics – period). Those days were principally associated with the development of Economics as a separate Tripos[1] from 1903 on and ending with the retirement, then deaths of the first generation of Keynes's 'pupils' and/or close colleagues – Piero Sraffa, Joan Robinson, Austin Robinson, Richard Kahn, James Meade, Nicky Kaldor, David Champernowne and Brian Reddaway – in the 1980s and 1990s.[2]

The dominant group in the Faculty at present seems to wish the Faculty to be a clone of the leading United States departments, especially Harvard, MIT, Stanford and Yale, for example, but certainly not Chicago. In doing so it seems to have forgotten two important principles of good economics: comparative advantage and a role for differentiated products. As a liberal educator I strongly support teaching students what is going on at the frontiers of mainstream research in a discipline, even if it is done in a critical manner (after all, we are talking about *university* education); but I also think it sensible, indeed necessary, to preserve what elsewhere I have called the Cambridge tradition, in which I was brought up in Australia in the early 1950s and to which I have tried to contribute over my working life (still going on) at Adelaide,

* Originally published as Geoffrey Harcourt (2007), 'What Is the Cambridge Approach to Economics?' in Eckhard Hein and Achim Truger (eds), *Money, Distribution and Economic Policy. Alternatives to Orthodox Macroeconomics*, Cheltenham, UK and Northampton, MA: Edward Elgar Publishing, pp. 11–30.

Cambridge and elsewhere; see Harcourt (2001a, 2001b, 2003, 2006), Harcourt and Kerr (2003), for example. In this chapter I concentrate on the approaches and methods which are characteristic of economists steeped in the Cambridge tradition.

Malthus

I start with Thomas Robert Malthus, a Fellow of my college, Jesus, the person called by Keynes 'The first of the Cambridge economists', (Keynes [1933] 1972, p. 71) – by which he meant the first person to think like Keynes (Keynes never considered modesty a virtue). Keynes admired the first edition of the *Essay* on population (Malthus 1798) more than the second edition (1803) because, though it was mostly deductive in form, it was so all-of-a-piece that its message came through loud and clear, at times in an extremely witty fashion. In the second edition, this clarity was rather overlaid by copious empirical evidence and qualifications of ifs and buts – see Keynes ([1933] 1972, pp. 34–35).[3]

Marshall and his legacy

This last was also an outstanding characteristic of Keynes's other mentor in economics, Alfred Marshall, whose capacity for putting up fog-like smoke screens when weak points in an argument, or unpalatable conclusions were present, was second to none. I thoroughly agree with Joan Robinson. She wrote: 'The more I learn about economics the more I admire Marshall's intellect and the less I like his character' (Joan Robinson [1953b] 1973, p. 259). Her judgment is amply confirmed with detailed evidence, evidence which does *not* detract from the essential message, by my former PhD student and distinguished Marshall scholar, Rita McWilliams Tullberg. Rita coupled her evaluation of Marshall with her admiration (universally shared in the profession, I would guess) of Mary Paley Marshall, whose treatment by Marshall after they married is a major scandal of our trade; see, for example, McWilliams Tullberg 1990, 1991, 1992, 1995.

Be that as it may, Marshall *was* a really great economist. He bequeathed to us his development of demand and supply analysis as a means of handling that elusive but fundamental concept, time, by his partial equilibrium approach incorporating three different analytical periods – market, short and long. Not that this allowed him ever fully to overcome the basic inconsistency in his 'vision'. On the one hand, there is his understandable pride in his development of static, partial equilibrium analysis with its judicious use of the *ceteris paribus* pound in order to illuminate complex real-life situations. On the other hand, there is his 'vision' of economies as evolving organic systems so that biology and its method, rather than (classical) physics and its method, were the appropriate analogy and framework.

In one sense it has been the endeavour to break out of the first approach and form ways of working within the second that has been the greatest challenge and organiser of the contributions of the people I have placed in the Cambridge tradition. Naturally enough, no one has been completely successful but all saw the problem clearly and worked away at providing solutions. To my mind, the two who have come closest, and so bequeathed to us the most promising ways forward, are Richard Goodwin and Kalecki. They developed their ideas pretty much independently of each other but had in common some of the same mentors – Smith, Marx and Keynes, for example.[4]

Marshall also worked with a dichotomy between the real and the monetary. Breaking out of this in order to analyse the nature of a monetary production economy was the greatest challenge that Marshall's most illustrious pupil, Keynes, was to face. Marshall also provided the ingredients but was very timid about using them himself for the other major strand that came out of his work – the rise of the economics of welfare through his successor in the Chair of Political Economy, A. C. Pigou, and continued to this day by, for example, Tony Atkinson and, of course, Amartya Sen. Atkinson acknowledges James Meade's influence and example – part of Meade's great range of contributions was his deep concern with equity and equality in economic policy and political life generally. Sen is an obvious successor to Pigou in this strand of Marshall's influence.[5] But I shall leave this strand for others to write on as I want to concentrate on Keynes and his contributions and on those of his followers, not only because macroeconomics is the subject of the conference[6] but also because it is the developments associated with it that I am most familiar with from teaching and research.

Both strands reflect Marshall's desire that even more than light-bearing, economics should be fruit-bearing, that is to say, have sensible applications to the making of policy. Pigou's *Economics of Welfare* (1920) was one of the first major examples of this philosophy; and, of course, Keynes's approach is the example *par excellence*, the inspiration and example for many of the people whose contributions I discuss below.

Keynes

Keynes was Marshall's pupil after he graduated in 1905 and was preparing for the Civil Service examinations. As an undergraduate, though, he read mathematics and spent much time on philosophy, including moral and political philosophy. G. E. Moore and Edmund Burke were major influences on him at that time and subsequently. He always regarded economics as a branch of moral philosophy, even though Marshall, after a long battle, had created a separate Economics Tripos by the time Keynes became his pupil. Incidentally, the first major book in political economy that Keynes read was William Stanley Jevons's *The Theory of Political Economy* (1871). He remained an admirer of Jevons, who 'chiselled in stone', as opposed to Marshall (whose *Principles* he also admired) who 'knitt[ed] in wool' (Keynes [1933] 1972, p. 131). Until after the publication of *A Treatise on Money* in 1930, Keynes claimed to be working within the Cambridge and especially the Marshallian approach to economics, using supply and demand analysis, distinguishing between market, short and long periods, accepting at least for the long period, a dichotomy between the real and the monetary so that in monetary matters the quantity theory of money explained the general price level, and viewing markets and systems as equilibrating mechanisms.

The role of the economic analyst was to explain the conditions of equilibrium, the forces that would return the system to equilibrium if it had been shocked away from it, and the mode of transition between one equilibrium position and another new one when the values of the fundamentals determining the equilibrium position changed. In what was intended to be his masterpiece, a definitive treatise on money, Keynes wrote:

> My object has been to find a method which is useful in describing, not merely the characteristics of static equilibrium, but also those of disequilibrium, and to discover the dynamical laws governing the passage of a monetary system from one position of equilibrium to another. (Keynes [1930] 1971, p. *xvii*)

It is true that early on after the end of World War I Keynes was putting more emphasis on short-term malfunctions and the need for theory and policy to cope with them than did Marshall—hence Keynes's best known remark about the long run and mortality, which was included in the passage in *A Tract on Monetary Reform* [1923] (1971) where he was cheeking his old teacher.[7] But in *A Treatise on Money* he still felt inhibited about tackling in too great detail, the intricate analysis of short-period output in aggregate because it was out of place in a treatise on money; see, for example, Keynes (1973a, pp. 145–46).

Yet events and the increasing realisation of the significance of what he had learnt from his philosophical musings, together with the influence of Richard Kahn in particular[8] and the members of the 'circus' in general, his close association with Dennis Robertson in the 1920s and arguments with Ralph Hawtrey, led Keynes increasingly to change his approach. He brought into play three main philosophical tenets for a subject such as economics. Their source is *A Treatise on Probability* (Keynes [1921] 1973), the published version of his fellowship dissertation for King's College, Cambridge, in 1908–1909. He argued that, in certain disciplines, of which economics is a leading example, the whole need not be only the sum of the parts. Keynes's realisation of this, that overall systems could have separate lives of their own, that the behaviour of parts could itself be constrained by overall relationships, and that profound implications follow from this, played an increasingly important influence in his subsequent work in economics. His full and mature realisation of all this came to fruition in *The General Theory* (Keynes [1936] 1973), especially in one of the meanings that he gave to the term 'general', and his repeated stress on the need to avoid the fallacy of composition when the workings of the economy as a whole are analysed. In the preface to the French edition (20 February 1939) he wrote:

> I mean [by a *general* theory] that I am chiefly concerned with the behaviour of the economic system as a whole … I argue that important mistakes have been made through extending to the system as a whole conclusions which have been correctly arrived at in respect of a part of it taken in isolation. (Keynes 1973, p. xxxii)

Another issue which preoccupied Keynes in *A Treatise on Probability* was his systematic pondering on the principles of reasonable behaviour in an uncertain environment. This fitted with Marshall's stress, which runs through the *Principles* (Marshall [1890] 1961), on the nature of reasonable behaviour of businesspeople, particularly in their own uncertain environments. Of course, Keynes also discussed not too sensible or reasonable behaviour by decision makers of all kinds in a similar environment and their implications for systemic behaviour. Ted Winslow (2005) puts far more stress on economic decision making being *not* sensible and on Keynes arguing this than I have. After reading his closely argued and documented paper I am more inclined to agree with his emphasis.

Keynes's philosophical reasoning also discerned many different appropriate languages for different situations, issues and aspects or dimensions of both of them. In effect he believed there was a spectrum of such languages running all the way from poetry and intuition through lawyer-like arguments to mathematics and formal logic. All these were consistent in their appropriate settings with arguments being possible and knowledge being acquired (see Harcourt 1987, Sardoni 1992).

The major outcome of these endeavours was the publication of *The General Theory* in 1936. It contains Keynes's analysis of a monetary production economy in which the dichotomy between the real and the monetary has been scrapped, money being integrated in the analysis right from its start. The equilibrium method was retained, but the equilibrium of the system – perhaps rest state is a better phrase – need not be the special case of full employment; investment leads and saving responds, mostly through changes in income associated with the working of the Kahn-Meade multiplier, with the rate of interest being determined principally in the money market by reconciling the demand for and supply of money; and the expected rates of profit on investments having to match up to the nominal rate of interest (rather than as in 'classical' thought, the nominal rate being consistent with the natural rate in order to avoid cumulative inflations or deflations, a Wicksellian as well as Keynesian insight). The general price level was principally determined in the short term by the productivity of variable factors, primarily labour and the level of the money wage. In 1937, Keynes added the finance motive as an important determinant of the demand for money, drawing attention to the availability of finance as the ultimate constraint on investment expenditure rather than the willingness to save; see Keynes (1973b, pp. 201–26). Meade put it very well when he wrote that 'Keynes's intellectual revolution was to shift economists from thinking normally in terms of a model of reality in which a dog called *savings* wagged his tail labelled *investment* to thinking in terms of a model in which a dog called *investment* wagged his tail labelled *savings*' (Meade 1975, p. 82, emphasis as original).

Though Keynes remained essentially a Marshallian equilibrator in method, he did take us a considerable way towards tackling dynamic processes and tendencies with his method and theory of shifting equilibrium (Keynes [1936] 1973, pp. 293–94). By it he allowed feedbacks from one set of determinants of rest states to other sets if, initially, the rest states, in particular the point of effective demand, were not achieved; see Kregel (1976). This constituted a bridge which partly allowed the profession to move from static analysis to more evolutionary, dynamic analysis of the second part of Marshall's 'vision' and provided the base on which the post-war developments by Keynes's colleagues principally were to build. Keynes also adapted the apparatus of *The General Theory*, the use of aggregate demand and supply relationships, to analyse inflationary situations such as were expected to arise in wartime; see 'How to pay for the War' (Keynes 1978, ch. 2). This illustrates that, theoretically and subsequently through wartime policies, he had indeed created a *general* theory of employment, interest and money, and now prices as Omar Hamouda (1997) pointed out. Finally, David Vines makes crystal clear in his splendid review article (2003) of Robert Skidelsky's third volume of his majestic biography of Keynes (Skidelsky 2000), that, in his wartime writings for the Treasury and for Bretton Woods, Keynes laid the conceptual foundations for post-war international macroeconomic analysis and policy.

Joan Robinson and colleagues

During the 1920s and 1930s both Kahn and Joan Robinson used Marshall's approach and method in their pioneering contributions to the theory of imperfect competition – Kahn in *The Economics of the Short Period* ([1929] 1989),[9] Joan Robinson in *The Economics of Imperfect Competition* (1933a). They were both tackling a real question: why did firms survive in prolonged slump conditions, albeit with excess capacity, when the implications of Marshallian/Pigouvian analysis of competitive conditions was either full capacity working or complete shut down. But, as we shall see, Joan Robinson subsequently repudiated the method of her book, saying it was 'a shameless fudge', to wit, that the equilibrium price and quantity for each mini-monopoly in a competitive environment waited patiently 'out there' to be found by trial and error, the groping process of business people's price setting and production and employment decisions. That is to say, there is a denial of path-dependence processes so that where the firm ended up was independent of the path that it took to get there; see, for example, Joan Robinson ([1953a], 1960, p. 234) for a succinct statement of her argument. In the first ever issue of what Dennis Robertson called 'the Green Horror', the *Review of Economic Studies*, Kaldor clearly outlined the nature of path dependence in what must have been one of his earliest published papers (1934).[10] Kahn, Meade, Austin and Joan Robinson and Piero Sraffa were continuously criticising and helping Keynes as he moved from *A Treatise on Money* to the making of *The General Theory* (see Keynes, 1973a, Harcourt 1994; 1995). Kahn provided an essential ingredient with his (and Meades's) concept of the multiplier; Joan Robinson provided two preliminary reports (Joan Robinson 1933b, 1933c).[11] After the publication of *The General Theory*, she published her 'told to the children' version of the new theory, (Joan Robinson [1937a] 1969), and a selection of essays (Joan Robinson [1937b] 1947), which extended the theory to the open economy, foreign exchange markets and the Marshallian long period at the level of the economy as a whole. She still used Marshall's method and orthodox concepts, for example, the then fashionable concept of the elasticity of substitution between capital and labour in an explanation of the distribution of income between profits and wages in the Keynesian consumption function. Austin Robinson wrote an illuminating review of *The General Theory* in *The Economist* in 1936; his own work after that was very much the application in a common but deep sense of what he found in Marshall's *Principles* and *The General Theory* (see Harcourt 1997, 2001a).[12]

Joan Robinson and Sraffa

Sraffa was rather intellectually aloof from these contributions. He, of course, provided criticism – he was already renowned for his remorseless logic and critical skills – but he was preoccupied with the edition of Ricardo's works and correspondence (which finally emerged in 1951!) and his conceptual critique of the foundations of the neoclassical theory of value and distribution combined with the rehabilitation of Classical economics, especially its organising concept of the surplus and its long-period method (Sraffa 1960). He had mounted a devastating attack on Marshall's partial equilibrium method and its limited application to the real world in his 1925, 1926 and 1930 articles and his lectures at Cambridge at the end of the 1920s. His 1926 article served as an impetus to Joan Robinson to write her 1933 book. He also, at this time, developed at least one basic aspect of the critique of Neoclassical capital theory in the 1950s–1970s (see Bradford and Harcourt 1997, p. 131). Sraffa did ruthlessly and enthusiastically support Keynes in the fight back against Hayek's criticisms of *A Treatise on Money* (see Sraffa 1932).

Joan Robinson first met Kalecki in 1936 and quickly recognised that he had independently discovered the principal propositions of *The General Theory*: furthermore, his discoveries were placed in a more appropriate setting, a Marxian analysis of capitalism using the departmental schema of production and reproduction. This became even more clear to her after she read Marx at the beginning of the war and wrote her 1942 *An Essay on Marxian Economics*. By the time she wrote *The Accumulation of Capital* (Joan Robinson [1956] 1969) she was mainly working within a Kaleckian framework.

Post-war developments

In the post-war period there were two, possibly three major developments in Cambridge concerning approaches and topics.[13] The first is what Joan Robinson called 'the generalisation of *The General Theory* to the long period'. This had two major stimuli: the seminal writings on dynamic theory by Roy Harrod in his 1939 article and 1948 book; and the awakened interest in the post-war era in development problems in both war-torn Europe and in the developing countries themselves. The major contributors to this in Cambridge were Joan Robinson, Kaldor, Kahn, Goodwin, Allan Brown and Richard Stone, and in my generation, Luigi Pasinetti.[14] Kalecki independently tackled similar problems.

The developments were a new look at the old Classical and Marxian preoccupations with distribution, accumulation and growth, tackled afresh in the light of the 'Keynesian' revolution. For Kahn and Joan Robinson, two steps were involved: first, working within a 'Golden Age' framework – the analysis of mythical situations – in order to set out precise definitions of core concepts, and of the relationships between them, in order to get a 'feel' on the nature of development and its accompanying interrelationships within a mostly competitive capitalist structure, (though the economics of planned economies, usually of a democratic socialist variety, were not completely neglected).

The analysis that was most difficult technically yet said by Joan Robinson to be of secondary importance in an analysis of the growth process was the analysis of the choice of techniques in the investment decision at the level of the economy as a whole. It was, though, linked on to the second preoccupation, the critique of the conceptual foundations of the neoclassical theory of value and distribution, in Cambridge associated with Joan Robinson and, most fundamentally, with Piero Sraffa in what became known as the Cambridge – Cambridge controversies in the theory of capital (see Harcourt 1969, 1972, Cohen and Harcourt 2003, Bliss *et al.* 2005). There were again two strands to this: a doctrinal critique of concepts within the framework of either stationary states or steadily growing Golden Ages; and a methodological critique associated with using 'differences' to analyse 'changes'. This procedure, it was argued, was common to the method associated with the revival of Classical political economy by, for example, Sraffa, and to Neoclassical procedures associated with comparative statics analysis.[15]

Returning to the first theme, Golden Age analysis was a preliminary to the more satisfyingly fruitful task of analysing situations in historical as opposed to logical time. In logical time we try to answer questions framed as 'what would be different if ...'. In historical time we ask 'what would follow if ...'.[16] Here Kahn and Joan Robinson, on the one hand and Kaldor, on the other, diverge.

From the very start Kaldor intended his analysis to relate exclusively to the second theme. He started from his famous concept of 'stylized facts'

– observed empirical regularities on development and distribution that needed to be explained by the then emerging models of growth, many of them his. He had in common with Sraffa, Joan Robinson and Kahn dissatisfaction with mainstream theories of value, distribution and growth, as witnessed to in probably his best known paper, 'Alternative theories of distribution' (Kaldor 1955–56). In it, having set out and dismissed all that had gone before, he set out his version of a 'Keynesian' macroeconomic theory of distribution, albeit set in the long period and assuming full employment. Kalecki had already in the 1930s provided such a theory for the short period and without assuming full employment while explicitly including microeconomic pricing behaviour; see especially Kalecki (1936). Also, in common with Joan Robinson and Kahn, Kaldor provided a solution to one of Harrod's problems, whereby if there was a divergence between the warranted rate of growth, g_w, and the natural rate of growth, g_n, a change in distribution would so change the value of the overall saving ratio (because of the different saving behaviour at the margin of wage-earners and profit-receivers) as to make g_w approach g_n in value.

Joan Robinson set out the methodological critique very clearly but never solved the problem of analysis in historical time itself. She wrote:

> The short period is here and now, with concrete means of production in existence. Incompatibilities in the situation ... will determine what will happen next. Long-period equilibrium is not at some date in the future; it is an imaginary state of affairs in which there are no incompatibilities in the existing situation, here and now. (Joan Robinson 1962b, p. 690; 1965, p. 101 in the 1965 reprint)

By the late 1960s Kaldor decided that he had failed to solve the same problem. He changed direction for the rest of his life, incorporating an insight from his teacher at the London School of Economics (LSE), Allyn Young, the concept of cumulative causation,[17] about which I say more below.

Capital theory critique

As I noted, there were two aspects to the capital theory critique. The first was in effect a doctrinal critique in which it was legitimate to use highly abstract constructions in order to express in an ideal setting the fundamental stance of an approach, for example, that in neoclassical economics price is an index of scarcity. The object is to see whether in these settings, the insight rigorously goes through, that the theory meets Sraffa's stringent conditions for a theory to be logically robust. He stated the conditions in his intervention in the discussion at the Corfu Conference on capital theory.

> [O]ne should emphasise the distinction between two types of measurement. First, there was one in which the statisticians were mainly interested. Second, there was measurement in theory. The statisticians' measures were only approximate and provided a suitable field for work in solving index number problems. The theoretical measures required absolute precision. Any imperfections in these theoretical measures were not merely upsetting, but knocked down the whole theoretical basis... The work of J. B. Clark, Böhm-Bawerk and others was intended to produce pure definitions..., as required by their theories... If we found contradictions, ... these pointed to defects in the theory. (Sraffa 1961, pp. 305–6)

The capital-reversing and reswitching results were taken to undermine the conceptual foundations of the Neoclassical theory of distribution, especially in its aggregate production function and marginal productivity forms, but also, Sraffa, Krishna Bharadwaj, Garegnani and Pasinetti would argue, in all its forms. Bliss, Hahn, Samuelson and Solow, for example, while accepting the results, deny that they constitute a fundamental critique of the highest form of Neoclassical theory (see Dixit 1977). As Cohen and Harcourt (2003, 2005) point out, the disagreement rumbles on.

Joan Robinson, though, increasingly concentrated on the second strand of history versus equilibrium, a strand not acceptable to the Sraffians (neo-Ricardians). (We shall probably never know what Sraffa himself thought.) Her stance is, ironically, increasingly accepted now by the most sophisticated mainstreamers, for example, by Franklin Fisher, at least as far as the application of aggregate production functions to real-world data is concerned and by Bliss, at least as far as high theory is concerned; see Bliss's introduction to Bliss *et al.* (2005).[18]

Of course, the debates were not confined to capital theory because Neoclassical growth models associated with Solow and Swan (eminent Keynesians, I should add) were developed alongside the Cambridge capital theory controversies. As we know they stressed Marshall's 'dynamical principle of "Substitution"... seen ever at work' (Marshall [1890] 1961, p. xv) as a possible solution to Harrod's problems of instability if the economy was not on g_w and how it would approach g_n if initially, they were not equal to one another. 'New' endogenous growth theory is still Neoclassical in inspiration and analysis but also draws on Schumpeter explicitly and later Kaldor (sometimes without knowing it); see Kurz (1997).

To my mind the most promising solution so far to the conundrum in Marshall's approach and the issues raised by Joan Robinson in particular are to be found in Kalecki's later writings and, independently, in Goodwin's writings, especially those which come out of his classic 1967 paper, 'A growth cycle', in the Dobb *Festschrift* volume (Feinstein 1967). In Kalecki's last paper on these issues, published in the *Economic Journal* in 1968, he wrote 'the long-run trend is only a slowly changing component of a chain of short-period situations ... [not an] independent entity' (Kalecki 1968; 1971, p. 165). This viewpoint on method embraces Goodwin's approach of cyclical growth, with trend and cycle indissolubly mixed as well and does, it seems to me, tackle directly Marshall's conundrum. It is, moreover, consistent with the later Kaldor's stress on cumulative causation processes.

As many of you may know, I illustrate these processes and their contrast with the mainstream approach, at least before some convergence between the two started, with the modern writings on path-dependent equilibrium and hysteresis processes, by the analogy of a wolf pack. There are two major views on the workings of markets and economies. The dominant one is akin to a wolf pack running along. If one or more wolves get ahead or fall behind, powerful forces come into play which return them to the pack. (The parallels with the existence of an equilibrium position that is unique and stable, and that the forces responsible for existence are independent of those responsible for stability are, I hope, obvious.) The other view has the forces acting on the wolves who get ahead or fall behind making them get further and further ahead or fall further and further behind, at least for long periods of time. This captures the notions of virtuous or vile processes of cumulative causation.

I submit that theories incorporating these views, plus Kaldor's analysis of markets where stocks dominate flows, and expectations by transactors on both sides of markets dominate the more usual factors determining supply and demand and price setting, as set out in Kaldor (1939), help us to make much more sense of the recent behaviour of foreign exchange, stock and property markets and indeed of whole systems than do the currently fashionable macroeconomic theories. The latter include the use of Frank Ramsey's benevolent dictator model (in a completely inappropriate setting for which it was never intended), representative agent models, real business cycle theory and New Keynesian analysis.[19]

Economic history

Cambridge also has a long and distinguished history associated with contributions to economic history, history of economic theory, and applied and policy work. As to economic history, there is the pioneering work of John Clapham, Maurice Dobb (from a Marxist standpoint), Phyllis Deane, Charles Feinstein, Robin Matthews and Brian Mitchell, principally in a Keynesian setting. Dobb, of course, was the leading Marxist economist in the United Kingdom for many decades; he bequeathed to us a rich legacy of careful scholarship in economic history and history of economic theory with at least two classics, *Political Economy and Capitalism* (Dobb [1937] 1940) and his last book, *Theories of Value and Distribution since Adam Smith* (Dobb 1973), as well as insightful, beautifully written articles on the economic history of Russia and on the problems of developing economies. In addition to her pioneering work on the history of the industrial revolution, Phyllis Deane took over Dobb's lecture slot on the history of theory when he retired and wrote her wonderful little volume, *The Evolution of Economic Ideas* (Deane 1978), which was set in the framework of Kuhn's paradigm explanation of the nature of scientific development. Both Dobb and Deane thought it impossible to make sense of a subject such as economics without analysis of theories, applications, policies and people within their historical context, a point of view which I heartily endorse and try to follow in my teaching and research; see, for example, Harcourt (2006).

The Directors

The Department of Applied Economics (DAE) at Cambridge, alas now no more, has had four outstanding but very different Directors – Richard Stone, Brian Reddaway, Wynne Godley and David Newbery. As my colleague, Michael Kitson, wrote in our joint article reviewing the achievements of 50 years of the National Bureau of Economic Research, (Harcourt and Kitson 1993, Harcourt 2001a), all of their approaches could be placed under the following rubric (with, of course, different emphases).

The Cambridge approach to applied economics ... stresses the limitations of much of orthodox neoclassical theory, however elegant, in explaining economic phenomena in the real world. Instead, it emphasises the importance of relevance in economics, incorporating the lessons of history, the institutional context and prevailing social and political conditions. Theory and measurement are thus mutually interdependent as robust empirical analysis is dependent on relevant theory, which in turn depends on reliable observations. Cambridge advances in theoretical and applied economics have, therefore, gone hand in hand. Furthermore, techniques have never been allowed to obscure the analysis – the medium is not the message. (Harcourt and Kitson 1993, Harcourt 2001a, p. 221)

When Stone ceased to be Director in 1955 he directed and developed with Allan Brown the Cambridge growth project. It combined in an integrated whole previous work on demand analysis, input-output analysis and the national accounts, all of which featured in the research of the DAE under Stone's Directorship. Reddaway and Godley shared an affinity in that Marshall and Keynes were their principal mentors. Reddaway presided over down-to-earth, common sense applied projects, usually with implications for policy. Respect for what data actually means and what it could and could not tell us, and a healthy scepticism about techniques divorced from what the basic data could take predominated. Godley drew on Marshall's concept of the long period and Keynes's analysis of the processes at work in modern capitalism to provide a logical framework of relationships incorporating the profit and loss account, the balance sheet and funds statement, macroeconomic constraints that must always bind in empirical work on explanation and policy. Newbery is very much a sophisticated Marshallian interested in applied microeconomic problems and also in developing economies and, now, the problems of transition economies.

In his later years Meade returned to his Keynesian roots and combined his humane civilised outlook with the use of the techniques of control engineers. (He first came across these in the work of his great friend and protégé at the LSE, Bill Phillips.) Meade worked with Andrew Blake, David Vines and Martin Weale as well as with control engineers (see Meade 1982, Vines *et al.* 1983, Weale *et al.* 1989).

The Cambridge tradition today

There are still some colleagues in the Faculty at Cambridge working within the Cambridge tradition as I have defined it – Gabriel Palma, Bob Rowthorn, Ajit Singh, Frank Wilkinson, for example – and on method, principally through Tony Lawson's influential contributions to critical realism; see, for example, Lawson (1997, 2003). As I often tell Lawson, the central core of truth in critical realism is to be found in Marx's method and Keynes's methodological critique of Tinbergen's early econometric work on investment – but I would say that, wouldn't I.

Frank Hahn is not within this tradition, at least not consciously. But his courageous attacks on the Monetarists and New Classical macroeconomics seem to suggest that he recognises aspects of Keynes's method when he writes that he finds himself at times able only to provide 'arguments that are merely plausible rather than clinching' (Hahn 1982, p. xi).

Here I must close if only for reasons of space and exhaustion. I hope I have written enough to encourage readers to chase up at least some of the readings in the references at the end of the chapter.

Notes

1. Previously Economics was part of the Moral Sciences Tripos.
2. Though sadly Michal Kalecki never had a permanent post in the Faculty, his influence on Joan Robinson in particular, and his remarkable contributions were so great that he must play a major role in the narrative. Personally, I regard him as the greatest all-round political economist of the twentieth century.
3. Let me quote what Keynes said of Malthus's approach, for the latter is still a role model for economists to follow, and Keynes's beautifully written paragraph is a succinct, lucid description of the Cambridge approach to economics: Malthus was

    above all, a great pioneer of the application of a frame of formal thinking to the complex confusion of the world of daily events. Malthus approached the central problems of economic theory by the best of all routes. He began ... as a philosopher and moral scientist, ... brought up in the Cambridge of Paley, applying the *a priori* method of the political philosopher. He then immersed himself ... in the facts of economic history and of the contemporary world, applying the methods of historical induction and filling his mind with a mass of the material of experience ... finally he returned to *a priori* thought, ... to the pure theory of the economist proper, and sought ... to impose the methods of formal thought on the material presented by events, ... to penetrate these events with understanding by a mixture of intuitive selection and formal principle and thus to interpret the problem and propose the remedy. In short, from being a caterpillar of a moral scientist and a chrysalis of an historian, he could at last spread the wings of his thought and survey the world as an economist! (Keynes [1933] 1972, p. 107)
4. In Goodwin's case we should add Knut Wicksell, Roy Harrod, Wassily Leontief and Joseph Schumpeter.

5. Sen was my exact contemporary as a PhD student at Cambridge in the 1950s. I always thought he would be the first person among my contemporaries at Cambridge who would get the Nobel Prize. Another contemporary who should have but I fear will not, is Luigi Pasinetti, probably the last of the great system builders in our profession and, today, the senior living heir to the Cambridge tradition discussed here.

6. I should say that, as with my mentor Joan Robinson, I regard the dichotomy between micro and macro a major error, a distinction which cannot be defended logically. There is always a macroeconomic background to microeconomic behaviour and vice versa. I think the Marxist view that the macroeconomic foundations of microeconomics are of fundamental importance is a vital insight, see Crotty (1980), and, though not coming from Marx but from Marshall and Keynes, the work of Wynne Godley.

7. 'But this *long run* is a misleading guide to current affairs. *In the long run* we are all dead. Economists set themselves too easy, too useless a task if in tempestuous seasons they can only tell us that when the storm is long past the ocean is flat again.' (Keynes [1923] (1971), p. 65)

8. Kahn wrote a fellowship dissertation for King's in 1928–29 on the economics of the short period and was always sceptical of the quantity theory of money as a causal explanation of the general price level; see note 9.

9. Kahn's dissertation was not published in English until 1989 just after his death. (An Italian translation was published in 1983 due to the efforts of Marco Dardi.) Had it been published in the 1930s, it and his 1931 *Economic Journal* article (Kahn 1931) on the multiplier would surely have seen him receive the Nobel Prize.

10. Kaldor was at the LSE in the 1930s but joined the Cambridge Faculty after the Second World War when he was already well known as an enthusiastic and original Keynesian who had broken with Robbins's and Hayek's approach at the LSE.

11. One was written in 1931 but only published in 1933.

12. He wrote two classics on industrial organisation in the 1930s and 1940s, both using Marshall's methods and incorporating detailed observations on and knowledge about production methods and market structures (Austin Robinson [1931] 1953 and [1941] 1956).

13. I abstract from the influence of Frank Hahn who came to Cambridge in the early 1960s and who, according to Bob Solow, single-handedly pulled the Faculty, kicking and screaming, reluctantly into the 20th century.

14. Maurice Dobb and Amartya Sen also made important contributions, which, however, were on the whole separate from those of the people in the text. Frank Hahn's and Robin Matthews's 1964 survey of growth theory provided the definitive model for survey articles ever afterwards.

15. This is not an uncontroversial view. The most sophisticated neo-classical have a neoclassical (Irving) Fisherian 'vision' of the accumulation process but are often and increasingly suspicious of comparative statics results. Franklin Fisher is an outstanding proponent of this view as is Christopher Bliss. Joan Robinson and the neo-Ricardians shared a classical–Marxian–Keynesian 'vision' of the accumulation process but differed radically on method. The latter argue that the long-period method is the only legitimate

way of doing precise rigorous theory, which Joan Robinson rejects as far as descriptive analysis in historical time is concerned.

16. For a further discussion of the differences, see Joan Robinson (1962a, pp. 23–26).

17. It was independently developed by Gunnar Myrdal and was, of course, to be found in Adam Smith and Thorstein Veblen.

18. My own view veers towards that of Joan Robinson but not completely. I still see a useful and valid role for the classical concept of centres of gravitation as *sometimes* useful short cuts, especially in short-period analysis; see Harcourt (1981; 1982) for why and Harcourt (1965; 1982) and Harcourt and Kenyon (1976) for applications.

19. For a further statement of my views on all this, see Harcourt (2004; 2006).

References

Bliss, C. (2005), 'Introduction: The Theory of Capital: A Personal Overview', in Bliss, C., A. J. Cohen and G. C. Harcourt (eds) (2005), *Capital Theory*, Vol. 1, Cheltenham, UK and Northampton, MA, USA: Edward Elgar, pp. xi–xxvi.

Bliss, C., A. J. Cohen and G. C. Harcourt (eds) (2005), *Capital Theory*, 3 vols, Cheltenham, UK and Northampton, MA, USA: Edward Elgar.

Bradford, W. and G. C. Harcourt (1997), 'Units and Definitions', in Harcourt, G. C. and P. A. Riach (eds), *A 'Second Edition' of The General Theory*, Vol. 1, London: Routledge, pp. 107–31.

Cohen, A. J. and G. C. Harcourt (2003), 'Whatever Happened to the Cambridge Capital Theory Controversies?' *Journal of Economic Perspectives*, 17, 199–214.

Cohen, A. J. and G. C. Harcourt (2005), 'Introduction: Capital Theory Controversy: Scarcity, Production, Equilibrium and Time', in Bliss, C., A. J. Cohen and G. C. Harcourt (eds) (2005), *Capital Theory*, Vol. 1, Cheltenham, UK and Northampton, MA, USA: Edward Elgar, pp. xxvii–lx.

Crotty, J. R. (1980), 'Post-Keynesian Theory: An Overview and An Evaluation', *American Economic Review*, 70, 20–25.

Deane, P. M. (1978), *The Evolution of Economic Ideas*, Cambridge: Cambridge University Press.

Dimand, Mary Ann, Robert W. Dimand and Evelyn L. Forget (eds) (1995), *Women of Value: Feminist Essays on the History of Women in Economics*, Aldershot, UK and Brookfield, US: Edward Elgar.

Dixit, A. (1977), 'The accumulation of capital theory', *Oxford Economic Papers*, 29, 1–29.

Dobb, M. H. [1937] (1940), *Political Economy and Capitalism: Some Essays in Economic Tradition*, London: Routledge.

Dobb, M. H. (1973), *Theories of Value and Distribution since Adam Smith*, Cambridge: Cambridge University Press.

Feinstein, C. H. (ed.) (1967), *Socialism, Capitalism and Economic Growth: Essays Presented to Maurice Dobb*, Cambridge: Cambridge University Press.

Goodwin, R. M. (1967), 'A Growth Cycle', in Feinstein, C.H. (ed.) (1967), *Socialism, Capitalism and Economic Growth: Essays Presented to Maurice Dobb*, Cambridge: Cambridge University Press, pp. 54–58.

Hahn, F. H. (1982), *Money and Inflation*, Oxford: Basil Blackwell.

Hahn, F. H. and R. C. O. Matthews (1964), 'The Theory of Economic Growth: A Survey', *Economic Journal*, 74, 779–902.

Hamouda, O. F. (1997), 'The General Theory of Employment, Interest and Money and Prices', in Arestis, P., G. Palma and M. Sawyer (eds) (1997), *Capital Controversy, Post-Keynesian Economics and the History of Economics: Essays in Honour of Geoff Harcourt*, Vol. 1, London: Routledge, pp. 226–34.

Harcourt, G. C. (1965), 'A Two-Sector Model of the Distribution of Income and the Level of Employment in the Short Run', *Economic Record*, 41, 103–17, reprinted in Sardoni, C. (ed.) (1992), *On Political Economy and Modern Political Economists: Selected Essays of G. C. Harcourt*, London: Routledge, pp. 83–98.

Harcourt, G. C. (1969), 'Some Cambridge Controversies in the Theory of Capital', *Journal of Economic Literature*, 7, 369–405.

Harcourt, G. C. (1972), *Some Cambridge Controversies in the Theory of Capital*, Cambridge: Cambridge University Press.

Harcourt, G. C. (1981), 'Marshall, Sraffa and Keynes: Incompatible Bed-Fellows?' *Eastern Economic Journal*, 5, 39–50, reprinted in Harcourt, G. C. (1982), *The Social Science Imperialists: Selected Essays*, edited by Prue Kerr, London: Routledge, pp. 250–64.

Harcourt, G. C. (1982), *The Social Science Imperialists: Selected Essays*, edited by Prue Kerr, London: Routledge.

Harcourt, G. C. (1987), 'Theoretical Methods and Unfinished Business', in Reese, D. A. (ed.), *The Legacy of Keynes: Nobel Conference*, XXII, San Francisco: Harper & Row, pp. 1–22, reprinted in Sardoni, C. (ed.) (1992), *On Political Economy and Modern Political Economists: Selected Essays of G.C. Harcourt*, London: Routledge, pp. 235–49.

Harcourt, G. C. (1994), 'Kahn and Keynes and the Making of *The General Theory*', *Cambridge Journal of Economics*, 17, 11–23, reprinted in Harcourt, G. C. (1995), *Capitalism, Socialism and Post-Keynesianism: Selected Essays of G. C. Harcourt*, Aldershot, UK and Brookfield, US: Edward Elgar, pp. 47–62.

Harcourt, G. C. (1995), *Capitalism, Socialism and Post-Keynesianism: Selected Essays of G. C. Harcourt*, Aldershot, UK and Brookfield, US: Edward Elgar.

Harcourt, G. C. (1997), 'Edward Austin Gossage Robinson, 1897–1993', *Proceedings of the British Academy*, 94, 1996 *Lectures and Memoirs*, 707–31, reprinted in Harcourt, G. C. (2001a), *50 Years a Keynesian and Other Essays*, London: Palgrave Macmillan, pp. 131–56.

Harcourt, G. C. (2001a), *50 Years a Keynesian and Other Essays*, London: Palgrave Macmillan.

Harcourt, G. C. (2001b), *Selected Essays on Economic Policy*, London: Palgrave Macmillan.

Harcourt, G. C. (2003), 'Cambridge Economic Tradition', in King, J. E. (ed.), *The Elgar Companion to Post Keynesian Economics*, Cheltenham, UK and Northampton, MA, USA: Edward Elgar, pp. 44–51.

Harcourt, G. C. (2004), 'The Economics of Keynes and Its Theoretical and Political Importance: Or, What Would Marx and Keynes Have Made of the Happenings of the Last 30 Years?' In Magnusson, G. and J. Jespersen (eds), *Keynes's General Theory and Current Views: Methodology, Institutions and Policies*, Reykjavik, Iceland: Faculty of Economics and Business Administration, University of Iceland, pp. 17–32.

Harcourt, G. C. (2006), *The Structure of Post-Keynesian Economics: The Core Contributions of the Pioneers*, Cambridge: Cambridge University Press.

Harcourt, G. C. and P. Kenyon (1976), 'Pricing and the Investment Decision', *Kyklos*, 29 (3), 449–77, reprinted in Sardoni, C. (ed.) (1992), *On Political Economy and Modern Political Economists: Selected Essays of G. C. Harcourt*, London: Routledge, pp. 48–66.

Harcourt, G. C. and P. Kerr (2003), 'Keynes and the Cambridge School', in Samuels, W. J., J. E. Biddle and J. B. Davis (eds) (2003), *A Companion to the History of Economic Thought*, Oxford: Blackwell, pp. 343–59.

Harcourt, G. C. and M. Kitson (1993), 'Fifty Years of Measurement: A Cambridge View', *Review of Income and Wealth*, 39(4), 435–47, reprinted in Harcourt, G. C. (2001a), *50 Years a Keynesian and Other Essays*, London: Palgrave Macmillan, pp. 219–37.

Harcourt, G. C. and P. A. Riach (eds) (1997), *A 'Second Edition' of The General Theory*, 2 Vols, London: Routledge.

Harrod, R. F. (1939), 'An Essay in Dynamic Theory', *Economic Journal*, 49, 14–33.

Harrod, R. F. (1948), *Towards a Dynamic Economics: Some Recent Developments of Economic Theory and Their Application to Policy*, London: Macmillan.

Jevons, W. S. (1871), *The Theory of Political Economy*, London: Macmillan.

Kahn, R. F. [1929] (1989), *The Economics of the Short Period*, Houndmills, Basingstoke: Macmillan.

Kahn, R. F. (1931), 'The Relation of Home Investment to Unemployment', *Economic Journal*, 41, 173–98.

Kaldor, N. (1934), 'A Classificatory Note on the Determinates of Equilibrium', *Review of Economic Studies*, 1, 122–36.

Kaldor, N. (1939), 'Speculation and Economic Stability', *Review of Economic Studies*, 7, 1–27.

Kaldor, N. (1955–56), 'Alternative Theories of Distribution', *Review of Economic Studies*, 23, 83–100.

Kalecki, M. (1936), 'Pare uwag o teorii Keynesa', *Ekonomista*, 3, 18–26, English translation by Targetti, F. and B. Kinda-Hass (1982), 'Kalecki's review of Keynes' General Theory', *Australian Economic Papers*, 21, 245–53.

Kalecki, M. (1968), 'Trend and Business Cycles Reconsidered', *Economic Journal*, 78, 263–76, Reprinted in Kalecki, M. (1971), *Selected Essays on the Dynamics of the Capitalist Economy, 1933–70*, Cambridge: Cambridge University Press, pp. 165–83.

Kalecki, M. (1971), *Selected Essays on the Dynamics of the Capitalist Economy, 1933–70*, Cambridge: Cambridge University Press.

Keynes, J. M. [1921] (1973), *A Treatise on Probability: Collected Writings*, Vol. VIII, London: Macmillan.

Keynes, J. M. [1923] (1971), *A Tract on Monetary Reform: Collected Writings*, Vol. IV, London: Macmillan.

Keynes, J. M. [1930] (1971), *A Treatise on Money, Collected Writings*, vols. V, VI, London: Macmillan.

Keynes, J. M. [1933] (1972), *Essays in Biography: Collected Writings*, Vol. X, London: Macmillan.

Keynes, J. M. [1936] (1973), *The General Theory of Employment, Interest and Money: Collected Writings*, Vol. VII, London: Macmillan.

Keynes, J. M. (1973a), *The General Theory and After: Part I, Preparation: Collected Writings*, Vol. XIII, London: Macmillan.

Keynes, J. M. (1973b), *The General Theory and After: Part II, Defence and Development: Collected Writings*, Vol. XIV, London: Macmillan.

Keynes, J. M. (1978), *Activities 1939–45: Internal War Finance: Collected Writings*, Vol. XXII, London: Macmillan.

Kregel, J. A. (1976), 'Economic Methodology in the Face of Uncertainty: the Modelling Methods of Keynes and the Post-Keynesians', *Economic Journal*, 86, 209–25.

Kurz, H. D. (1997), 'What Could the "New" Growth Theory Tell Smith Or Ricardo?' *Economic Issues*, 2, 1–20.

Lawson, T. (1997), *Economics and Reality*, London: Routledge.

Lawson, T. (2003), *Reorientating Economics*, London: Routledge.

Lutz, F. A. and D. C. Hague (eds) (1961), *The Theory of Capital*, London: Macmillan.

Malthus, T. R. (1798), (First Essay) *An Essay on the Principles of Population*, London: J. Johnson.

Malthus, T. R. (1803), (Second Essay) *An Essay on the Principles of Population*, London: John Murray.

Marshall, Alfred [1890] (1961), *Principles of Economics*, London: Macmillan.

McWilliams Tullberg, R. (1990), *Alfred Marshall in Retrospect*, Aldershot, UK and Brookfield, US: Edward Elgar.

McWilliams Tullberg, R. (1991), 'Alfred Marshall and the Male Priesthood of Economics', *Quaderni di Storia dell'Economia Politica*, 9(2–3), 235–68.

McWilliams Tullberg, R. (1992), 'Alfred Marshall's Attitude to the *Economics of Industry'*, *Journal of the History of Economic Thought*, 14(2), 257–70.

McWilliams Tullberg, R., T. Raffaelli and E. Biagini (eds) (1995), *Alfred Marshall's Lectures to Women: Some Economic Questions Directly Connected to the Welfare of the Laborer*, Aldershot, UK and Brookfield, US: Edward Elgar.

Meade, J. E. (1975), 'The Keynesian Revolution', in M. Keynes (ed.), *Essays on John Maynard Keynes*, Cambridge: Cambridge University Press, pp. 82–88.

Meade, J. E. (1982), *Stagflation Volume 1: Wage-Fixing*, London: George Allen and Unwin.

Pigou, A. C. (1920), *The Economics of Welfare*, London: Macmillan.

Robinson, E. A. G. [1931] (1953), *The Structure of Competitive Industry*, Cambridge: Cambridge University Press.

Robinson, E. A. G. (1936), 'Mr Keynes on Money', *The Economist*, 24 February, 471–72.

Robinson, E. A. G. [1941] (1956), *Monopoly*, Cambridge: Cambridge University Press.

Robinson, J. (1933a), *The Economics of Imperfect Competition*, London: Macmillan.

Robinson, J. (1933b), 'A Parable of Saving and Investment', *Economica* (N.S.), 13, 75–84.

Robinson, J. (1933c), 'The Theory of Money and the Analysis of Output', *Review of Economic Studies*, 1, 22–26.

Robinson, J. [1937a] (1969), *Introduction to the Theory of Employment*, London: Macmillan.

Robinson, J. [1937b] (1947), *Essays in the Theory of Employment*, Oxford: Blackwell.

Robinson, J. [1942] (1966), *An Essay on Marxian Economics*, London: Macmillan.

Robinson, J. (1953a), 'Imperfect Competition Revisited', *Economic Journal*, 63, 579–93; reprinted in Robinson, J. (1960), *Collected Economic Papers*, Vol. II, Oxford: Basil Blackwell, pp. 222–38.

Robinson, J. (1953b), 'A Lecture Delivered at Oxford by a Cambridge Economist', in Robinson, J., *On Re-reading Marx*, Cambridge: Students Bookshop, reprinted in Robinson, J. (1973), *Collected Economic Papers*, Vol. IV, Oxford: Basil Blackwell, pp. 254–63.

Robinson, J. [1956] (1969), *The Accumulation of Capital*, 3rd edn, London: Macmillan.

Robinson, J. (1962a), *Essays in the Theory of Economic Growth*, London: Macmillan.

Robinson, J. (1962b), 'Review of H. G. Johnson, *Money, Trade and Economic Growth*', *Economic Journal*, 72, 690–92, reprinted in Robinson, J. (1965), *Collected Economic Papers*, Vol. III, Oxford: Basil Blackwell, pp. 100–2.

Sardoni, C. (ed.) (1992), *On Political Economy and Modern Political Economists: Selected Essays of G.C. Harcourt*, London: Routledge.

Skidelsky, R. (2000), *John Maynard Keynes, Volume Three: Fighting for Britain 1937–1946*, London: Macmillan.

Sraffa, P. (1925), 'Sulle relazioni fra costo e quantità prodotta', *Annali di Economica*, II (1), 277–328.

Sraffa, P. (1926), 'The Laws of Returns Under Competitive Conditions', *Economic Journal*, 36, 535–50.

Sraffa, P. (1930), ' "A Criticism" and "Rejoinder" in "Increasing Returns and the Representative Firm: A Symposium" ' *Economic Journal*, 40, 89–92, 93.

Sraffa, P. (1932), 'Dr Hayek on Money and Capital', *Economic Journal*, 42, 42–53.

Sraffa, P. (1960), *Production of Commodities by Means of Commodities: Prelude to a Critique of Economic Theory*, Cambridge: Cambridge University Press.

Sraffa, P. (1961), 'Comment', in Lutz, F. A. and D. C. Hague (eds), *The Theory of Capital*, London: Macmillan, pp. 305–6.

Vines, D. (2003), 'John Maynard Keynes 1937–1946: the Creation of International Macroeconomics', *Economic Journal*, 113, 338–61.

Vines, D., J. M. Maciejowski and J. E. Meade (1983), *Stagflation Volume 2: Demand Management*, London: George Allen and Unwin.

Weale, M., A. Blake, N. Christodoulakis, J. Meade and D. Vines (1989), *Macroeconomic Policy: Inflation, Wealth and the Exchange Rate*, London: Unwin Hyman.

Winslow, T. (2005), *Keynes's Economics: A Political Economy as Moral Science Approach to Macroeconomics and Macroeconomic Policy*, mimeograph, Berlin, 28–29 October, 2005.

Part VI
Policy

13
Markets, Madness and a Middle Way Revisited (2007)*

May I thank the original inhabitants of the land on which we now meet, for their courtesy in having us as their guests?[†]

Just over 14 years ago, I gave the second Donald Horne Address on 'Markets, Madness and a Middle Way' (I have a horrible feeling it was also the last Horne Address). Tonight I want to revisit some of the themes and issues I raised then. February 1992 was a strategic time in which to reflect upon and assess the emerging or emerged effects of the Monetarist experiment in many advanced capitalist economies, together with the rise to dominance of neo-liberal policies backed up by the arguments of economic rationalists. It was also an appropriate time to try to persuade the then Prime Minister, Paul Keating, to have second thoughts about some old-fashioned theories and policies which the ALP government had jettisoned almost entirely but nevertheless were still maintaining relatively open minds about, as the law of unintended consequences began to emerge explicitly and openly.

Though Mrs. (as she then was) Thatcher and President Reagan were credited with being the first to implement the 'Monetarist Revolution,' as far as policy is concerned, in the 1980s, I would argue that they were preceded by yet another great Aussie first in the last year of the Whitlam government (1975) and then again in the years of the Fraser coalition government prior to the election of the Hawke ALP government in 1983. Years of thorough preparation culminated in the ideas

---

* Originally published in *Economic and Labour Relations Review*, vol. 17, April, 2007, pp. 1–10. Corrected version in vol. 18, November, 2007.

advanced through the late 1970s ALP National Committee of Enquiry (on which I was the economist). These ideas were preceded years earlier by the courageous stances of Ralph Willis in the political sphere and Laurie Carmichael in the industrial/ union sphere. They were taken on board by academics such as my great mentor and friend, the late Eric Russell, and had a significant influence on policy at least for the first years of the Accord. As I often remark (at 75, a legitimate procedure) the broad suggestions of Discussion Paper No. 6 on 'Economic Issues and the Future of Australia' (1979) were accepted by Bob Hawke for at least half an hour after he became Prime Minister.

In the 1970s I was openly critical of those Australian economists who, largely innocent of the insights bequeathed to us by Marx, Keynes and Kalecki, provided 'respectable' academic support for Monetarist and like-minded policies. At that time, Paddy McGuiness was critical of those he dubbed 'Kindergarten Marxists'; I adopted his phrase making in talking of our Kindergarten Macroeconomists' (no names, no pack drill). In doing so, I was joining forces with Tommy Balogh and Nicky Kaldor in the UK. Balogh called Monetarism 'the incomes policy of Karl Marx': the need to recreate a reserve army of labour and make the sack an effective weapon again after the years of the Long Boom (the Marxist description) or Golden Age of Capitalism (Julie Schor's, Alan Hughes's and Ajil Singh's description) had swung economic, political and social power from capital to labour. This swing resulted in the relatively short-lived but powerfully irresponsible behaviour of trade unions in many advanced capitalist economies, which was at least partly responsible for the accelerating inflation and then the stagflation episodes of those years. These developments explicitly illustrated the extraordinarily prescient insights of Kalecki's 1943 (!!) classic, *Political Aspects of Full Employment*. Kalecki distinguished sharply between the political economy of getting back to full employment after a prolonged slump, when all classes and pressure groups were in at least temporary agreement about its desirability on the one hand, and sustaining full employment on the other, when profound differences emerged cumulatively (I have discussed these issues more fully in a recent paper on what would Marx and Keynes have made of the last 30 years and more; see Harcourt (2007)).

Tonight I want to concentrate on three issues of topical interest in Australia and elsewhere: the systemic effects of the new objectives and industrial relations legislation of the Howard government; some systemic aspects of the so-called pension crises facing advanced countries, especially those in which population growth is stagnant or declining; and the role of monetary policy in package deals of policies designed to secure full employment, reasonable rates of growth in a stable environment (shades of Gordon Brown) and equitable distributions of income and wealth, not least through the public sector. 'Call me old-fashioned but ...'

II

Before discussing these three topics, let me make a brief but vital methodological statement. What are considered to be to the dominant processes at work in individual markets and indeed whole systems (including ultimately the world as a closed system), make a great difference to the sorts of policies that logically may be advocated. As some of you know, I like to illustrate the two dominant 'visions' of how markets/systems work by a wolf pack analogy. I always add the proviso that as I am not a zoologist I may be completely up the creek about wolf pack behaviour. But as I am also an economist (even though half the people at Monash Economics in 1982 thought I was a sociologist), let me assume that I am right. The mainstream 'vision' (even allowing for path-dependent processes) views market systems as a wolf pack running along. If one or more wolves stray, very powerful forces come into play and quickly (or at least ultimately) bring them back to the pack. The other 'vision', which, though alternative, has most respectable ancestors in Adam Smith, Marx, Thorstein Veblen, Allyn Young, Kaldor and Gunnar Myrdal (in fact even the New Testament: 'For unto everyone that hath shall be given, and he shall have abundance; but from him who hath not shall be taken away even that which he hath' (St Matthew, 25, 28–29)). Within it, if one or more wolves stray, they get further and further ahead of, or fall further and further behind the pack, at least for long periods of time. I hope there is an obvious resemblance between the first scenario and the argument in competitive situations for long-period stable equilibrium positions, in which the powerful forces responsible for existence are independent of those responsible for global and local stability. Similarly, I hope this scenario is also obviously related to the view that time series may be broken down into trend and cyclical components, with the factors responsible for each being largely independent of one another.

The other 'vision' of virtuous or vile cumulative causation processes rejects both the distinction between existence (whether unique or multiple) and stability, indeed often the concept of equilibrium itself, in describing economic processes. It sees, or is at least consistent with seeing, the cycle and trend as indissolubly mixed, separable at best only for statistical reasons, mutually determined so as to make for the cyclical growth processes. This view was pioneered by Richard Goodwin (1967) and Kalecki (1971), independently of one another.

As for the implications for policy, I like to illustrate this by referring to Milton Friedman's 1953 argument for floating exchange rates. Because of his strong Chicago belief in the existence of competitive stable long-period equilibrium positions, he argued that free floats would allow exchange rates quickly to find and then hold to their long-period equilibrium patterns. He argued that speculators, because of their superior knowledge and their greater willingness than mere mortals to take risks, would by their activities hasten both the attainment of such patterns and the return, should there be shocks which temporarily took exchange rates away from them.

But if foreign exchange markets are characterised by cumulative causation processes, not only is there not a stable long-period pattern out there to be found by the operation of competitive markets, but also speculators, by making fluctuations even more extreme and volatile than they otherwise would have been, are systemically harmful, not beneficial. I rest my case as to which scenario makes better sense of the happenings of the 30 years and more since the Bretton Woods rules were abandoned. We also have here a rationale for the various schemes based on the Tobin Tax proposals. My own variant was thought out quite innocently of Tobin's 1970s suggestions, i.e., I was not aware of them, but it is in some sense a generalisation of them. It may be found in my 1994 paper, 'A "Modest Proposal" for taming speculators and putting the world on course to prosperity'. It grew out of an equally modestly titled paper, 'The Harcourt plan to "save" the world', which I wrote in the early 1990s for the first issue of the Cambridge undergraduate Marshall Society's journal, *At the Margin*.

III

I have arrived in Australia this time just as the debates about the new industrial relations legislation and its implementation seem to have come to the boil, not least with the ALP's pledge to scrap AWAs if elected in 2007. Claims and counter claims abound but I want to concentrate on the possible systemic effects of scrapping our time-honoured institutions and encouraging extreme microeconomic bargaining arrangements over wages and other conditions. Let me remind you that our Patron Saint, Adam Smith, stressed that competitive markets only work efficiently and equitably if power is diffused equally on both sides of the market with no one having any individual power at all (he provided many other provisos but this was fundamental). Clearly this condition is not true of Australian labour markets, not only because of their individual characteristics, but also because we have had levels of unemployment which, while not high relatively to much of Europe (for example), are still high enough to do the traditional job of the reserve army of labour. These unemployment levels are sufficient to make the sack effective and to allow the implementation of the 'let managers manage' philosophy so beloved of our political masters and our role models in U.S. capitalism. Incidentally, as Keith Hancock pointed out to me a few weeks ago in Adelaide, history seems to be a forgotten subject – unemployment rates of under five per cent and going down were evidently heralded in the media as the lowest rates ever! I reminded Keith that the remark that most dates my first book, *Economic Activity*, written with Peter Karmel and Bob Wallace and published in 1967, was the claim in chapter 15 (on policy) that any Federal Government that allowed unemployment to rise above two per cent would be unlikely to survive. We had in mind the experience in the early 1960s when a credit squeeze left the Menzies government dependent, I believe, on Communist Party preferences in North Queensland, where Jim Killen was the MP, for the re-election of the coalition government with a tiny majority.

In a special issue of *The Economic and Labour Relations Review* of May 2006, Braham Dabscheck[1] brilliantly analyses the double think, Brave New World aspects of Howard's claims for his legislation. Dabscheck shows clearly how strong the employers' and weak the employees' positions in general are, again echoing Adam Smith's views on the nature of bargaining in labour markets. I do not think Marx would have found much strange or unexpected in Dabscheck's and the other essays on the detailed characteristics of what is proposed, all directed at maximising the potential surplus to be obtained from control of the lengths and intensities of working weeks. Of course, lip service is paid to the virtues of cooperation, of getting together as a team, but in reality it is almost always lip service only. The lot of those workers most directly affected is indeed not a happy one.

But the legislation and new institutions are just extreme characteristics of the creation of so-called flexible labour markets. Obviously, I am not against the creation of institutions which allow inevitable structural changes to be handled with a minimum of social disruption – something Scandinavian countries have been successful, overall, in achieving. They have always understood that social and economic changes take time, sometimes much time, and that the transition has to be underlaid and sustained by all sorts of retraining and relocating measures, as well as by measures to preserve historical communities and their associated infrastructures. As Eric Russell used to say, there is a world of difference between the precise algebra of models of economic phenomena, in which time enters usually only in so far as it has the same dimension as space, and the often painful, time-extended processes of reality. People who advocate major changes on the basis of such guides while holding tenured posts really should ask themselves, every now and then, what *exactly* are they doing.

The late Wilfred Salter, with Eric Russell, played a large part in setting the ground rules for changes in money incomes within package deals of policies in Australia. These packages were designed to maintain full employment without accelerating inflation tending ultimately to take over and make untenable, on Kaleckian grounds, full employment. Kalecki wrote:

> The *maintenance* of full employment would cause social and political changes which would give a new impetus to the opposition of business leaders... 'the sack' would cease to play its role as a disciplinary measure. The social position of the boss would be undermined and the self assurance and class consciousness of the working class would grow. Strikes for wage increases and improvements in conditions of work would create political tension... true... profits would be higher... and even the rise in wage rates... is less likely to reduce profits than to increase prices.... But 'discipline in the factories' and 'political stability' are more appreciated by business leaders than profits. Their class instinct tells them that lasting full employment is unsound from their point of view... that unemployment is an integral part of the normal capitalist system (Kalecki 1943; 1971: 140–41, emphasis in original).

He added: 'big business... would probably find more than one economist to declare that the situation is manifestly unsound' (*ibid* 144).

As ought to be known but is now too often forgotten, Salter published one of the great modern classics of our trade, *Production and Technical Change*, in 1960. The book was based on his PhD at Cambridge in the early 1950s, written under the supervision of Brian Reddaway and brought to fruition by a year at John Hopkins and then by Trevor Swan's careful guidance at the ANU.

Salter developed Marshall's analysis to explain why old and new machines of different vintages, when the latter had greater expected quasi-rents and were more cost-effective, could nevertheless operate side by side in firms and industries. Basically it was because the older vintages only had to expect to cover their variable costs (bygones are bygones) in order to continue operating whereas new machines have to be expected to cover *total* expected costs in order to be installed. The core of the macroeconomic and systemic consequences of this finding is that the overall productivity regime to be established, both level and rates of increase, depends upon the rate at which average wage levels (with their accompanying relative wage structures) increase over time. If they rise at the rate determined by overall productivity (plus prices) then high productivity industries will be encouraged to expand, and low productivity industries will be forced to contract or even shut down. The overall result will be the maximum rate of increase possible in overall productivity in the given situation, as well as in accompanying real incomes. By contrast, if money incomes were to be adjusted by individual levels and rates of increase of productivity, the expansion of high productivity industries would be discouraged while low productivity industries, often already declining, would be able to linger on well past their sell-by dates. The overall productivity regime would *not* allow nearly as high rates of increase of *real* incomes as could have occurred in the alternative scenario. This, in turn, would reinforce the coming into play of Kalecki's scenario and the creation of higher levels of unemployment via policy – so-called short sharp shocks – to push unemployment above its so-called natural rate and so change inflationary expectations, in reality, reversing the distribution of power between labour and capital. You will all remember 'the recession we had to have', to quote a well-known brand of Wrigley's chewing gum – PK.

The Russell–Salter rule thus may be seen to be both efficient and equitable. It is efficient, because it makes the most favourable productivity scenario possible. It is equitable because at the level of the economy as a whole, capital and labour are complements in the production of the national product, and so all classes should be able to receive, at least as a starting point, the same rate of increase of money incomes, to enable them to command the increase in the real fruits of progress forthcoming. Of course, there are all sorts of provisos and exceptions and modifications that need to be taken into account – that is why we had arbitration institutions for so many decades even if John Howard does not understand or appreciate this – but the major starting point needs to be those processes. And it is exactly that starting point that will become impossible under the new 'rules of the game' and Australia will enter – indeed, is more or less already there because of reforms such as enterprise bargaining – the second scenario sketched above. This makes the attainment and sustaining of full employment without undue or accelerating inflation a most difficult if not impossible task. (I am not claiming that the first scenario will *necessarily* go through and the Kaleckian dilemma be solved, only that it would offer a better chance for these desirable outcomes to occur.) Such is the price to be paid for transferring emphasis to narrowly self-interested behaviour from community-wide, cooperative attitudes of citizens in a democracy, acting together through appropriate institutions for the common good of all.

IV

Hazel Bateman and Geoffrey Kingston have most kindly allowed me to read their extremely informative 2006 paper, 'Comparative performance of retirement income schemes in the Anglosphere[2]: An update'. They give a comprehensive account of the retirement institutions and provisions, and of the policies, public and private, of these economies/societies and evaluate their performances, limitations and achievements. Their very careful and detailed analysis puts the so-called pension crisis of the western world into perspective. There clearly problems that have to be tackled but the orders of magnitude, even when there are declining rates of population increase relatively to those of the Baby Boomer era, do not involve insuperable problems.

Because most of the analysis in this whole area implicitly at least assumes a neoclassical world of full employment, the emphasis is mostly on how to raise saving ratios, both private and public. Much of the detailed analysis makes good sense and there is no doubt that some increase in both public and private saving and in taxation rates will need to occur. All this is discussed carefully and in great detail by Bateman and Kingston and also in the recent Turner Report in the United Kingdom (Turner 2006). The latter is noteworthy for arguing for the restoration of the adjustment of state pensions by the rate of increase of earnings (under certain conditions this is the equivalent of following the Russell–Salter rule) rather than by the rate of increase of prices, a 'reform' disgracefully brought in by Mrs. Thatcher near the start of her reign (remember she once said: 'We are a grandmother'). Turner also suggests that the retirement age will have to be modestly increased, a perfectly sensible reform in the round for as longer lengths of life come to be expected, it seems sensible to keep the ratio of working life to retirement life constant, with provisos, of course, for the special needs of specific occupations.

Because of the neoclassical setting of the arguments, one vital consideration is often overlooked, a consideration which though old-fashioned is nevertheless highly relevant. It comes obviously under the rubric of the paradox of thrift – from Mandeville through Malthus and Keynes to the present day. There is no point in devising all sorts of fancy schemes, public and private, for raising the overall rates of saving out of *given* levels of income if we ignore the fact that achieving them *by themselves* may well result in no increase at all in aggregate saving (as opposed to rates) or, indeed, even in a fall in aggregate saving unless steps are taken simultaneously to induce greater rates of investment in both the public and private sectors. It cannot be stated too often that both in industrial economies and in the economic world as a whole, investment leads and saving follows, and that this is as true (with suitable provisos) of situations of full employment as it is of those with unemployment: a simple but profound point, I believe, put beautifully by the late James Meade in what must have been one of his last published statements. Meade wrote:

> In a national closed economy, an increase in investment which takes place in one county (e.g. Somerset) may cause a regional movement of capital funds, and a regional movement of goods from another county (e.g. Dorset), the net movement of capital funds of one kind or another being necessarily equal to the net movement of goods and services. The world economy is a closed economy, and this same net movement of capital funds and goods and services takes place from one country to another, the total multiplier being simply what happens in a closed world economy (Meade 1997: 82).

This paragraph, vintage Meade, succinctly states the themes of Dalziel and Harcourt (1997), Harcourt (2001b), which it took the latter 16 pages to make! See also Meade (1975; 1993).

Coupled with this is the distinction that should always be made, when discussing the process of accumulation, between finance, investment and saving. It is finance that makes investment possible, given satisfactory expected private (and social) returns and sufficient productive capacity; investment in turn creates the saving that accompanies it by induced changes in income. So all the fancy funds being set up in various pension schemes and so on will require the saving created by investment which was prior created by finance as possible vehicles to hold and absorb the new securities so issued (as well as take part in rearrangements of existing portfolios). And it is the level and rate of growth of real resources and capacity to produce which make these possible that has to be matched by the consumption, investment, government spending and net exports occurring, regardless of whether given pension schemes have been 'fully funded' or, in the case of state pensions, met by redistributive taxation, taxing the active to support the previously active who are now having a well-deserved retirement. The latter should be a characteristic of any decent society, as opposed to the view of 'Poor old Dad, too old to work, so we took him outside and shot him.'

V

Finally, I want to make some remarks on monetary policy and monetary / real interactions generally which follow on from the finance → investment → saving nexus I mentioned above. I draw on a contribution I made to the volume in honour of the late Hy Minsky (Harcourt 2000). For me, the essence of Minsky is the following, even though he attributed it – with generous poetic licence, I believe – to Keynes. Production, employment and, especially, investment decisions in firms *have* to be made on the basis of *expected* cash flows. The decisions lead (amongst other things) to financial decisions that imply the locking-in of *certain, inescapable* payments of interest and principal (or their equivalents) which are reflected on the liabilities side of the balance sheets of the firms involved. Expectations usually turn out to be wrong, even though, as Keynes argued, in order to *do* anything at all, rather than starve to death like the stupid ass of antiquity, we have to base our decisions on the convention that the future will be the same as the immediate past and present, unless there are very strong reasons for supposing otherwise. Because of the resulting discrepancies arising from over-realised or under-realised cash flows and committed payments, the consequent actions of business people turn out to be different, often vastly so, than they would have been had expectations been realised. This gives rise to an endogenous cyclical mechanism arising from financial and real factor interactions, with greater amplitudes and deeper and more maintained slumps that would be implied by the inescapable real rhythms in the economy. In recent years the extension of 'credit for all' to consumers has added another set of factors making for even greater instability.

Keynes though, is, as always, relevant: he followed up *The General Theory* with his important articles on the finance motive in 1937. Keynes saw the typical sequence in the accumulation process in a firm and then in the economy as a whole in his time and especially in the UK as follows. An investment project is evaluated by its would-be implementer. An approach is then made to a bank for a short-term loan in order to implement it. The loan may or may not be supplemented from the firm's *past* saving: yesterday's saving may help to determine today's investment and today's saving may help to determine tomorrow's investment, but it is today's investment which determines today's saving. If the expected profits and accompanying cash flows turn out to be correct, the loan may be repaid by floating new equities or debentures without adversely affecting their existing values on the stock exchange. The balance sheet then shows the new investment on the assets side and the short-term liability is transformed into a long-term liability or a rise in shareholders' funds on the other side.

If we generalise to the economy as a whole and postulate a *rise* in total planned investment expenditure, so that Keynes's revolving fund of finance which supports a constant flow of investment no longer suffices, part of the demand for the new flow of securities and debentures comes from the placement of new saving created by the higher levels of investment and induced higher levels of income generated through the multiplier process (remember it?).

As we saw, Minsky superimposed on the real cyclical processes the additional amplitudes associated with unrealised cash flows and the impact on confidence, the 'animal spirits' of business people. How may the banking system ameliorate these sources of instability? To answer, we draw on Marshall and a distinction which J. R. Hicks (as he then was) made in commenting upon Roy Harrod's work on imperfect competition in the 1950s. Hicks distinguished between 'snatchers', those firms that take up all short-term profit opportunities available in an imperfectly competitive environment, regardless of possible long-term adverse effects on their future profits, and 'stickers', those firms that keep long-term profits prospects always at the forefront of their minds and so willingly forego some immediate gains if they are felt to have undesirable long-term effects.

My contention is that trading banks and other providers of finance tend more to be snatchers than stickers. They amplify further Minsky-type fluctuations by being euphoric in the up turn, slack on credit-worthy requirements, but deeply depressed in the down turn, acting in ways that harm the activities of firms, the long-term prospects of which are almost certainly viable, despite their short-term situations. We should therefore encourage banks and other providers of finance to have well stocked research departments that can distinguish between the Marshallian short period and long period, expertly assess long-term prospects and recommend support in the down turn and caution in the up turn, so serving to reduce the effects and size of Minsky-type fluctuations. No one bank can step out of line and expect to survive so the system will have to be induced by Central Bank carrots and sticks to behave in the ways I have suggested.

No doubt much of this is old hat but I felt it a good idea to raise these issues and suggestions, some of which were implicit or even explicit in the Horne Address of over 14 years ago.

Notes

† A lecture delivered at a Public Meeting of the Centre for Applied Economic and Policy Research, held at Swinburne University of Technology, Melbourne on 10 July 2006.

1. The examination of Braham's Masters dissertation on the payment of Aussie Rules footballers was one of the most pleasant tasks I have ever had to do.
2. The Anglosphere includes Australia, Canada, New Zealand, the United Kingdom and the USA.

References

Bateman, H. and Kingston, G. (2006) 'Comparative Performance of Retirement Income Systems in the Anglosphere: An Update', School of Economics, roneo, UNSW.

Bellofiore, R. and Ferri, P. (eds) (2000) *Financial Fragility and Investment in the Capitalist Economy: The Economic Legacy of Hyman Minsky*, Edward Elgar, Cheltenham.

Discussion Paper no. 6 (1979) 'Economic Issues and the Future of Australia', in Australian Political Studies Association, Australia Labor Party National Committee of Inquiry, *Discussion Papers*, APSA Monograph no. 23, Flinders University, Adelaide.

Dabscheck, B. (2006) 'Introduction' and 'The Contract Regulation Club', *Economic and Labour Relations Review*, 16(2), pp. 1–2, 3–24.

Dalziel, P. and Harcourt, G. C. (1997) 'A Note on "Mr Meade's Relation" and International Capital Movements', *Cambridge Journal of Economics*, 21, pp. 621–31, reprinted in Harcourt (2001b), 72–87.

Feinstein, C. (ed) (1967) *Socialism, Capitalism and Economic Growth: Essays Presented to Maurice Dobb*, Cambridge University Press, Cambridge.

Friedman, M (1953) 'The Case for Flexible Exchange Rates', in M. Friedman, *Essays in Positive Economics*, Chicago University Press, Chicago, pp. 157–203.

Goodwin, R. (1967) 'A Growth Cycle', in Feinstein (ed.) (1967), pp. 54–58.

Harcourt, G. C. (1992) 'Markets, Madness and a Middle Way', The Second Donald Horne Address, reprinted in *The Cambridge Review*, 114, 1993, pp. 40–45.

Harcourt, G. C. (1993) 'The Harcourt Plan to "Save" the World', *At the Margin*, 1, pp. 2–5.

Harcourt, G. C. (1994) 'A "Modest Proposal" for Taming Speculators and Putting the World on Course to Prosperity', *Economic and Political Weekly*, xxix, 2490–92, reprinted in Harcourt (2001a), pp. 255–62.

Harcourt, G. C. (2000) 'Investment Expenditure, Unrealised Expectations and Offsetting Monetary Policies', in Bellofiore and Ferri (eds) (2000), pp. 69–75, reprinted In Harcourt (2001b), pp. 197–205.

Harcourt, G. C. (2001a) *Selected Essays on Economic Policy*, Palgrave Macmillan, Houndmills, Basingstoke.

Harcourt, G. C. (2001b) *50 Years a Keynesian and Other Essays*, Palgrave Macmillan, Houndmills, Basingstoke.

Harcourt, G. C. (2007) 'The Theoretical and Political Importance of the Economics of Keynes; Or, What Would Marx and Keynes Have Made of the Happenings of the Past 30 Years and More?' In Mathew Forstater, Gary Mongiovi and Steven Pressman (eds) (2007), *Post-Keynesian Macroeconomics: Essays in Honour of Ingrid Rima*, New York: Routledge 2007, pp. 56–69.

Harcourt, G. C., Karmel, P. H. and Wallace, R. H. (1967) *Economic Activity*, Cambridge University Press, Cambridge.

Hicks, J. R. (1954) 'The Process of Imperfect Competition', *Oxford Economic Papers*, 6, pp. 51–54, reprinted as 'Stickers and Snatchers', ch. 12 of John Hicks (1983), *Classics and Moderns, Collected Essays on Economic Theory*, Vol. III, Basil Blackwell, Oxford, pp. 163–78.

Kalecki, M. (1943) 'Political Aspects of Full Employment', *Political Quarterly*, 14, pp. 322–31, reprinted in Kalecki (1971), pp. 138–45.

Kalecki, M. (1971) *Selected Essays on the Dynamics of the Capitalist Economy 1933–70*, Cambridge University Press, Cambridge.

Keynes, J. M. (1937a) 'Alternative Theories of the Rate of Interest', *Economic Journal*, 47, pp. 241–52, reprinted in *Collected Writings*, vol. XIV (1973), pp. 201–15.

Keynes, J. M. (1937b) 'The "Ex-Ante" Theory of the Rate of Interest', *Economic Journal*, 47, pp. 663–69, reprinted in *Collected Writings*, vol. XIV (1973), pp. 215–23.

Meade, J. E. (1975) 'The Keynesian Revolution', ch. 10 in Keynes, M. (ed.), *Essays on John Maynard Keynes*, Cambridge University Press, Cambridge.

Meade, J. E. (1993) 'The Relation of Mr Meade's Relation to Kahn's Multiplier', *Economic Journal*, 103, pp. 664–65.

Salter, W. E. G. (1960) *Productivity and Technical Change*, Cambridge University Press, 2nd ed., with an Addendum by W.B. Reddaway (1966), Cambridge University Press, Cambridge.

Turner, A. et al. (2006) Implementing an Integrated Package of Pension Reforms, The Final Report of the Pensions Commission, Pensions Commission, available http://www.pensionscommission.org.uk/publications/2006/final-report/final_report.pdf.

14

Finance, Speculation and Stability: Post-Keynesian Policies for Modern Capitalism (2010)

I

Maynard Keynes's best known remark is: '*In the long run* we are all dead' (Keynes (1923); *C.W.*, vol. IV, 1971, 65, emphasis in original). This led an IMF wit some years ago to crack: 'Well, he's dead and we're in the long run.' Though Keynes's remark is well known, its context is not. It occurs in his 1923 *Tract on Monetary Reform* in which he is cheeking his old teacher, Alfred Marshall. For he continued: 'Economists set themselves too easy, too useless a task if in tempestuous seasons they can only tell us that when the storm is long past the ocean is flat again' (65). He was arguing for a change in emphasis, from concentrating on the economics of the long period, of the long-period determination of normal competitive equilibrium prices and quantities by the forces of supply and demand, Book V of Marshall's *Principles*, then the bible of most English-speaking economists, to more attention to analysis of, and policy for short-run happenings. But, just before he died, in his last article in the *Economic Journal*, in speeches to the House of Lords and at his Political Economy Club at Cambridge (by then presided over by Dennis Robertson), he bemoaned the fact that the pendulum had swung too far the other way, to an undue concentration on the short period and the neglect of fundamental and lasting truths to be found in the insights of our founder Adam Smith and Keynes's own mentor, Marshall.[1]

If all this has a familiar and topical ring to it, so it should, as we are in the middle of the most serious crisis in the interrelated capitalist world since the 1929–1930s depression years. We have witnessed in recent decades undue concentration by decision-makers, not least in the private sector, the stock exchanges and the foreign exchange markets, on the short term and a relative neglect of the long-term consequences of their decisions. This has been reinforced by technical innovations which have had the effect in many areas of shrinking the length of the short run from months, or even years to weeks, or even days or hours. While these 'real world' events have been unfolding we have also seen a major change in the characteristics of the dominant mainstream analysis of the economy, a return to what Joan Robinson (1964) called many years ago, 'Pre-Keynesian theory after Keynes'. Starting with Friedman and the monetarists, and reinforced by Hayek's philosophical views, we have seen, if not the overthrow then at least the very considerable downgrading of Keynes's and the Post-Keynesian's 'vision' and analysis of the world. At the same time the contributions of another great interpreter of the essential fundamentals of the capitalist process have virtually vanished, for illogical reasons. The overthrow of the so-called socialist economies of Eastern Europe and of the Communist regime of the former USSR do not in themselves refute Marx's insights into how capitalism works, though it was and is so interpreted, not least by Mrs Thatcher as she then was. Yet I have argued that Keynes, Kalecki and Marx, were they still with us, would have made far more sense of what has been happening over the last 30 years and more than do the Lucasians, modern classical macroeconomists, the inappropriate application of Frank Ramsey's model, or even the New Keynesians' concentration on imperfections. Not least does Marx come into his own with his insight that when financial capital is out of kilter with industrial and commercial capital, instability and crises are likely to result; see Harcourt (2007a).

II

Before setting out the framework of analysis that lies behind the policy proposals I shall tentatively suggest, I first pay tribute to, in particular, my Australian mentors, Eric Russell and Wilfred Salter. Because they both died far too young (Salter when he was 34, Eric at 55) and because Eric did not publish a lot, their contributions may not be as well known as they should be. What I write is very much influenced by them and by my Cambridge mentors, especially Joan Robinson, Richard Kahn, Nicky Kaldor, Piero Sraffa, Dick Goodwin and Luigi Pasinetti. Last but certainly not least, discussions with Philip Arestis and reading his papers have much influenced my approaches to economic theory and policy.

Before setting out policies, I need to sketch the characteristics of a post-Keynesian analysis of the processes at work in modern capitalism.

What Joseph Schumpeter called 'vision' and its implications for analysis have profound effects on what policies to propose.

I start by quoting Joan Robinson (1978; C.E.P., vol. V, 1979, 210): 'To me, the expression *post-Keynesian* has a definite meaning; it applies to an economic theory or method of analysis which takes account of the difference between the future and the past' (emphasis in original). So we start by asking how key decision-makers behave, sometimes sensibly, sometimes not, in an environment of inescapable uncertainty, themes about which Keynes wrote incisively in *The General Theory*. Witness his account in chapter 12 of the working of the stock exchange in different situations and economies:

> If I may be allowed to appropriate the term *speculation* for the activity of forecasting the psychology of the market, and the term *enterprise* for the activity of forecasting the prospective yield of assets over their whole life, it is by no means always the case that speculation predominates over enterprise. As the organisation of investment markets improves, the risk of the predominance of speculation does, however, increase. In ... New York, the influence of speculation ... is enormous. Even outside the field of finance, Americans are apt to be unduly interested in discovering what average opinion believes average opinion to be; and this national weakness finds its nemesis in the stock market. It is rare ... for an American to invest, as many Englishmen still do, 'for income'; and he will not readily purchase an investment except in the hope of capital appreciation. This is only another way of saying that, when he purchases an investment, the American is attaching his hopes, not so much to its prospective yield, as to a favourable change in the conventional basis of valuation, *i.e.* that he is ... a speculator. Speculators may do no harm as bubbles on a steady stream of enterprise. But the position is serious when enterprise becomes the bubble on a whirlpool of speculation. When the capital development of a country becomes a by-product of the activities of a casino, the job is likely to be ill-done. The measure of success attained by Wall Street, regarded as an institution of which the proper social purpose is to direct new investment into the most profitable channels in terms of future yield, cannot be claimed as one of the outstanding triumphs of *laissez-faire* capitalism – which is not surprising, if ... the best brains of Wall Street have been in fact directed towards a different object. (Keynes 1936; *C.W.*, vol. VII, 1973, 158–59, emphasis in original)

Secondly, there is a vast divide between how post-Keynesians think of how markets, indeed, systems as a whole, behave, on the one hand, and the mainstream view, on the other (though there has been *some* convergence in recent years with the emergence of path-dependent processes, hysteresis, and so on). Nevertheless, there is still a stranglehold of equilibrating notions on the mainstream in contrast to the increasing emphasis on cumulative causation processes by post-Keynesians. (Cumulative causation originated in Adam Smith's writings, was brought into the modern age by Thorstein Veblen, Kaldor's teacher at LSE, Allyn Young, Kaldor himself, and, independently, by Gunnar Myrdal.) For many years I have illustrated the difference by a wolf pack analogy (which may be untrue of their actual behaviour – I am not a zoologist) but is, I believe, an accurate description of the respective economic theories).

The mainstream approach is that akin to a wolf pack running along. If one or more wolves get ahead or fall behind, powerful forces come into play which return them to the pack. (The parallels with the existence of a unique equilibrium that is stable, and that the forces responsible for existence are independent of those responsible for stability are, I hope, obvious.) The other approach has it that the forces acting on the wolves who stray make them get further and further ahead or fall further and further behind, at least for long stretches of time. (This also corresponds with Goodwin's and the late Kalecki approach that the trend and cycle are indissolubly mixed, not separable concepts determined by independent factors; see, for example, Goodwin (1967), Kalecki (1968), Harcourt (2006)).

Why does the difference matter for policy? Let me illustrate this with Friedman's case for freely floating exchange rates (Friedman (1953)). Underlying his arguments is the first wolf pack analogy, that in a competitive setting there exists a set of stable long-period exchange rates that quickly would be found and kept by a free float. In this setting the systemic effects of speculation would be beneficial, for speculators with their superior knowledge, intelligence and information would help the market to reach the equilibrium pattern more quickly than in their absence, and to sustain it there.

But suppose the second scenario is at least the more correct description of how foreign exchange markets work. Then there is no set of stable long-period rates 'out there' waiting to be found so that now a float combined with speculation will be systemically harmful, accelerating the movements away in both directions of exchange rates from one another and also of systems, at least for long periods of time. The second scenario is more akin to what has happened over recent decades, and provides the rationale for various schemes suggested to curb the actions of speculators.

Next, consider a lesson from Marx, Keynes and Kalecki which was put most neatly by James Meade: 'Keynes's intellectual revolution was to shift economists from thinking normally in terms of a model of reality in which a dog called *savings* wagged his tail labelled *investment* to thinking in terms of a model in which a dog called *investment* wagged his tail labelled *savings*' (Meade 1975, 82, emphasis in original). This profound insight is often forgotten in, for example, discussions of the coming pensions crisis, whereby all sorts of ingenious schemes are suggested to induce more saving over people's working lives but little, if any, mention is made of the necessary condition for them to be successful is that simultaneously there has to be accompanying private and public investment expenditure, otherwise the paradox of thrift will come into its own; see Harcourt (2007b).

Next, in view of the over-, or even sole, reliance in recent years on the rate of interest to control the economy, especially as an anti-inflationary measure, let me paraphrase a wise saying from a very fine but much neglected economist, the late Sir Dennis Robertson: 'People tell me that the bank rate is a beautiful and delicate instrument but I think it is coarse and blunt.' With this should be coupled the insightful comment of the late Tommy Balogh that 'Monetarism is the incomes policy of Karl Marx' (Balogh 1982, 77). He meant, of course, that the manipulation of either the quantity of money and/or the rate of interest through monetary policy has its (uncertain) effects on inflation and activity by its impact on employment, that the creation of a cowed and quiescent workforce by making the sack an effective weapon reduces money-wage demands and so reduces one major cause of inflation.

Michal Kalecki was one of the first political economists to articulate this truth. In his famous paper, 'Political aspects of full employment' (published in 1943!), he analysed the essential difference in the political economy of getting back to full employment after a deep slump when all classes and vested interests would be in an (uneasy) accord, on the one hand, and the political economy of sustaining full employment, on the other, when what I call the Kaleckian dilemma occurs. Kalecki wrote of the second situation:

> the *maintenance* of full employment would cause social and political changes which would give a new impetus to the opposition of the business leaders [to full employment]. Indeed, under a regime of permanent full employment, the sack would cease to flag its role as a

disciplinary measure. The social position of the boss would be undermined and the self-assurance and class-consciousness of the working class would grow. Strikes for wage increases and improvements in conditions of work would create political tension ... true ... profits would be higher under a regime of full employment than they are on average under *laisser-faire*, and even the rise in wage rates resulting from the stronger bargaining power of the workers is less likely to reduce profits than to increase prices, and thus affect adversely only ... rentier interests. But 'discipline in the factories' and 'political stability' are more appreciated than profits by the business leaders. Their class instinct tells them that lasting full employment is unsound from their point of view, and that unemployment is an integral part of the normal capitalist system. (Kalecki 1943;. *C.W.* Vol. I, 1990, 351, emphasis in original)

I now draw on an insight by another great economist, John Hicks, whose insight concerning 'Snatchers' and 'Stickers', when writing on imperfect competition in the 1950s, Hicks (1954), helps to illuminate the recent behaviour of banks and other financial intermediaries. If I may be indulged, I quote here from the paper I presented in 1998 at the Conference in Bergamo in honour of Hy Minsky (Harcourt 2000; 2001a, 201–2).

Hicks presented a period analysis of price setting and identified when it would be 'safe' always to maximise short-period or immediate expected profits ... to snatch completely what was *immediately* available, regardless of the consequences ....This ... was contrasted with [a situation] where it would be necessary to take into account the longer-term consequences of snatching now ... [T]he objective then became the maximisation of *long-term* expected profits, to stick [not] snatch, so foregoing some immediate opportunities because of ... negative feedbacks on consumer goodwill, for example, in future periods. I cite Hicks's article ... because ... commercial banks all around the world ... have behaved more like Snatchers than Stickers in their lending behaviour, notably over the past twenty to thirty years [and more]. This has had disastrous consequences ... for their customers and even themselves, [and] for the performance of the system as a whole .... [T]he conventional view of bankers [used to be] that they are sound, cautious, conservative people ... But their actions in recent years belie such a stereotype; in fact they [are] either over optimistically euphoric about economic situations and lend accordingly – lots – without proper assessments of risks or credit-worthiness generally, or they are unduly pessimistic..., calling in loans without any regard to the medium- to long-term viability and soundness of their customers' situations. This behaviour... has also been characteristic of non-banking financial institutions over the same period... [T]heir behaviour has served significantly to reinforce the cyclical processes which Minsky identified in Keynes's system.

The essence of Minsky's message was that investment expenditure is planned in anticipation of future cash flows, that finance is raised to make the investment possible, so building *inescapable* future commitments into balance sheets, extra liabilities on which extra interest and other payments have to be paid regardless of actual outcomes. One of Keynes's greatest insights, on which Minsky has built, was that apart from the state of long-term expectations, availability of finance, not saving, is the binding constraint on investment expenditure – a corollary of Meade's remark quoted above and set out by Keynes in 1937 in his discussions of the finance motive; see Keynes 1937a, 1937b; *C.W.*, vol. XIV, 1973, 201–23. So a major post-Keynesian tenet is that there is an inescapable logical sequence of finance →investment→saving, a proposition going by default in much recent discussion of both national and international processes; see Dalziel and Harcourt 1997; Harcourt 2001a, 72–87.

Returning to Minsky's analysis, if therefore actual cash flows turn out to be different from what was expected, because of the certain commitments, their effect is to accentuate the inescapable real fluctuations of the economy (if actual events exceed expected, in an upward direction, if they are less, in a downward direction). With banks and other financial intermediaries being overall often irresponsible Snatchers, fluctuations both real and financial have been greatly enhanced.

A final consideration which characterises post-Keynesian analysis arose first in the work of Roy Harrod who laid the foundations of the modern theory of growth. In his pioneering article (1939) and book (1948), he distinguished between the demand side of growth, principally with his concept of the warranted rate of growth (g_w) and the supply side with his concept of the natural rate of growth (g_n). The factors which determined g_n were argued to be (or at least treated as if they were) independent of those determining g_w. g_n itself summed up the potential for long-term growth of the economy in terms of the growth and improvement of economies' labour forces. But the separation of g_n from g_w (and the expected and actual rates of growth) is not acceptable for reasons cogently put forward by, especially, Salter's analysis of the rate of embodiment of new methods through investment in capital stocks; see Salter 1960, 1965. Clearly the size of g_n must be related to this. As I mentioned before, post-Keynesians go even further by their rejection of the distinction between trend and cycle, putting in their place theories of cyclical growth. This contrasts strongly with modern mainstream practice where growth is discussed in supply terms independently of demand, as though short-term fluctuations occur around a full employment trend, that is to say, g_n.

III

With this as background, what would a package deal of post-Keynesian policies look like? (While I shall not discuss climate change policies explicitly, I assume that the policies I suggest will take proper account of the long-term constraints that global warming and responses to it entail.) It is to be hoped that there will be international cooperation with, and coordination of, some of the individual policies, otherwise they would not have a chance to succeed. It may be that unfolding current events are making these possible; but I would not bet on it.

While it will never be possible entirely to escape from cyclical fluctuations – Dennis Robertson again made this clear in his criticism of Keynes's *General Theory* and the early Keynesians' emphasis on trying always to be at full employment (see Anadike-Danes (1985)) –, the aim should be to minimise the amplitude of fluctuations and to keep average levels of employment as near as possible to full employment, allowing for frictional, and seasonal unemployment and the necessary flexibility associated with restructuring processes. These last may take years to work themselves out but here Scandinavian practices are excellent guides – retraining, early pensions, keeping communities together.

For the banking system, an implication of Minsky's analysis for policy is that central banks should encourage trading banks to use their research departments to evaluate the medium- to long-term prospects of those who borrow from them for both investment and consumption purposes. This would make the granting of loans in the upturn more cautious and responsible and the pulling of plugs in the downturn, because of short-term cash flow problems, less frequent so, overall, reducing the amplitude of fluctuations in activity to its inescapable real patterns. The UK government has recently (January 2009) taken some faltering steps to implement these ideas (but not any more with the government of Cameron-lite and Boy George Osborne).

For non-banking financial intermediaries, we need to induce similar behaviour from both lenders and borrowers. The problem is that innovations in financial instruments have been so fast and complicated that credit-rating agencies have not the skills to make authoritative assessments of various instruments. This is especially true of derivatives and the behaviour of hedge funds. Yet, in principle, it should be possible to classify activity in these instruments and institutions into acceptable and not, and design tax impositions accordingly. Indeed, if this is not possible, their activities will continue to plague the stability of economies and attempts through policy to overcome instability and crisis.

One of the greatest tragedies of the twentieth century was that the Americans (in the person of Harry Dexter White) won out over the United Kingdom (in the person of Maynard Keynes) at Bretton Woods. Had the latter prevailed, there would have been pressure on creditor nations to behave, so removing inbuilt contractionary forces which have plagued the system, and we would have had a world central bank and a world currency for settling international transactions. Moreover, the world would have moved towards freer trade with out necessarily accompanying free capital movements. This would have allowed a system of fixed exchange rates with a provision for moveable pegs to have prevailed without being destroyed by speculators with their massive inflows and outflows of 'hot money'.

Today we have relatively free international capital movements but not a world central bank or a world currency. This is an inherently unstable situation which benefits developed economies, especially large ones, but harms developing economies, especially those only starting development and those which are small but open. Arestis, Basu and Mallik (2005) have argued the case for a world central bank playing a central coordinating and regulatory role, and a world currency as a second-best solution, the only way to have 'true financial globalisation'. But, given the choice, they would not have started from there in the first place.

As a general rule I have come to favour spending by governments on infrastructure being determined by medium- to long-term needs (given the philosophical stances of the governments in power), with short-term aggregate demand puzzles being tackled by changes in taxation. An overall tax structure which reflects equity and efficiency should be designed and the whole structure should be jacked up or down according to the anticipated state of aggregate demand from other sources. This view, however, has to be modified in the present crisis, as indeed has already occurred in Australia, China, Continental Europe, the United States and the UK (with varying degrees of enthusiasm and competence). Increases in government expenditure associated with bringing forward plans already in the pipeline, or waiting their turn, makes good sense. We have been presented with a golden opportunity to do something substantial about deficiencies in social housing, city infrastructure, out-of-date or inadequate school buildings and hospitals, transport inadequacies and so on, not to mention reducing student–staff ratios in schools and in universities and increasing the provision of trained people to tackle reading and writing problems, and care for the disabled and elderly. For those who are worried about rising (especially external) debt to income ratios, may I suggest that until unemployment falls to levels relatively close to full employment, extra government expenditure should be financed by writing cheques on the central banks, not by issuing new debt?

Like Keynes, Kalecki, Kaldor and Robertson, I am very sceptical about over-reliance on changes in the rate of interest as an effective policy measure. The fiscal fine-tuners of earlier years were undoubtedly over optimistic but what of the monetary fine-tuners of independent central banks in more modern times? There is a lot to be said, within given constraints, of setting relatively low interest rates and keeping them there, using other measures to tackle short-term fluctuations and long-term needs.

In Australia we have been blessed over the years with deep analysis of a permanent incomes policy, very much influenced by the contributions of Eric Russell and Wilfred Salter. Their arguments used to be well known. Allied with maintaining full employment, we need institutions which as a start allow money incomes to be adjusted for prices and *overall* productivity (reflecting the terms of trade in open economies). This would allow all citizens to share in the rising prosperity associated with the complementary relationship between capital and labour at the economy level. (On occasions they would take their fair share of any decline in real standards.) Not only would this be equitable, it would also be efficient because it hastens the disappearance of low productivity, often declining industries and enhances the growth of high productivity, often expanding industries. The associated faster growth of *overall* productivity when reflected in the increase in money incomes may serve to tackle the Kaleckian dilemma of sustaining full employment alongside the accompanying shift of economic, social and political power from capital to labour; see Harcourt (1997; 2001b). Post-Keynesians are 'horses for courses' analysts and so each economy would need to try to achieve this goal through institutions which suited its sociological and historical experiences. (In Australia we have all but destroyed the institutions which could have delivered this goal.) The most difficult task in all these economies will be getting the currently grossly overpaid captains of industry and finance to accept such a rule.

If we accept a cumulative causation view of the workings of markets and systems, there is a strong case for arguing that speculation is systemically harmful, not beneficial, in many markets. Therefore we have to design Marshallian/Pigovian carrot and stick measures to reduce overall the amount and therefore effects of speculation. (We do not have the luxury of authoritarian states of locking speculators up.) Here the tax system comes into play. The Tobin tax on foreign exchange transactions is an early example of this. The overall aim should be to reward legitimate, systemically beneficial economic activity and punish systemically harmful activity.

In foreign exchange markets, this requires classifying overall transactions (turnovers) on both sides of the market into useful economic purposes – trade, investment, consumption – with the residual being *prima facie* speculative transactions. Overall, tax rates on transactors' incomes should reflect penal rates associated with speculation; see Harcourt (1995). Of course, it may still be thought profitable for individuals to speculate but the inducement is not to. Obviously there is need for international agreement on such measures, otherwise domestic taxpayers are induced to go offshore.

In housing markets again the tax system could be directed towards encouraging economically and socially beneficial transactions – buying and selling (or letting and renting) houses because of changes in employment, arrival of a family, parents coming home to live – and discouraging speculative purchases where again penal rates of tax on incomes would apply to both buyers and sellers. On stock exchanges Keynes advocated measures which encourage buyers to look at the medium to long-term prospects of companies, the shares of which they were thinking of buying or selling, that is, being Stickers. This required rewards for the length of time shares were held, so offsetting the trend decline in the number and lengths of marriages by making portfolios more durable and lasting; see Keynes (1936; *C.W.*, vol. VII, 1973, 160–61).

IV

I hope I have set out some ideas that other people might like to take up. I recently read John King's superb new book on Nicky Kaldor (King (2009)), and I noted the overlap with his policy proposals, especially in his last book (Kaldor (1996)), which contained his 1984 Matteoli lectures. (In addition, he wanted buffer stock schemes to stabilise the prices of primary products and two-tier exchange rates.) Keynes wanted to save capitalism from itself; Marx (and Kalecki) thought that was impossible. Progressive people backed by Keynes's sensible analysis will be more likely to make Keynes's aims achievable and prove Marx and Kalecki wrong. (In this category I include Philip Arestis, a post-Keynesian optimist *par excellence*.) Had any society been prepared to accept and allow Kalecki's plans for democratic socialism to prevail, that would have been a first-best solution. But, in the present circumstances, that time sadly is past, as Prue Kerr and I recognised in our 1980 paper, 'The mixed economy'. So capitalism with a more human face is the most we can realistically hope for.

Note

1. See, for example, Keynes (1946), 185–86. In the House of Lords Keynes claimed that 'There is an attempt to use what we have learnt from modern experience and modern analysis, not to defeat, but to implement the wisdom of Adam Smith' (186). See also Keynes's last time at the Political Economy Club: Editorial Introduction (2006), and Lloyd (2006).

References

Anadike-Danes, M. K. (1985), 'Dennis Robertson and Keynes's *General Theory*', in G. C. Harcourt (ed.) (1985), *Keynes and His Contemporaries*. Houndmills, Basingstoke, Hampshire: Macmillan.

Arestis, Philip, Santanou Basu and Sushanta Mallick (2005), 'Financial Globalization: the Need for a Single Currency and a Global Central Bank', *Journal of Post Keynesian Economics*, 27, 507–31.

Balogh, T. (1982), *The Irrelevance of Conventional Economics*, London: Weidenfeld & Nicolson.

Editorial Introduction (2006), 'Keynes's Last Time at the Political Economy Club: Editorial Introduction', *Cambridge Journal of Economics*, 30, 1.

Dalziel, P. C. and G. C. Harcourt (1997), 'A Note on "Mr Meade's Relation" and International Capital Movements', *Cambridge Journal of Economics*, 21, 621–31, reprinted in Harcourt (2001a), 72–87.

Goodwin, R. M. (1967), 'A Growth Cycle', in Feinstein, C. H. (ed.) (1967), *Socialism, Capitalism and Economic Growth: Essays Presented to Maurice Dobb*, Cambridge: Cambridge University Press.

Harcourt, G. C. (1995), *Capitalism, Socialism and Post-Keynesianism: Selected Essays of G.C. Harcourt*. Cheltenham: Edward Elgar.

Harcourt, G. C. (1997), 'Pay Policy, Accumulation and Productivity', *Economic and Labour Relations Review*, 8, 78–89, reprinted in Harcourt (2001b), 263–75.

Harcourt, G. C. (2000), 'Investment Expenditure, Unrealised Expectations and Offsetting Monetary Policies', in R. Bellofiore and P. Ferri (eds), (2000) *Financial Fragility and Investment in the Capitalist Economy. The Economic Legacy of Hyman Minsky*, Cheltenham: Edward Elgar, 69–75, reprinted in Harcourt (2001a), 197–205.

Harcourt, G. C. (2001a), *50 Years a Keynesian and Other Essays*, Houndmills, Basingstoke, Hampshire: Palgrave Macmillan.

Harcourt, G. C. (2001b), *Selected Essays on Economic Policy*, Houndmills, Basingstoke, Hampshire: Palgrave Macmillan.

Harcourt, G. C. (2006), *The Structure of Post-Keynesian Economics: The Core Contributions of the Pioneers*. Cambridge: Cambridge University Press.

Harcourt, G.C. (2007a) 'The Theoretical and Political Importance of the Economics of Keynes: Or, What Would Marx and Keynes Have Made of the Happenings of the Past 30 Years and More', in Mathew Forstater, Gary Mongiovi and Steven Pressman (eds), *Post-Keynesian Macroeconomics. Essays in honour of Ingrid Rima*, London and New York: Routledge, 56–69.

Harcourt, G. C. (2007b), 'Markets, Madness and a Middle Way Revisited', *Economic and Labour Relations Review*, 17, April, 1–10, corrected version in 18, 2007, 1–10.

Harcourt, G. C. and Prue Kerr (1980), 'The Mixed Economy', in Jane North and Pat Weller (eds) (1980), *Labor*, Sydney: Ian Novak.

Harrod, R. F. (1939) 'An Essay in Dynamic Theory', *Economic Journal*, 49, 14–35.

Harrod, R. F. (1948), *Towards a Dynamic Economics: Some Recent Developments of Economic Theory and their Applications to Policy*, London: Macmillan.

Hicks, J. R. (1954), 'The Process of Imperfect Competition', *Oxford Economic Papers*, 6, 41–54, reprinted as 'Stickers and Snatchers', ch. 12 of John Hicks (1983), *Classics and Moderns, Collected Essays on Economic Theory*, vol. III, Oxford: Basil Blackwell, 163–78.

Kaldor, N. (1996), *Causes of Growth and Stagnation in the World Economy*, Cambridge: Cambridge University Press.

Kalecki, M. (1943), 'Political Aspects of Full Employment', *Political Quarterly*, 14, 322–31, *C.W.*, vol. I, 1990, 347–56.

Kalecki, M. (1968), 'Trend and Business Cycles Reconsidered', *Economic Journal*, 78, 263–76; *C.W.*, vol. II, 1991, 435–50.

Keynes, J. M. (1923), *A Tract on Monetary Reform*, London: Macmillan; *C.W.*, vol. IV, 1971.

Keynes, J. M. (1936), *The General Theory of Employment, Interest and Money*, London: Macmillan; *C.W.*, vol. VII, 1973.

Keynes, J. M. (1937a), 'Alternative Theories of the Rate of Interest', *Economic Journal*, 47, 241–52; *C.W.*, vol. XIV, 1973, 201–15.

Keynes, J. M. (1937b), 'The "Ex Ante" Theory of the Rate of Interest', *Economic Journal*, 47, 663–9; *C.W.*, vol. XIV, 1973, 215–26.

Keynes, J. M. (1946), 'The Balance of Payments of the United States', *Economic Journal*, 56, 172–87.

King, J. E. (2009), *Nicholas Kaldor*, Houndmills, Basingstoke, Hampshire: Palgrave Macmillan.

Lloyd, Ian (2006), 'Summary of an Address by Lord Keynes to the Political Economy Club, Trinity College, Cambridge on the 2nd of February 1946', *Cambridge Journal of Economics*, 30, 2–6.

Meade, J. E. (1975), 'The Keynesian Revolution', in Milo Keynes (ed.) (1995), *Essays on John Maynard Keynes*, Cambridge: Cambridge University Press, 82–88.

Robinson, Joan (1964), 'Pre-Keynesian theory after Keynes', *Australian Economic Papers*, 3, 25–35.

Robinson, Joan (1978), 'Keynes and Ricardo', *Journal of Post-Keynesian Economics*, 1, 12–18, reprinted in *C.E.P.*, vol. V, 1979, 210–16.

Salter, W. E.G. (1960), *Productivity and Technical Change*, Cambridge: Cambridge University Press, 2nd edn, 1966.

Salter, W. E. G. (1965), 'Productivity Growth and Accumulation as Historical Processes', in E. A. G. Robinson (ed.), (1965) *Problems in Economic Development*, London: Macmillan, 266–91.

Part VII

Intellectual Biographies and Tributes

15
The Contributions of Tom Asimakopulos to Post-Keynesian Economics (2008)*

Introduction

Tom and I knew one another for 35 years.[†] Our close friendship dates from the late 1960s, after Tom had made a major shift in his approach to economics. This followed his year at MIT in 1965–66 where, listening to Bob Solow's lectures, the significance of Joan Robinson's critique of neo-classical theory and method fell into place (see Harcourt, 1991, 42, and Abe Tarasofsky's moving account of this episode quoted in the Preface of Harcourt et al. (eds), 1994, xii). Tom immediately took up the implications of the critique and started to spell them out in his own work. This was a courageous decision. It removed him from being regarded as one of the most promising young theorists in mainstream economics in Canada to an unpopular maverick position for which there was little understanding and even less tolerance among his peers.

When Tom and I were research students at King's College in the 1950s, he worked with Harry Johnson. My supervisors were Nicky Kaldor and then Ronald Henderson, but I was very much influenced by Joan Robinson, especially by *The Accumulation of Capital* (1956). I read her *magnum opus* in my second year as a research student, having been to her lectures on it the year before with Tom and our mutual friend and my former teacher at Melbourne University, Keith Frearson. Tom and Keith worked carefully through their lecture notes and the book

---

* Originally published as chapter 5 in L. Randall Wray and Mathew Forstater (eds), *Keynes and Macroeconomics after 70 Years, Critical Assessments of The General Theory*, Cheltenham, UK and Northampton, MA: Edward Elgar Publishing, pp. 64–79.

itself when it was published. Tom was puzzled and irritated by her arguments, and by her criticisms of the orthodox theories of value and distribution and neoclassical methodology on which he had been brought up. I did not have many talks with Tom about economics but I did observe with awe the worksheets for his PhD dissertation in the (old) Marshall Library; they were an appropriate index of his systematic thoroughness and command of technique. His research topic was a three-commodity, three-country study in international trade theory entitled 'Productivity Changes, the Trade Balance and the Terms of Trade'. It required painstaking, voluminous calculations in calculus.

His first mentor was Jack Weldon, and Murray Kemp was also an important influence (see Harcourt, 1991, 42, n. 2). I imagine (but I don't know) that Tom was taught Keynes from *A Treatise on Money* and *The General Theory* and Marshall from the *Principles* by Jack, together with Joan Robinson and Edward Chamberlin (1933) from the originals and Piero Sraffa from the 1926 *Economic Journal* article, just as I was in Melbourne. I expect that he came to know J. R. Hicks from *Value and Capital* (and the *Trade Cycle?*), Roy Harrod from his 1939 article and 1948 book, Paul Samuelson from the *Foundations* (1947) and his published articles, and, I also imagine, some original D. H. Robertson. Reading Jack Weldon's superb chapter on the classical theory of distribution in Tom's book on income distribution (1988a), in retrospect I am not surprised that Tom came to the later views that he did, for the crucial seeds were sown early on by Jack. Nevertheless, in the 1950s and early 1960s, his overall structure of analysis differed from what it was to become, now reflected in the volume of selected papers (Asimakopulos, 1988b), the introduction to and his chapter in the edited book on income distribution, his microeconomics text (1978a), and his last book (1991). There, the views he had developed over the years in teaching Keynes, Harrod and Joan Robinson to his students, were set out lucidly and in full for posterity.

Tom's published writings show more than any other scholar's work I know well[1] the great value of developing books and articles from teaching material, which is how the bulk of Tom's published work originated. The need to explain explicitly and clearly the assumptions of the analysis, to understand other authors' views, the need to present a perspective and to explain the origins and relevance of concepts – all the demands on a good teacher were supplied in Tom's writings. They were built up from years of experience of lecturing on the issues, often at different levels. So, in speaking of Tom the economist I must also speak on Tom the man; the two were inseparable.

His attitudes to teaching and research reflected his philosophy of life in general. The most admirable aspect of his economics was that teaching was the top priority. He loved teaching the microeconomics course to the Honors students at McGill University. Even though he had a teaching assistant for the course, he made sure that from time to time he gave tutorials himself. A particularly poignant instance is that during his last illness he gave tutorials in the hospital amphitheatre a few weeks before his death. I have rarely known a teacher so thorough in the preparation of background notes in which the assumptions and arguments would be laid out clearly, simply and with great force. Tom's careful scholarship unobtrusively shone through in appropriate quotes, citations and sensible reading lists.

Another characteristic of Tom's work was his ability to retain the essential message and thrust of great authors, and to pass their message on, fully and fairly. At the same time he ironed out mistakes, inconsistencies, muddles and the blurred vision which inevitably must characterise the work of innovative original thinkers, charting new and/or unfamiliar territories. Because Tom did this for the great authors whose work he read, analysed and taught, the structure of his own thought is a model of coherence, clarity and logical consistency.

Tom wrote to me on 26 April 1984, soon after the death of Joan Robinson, that he had written 'a "critical" review [of her contributions (Asimakopulos, 1984), because she was] too important an economist to be treated any other way, but the basis for [all his] criticism [came] from her own critical writings'. Joan was as hard on herself as she was on others, that is to say, very hard indeed. Tom too had exacting standards. The more he liked and respected a person, especially a student, the harder he would be. I am sure he would wish the same attitudes to be present in evaluations of his contributions. It is more difficult to fault him by these standards than it was Joan Robinson. I attribute this partly to differences in temperament, especially as Joan grew older, but mainly to Tom's conscientious attention to detail in classes, where he would often be teaching less gifted pupils than those whom Joan taught for most of her life.

Tom's approach in teaching and writing

Tom insisted that all discussions of economic issues be grounded in the nitty-gritty of reality, of a recognisable economy with its specific history, institutions and 'rules of the game', as Joan Robinson used to put it. This was true not only of his discussions of employment and growth theories but also of his microeconomic lectures and the textbook (1978a) that grew out of them. The chapters are full of real-world examples; the theory is assessed by how well it illuminates them. Tom deplored the habit in modern macroeconomics of ceasing to distinguish, in models which are supposed to relate to capitalist economies, between the capital goods sector and the consumption goods sector, with the different motives and financial power of the decision makers in, and the purchasers of the products of, each sector. This failure meant that the differential impacts of their behaviour as a group or class on economic processes were missed out. He was critical of Martin Weitzman's influential article in 1982 on increasing returns and involuntary unemployment, just because the model in the article was not recognisable as one of a capitalist economy because these essential features were missing in its specification. (Nicky Kaldor loved it – or, at least, he loved its conclusions.) Tom wrote: 'There is no investment in this model...and it thus cannot even begin to analyse the question of the determinants of the levels of, and fluctuations in, output and employment in modern economies' (Asimakopulos, 1985, 352). 'The model does not contain workers or capitalists, but only units of a single "composite" factor of production, and there can thus be no wages or profits, even though the terms are used' (352). The production units are referred to by Weitzman 'as "firms or plants" (795), but they are no more...than a combination of factor units come together to produce goods...There is [therefore] no factor unit doing the "hiring" with the others being "hired"...Weitzman ignores the specification of his model and uses the verb "to hire"' (788) (Asimakopulos, 1985, 352–53). Tom points out that Weitzman attributes 'persistent involuntary underutilization of the major factors of production' to insufficient overall demand, itself traceable in turn to the unemployed lacking 'the means to communicate or make effective their potential demands' (Weitzman, 1982, 787). But for Keynes, such communication was not sufficient 'for an increase in employment to be self-sustaining, because the value of the increased output contains a profit component. Investment, as well as consumption, must increase in order to establish a higher equilibrium level of output and employment' (Asimakopulos, 1985, 353–54). Tom concludes: 'Weitzman is unable to deal with Keynes's approach, or to examine its micro-foundations because there is no investment in Weitzman's model' (354).

Again, when Tom (1978b) contrasted the model(s) of the firm implied in Kinut Wicksell's and Alfred Marshall's writings, he much preferred Marshall's model because its essential features were more recognisably those of actual firms in a historically real, capitalist economy. One of Wicksell's specifications, by contrast, was much more abstract and idealised and so did not give rise to categories of income and classes of persons to be found in actual firms, or to results which were legitimately comparable with those from Marshall's model. The setting for Tom's critique was the discussion in the modern literature 'concerning the appropriate criterion for firms to use in choosing the optimal technique for investment...maximization of the internal rate of return on the amount invested and maximization of the present value of the investment' (Asimakopulos, 1978b, 51). Tom points out: 'The decision-makers in each of these models have different roles [and so] each...refers to a different reality' (51). He adds: 'the failure to appreciate this difference is due to the absence in much of current economic theory of specifications of the institutional settings for the analyses...A necessary element in a theoretical model, if it is to be used to gain insights into the operation of actual economies, is the specification of the social relations of production which pertain to those economies' (51–52).

Tom argued that Marshall included two important features of modern economies in his model: first, the concept of ownership of the means of production by a minority (the 'capitalists') which allowed them to organise and control production and purchase the labour power of the majority (the 'workers'); second, two types of capitalists, entrepreneurs who use their own as well as borrowed capital to organise production, and rentiers who lend their capital but are otherwise passive as far as production is concerned. Wicksell had only one, or sometimes, none of these features in his model.

Tom's later approach

In his later approach Tom took a stance which reflected those of his first mentor, Jack Weldon, and his second major mentor, Joan Robinson and, through her, Kalecki. In his chapter on the classical theory of distribution (Weldon, 1988), Jack stresses that there were recognisable macroeconomic processes in classical thought to which was linked the crucial organising concept of the surplus, its creation, extraction, distribution and use. This became central to Tom's thought, too, though he was most interested in what was happening in the sphere of distribution and exchange. There he traced the interrelationships between the theory of effective demand, especially of investment, and employment and distribution, their links back to underlying pricing mechanisms, and also (with John Burbidge) how a theory of tax incidence could be developed within this framework.

The crucial change in Tom's structure of analysis occurred when he fully comprehended Joan Robinson's distinction between logical time and historical time. This was associated with her methodological critique of neoclassical theory as she saw it, the illegitimacy of applying propositions drawn from a comparison of differences to an analysis of processes involving actual changes occurring. (She eventually summed this up in the graphic phrase 'History versus Equilibrium'.) Joan wrote about all this in an intuitive manner, criticising those economists who argued for a tendency towards equilibrium, whereas, she argued, either an economy (or a market or an industry or a firm) is *in* equilibrium and has been for a long time, logically since the expulsion from the Garden of Eden, *or* it is not. In the latter case, economists observe a specific situation with a particular history, structure and set of expectations. Their role is to analyse what happens next when a change is imposed on the existing situation. Joan often used the analogy of a pendulum, the ultimate resting place of which is independent of whether it is given a slight nudge or arbitrarily lifted high and let go. In physics it ends up at the same place but in any economic system the analogy does not apply. Even in the first case it might not be true that an economy (et al.) would return after a slight nudge, unless the traders responsible for making the market and setting the prices had had such a long time to experience the realisation of equilibrium prices that they did not panic when the (small) nudge occurred. But if the economy had never reached an equilibrium position in the past, how could it be argued that people will ever have the experience to know that they will reach one in the future? Analytically, Joan Robinson (and Kaldor) were talking about path-dependent equilibria – where an economy ends up depends on the path taken on the way. In Joan Robinson's case, she thought that it was often unlikely that it would *ever* end up in an equilibrium position though it might remain in a tranquil position for a while, one which superficially seemed to have equilibrium characteristics.

These insights underlay much of Tom's later work. An early example is Tom's article, 'Keynes, Patinkin, historical time and equilibrium analysis' (1973, 47–76). Here he contrasts the economic model examined in Patinkin's 1956 book (which acknowledged an 'obvious dependence...on the...concepts and techniques [of *The General Theory*])' with the model underlying *The General Theory*. This difference is reflected in the treatment of historical time, expectations, and the forces leading to positions of full-employment equilibrium.

> Keynes' model is...a causal model...deals with a particular situation at a particular period of time. Given...the...features of the particular situation examined,...the model works out what will happen next...may not be one of full employment...expectations may be disappointed with repercussions on behavior in future periods. Patinkin's model...is an equilibrium model. Attention is concentrated

on equilibrium relations ... embodies the assumption that forces will move the system to equilibrium if the position examined [is] one of disequilibrium. (Asimakopulos, 1973, 179)

Keynes's 'essentially static' analysis is nevertheless 'concerned with a segment of actual, historical time ... The *memory* of past states and previous transaction prices affect present attitudes ... Patinkin's model ... deals with a very different "world" ... more readily described in terms of simple equations' (180, emphasis in original). In particular, expectations continue to be held with certainty, even though they may be disappointed and 'the basis on which expectations are formed' is seen to be responsible. 'Patinkin's model is ... essentially "timeless", with the economy's history having no role in [its] development ... [it] does not provide a useful theoretical basis for understanding the workings of the economies for which Keynes' model was developed' (181).

These arguments are reflected in Tom's discussion of local and global stability in his microeconomics textbook (1978a). He gives a clear account (82–87) of the differences between Marshallian and Walrasian stability in a competitive market. He then points out the limited nature of the concepts – local and global, Marshallian or Walrasian, or any combination of these. For *always*, the equilibrium sits there waiting to be found while the stability analysis does its thing, whereas the essence of the Robinsonian critique is that the very act of seeking the equilibrium position changes the equilibrium position itself. In the section 'limitations of standard stability analysis', Tom writes:

The standard methods ... are mechanical. Expectations and the passage of time are ignored ... the experience of non-equilibrium situations does not affect the positions of the demand and supply curves ... the experience of changing prices does not change the expectations about future conditions ... There is no time ... other than a representation of demand and supply conditions for [a] particular slice of time. They cannot be used to trace a movement over a series of such slices, or during this particular period ... if the initial price is not an equilibrium price, without additional assumptions concerning ... the foundation of expectations, the holding of stocks, and possible changes over time in the values of the parameters. (Asimakopulos, 1978a, 86–87)

In terms of Jan Kregel's classic paper (1976) on the various models in *The General Theory*, as well as the papers after it, the shifting equilibrium method emerges as the dominant one. In Keynes's theory, not only were short-term expectations not immediately fulfilled, but also their very non-fulfilment was allowed to feed back into the formation of long-term expectations and so change the implied equilibrium (rest state) position associated with the point of effective demand itself. Grappling with this issue led to some of Tom's most incisive work, such as his critique of Keynes's theory of investment and the two-sided relationships between accumulation and profits which he put in its place (scrupulously acknowledging the influence of Kalecki and Joan Robinson on his 1971 paper); his exposition of Kalecki's theory of investment (1977), where, by the time the chain of reasoning had been gone through, he had returned again to the arbitrary position from which, for convenience, he had started the analysis and had explicitly handled any problems raised by his discussion at each point on the way, so making sure that the analysis *was* set in historical time. Again, in Asimakopulos and Burbidge on tax incidence (1974; Asimakopulos, 1988b), all these issues are faced fairly – and dealt with. The conclusion is a model of clarity and modesty.

> We have obtained results on the incidence of taxation by concentrating on situations of short-period equilibrium. This is appropriate for comparisons with the neoclassical models because they deal only with equilibrium positions and it is in line with Kalecki's work in this area. It is only a first step, however, and a fuller treatment of the subject would require the tracing of the effects of tax changes over time. A change in tax at the beginning of a short period, even if we assume that it does not affect current investment, would probably work itself out over more than one short period. The resulting changes in output, prices, profits etc. will affect investment decisions and these will lead to further changes. In order to assess the longer-term effects of tax changes the analysis must be carried out within the context of a fully articulated growth model that permits the effects of the changes to be traced out over time (Asimakopulos and Burbidge, 1974; Asimakopulos, 1988b, 70).

Finally, in his 1983 paper for the Joan Robinson Memorial issue of the *Cambridge Journal of Economics*, which precipitated one of the most prolonged controversies of the 1980s in Post-Keynesian theory, Tom discussed the deficiencies of Keynes's and Kalecki's modes of attack on the interrelationship between finance, saving and investment. In Keynes's 1937 articles on the rate of interest (*CW*, vol. XIV, 1973) in which he discussed his neglect in *The General Theory* of the finance motive as an additional reason for demanding money, he reached the startling conclusion that: 'the investment market can become congested through shortage of cash [but]never...through shortage of saving...the most fundamental of my conclusions within this field' (*CW*, vol. XIV, 1973, 22).

Tom re-examined Keynes's arguments and also Kalecki's, for he discerned a similarity between Keynes's concept of a 'revolving fund' of finance and Kalecki's 'image' of the circle of finance which closes itself (Kalecki, 1935, 343). Tom wished to show that their models were not general but rather assumed a situation of considerable unemployment and undercapacity utilisation of existing plant, with ample unused finance in the banking system, so that output and prices (perhaps) could be changed without pressure on interest rates. Moreover, it would be legitimate to proceed as if income had risen to give the new desired saving equal to the new desired investment immediately. That is to say, it was allowable to slide over the distinction between the existence of a short-period rest state (with unemployment) and the process by which it was attained, a procedure which was not generalisable to all situations of the economy. In a sense Tom was to side with Ralph Hawtrey and, later, Hicks (in *The Crisis in Keynesian Economics*, 1976), in their reluctance to accept Keynes's short-cut method whereby the short-period rest state point could be used to 'explain' critical observations on the economy (see Harcourt, 1981; Sardoni (ed.) 1992, 250–64).

Tom insisted that, for Post-Keynesian analysis to be operational, it must be done in terms of periodic analysis. He criticised Joan Robinson's later views in which she changed the definition of the short period so that it became 'not a length of time but a state of affairs'. She argued that the expressions, 'short period' and 'long period', should be used 'as adjectives, not as substantives' (Joan Robinson, 1971, 17–18). Tom objected to this approach because it took away 'the setting for Keynes's theory since there is no time available to permit variations in the utilisation of productive capacity in response to changing short-term expectations' (Asimakopulos, 1988b, 196). (The simplification then required for Keynes's theory, which he himself shied away from, is to suppose that most production and gestation periods in the economy are of much the same length and that decisions about production, and about investment, are synchronised.) Joan Robinson's views are, I think, connected to the insights contained in Hugh Townshend's 1937 paper in the *Economic Journal*, 'Liquidity-premium and the theory of value' and to those in Nicky Kaldor's 1939 paper, 'Speculation and economic stability'. The arguments of both of these papers, together with those of Keynes himself in his 1937 papers, lie behind, for example, Snippe's 1985 critique of Tom's article. Victoria Chick, in her entry on Townshend in the *New Palgrave*, has put the essence of the position very well indeed:

> Townshend's note takes issue with Hicks's [subsequent] attempt to transform the theory of liquidity preference into a mirror image of the loanable funds theory by Walras's Law. Townshend saw that this was an attempt to retain the link between prices and flow concepts of cost and demand ... [He argued] that it was in the nature of Keynes's ... theory that expectations of the future could change the value of assets overnight and be reflected in the market prices of those assets even in the absence of actual trading. Thus current prices could be determined by subjective as well as objective fact and future prices were indeterminate. (1987, 662)

This leads into Kaldor's analysis in which he discusses, in effect, the characteristics of those markets where stocks dominate flows, and expectations dominate tangible economic factors, in the determination of prices, so that the analysis must concentrate on a moment in time before being extended to illuminate periods of time. Tom drew on Kaldor's analysis in order precisely to define those conditions which must hold in the financial sectors in order that the simple multiplier story of Keynes and Kalecki went through. It involves taking a view of what is the typical way in which an investment project is financed over its lifetime; that is, to get it off the ground in the first place and, then, to build the financial aspect of it into the liability side of the firm's balance sheet in a permanent form. For the economy as a whole, this requires consideration of both how banks behave in aggregate and how new saving from newly created income associated with new investment expenditure and secondary rounds of consumption expenditure is held. This requires, in turn, a consideration of the term structure of interest rates (and, increasingly, the factors which lie behind the holding of equities and the issue of new ones). Kaldor postulated a group of speculators who needed to take a view on the long-term rate of interest (and presumably the prices of equities) in order that they could 'do their thing' and so keep the long-term rate of interest at levels it would have attained anyway, had there not been a rise in aggregate expenditure in the first place.

Tom was very careful to distinguish between the identity, $S \equiv I$ and the equilibrium condition, $S = I$, something which neither Keynes nor Kalecki ever had really clear in their own minds. But there was a faint blur in Tom's discussion of saving which literally is a decision not to spend, not a provision of finance as such. Kregel points this out in his comment in the *Journal of Post Keynesian Economics* (1986); he argues that what Tom identified as temporary or undesired savings are in fact cash balances arising from decisions to hold or to disgorge (96; see also Kregel's essay in Harcourt et al., 1994 (eds)). This pushes the argument back to the crucial role of the banks in allowing the new investment process to go through in its entirety, that is, to Keynes's original position.

To help settle the arguments, may I ask whether the following statement can be given a rigorous precise meaning within the context of these exchanges? 'Yesterday's' saving may influence 'today's' investment, and 'today's' saving may influence 'tomorrow's' investment, but it is 'today's' investment which is responsible for 'today's' saving. This both reveals a deep Keynesian insight and is *not* precise, for the distinction between 'desired' and 'actual' remains blurred. In sorting this out Tom's approach was invaluable, even if he lost sight of some of the elements in the argument whereby a 'moment' of time really was the proper vantage point from which to begin the analysis.

Tom on Keynes, Harrod and Joan Robinson

In his last book (Asimakopulos, 1991), Tom dealt with the contributions of Keynes, Harrod and Joan Robinson. He examined the work of the last two scholars because both of them, in their own distinctive ways, were attempting to 'generalize *The General Theory* to the long period'. In Tom's reading, both conceded, in the end, that they failed. While it could plausibly be argued that the analysis of *The General Theory* is directly applicable to actual economies in the here and now[2] even when simplified to rest state analysis, Tom nevertheless agreed with Keynes's judgment: 'I should, I think, be prepared to argue that, in a world ruled by uncertainty with an uncertain future linked to an actual present, a final position of equilibrium, such as one deals with in static economics, does not properly exist' (*CW*, vol. XXIX, 1979, 222). From this standpoint, both Harrod's warranted rate of growth and Joan Robinson's Golden Ages were *not* the operational counterparts in growth theory of the aggregate demand and supply schedules (and their intersection) of *The General Theory*. Kalecki's (1968) (and R.M. Goodwin's) cyclical growth models, in which long- and short-period factors impinge *simultaneously* on the economic decisions of the here and now to create activity, employment and distribution, were, I conjecture, Tom's favoured way forward.

Because of this, Tom was impatient with, and sceptical of the neo-Ricardian long-period method (outside the domain of doctrinal debates, where even Joan Robinson would allow its use if it exposed lack of logic in her opponents' propositions). Far from accepting that general theory could only be done using the long-period method, whereby general propositions could be made about the interrelationships between persistent forces at work in economies, Tom denied that, in general, there could be either convergence on or fluctuations around such centres of gravitation. He thus rejected the Milgate–Eatwell–Garegnani interpretation of *The General Theory* (1983) as a long-period theory (only to be labelled an imperfectionist for doing so!). By doing so, he also rejected Marshall's view that short-period normal equilibrium positions could be regarded as stations on the way to the central long-period normal equilibrium cross.

Tom's relationship with Piero Sraffa

What then of Tom's relationship to the work of our mutual pastor of Cambridge research students from the 1950s, Piero Sraffa? I have deliberately separated this from his attitudes to the approach of the neo-Ricardians for, while they explicitly claim kinship with Sraffa, they have moved on in directions which are not obviously associated with Sraffa himself. Sraffa's writings are relevant for Tom's approach in two ways. First, Tom took on board the technical aspects of Sraffa's 1926 article in the *Economic Journal*; that is, the conditions which have to be satisfied in the real world for Marshall's partial equilibrium procedure to be applied legitimately. As a result, Tom is one of the few economists who have tackled successfully the aggregation problems in *The General Theory*, by making explicit the conditions which have to be satisfied before both the aggregate demand schedule and the aggregate supply schedule may be regarded as coherent concepts. In doing this, Tom expunged the confusions in Keynes's presentation of aggregate demand in *The General Theory* – the two different concepts, only one of which survives as coherent (see Asimakopulos, 1991, 20–23), as well as explaining how the aggregate supply curve could be constructed without running foul of, among other things, the Sraffa critique (see, in particular, Asimakopulos, 1988b, 104–13).

Tom thus carefully absorbed the technical critique but he did not go the whole way with Sraffa in the latter's conceptual critique of supply and demand theory. This is clear in Tom's (1988b) chapter on Sraffa and Keynes. Tom comments (129) that, in the system of *Production of*

Commodities by Means of Commodities (1960), Sraffa had left 'formally open' the question whether demand could affect the prices of production in a complete economic system 'even though the general thrust of Sraffa's work implied that demand is not important in this context or, at least, that its influence on price is "not comparable" with those of labour and material inputs.' In a footnote (n. 3, 142), Tom amplifies this and reports Sraffa's response:

I had written to Sraffa in 1971 and had observed that his theoretical framework did not permit any conclusions about the effects of demand on prices unless the assumption of constant returns to scale were added. He responded in a letter dated 11 July 1971: 'You say "I don't see how demand can be said to have no influence on prices, unless constant returns ..." I take it that the drama is enacted on Marshall's stage where the claimants for influence are utility and cost of production. Now utility had made little progress (since the 1870s) towards acquiring a tangible existence and survives in textbooks at the purely subjective level. On the other had, cost of production has successfully survived Marshall's attempt to reduce it to an equally evanescent nature under the name of "disutility", and is still kicking in the form of hours of labour, tons of raw materials, etc. This, rather than the relative slope of the two curves, is why it seems to me that the "influence" of the two things on price is not comparable.'

Tom was probably too sympathetic to the approaches of Marshall and Keynes completely to agree with Sraffa, even though, in Tom's later writings, agreement with Marx and Kalecki on other matters was evident.[3] This *may* mean that Tom would have agreed with Joan Robinson's (nearly final) statement on the connection between Sraffa's approach and those of Marx in 'Accumulation and exploitation: an analysis in the tradition of Marx, Sraffa and Kalecki' (Bhaduri and Joan Robinson, 1980). They argued that Sraffa's target (in his prelude to a critique) was not 'current neoclassical teaching rooted in general equilibrium and "scarce means with alternative uses" [but] the amorphous moralizing of Marshallian theory of "factors of production" receiving "rewards" consonant with their respective productivities'. They claimed that Sraffa showed 'that the influence upon distribution in capitalist industry must be divided into two separate elements. On the one side are the technical factors... [on the other] the share of wages in net output (and therefore the potential ratio of profit on capital) [which] depends upon commercial, social and political influences and the class war' (111).

Production potential and actual output coincide or diverge according to the state of effective demand, itself affected by the distribution of income. Sraffa's particular contribution was to establish that 'In principle, a given technical situation is compatible with any proportion of relative shares [thus ruling] out the notion of earnings determined by productivity' (111). In Joan Robinson's view, the second half of the story is easily released into historical time. It is the challenge of the 'first half of the story – the influence of changes in technology on demand for labour, on accumulation and on effective demand – [which needs to be taken up afresh]' (111). Those scholars who respond to this challenge will be continuing in a tradition to which not only Tom's two mentors contributed so much but also Tom himself.

Conclusion

To sum up: Tom has left a fine legacy in print. As interpretations of Keynes, Kalecki, Harrod and Joan Robinson and (to a lesser extent) Sraffa, his books and papers will continue to be invaluable. Tom stands fair and square with these scholars as an economist who deeply understood the economic and political processes at work in capitalism and how they may best be modelled. His outstanding papers included the path-breaking work on short-period tax incidence (written with John Burbidge: Asimakopulos and Burbidge 1974; Asimakopulos, 1988b), his critical analysis of Keynes's investment theory (1971), his stalwart defence of Keynes's contributions as set in a short-period context (1984, 1985, 1989), and his paper on saving, investment and finance in Keynes and Kalecki in the 1983 Joan Robinson Memorial issue of the *Cambridge Journal of Economics* (1983, 1988b).

His writings on pensions will also continue to instil common sense and provide relevance. Along with Weldon, Tom stressed that public pension schemes involve redistribution through taxes, and thus command over resources, from the working to the retired (or ill or widowed) in the here and now. They are not associated with a process of saving now for dissaving later on. Moreover, because any ongoing scheme of necessity must exist in an environment of uncertainty about the future, analysis should not be based on models which assume away uncertainty, as virtually all the well-known models in the literature do.

It would be wrong to end here for the most important thing in Tom's life was his family. Tom was strict but he doted on 'his girls' – all three, Marika, Anna and Julia. Their friends noted what a united, supportive, loving, happy family they were, no more so than in the last years of Tom's life. After Tom died (Cambridge University Press accepted his 1991 book in the last week of his life), Marika saw through its preparation just as she had been the ever-present helpmate with his earlier books.

Notes

† In writing this chapter, I have drawn heavily on my chapters in Harcourt et al. (eds) (1994) and Arestis and Sawyer (eds) (1992 [2000]). I acknowledge the criticisms on a draft of this chapter by an anonymous referee who is not responsible for my response or lack of response to them.

1. The one possible exception is Eric Russell, but I can assure you that that is praise indeed!
2. We have seen that there is a dispute as to whether we mean a moment or a stretch of actual time.
3. For another view on these issues, see the essay by Neri Salvadori in Harcourt et al. (1994).

References

Arestis, P. and M. Sawyer (eds) (1992 [2000]), *A Biographical Dictionary of Dissenting Economists*, Cheltenham, UK and Northampton, MA, USA: Edward Elgar.

Asimakopulos, A. (1971), 'The Determination of Investment in Keynes' Model', *Canadian Journal of Economics*, 4, 382–88.

Asimakopulos, A. (1973), 'Keynes, Patinkin, Historical Time, and Equilibrium Analysis', *Canadian Journal of Economics*, 6, 179–88.

Asimakopulos, A. (1977), 'Profits and Investment: a Kaleckian Approach', in G. C. Harcourt (ed.), *The Microeconomic Foundations of Macroeconomics*, London: Macmillan, pp. 328–42.

Asimakopulos, A. (1978a), *An Introduction to Economic Theory: Microeconomics*, Oxford: Oxford University Press.

Asimakopulos, A. (1978b), 'The Non-Comparability of Criteria for the Choice of Optimal Technique', *Australian Economic Papers*, 17, 51–62.

Asimakopulos, A. (1983), 'Kalecki and Keynes on Finance, Investment and Saving', *Cambridge Journal of Economics*, 7, 221–33.

Asimakopulos, A. (1984), 'Joan Robinson and Economic Theory', *Banca Nazionale Del Lavoro Quarterly Review*, December, 381–409.

Asimakopulos, A. (1985), 'The Foundations of Unemployment Theory: A Comment', *Journal of Post Keynesian Economics*, 7, 352–62.

Asimakopulos, A. (ed.) (1988a), *Theories of Income Distribution*, Boston, MA: Kluwer Academic.

Asimakopulos, A. (1988b), *Investment, Employment and Income Distribution*, Oxford: Polity Press.

Asimakopulos, A. (1989), 'The Nature and Role of Equilibrium in Keynes's *General Theory*', *Australian Economic Papers*, 28, 16–28.

Asimakopulos, A. (1991), *Keynes's General Theory and Accumulation*, Cambridge: Cambridge University Press.

Asimakopulos, A. and J. B. Burbidge (1974), 'The Short-Period Incidence of Taxation', *Economic Journal*, 84, 267–88, reprinted in Asimakopulos (1988b).

Bhaduri, A. and J. Robinson (1980), 'Accumulation and Exploitation: An Analysis in the Tradition of Marx, Sraffa and Kalecki', *Cambridge Journal of Economics*, 4, 103–15.

Chamberlin, E. H. (1933), *The Theory of Monopolistic Competition*, Cambridge, MA: Harvard University Press.

Chick, V. (1987), 'Townshend, Hugh (1890–1974)', in John Eatwell, Murray Milgate and Peter Newman (eds), *The New Palgrave Dictionary of Economics*, vol. IV, London: Macmillan, p. 662.

Eatwell, John and Murray Milgate (eds) (1983), *Keynes's Economics and the Theory of Value and Distribution*, London: Duckworth.

Goodwin, R .M. (1967), 'A Growth Cycle', in C. H. Feinstein (ed.), *Socialism, Capitalism and Economic Growth: Essays Presented to Maurice Dobb*, Cambridge: Cambridge University Press, pp. 54–58.

Harcourt, G. C. (1981), 'Marshall, Sraffa and Keynes: Incompatible Bedfellows?' *Eastern Economic Journal*, 7, 39–50, reprinted in Sardoni (ed.) (1992), pp. 250–64.

Harcourt, G. C. (1991), 'Athanasios (Tom) Asimakopulos 1930–1990: A Memoir', *Journal of Post Keynesian Economics*, 14, 39–48.

Harcourt, G. C., A. Roncaglia and R. Rowley (eds) (1994), *Income and Employment in Theory and Practice: Essays in Memory of Athanasios Asimakopulos*, Basingstoke: Palgrave Macmillan.

Harrod, R. F. (1939), 'An Essay in Dynamic Theory', *Economic Journal*, 49, 14–33.

Harrod, R. F. (1948), *Towards a Dynamic Economics*, London: Macmillan.

Hicks, J. R. (1939), *Value and Capital*, Oxford: Clarendon Press.

Hicks, J. R. (1950), *A Contribution to the Theory of the Trade Cycle*, Oxford: Clarendon Press.

Hicks, John (1976), *The Crisis in Keynesian Economics*, Oxford: Clarendon Press.

Kaldor, N. (1939), 'Speculation and Economic Stability', *Review of Economic Studies*, 7, 1–27.

Kalecki, M. (1935), 'A Macrodynamic Theory of Business Cycles', *Econometricia*, 3, 327–44.

Kalecki, M. (1968), 'Trend and Business Cycle Reconsidered', *Economic Journal*, 78, 263–76.

Keynes, J. M. (1930), *A Treatise on Money*, 2 vols, London: Macmillan.

Keynes, J. M. (1936), *The General Theory of Employment, Interest and Money*, London: Macmillan.

Keynes, J. M. (1937a, 1937b, 1973), *Collected Writings*, vol. XIV, London: Macmillan.

Keynes, J. M. (1979), *Collected Writings*, vol. XXIX, London: Macmillan.

Kregel, J. A. (1976), 'Economic Methodology in the Face of Uncertainty: The Modelling Methods of Keynes and the Post Keynesians', *Economic Journal*, 86, 209–25.

Kregel, J. A. (1986), 'A Note on Finance, Liquidity, Saving and Investment', *Journal of Post Keynesian Economics*, 9, 91–100.

Patinkin, D. (1956), *Money, Interest and Prices*, New York: Row Peterson.

Robinson, J. (1933), *The Economics of Imperfect Competition*, London: Macmillan.

Robinson, J. (1956), *The Accumulation of Capital*, London: Macmillan.

Robinson, J. (1971), *Economic Heresies: Some Old-fashioned Questions in Economic Theory*, Basingstoke: Palgrave Macmillan.

Samuelson, P. A. (1947), *Foundations of Economic Analysis*, Cambridge, MA: Harvard University Press.

Sardoni, C. (ed.) (1992), *On Political Economists and Modern Political Economy, Selected Essays of G. C. Harcourt*, London: Routledge.

Snippe, J. (1985), 'Finance, Savings and Investment in Keynes's Economics', *Cambridge Journal of Economics*, 9, 257–69.

Sraffa, P. (1926), 'The Laws of Returns Under Competitive Conditions', *Economic Journal*, 36, 535–50.

Sraffa, P. (1960), *Production of Commodities by Means of Commodities. Prelude to a Critique of Economic Theory*, Cambridge: Cambridge University Press.

Townshend, H. (1937), 'Liquidity-Premium and the Theory of Value', *Economic Journal*, 47, 157–69.

Weitzman, M. L. (1982), 'Increasing Returns and the Foundations of Unemployment Theory', *Economic Journal*, 92, 787–804.

Weldon, J. C. (1988), 'The Classical Theory of Distribution', in Asimakopulos (ed.) (1988a), pp. 15–47.

16

Keith Septimus Frearson, 18 September 1922–2 February 2000: A Memoir and a Tribute (2000)*

Keith Frearson was born to store-keeper parents, William Allan Frearson and Olive Elizabeth, née Roberts, in the small wheat-farming town of Tammin in Western Australia. He was the sixth of eight children – he attributed his second name to the fact that his mother had lost count. He was a RAAF navigator in Lancasters in Bomber Command during World War II. He beat the odds many times in an exceptional number of flights over Germany (including the raid on Dresden) for which he was awarded the Distinguished Flying Cross (DFC). These horrific experiences undoubtedly affected him and his behaviour for the rest of his life though he rarely spoke of them except in typical Frearson jests.

After the war he did honours mathematics and economics at the University of Western Australia. He then taught Statistical Method (in Jean Polglaze's famous second year course) and Mathematical Economics at Melbourne (1952–54) before going to Clare College, Cambridge for the years 1954 to 1956. There, he was supervised first by Nicholas Kaldor and then by Robin Matthews. Angus Sinclair tells us that going to Cambridge for Keith was 'akin to a religious experience'. He found his inspiration in Joan Robinson; he went to her lectures on what was to become *The Accumulation of Capital* (1956) and fell under her spell. She 'provided the intellectual and emotional backing to confirm Keith's incipient belief in the human possibilities of economics…that [it] was nothing if it was not about social betterment;' (Sinclair 2000a, 1). He could not abide – and said so to their faces – those who treated the subject as just a technical exercise. Joan Robinson and Frearson became great friends and Frearson looked after her on her two visits to Australia

---

* Originally published in *Economic Record*, vol. 76, September 2000, pp. 297–300.

(1967 and 1975). Frearson subsequently spent most of his study leaves in Cambridge where he was a great favourite of the Faculty and students alike, as well as of his landlady in Maids' Causeway.

In 1956 Frearson returned to a lectureship at Melbourne. When Donald Cochrane set up the Faculty at Monash University, Frearson went with him as Senior Lecturer responsible for the economics statistics course. He also taught macroeconomics, especially economic growth. He stayed at Monash for the rest of his life, becoming an Associate Professor in the 1970s. He lived in Mannix College (and was also a frequent visitor to the Notting Hill pub, for, as everyone knew, Keith enjoyed a drink). Frearson kept a room in the Menzies building and continued to teach after he retired in 1987.

Frearson was a remarkable teacher, placing premiums on teaching and a pastoral role which remain unattainable goals for most university teachers. Completely on top of his material, he also had the knack of making it crystal clear. He always got to the core of issues. He used mathematics to illuminate, not obfuscate. By helping 'students to become familiar with the *mechanics* of a problem, [they could then] concentrate…upon its *economic* meaning and application'. Frearson, undated, ii, emphasis in original. His explanations of conceptual bases were as exciting as they were clearly explained.

Frearson was an extraordinarily funny, witty person (with a distinctive delivery often copied by his friends). He was incredibly kind and generous, willingly giving his time and money. He wrote like an angel, but, sadly, published little. The year 1964 was his *annus mirabilis*: he published three articles – a survey of growth theory in the June–December issue of *Australian Economic Papers*, 'The Law and the Lore', in the May 16 issue of *Nation*, and 'A Guide to make you happy. Reflections on leisure and economic growth' in the Autumn issue of *Dissent*. His lecture notes have survived and he wrote up his lectures on mathematics to first-year students as *Elementary Mathematics for Students of Economics*. He once wrote for the present author his views on Harrod's model 'Harrod's Dynamics – the F. T. version (as told to G.C.H.)' (He always referred to his students as F. T. – 'Frearson Trained'). He drew judiciously on arguments in *The General Theory* as well as on Harrod's writings. He emphasised that in long-period analysis it is reasonable to suppose that, for a given value of planned investment expenditure, short-term expectations may be taken as realised so that actual short-period income is always equilibrium short-period income. This allowed Harrod to bring out the destabilising effects on the economy in the long period of a gap between planned saving and investment at the expected level of sales, if the economy was not on the warranted rate of growth (g_w). Frearson carefully identified which concepts are actual, which expected, and the consequences of their non-equality. Thus, even if plans are always realised, it is *only* when the economy is on g_w that decision-makers are glad they made those plans in the first place; see Harcourt (2002).

In his 1964 survey he identified Arthur Lewis's and Joan Robinson's books (1955, 1956) as the major ones on growth. He thought a unified treatment of the then literature 'exceedingly difficult' – ' "A Complete Theory of Growth Involving Heterogeneous Models" would be beset with index number problems no less formidable than those involved in the theory of capital' (1). He nevertheless believed growth theory had achieved something – growth was a stated objective of policy and theory provided 'a method of thinking about current problems in the content of an expanding economy' (2).

Frearson used the models of Joan Robinson's *Accumulation of Capital* because simple models and clear thinking provide 'insight into the fundamental elements of an extremely complex process' (2). By concentrating on 'the purely economic strands in the process of development' light may be shed on otherwise dark corners, provide a practical guide to... understanding history, and [indicate] to planners...how best they might set about their task' (3). Frearson made wise remarks about both the measurement and meaning of capital and how ultimately, it is consumption per head (and its distribution) which is of supreme importance. He stated clearly what Harrod instability is – if the economy is not in initially on g_w it won't ever find its way there – and that full employment of capital and labour requires $g_n = g_w = g$. He is explicit that Joan Robinson's Golden Age is the dynamic counterpart of Marshall's stationary state and that both are mythical states of affairs. He stresses the Keynesian moral that growth of output depends on 'animal spirits' and a strong inducement to invest: failing these, increasing saving can be a positive impediment to growth. He has sensible things to say about technical progress, on how it impinges on modelling – and the economy.

In his discussion of the choice of technique he stated succinctly the Robinsonian critique concerning using differences to analyse changes:

> The production of Bigger and Better machines [in a transition process] calls into question the measurement of the stock of capital...To avoid this...capital [must be assumed to be] a fluid factor of production...or [we must assume] that there is instantaneous adjustment to each new technique introduced...not compatible with an analysis of [time-paths]...neglect [of] adjustments...is tantamount to applying comparative statics to a process in time. (19)

Frearson concluded that the arguments had clarified 'in some measure the sort of economic theory...appropriate for true dynamic economics'. The main casualties may well be 'the conventional production function...and marginal productivity theory' (24) – a right cause which has not triumphed! Frearson had strong likes and dislikes in economics and other walks of life – echoes of his time and place of birth could sometimes surface. His heroine was Joan Robinson, his heroes were Harrod, Colin Clark, Trevor Swan, Donald Cochrane and, of course, Keynes. He did *not* like Milton Friedman or his views. He greatly admired the United Kingdom, its institutions and traditions, especially those now passing away. He had 'an abiding respect for form and tradition [and while] firmly on the side of the underdog, [he was] respectful of those he judged to be exercising proper authority' (Sinclair (2000b, 7)).

Frearson had a great passion for Aussie Rules; he was the number one ticket holder for South Melbourne and then, when on the losing side of their move to Sydney as the Sydney Swans, a founder and often President of the Monash Football Club, as well as doing far more than a fair share of the chores associated with running amateur football clubs.

He became ill at the end of 1999 and died on 2 February 2000. Keith Frearson was truly a legend in his own life time. The tributes paid to him after he died were remarkable both for their numbers and for the sentiments expressed.

References

Frearson, K. S. (1960), 'Review of Hans Brems, *Output, Employment, Capital and Growth*, New York: Harper & Brothers, (1959)', *Economic Record*, 36, 295–300.
Frearson, K. S. (1964a), 'The Law and the Lore', *Nation*, 16 May, 6.
Frearson, K. S. (1964b), 'A Quid to Make You Happy: Reflections on Leisure and Economic Growth', *Dissent*, Autumn, 25–28.
Frearson, K. S. (1964a), 'Recent Developments in the Theory of Economic Growth', *Australian Economic Papers*, 3, 1–24.
Frearson, K. S. (undated), *Elementary Mathematics for Students of Economics*, mimeo, Monash.
Harcourt, G. C. (2002), 'Keith Frearson on Roy Harrod, as told to Geoff Harcourt', *History of Economics Review*, No 36, Summer, 76–84.
Harrod, R. F. (1948), *Towards a Dynamic Economics: Some Recent Developments of Economic Theory and their Application to Policy*, London: Macmillan.
Robinson, Joan (1956), *The Accumulation of Capital*, London: Macmillan.
Lewis, W. A. (1955), *The Theory of Economic Growth*, London: Macmillan.
Sinclair, A. G. (2000a), 'Keith Frearson', address at Frearson's funeral, mimeo.
Sinclair, A. G. (2000b), 'Keith Septimus Frearson. RAAF Navigator and University Lecturer 18.9.1922–2.2. 2000,' *Age*, 7 March, 7.

17
Reddaway [William] Brian, 1913–2002 (2004)*

Brian Reddaway was born on 8 January 1913 in Cambridge into a Cambridge 'gown' family. His father, William Fiddian Reddaway, was an historian (of Eastern Europe), a fellow of King's College and the first Censor of Fitzwilliam House. His mother was Kate Waterland Sills. Except for two years in Australia at the University of Melbourne (1936–38), Cambridge was always to be his base. He died in Cambridge on 23 July 2002 after a short illness.

Reddaway went to King's College School (1920–24), Lydgate House (Boarding) School, Hunstanton (1924–26) and Oundle School (1926–31). He came up to Cambridge (King's) as a Scholar in Natural Sciences in October 1931 and decided to read for Part I of the Mathematics Tripos before going on to read Chemistry in Part II of the Natural Sciences Tripos. Because he was 'inevitably much stirred by attempts to explain the slump and see a way out' (Harcourt, 1993, 153), coupled with a 'desire to understand why the world was suffering from "poverty in the midst of potential plenty"' (Reddaway, 1995, 31), the college agreed that he could forsake chemistry and read for Part II of the Economics Tripos. His supervisors in economics at King's were Richard Kahn and Gerald Shove; he also went once a fortnight to Maynard Keynes, who thought him the best pupil of his year in the Tripos. This opinion was confirmed by the Tripos examiners in 1934 who classed him as the only Ii of the year. Reddaway kept the essays he wrote for Keynes; on a memorable day in 1996 to mark 50 years on from Keynes's death, Reddaway read out Keynes's comments

* Originally published in *The New Palgrave: A Dictionary of Economics*, Vol. 4, London: Macmillan, 1987, pp. 108–109 and in Donald Rutherford (ed.), *The Biographical Dictionary of British Economists*, Volume 2, K-Z, Bristol: Thoemmes Continuum, 2004, pp. 998–1003

on his efforts to an audience of dons and students in a Mill Lane Lecture Theatre. There was a clear positive correlation between the answers to applied and policy questions (as compared to essays on theory) and the positiveness of Keynes's comments, a prescient omen indeed concerning Reddaway's subsequent career and contributions.

Reddaway joined the Bank of England as a special entrant in 1934. He went with his father to Russia before he started work at the Bank proper. This led to his first book, *The Russian Financial System* (1935), 'an "economist's" account of what [he] had learned in a month' (Reddaway, 1995, 5). The book is a little masterpiece (the essay on which it was based won the 1934 Adam Smith Prize at Cambridge). It is noted for its insight and its application, where relevant, of the then emerging analysis of Keynes's *General Theory*. Reddaway said that 'it was fascinating to find in what ways things worked similarly in Russia to the way they did in the West, and what were the important differences' (Reddaway, 1995, 4). For example, the study included an account of a tax system which provided the appropriate price level to ensure the purchase of the residual production of consumption goods once the level of accumulation had been decided, and given a socialist commitment to full employment of labour.

Subsequently his 'normal' duties at the Bank proved to be dull and slow moving. Reddaway asked Keynes for help just when Keynes received a letter from a former King's man, L. F. Giblin,, the Australian economist who held the Ritchie Chair of Economic Research at the University of Melbourne. Giblin was looking for an Economic Research Fellow to work with him as he had just been made a non-Executive Director of the Central Bank. Reddaway cites this as yet another example of himself as a lucky economist, to be in the right place at the right time when economists were faced with urgent and fundamental problems.

Reddaway left in January 1936 for two happy and productive years at the University of Melbourne, where he lived and tutored in Queen's College, as well as working with Giblin. He took with him an advance copy of *The General Theory* which he read on the ship (the voyage took 5.5 weeks). The Melbourne economists asked him to write what turned out to be the first published and one of the most perceptive reviews of *The General Theory*. (Reddaway's review was published in the June 1936 issue of the *Economic Record*.) His review is a lucid account of the main propositions of *The General Theory*; it only could have been written by someone who had absorbed and understood the contents of Keynes's *magnum opus*. It includes a footnote that is in essence IS/LM, an interpretation which its author only twigged on to some 50 years later when his attention was drawn to this by the historian of the IS/LM saga, Warren Young (1987). Reddaway criticised Keynes on this point, that he had not brought out enough 'the extent to which the variables *mutually determine one another*, rather than following a chain process' and on another, that Keynes should have used the 'cost of capital' rather than the rate of interest and taken quantity rationing of different borrowers into account (Reddaway, 1995, 6, emphasis in original). Keynes cheerfully took these criticisms on board without comment, writing to Reddaway that the review 'was very well done' (Reddaway, 1995, 6). In 1964, Reddaway returned to the review and wrote on issues he felt he had neglected: 'incorporation of government in the analysis; the static nature of the analysis; and the factors determining investment' (Reddaway, 1964, 108).

In 1937 Reddaway was subpoenaed to give evidence as an independent assessor (at the age of 24!) on the Trade Unions' submission to the 1937 Basic Wage Case. So effective was his evidence that the Commonwealth Arbitration Court accepted the Unions' case. The Basic Wage was returned to the real level it had before a large cut in 1931, together with a small addition. The 1937 Basic Wage judgment, known to this day as the Reddawage, prevailed for the next 15 years. Reddaway's reasons for the decision were not *that* Keynesian. He thought that real wages should be raised because otherwise the share of profits would be too great, fuelling an investment boom and resulting in sectoral imbalance.

Reddaway returned to England in January 1938 to take up a Fellowship at Clare College, Cambridge where he remained as a much respected and loved fellow for 64 years. In 1939 he was appointed to a university lectureship in the Faculty of Economics and Politics. He wrote (at the suggestion of John Hicks) one of his most original books, *The Economics of a Declining Population* (1939). Though his analysis of the longer-run effects of a declining population is orthodoxly neoclassical – a higher standard of living emerges because of higher capital per person than otherwise would have been the case – his discussion of the relationship between population growth and the level of employment is an astute application of the then, very new, Keynesian theory of employment. Moreover, the policy proposals read in a thoroughly modern manner, so that the impending reissue of his classic comes at a most opportune moment.

Reddaway experienced at this time his greatest stroke of luck of all: he wooed and won the hand of Barbara Augusta Bennett. The wonderfully happy partnership of 'Brian and Barbara' began with their engagement in June 1938 and marriage on 17 September 1938. Though Reddaway's relationship with his father was not anything like that between James and John Stuart Mill, there is no doubt that until he met Barbara, he felt that his emotional development and social confidence lagged far behind his intellectual prowess, development and confidence. The letter he wrote to Barbara when he became engaged is a moving testament to their love and to the emotions and happiness their relationship released for him. It also revealed that Reddaway had almost a 'new man' attitude, certainly for those times, to the respective roles of men and women in marriage, that is to say, an equal partnership in everything except with regard to men's employment; see Jacky Fisher in L. Reddaway, 2003, 26–27.

The second world war saw Reddaway working at the Board of Trade (1940–47), making his mark in the design and implementation of clothes rationing. As Richard Kahn related it, Reddaway, 'a highly conscientious man', thought that his involvement in the scheme's preparation must exclude him from benefiting from it. He burned his ration book each year. His clothes were in a dreadful state towards the end of the war, leading an American visitor to remark: 'These Brits certainly practise what they preach' (Marcuzzo, 1988, 28–29). He was a United Kingdom representative on a three-sided investigation by the Canadian, UK and US governments into the impact of the war on civilian consumption in these three countries, published in 1945. He also helped prepare an improved Census of Production and a new Census of Distribution. He represented the Board of Trade on the inter-departmental committee which drew up the new (post-war) index of retail prices. The Colonial Office subsequently sent him to Cyprus in 1949 and Sierra Leone in 1955 where 'ingenious common-sense and a careful discussion of problems with all the "parties" involved led to the smooth introduction of ... generally accepted [indexes]' (Reddaway, 1995, 8–9).

In 1947 Reddaway returned to the Faculty and Clare, but also took part in the sort of applied work – 'practical' jobs – he loved to do and in which his comparative advantage as an economist lay. First, he worked half-time at the Ministry of Fuel on a new 'rationing' problem, petrol this time, where Reddaway suggested an ingenious use of the price mechanism to complement the modest basic ration for all by making insurance half price for cars without supplementary coupons. Secondly, his most important 'practical' job, in 1951–52 he worked in Paris at the OECD on the Marshall Plan, writing a report concerned with liberalising trade between European countries and running the European Payments Union. From his experience he realised how important personal relationships are in international negotiations (Reddaway, 1995, 9–10).

In 1955 he was appointed Director of the Department of Applied Economics (DAE) at Cambridge, succeeding the founding Director, Richard Stone, who was made an offer he could not refuse, the P. D. Leake Chair of Finance and Accounting. Reddaway was promoted to an *ad hominem* Readership in Applied Economics in 1957. When James Meade retired in 1969 from the Chair of Political Economy (once held by Marshall), Reddaway (who was near the end of the compulsory tenure of the Directorship) was elected to succeed him, his 'usual good luck holding', he claimed (Reddaway, 1995, 10).

As Director he gave selflessly of his time to all working there, leaving his own detailed stamp, through prolonged written and verbal criticism, on the many careful, useful and down-to-earth books and papers that appeared under the imprint of the department under his Directorship. He was, the *Times* obituarist noted, 'an invaluable but ruthless critic [with] an exceptional capacity to master essential issues in any problem quickly' (L. Reddaway, 2003, 35). He was also to many 'something of a father figure' at the DAE, from whom they learnt a great deal, whose careers he helped to develop (as Keynes had his) and who valued him 'not only as a great economist but also as a good friend' (Ken George, in L. Reddaway, 2003, 57–58).

Reddaway himself headed two major research projects on 'the effects of direct overseas investment' (Reddaway, 1969, 1968) and 'the effects of the selective employment tax' (Reddaway, 1973), the 'climax to [his] work at the DAE' (Reddaway, 1995, 10). Martin Weale (in L. Reddaway, 2003, 38) points out that Reddaway was one of the first economists to address the question of foreign investment and assess its effect on the domestic economy: 'His conclusion was that it was worthwhile and should not be discouraged unless pressure on the foreign exchange reserves was particularly acute.' This last is an apt summary of the illumination provided by the Report. The second project was cut short when the incoming Conservative Government in 1970 scrapped the tax and withdrew the Treasury funds for financing the project – but not before Reddaway and his team had found by extremely hard work the positive effect on productivity that its originator, Nicholas Kaldor, had conjectured (though it was not as large as Kaldor had hoped would occur).

As well as these reports, Reddaway wrote a number of seminal papers. Two may serve as examples: 'Wage flexibility and the distribution of labour' (1959) and 'Rising prices for ever?' (1966). The first paper posed the question, what relocates labour, relative wages or job opportunities? Reddaway's carefully presented evidence strongly supported the latter. His analysis and answer for that time certainly needs to be followed up now in the United Kingdom in which the unproven assertion that flexible labour markets (a euphemism for using unemployment to cowe labour, reduce money – wage increases and make them more flexible in order to drive inflation out of the system) are *the* keys to attaining efficiency and prosperity. The second paper (it argued that because of demand-pull and cost-push forces, the question mark should be scrapped) was read and liked by Aubrey Jones who offered Reddaway part-time membership of the Prices and Incomes Board. This proved to be 'a highly interesting experience' for him, even though often the results achieved, especially with regard to money-wages, were disappointing. Reddaway put his finger on the reason why: the cases referred to the Board were allowed increases in money-wages which, if applied generally, would have implied a zero rise in prices. This outcome was undone by rises *not* implying this in the cases *not* referred to the Board.

His insight anticipated the thrust of the sequel to his paper, Reddaway (1997). There, unlike Arthur Brown (1997) who sided with Keynes's desire for long-term constancy of the general price level, Reddaway argued that there were sufficient flexibility and institutional structures in the system to allow most sections of the community to protect their real incomes so that the stimulus to investment and activity of gently rising prices could be allowed to operate.

Reddaway was an outstanding development economist. He visited many developing countries in the post-war years, 'a tireless globetrotter, advising national governments and bodies' (Michael Posner in L. Reddaway, 2003, 42), travelling abroad well into his eighties (his last visit was to Vietnam accompanied as ever by Barbara). He had great sympathy for the problems and inequities of the developing countries. His work on their problems was built up from first principles, themselves founded in keen common-sense observations and empirical generalisations. The appendix to *The Development of the Indian Economy* (Reddaway, 1962) on the importance of lags in the investment decision contains one of his most important insights. His policy recommendations were directed straight-forwardly to the problems in hand, always relevant if sometimes lacking in political nous, yet always showing, as Michael Posner puts it (L. Reddaway, 2003, 42): 'His quietly passionate concern to help the poorer countries to climb out of poverty.' Valerie Taylor, Co-ordinator, Centre for Rehabilitation of the Paralysed (CRP), Bangladesh, writes that, on learning of his death, 200 staff members stood for a moment's silence in Reddaway Hall 'built with the extremely generous gift that Brian and Barbara Reddaway gave for the work of CRP' (Taylor in L. Reddaway, 2003, 64).

Next, mention must be made of two activities dear to his heart – the editorship of the *Economic Journal* with his life-long friend David Champernowne (1971–76) and with Phyllis Deane as review editor; and his regular column as 'academic investor' in *The Investors Chronicle* in which he bared all on how his own and his college's portfolio had fared. The years as editor were remarkable ones. The demands on authors for clarity and detailed care could never have been greater. Reddaway was not widely read in the modern literature and neither knew nor cared who was who in the profession. Contributors were forced to state and restate their arguments, often up to five drafts, in order to get them past one of the highest natural intelligences our profession has seen. (Champernowne was the perfect complement in this activity.) Though often chastened by their attention, authors were nevertheless grateful for either much improved final products or for escaping making asses of themselves in the public domain.

An index of the enthusiasm with which Reddaway viewed the second activity is that he gave more space to it than to virtually any other episode in his 1995 autobiographical essay. The approach to portfolio management Reddaway persuaded his college to take is a slight variant on Keynes's own successful method when in the 1930s he changed his tactics and became a rich man as a result. In the 1920s he mostly speculated on the futures and forward exchange markets and ended up losing. He ceased to be a Hicksian 'snatcher' and became a Hicksian 'sticker' – create a portfolio with a few enough items in it to allow its holder to have considerable information about each item and stick to this choice unless there are very good reasons for changing, i.e., selling out or buying more of particular shares. The relevant committee of Reddaway's college met once a year from 1953 on to implement their policy of 'inactive management', a strategy that proved to be remarkably successful (see Reddaway, 1995, 15–16), not least because it allowed Clare College to fund the establishment of Clare Hall, a college for research students, in the early 1960s.

Reddaway was much respected as a teacher – he lectured well into his eighties. One of the last courses he gave was his first ever lectures on the principles of macroeconomics to Part I. He loved to lecture on statistics and generations of Tripos students have been brought up on the 'Reddaway method' and 'Reddaway questions' – know and understand your data, strengths and limitations, never use sophisticated methods if simple ones, scatter diagrams, free hand curves, for example, will tell you what you need to know. There is also a Reddaway technique for deseasonalising time series data. A most popular course in the 1970s was one on policy issues, presented as a dialogue with Champernowne. They would set up the problems, Champernowne would then provide the theoretical framework, Reddaway the necessary empirical ingredients and together they would set out the solutions, stressing as ever limitations as well as strengths. Reddaway supervised generations of Clare undergraduates, all of whom would have agreed with the assessment made by Bill Humphrey of 'Brian the Teacher' at Reddaway's Memorial Service. Humphrey was allowed to choose his own topics for his weekly essay, Reddaway would read the essay carefully beforehand, start with a word of encouragement – 'stout effort' – then gently probe and summarise with clarity and common sense. He discouraged jargon, was impatient of theory with little application and 'taught [Humphrey] not to strive after spurious accuracy'. His pupils deduced that 'he felt the ultimate reason for studying economics was to make the world a better place', 'that economic policies should be judged by the impact they have on the quality of people's lives' (Humphrey in L. Reddaway, 2003, 28–29).

Reddaway was also greatly in demand as a supervisor (if not examiner) of Ph.D dissertations. The most famous of the many he supervised over the years was the dissertation that formed the basis of W. E. G. Salter's classic book, *Productivity and Technical Change* (1960). (A second edition was published in 1966 with an addendum by Reddaway following Salter's tragically early death at the age of 34 in 1963.)

Brian Reddaway was fundamentally a kind and generous person, despite (or even because of) his blunt honesty and brutally frank criticisms of other's work (as well as his own) and his legendary carefulness over small amounts of money and other resources. Thus his manuscripts were usually written on the backs of past examination scripts. An incident related to Peter Reddaway illustrates beautifully Brian's integrity, honest and carefulness. His successor as Director of the DAE, Wynne Godley, asked Brian about his 'occasional claims' to be reimbursed the cost of a train ticket to London. Reddaway explained that he was being paid large amounts for the advice to the Confederation of British Industry (CBI) and attending their quarterly meetings in London. He donated those amounts anonymously to the DAE's research fund but felt that he did not 'deserve to be actually out of pocket' – hence the claims to be reimbursed (P. Reddaway in L. Reddaway, 2003, 46).

To sum up: Reddaway was a fine example of an applied economist in the tradition of Marshall and Keynes. He had one of the finest critical minds in the profession, remorselessly revealing flaws in logic and ignorance of the nature and use of data alike. He was severely practical

– the philosophical and speculative aspects of the discipline had no appeal to him and he had no use for theory for its own sake. He liked to be given questions and/or problems to solve: he produced reports noted for their innovative approach and clarity. Though in the years of monetarism he played a prominent role in defending Keynesian theory and policies from their monetarist critics, he was nevertheless an open-minded eclectic, willing to accept ideas from any approach provided they accorded with common sense and had an empirical foundation.

Brian Reddaway died in Cambridge on 23 July 2002. Barbara predeceased him, dying in Adenbrooke's hospital on 15 September 1996. He told his granddaughter Lucy Crampin in 1997 that he thought about Barbara 'every second of every day' (Crampton in L. Reddaway, 2003, 51). They had four children, 11 grandchildren and one great grandchild. The tributes in the booklet edited by Lawrence Reddaway (2003) testify to what remarkable parents and grandparents they were, and to the stable, loving family environment they created. Both Barbara and Brian came from the English upper-middle, professional class, members of which seem to be either the best or the worst of human beings, with little in between. The Reddaways were in all ways the best. Just as Brian thought himself a lucky person, so too their many friends and his colleagues were extremely lucky to have had them as friends and mentors.

References

Brown, A. J. (1997), 'The Inflationary Dimension', in Harcourt and Riach (eds), vol. 2 (1997), 41–60.

Crampton, Lucy (2003), 'Recollections by Lucy Crampton (granddaughter)', in L. Reddaway (2003), 50–51.

Eatwell, John, Murray Milgate and Peter Newman (eds) (1987), *The New Palgrave Dictionary of Economics, vol. 4, Q to Z*, London: Macmillan; New York: Stockton Press; Tokyo: Maruzen Company Limited.

Fisher, Jacky (2003), 'Readings from Letters by Brian Reddaway', in L. Reddaway (2003), 24–27.

Harcourt, G. C. (1987), 'Reddaway, Brian William (born 1913)', in Eatwell, Milgate and Newman (eds), vol. 4 (1987), 108–9.

Harcourt, G. C. (1993), *Post-Keynesian Essays in Biography: Portraits of Twentieth-Century Political Economists*, London: Macmillan.

Harcourt, G. C. and P. A. Riach (eds) (1997), *A 'Second Edition' of The General Theory*, 2 vols, London: Routledge.

Humphrey, Bill (2003), 'Reflection: Brian the Teacher', in L. Reddaway (2003), 27–29.

Lekachman, Robert (ed.) (1964), *Keynes's General Theory, Reports of Three Decades*, London: Macmillan; New York: St Martin's Press.

Marcuzzo, Cristina (1988), 'Richard F. Kahn: A Disciple of Keynes', *mimeo*, Modena.

Posner, Michael (2003), (Obituary from *Guardian* 5 September 2002), 'Brian Reddaway', in L. Reddaway (2003), 40–42.

Reddaway, Lawrence (ed.) (2003), *William Brian Reddaway, 08 January 1913 – 23 July 2002 and Barbara Augusta Reddaway, 15 August 1912 – 15 September 1996. Memories.*

Reddaway, Peter (2003), 'Reflections on Dad's Life', in L. Reddaway (2003), 45–50.

Reddaway, W. B. (1935), *The Russian Financial System*, London: Macmillan.

Reddaway, W. B. (1936), 'General Theory of Employment, Interest and Money', *Economic Record*, 12, 28–36.

Reddaway, W. B. (1939), *The Economics of a Declining Population*, London: George Allen and Unwin.

Reddaway, W. B. (1959), 'Wage Flexibility and the Distribution of Labour', *Lloyds Bank Review*, 13, 32–48.

Reddaway, W. B. (1962), *The Development of the Indian Economy*, London: George Allen and Unwin.

Reddaway, W. B. (1964), 'Keynesian Analysis and a Mixed Economy', in Lekachman (ed.) (1964), 108–23.

Reddaway, W. B. (1966), 'Rising prices for ever?' *Lloyds Bank Review*, July.

Reddaway, W. B. (1967), *Effects of UK Direct Investment Overseas – Interim Report*, Cambridge: Cambridge University Press.

Reddaway, W. B. (1968), *Effects of UK Direct Investment Overseas – Final Report*, Cambridge: Cambridge University Press.

Reddaway, W. B. (1970, 1973), *Effects of Selective Employment Tax*, 2 vols, Cambridge: Cambridge University Press, HMSO.

Reddaway, W. B. (1997), 'The changing significance of inflation', in Harcourt and Riach (eds), vol. 2 (1997), 28–40.

Salter, W. E. G. (1960), *Productivity and Technical Change*, Cambridge: Cambridge University Press; 2nd edition with an Addendum by W. B. Reddaway, 1966.

Weale, Martin (2003), 'Obituary from *The Independent*, 31 July 2002', in L. Reddaway (2003), 37–42.

Young, Warren (1987), *Interpreting Mr. Keynes: The IS/LM Enigma*, Cambridge: Polity Press.

18
Sukhamoy Chakravarty, 26 July 1934–22 August 1990 (1991)*

with Ajit Singh

Sukhamoy Chakravarty, who died in Delhi on 22 August 1990, was internationally respected as an academic economist of the highest distinction. Like Maynard Keynes, he was one of those rare scholars who are able successfully to bridge the gap between the world of learning and practical affairs. For over 20 years he worked at the centre of Indian economic planning, either as a member of India's Planning Commission or as one of its chief advisers. At his death he was chairman of the Council of Economic Advisers to the Indian Prime Minister, having served three successive prime ministers, and was also a professor at the Delhi School of Economics (where he did a full stint as a devoted lecturer and researcher).

Chakravarty was a cultured, learned person. He was extremely well read in his chosen subject and also in philosophy, physics and mathematics. He saw parallels and inter-relationships within and between disciplines which eluded less gifted minds. He took great delight in clearing intellectual hurdles, always looking for fresh ideas to discuss and new papers to read. Chakravarty was an unassuming man, with a wry sense of humour, approachable by students, colleagues and friends alike, always wise good company. He had nevertheless a proper sense of his own abilities. He was courteous but firm in debate, and he took much pleasure in the simple verities – family life, the company of friends, the solitary pleasures of the scholar with his books.

After a brilliant undergraduate career, Chakravarty went to Rotterdam to work for a PhD under Jan Tinbergen, for whom he had the greatest respect and affection, attitudes which were warmly reciprocated by Tinbergen. His dissertation was on the theory of planning. After

---

* Originally published in *Cambridge Journal of Economics*, vol. 15, 1991, pp. 1–3.

Rotterdam, Chakravarty went to a teaching post at the Massachusetts Institute of Technology. There he impressed Paul Samuelson as an outstandingly intelligent and original economic theorist.

Although Chakravarty was a mathematical economist, he combined that subject with political economy, so that his distinction lay in providing a bridge between the different schools of thought in modern economics. He was a devoted admirer of his neoclassical mentors, Tinbergen and Samuelson, but in his scholarly work he had a special affinity to the classical economists and to the Cambridge school of Sraffa, Joan Robinson and Kaldor (Chakravarty, 1982).

A career in the United States 'Ivy League' universities would have been his for the asking as in the late 1950s and 1960s he wrote seminal papers in leading international journals as well as path-breaking books on optimal growth and the theory of planning (Chakravarty, 1959, 1969). But he chose instead to return to India, where he joined the Planning Commission. He combined the roles of gifted economist and concerned citizen in a democratic society, trying to ally growth processes with equity for all its citizens. His experience of the practical details and difficulties of planning, however, made him sceptical of the role of pure theory in concrete situations. Chakravarty established for himself a pragmatic structure within which to think about planning, taking into account political, sociological, and historical constraints, and he was able to maintain his independence and integrity throughout all the changes of those years.

Chakravarty was an economist of the Left. However, he was not a revolutionary, rather a democratic socialist who believed in planning the commanding heights of a mixed economy and in a pluralist democratic polity. Because he continued to work for the government even when he did not approve of particular government policies, in order to attempt to change these from within, he was often criticised by the Indian Left. The antipathy of the Right and of mainstream liberal economists to his economic and political stance was, of course, to be expected. In the Indian political system, economic policy formulation and, particularly, its implementation take place largely as a result of deliberations inside the government machinery. It is arguable, to say the least, whether Chakravarty would have accomplished more by working outside the government than by his non-public but vigorous advocacy from within the establishment of the economic policies in which he passionately believed.

Together with the late Professor P. C. Mahalanobis, Chakravarty was widely acknowledged to be one of two leading intellectual figures associated with the momentous experiment of Indian planning. However, unlike Mahalanobis, Chakravarty was involved not only in the technical and theorectical work of economic planning, but also directly in the implementation of the five-year Plans during the past two decades. Any overall assessment of Chakravarty's contribution, therefore, inevitably depends on one's views about the successes and failures of India's economic planning and of its pluralistic polity. This is, of course, a highly controversial subject, which arouses passionate feelings among otherwise sober scholars of economic development. Clearly, we are too near the events to provide anything like a definitive appraisal of this experience, which, it must be remembered, has involved a fifth of mankind. Chakravarty's own brief but thoughtful and articulate defence of India's traditional development strategy is contained in his Radhakrishnan lectures, delivered in Oxford in 1986 (Chakravarty, 1987).

During the 1980s, for reasons which it would be insppropriate to go into here, the powerful Indian bureaucracy and the political leadership, with encouragement from the international financial institutions as well as liberal economists at home and abroad, embarked on a new economic strategy. This involved internal and external liberation, as well as a dose of the usual 'supply side' policies.[1] Chakravarty disagreed deeply with this new strategy, specifically on questions of external liberalisation. He nevertheless continued to be the Chairman of the Indian Council of Economic Advisers. In the Council's reports to the Prime Minister and in government counsels, he is known to have warned against the serious dangers of pursuing these liberalisation policies.[2]

In his Radhakrishnan lectures Chakravarty had outlined a rather different overall strategy for the 1990s from the one above. Apart from the technical shortcomings of the latter (e.g. the likelihood that it would lead to an unsustainable debt-servicing ratio), Chakravarty was most concerned that such policies would tend greatly to enhance inequalities in the distribution of income and wealth and thus imperil the country's political system. In place of this pattern of growth led by urban middle class consumption – what Lance Taylor has called the Brazilian model – Chakravarty put forward an 'agriculture first' strategy. In this view, instead of allowing investment in car production and other consumer durables with import-intensive technologies, Chakravarty thought that the government should invest in agriculture, so as to spread the 'green revolution' technology from Punjab and Haryana to the rest of the country. He argued that this would lead to a large increase in agricultural productivity and to a rise in rural living standards.

Although Chakravarty sketched out the essential argument of the 'agriculture first' strategy, he unfortunately did not get a chance to analyse its implications fully before his untimely death.[3] Towards the end of his life he was also deeply concerned with the more general theoretical, as well as practical policy questions facing not only India but all developing countries today: what are the optimal degree and pattern of 'openness' for an economy? In what order and how much should an economy liberalise in relation to trade, to foreign investment, to migration, to education, to culture, to science?[4] Sukhamoy Chakravarty had expected to take these ideas further in subsequent work, an opportunity alas cut short by his unexpected death at the early age of 56.

Notes

1. See Singh and Ghosh (1988) for a fuller analysis of the alternative Indian economic strategies.
2. The Council's reports to the Prime Minister are not normally published. However, when V. P. Singh became Prime Minister in 1990 he invited Chakravarty to continue as Chairman of the Council and allowed its report to the new Prime Minister on the state of the economy to be published. This report contains many of Chakravarty's thoughts on these issues (Government of India, 1989).
3. For a discussion of this strategy and, in particular, for an analysis of how Chakravarty's views differed from those of Mellors' similar-sounding proposals of 'agriculture first', see Singh and Tabatabahai, 1993.
4. Chakravarty and Singh presented an initial paper on this subject at WIDER in Helsinki in 1988 (Chakravarty and Singh, 1988).

References

Chakravarty, S. 1959. *The Logic of Investment Planning*, Vol. XVIII of *Contributions to Economic Analysis*, Amsterdam, North Holland Publishing Company, reprinted 1968, translated into Spanish, Madrid (1966).

Chakravarty, S. 1969. *Capital and Development Planning*, with a foreword by Professor Paul Samuelson, Nobel Laureate, Cambridge, MA, MIT Press.

Chakravarty, S. 1982. *Alternative Approaches to a Theory of Economic Growth – Marx, Marshall, Schumpeter, R. C. Dutt Memorial Lectures*, Calcutta, Orient Longman.

Chakravarty, S. 1987. *Development Planning: The Indian Experience*, Oxford, Clarendon Press.

Chakravarty, S. and Singh, A. 1988. 'The Desirable Forms of Economic Openness for the South', mimeo.

Government of India 1989. *Report of the Economic Advising Council on the Current Economic Situation and Priority Areas for Action*, New Delhi, Ministry of Finance, December, 1988.

Singh, A. and Ghosh, J. 1988. Import liberalisation and the New Industrial Strategy, *Economic and Political Weekly*, vol. 23, nos 45–47, November.

Singh, A. and Tabatabahai, H. (eds) (1993) *Economic Crisis and Agriculture* Cambridge: Cambridge University Press.

19
David Gawen Champernowne, 1912–2000: In Appreciation (2001)*

David Champernowne died in Devon on 19 August 2000 at the age of 88.[†] Though he was not directly associated with the *Cambridge Journal of Economics*, his major contributions both belong to and serve to extend the approach to economics which the journal is dedicated to preserve and advance. We wish therefore to record our appreciation of his life and work.

Champernowne was born in Oxford on 9 July 1912. His family roots, though, were in Devon. He was to hold posts at the LSE, Cambridge and Oxford; indeed, he held chairs in both 'ancient universities'. His undergraduate college was King's. He read mathematics (he was supervised with Alan Turing who became a close friend and with whom he was to design and construct a chess computer, the 'Turochamp', which was capable of beating bright beginners).

Reading Marshall awakened his interest in economics, so, advised by Keynes whose supervision pupil he became, he took the Maths Tripos in double quick time, obtaining a First, and then switched to the Economics Tripos in which he also obtained a First. He wrote a Fellowship Dissertation for King's on income distribution; this was to be a lasting interest of Champernowne, who always cared strongly about economic and social injustices, wanting to know why they occurred and what could be done about them. His dissertation was published 36 years later in 1973 as *Distribution of Income between Persons*. He lectured at the LSE (where he was influenced by Beveridge) and then at Cambridge in the late 1930s on economic statistics (I think he must have succeeded Colin Clark when Clark went to Australia). He spent the war years, first,

* Originally published in *Cambridge Journal of Economics*, vol. 25, July, 2001, pp. 439–42.

in the statistical section of the Prime Minister's office under Cherwell, and then in the Ministry of Aircraft Production with Jewkes. He did not find it easy to work with Cherwell. He and David Bensusan-Butt, a contemporary and close friend from King's, showed moral courage by criticising saturation bombing on the grounds of whether it was effective (it was not) and moral (it was not).

Immediately after the war, Champernowne became Director of the Oxford Institute of Statistics (1945–48) and a Fellow of Nuffield, then Professor of Statistics in 1948. He returned to Cambridge in 1959 to a Readership in the Faculty and a Fellowship at Trinity. He was elected to a Personal Chair in 1970. He retired in 1978. In retirement, he worked with Frank Cowell on a major book, *Economic Inequality and Income Distribution*, published by Cambridge University Press in 1998. His last years were plagued by ill health and anxiety, ameliorated to some degree when he and Mieke – they had married in 1948 – returned to his roots in Devon to be near one of their sons and grandchildren.

From the point of view of this journal, as well as his seminal writings on income distribution and inequality, I think his major contributions were, first, what was in effect a review article of *The General Theory*, which was published in the *Review of Economic Studies* in 1936, when he was only 23; his 'child's guide' to von Neumann's growth model in the *Review of Economic Studies* in 1945–46; his remarkable comment on Joan Robinson's 1953–54 article in the same journal, 'The production function and the theory of capital', which started the two Cambridge debates in capital theory (his 'comment' was nearly as long as her article and, in it, he identified most of the substantial issues, their significance and some possible solutions); the Kahn–Champernowne formula (1953–54) which, unknown to Champ (as he was affectionately known), was to appear independently in Piero Sraffa's 1960 book; and his trilogy on investment and uncertainty, *Uncertainty and Estimation in Economics* published in 1969, which was firmly in the Cambridge tradition of Keynes. In a complementary piece to these volumes but published earlier in 1964, he wrote

Some economists such as … Irving Fisher had written as though each individual's decision to save now carried with it the decision when instead to spend the money on consumption goods. [Others] wrote as though the determination of interest rates and of prices throughout the future was a simple matter of supply and demand extended from present markets to a scheme of future markets covering the years ahead … completely misleading … such future markets exist only in rare cases...individuals do not commit themselves years in advance in respect of their expenditure. Consequently employers have to plan in a thick fog, enshrouding not only what each other's plans may be, but every other likely state of demand and supply in the distant future. ...because of his perception of the inefficiency of this feature of our method of organizing production...Keynes kept returning to the links between the economic future and the present. (Champernowne, 1964, pp. 201–2)

In his review article of *The General Theory*, Champernowne argued that, while Keynes was correct to stress that wage-earners and employers bargained over money-wages at any moment of time, yet it was expected and desired real wages that they had in mind, taking into account their present and expected future circumstances. If in the event the economy did not deliver the real wages they desired, their actions would be directed to achieving them. Therefore, he argued, the observed trend relationship between unemployment and real wages was determined by the latter actions. He analysed how they reacted in the short period if actual wages were above or below the trend, on which what he called the basic wage prevailed. These arguments have been interpreted as Champernowne saying that Keynes was right in the short period and the Classical economists in the long period when full employment prevailed. I do not think they imply this at all. It could even more plausibly be argued that they are consistent with Kalecki's mature views (Goodwin's too) on the indissolubility of trend and cycle, with no necessary tendency to establish full employment.

Champernowne's literary interpretation of von Neumann's model is lucidity itself. A possible interpretation of the model is that it is a growing Classical system with wages kept to the minimum level needed to keep labourers alive in perfectly elastic supply, constant returns to scale rule in all activities, land is not scarce and demand plays no part in determining prices or overall activity because it is assumed that the income-elasticity of demand for all products is unity. Labour does not share in the surplus, all of which is profits which are saved and reinvested. The production processes consist of goods producing goods, some of which are the wage goods consumed by the workers. Prices are determined by the technical conditions of production and the overall rate of profits. With these assumptions, it is intuitively clear that the rate of profits equals the rate of growth of the economy. In turn, the latter is constrained by the rate of expansion of those goods, the supply of which can be expanded least rapidly (all goods are basics in the sense of the first part of Sraffa's 1960 book). Champernowne suggested as examples, whales or mathematical wranglers. He makes explicit that von Neumann treated durable capital goods (fixed assets) as joint products. In Sraffa's discussion of depreciation and the value of capital (Sraffa, 1960, pp. 63–73), he shows that the value of a balanced stock of durable assets becomes greater as the value of the rate of profits is increased and that the limit to the value of capital as the value of the rate of profits is raised *without* limit is the aggregate value of all the machines in the stock when each was new – this is the Kahn–Champernowne formula of Joan Robinson's 1953–54 article. Sraffa regarded the findings as significant because they were another illustration of his critique of neoclassical theory, that it is impossible to have a measure of capital which is independent of distribution and prices. This implication is one of the puzzles that Champernowne tackled in his 1953–54 comment. It worried him that the same physical stock of assets could have different values according to which relative price and wage/rate of profits configuration ruled, and why what was obviously positive accumulation could appear to be negative purely because of a valuation procedure. To overcome this, he constructed his ingenious chain index measure of capital which in effect precipitated out the effects of different prices from the valuation of capital goods to reveal the underlying quantities. He argued that this allowed the analysis of the process of accumulation (admittedly by comparisons of long-period equilibrium positions applied to 'slow' rates of accumulation) and also restored the traditional theory whereby equilibrium factor prices measured and were measured by their respective marginal products. In establishing all this, Champernowne clearly identified the phenomena of capital-reversing and reswitching and constructed his examples so as to rule them out by assumption. He was thus more than well aware of the criticisms but, at that point in time anyway, he was also prepared to defend the traditional marginal productivity results.

Mention should be made of his time as joint editor of the *Economic Journal* with Phyllis Deane and Brian Reddaway in the 1970s. The detailed attention which manuscripts received from the editors puts many economists in their debt, not only for the vital improvements in the clarity of their published articles but also for saving them from serious errors which otherwise might have made their way into the public domain. This is only one example of the enormous amount of time and expert advice which Champernowne gave unselfishly to others.

Frank Cowell says of Champernowne that he

> proved to be a genuine pioneer both in economic theory and statistics. His King's fellowship dissertation ... laid the foundations for the application of stochastic process models to the analysis of income distributions. His pre-war interest in Frank Ramsey's theory of probability led on to work at Oxford on the application of Bayesian analysis to auto-regressive series (... when the Bayesian approach was decidedly unfashionable), and culminated in his major trilogy *Uncertainty and Estimation in Economics* (1969). (*The Independent*, 26 August 2000)

David Champernowne always had a schoolboy enthusiasm for life. At the age of 74, he and Meike climbed Sca Fell, the one top in the Lake District he had not climbed. It was, Mieke tells me (8 December 2000) 'by far the best climb [they] ever did'. Perhaps I may be allowed to add the story of his fulfilment of another ambition, to run the length of the Roman Road near Cambridge, of which I was reminded by Vincent Massaro today (5 October 2000). In the mid 1960s, Champ asked Vince and me to run with him along the road *at night*. Mieke drove us to one end, then drove off to wait for us at the other end. It was a moonless night, and we soon discovered that the road was full of potholes. We finished the course (10 miles, I think) and were picked up safely by Mieke; but I have often wondered how, if, say, Champ had broken a leg in a pothole, we could have explained to the police what exactly we were doing carrying a middle-aged man in athletic gear along the Roman Road at night!

David Champernowne was quirky and original. Most of all, as his former Ph.D. student Neville Norman writes (September 2000), he 'was completely unselfish ... always wanted to help others. His [writings] were done to advance "economics", or "thinking" rather than himself ... the dominant theme [of his life]'.

Note

† I am most grateful to Mieke Champernowne for her comments on a draft of this note.

References

Champernowne, D. G. 1936. Unemployment, Basic and Monetary: The Classical Analysis and the Keynesian, *Review of Economic Studies*, vol. 3, 201–16.

Champernowne, D. G. 1945–46. A Note on J. v. Neumann's Article on 'A Model of Economic Equilibrium', *Review of Economic Studies*, vol. 13, 10–18.

Champernowne, D. G. 1953–54. The Production Function and the Theory of Capital: a Comment, *Review of Economic Studies*, vol. 21, 112–35.

Champernowne, D. G. 1964. Expectations and the Links between the Economic Future and the Present, in Lekachman, R. (ed.), *Keynes' General Theory: Reports of Three Decades*, London, Macmillan, 153–74.

Champernowne, D. G. 1969. *Uncertainty and Estimation in Economics*, 3 vols, London, Oliver & Boyd, Holden Day.

Champernowne, D. G. 1973. *Distribution of Income between Persons*, Cambridge, Cambridge University Press.

Champernowne, D. G. and Cowell, F. A. 1998. *Economic Inequality and Income Distribution*, Cambridge, Cambridge University Press.

Kahn, R. F. and Champernowne, D. G. 1953–54. The Value of Invested Capital, *Review of Economic Studies*, vol. 21, 107–11.

Robinson, J. 1953–54. The Production Function and the Theory of Capital, *Review of Economic Studies*, vol. 21, 81–106.

Sraffa, P. 1960. *Production of Commodities by Means of Commodities. Prelude to a Critique of Economic Theory*, Cambridge, Cambridge University Press.

von Neumann, J. 1945–46. A Model of General Economic Equilibrium, *Review of Economic Studies*, vol. 13, 1–9.

20
Robin Matthews: A Tribute (2010)*

Robin Matthews held the two most senior chairs of economics in the UK – the Drummond Chair at Oxford (1965–75, succeeding John Hicks) and the Chair of Political Economy at Cambridge, 'Marshall's Chair', (1980–91, succeeding Brian Reddaway). His many contributions to the discipline, the profession and the community make it abundantly clear why. He described his empirical work as economic history written in the style of an economist. His teaching, research and administrative duties over the years made him more and more aware of the inadequacies of 'the conventional model of rational individualistic utility maximisation, [so that increasingly his] interests moved toward the institutional and psychological underpinnings of economic behaviour'.

His wide-ranging interest and approaches are reflected in his major publications. Though he had no formal training in mathematics, he was a capable mathematician; he understood theory set out in a mathematical manner. His own writings, while they used mathematics relevantly and with mastery, also used them sparingly.

His earliest work was on the historical and theoretical aspects of the trade cycle in the UK. His first book, *A Study in Trade Cycle History* (1954), is far more than a complement to Walt Rostow's 1948 'Essays' on the *British Economy of the Nineteenth Century*. His Cambridge Economics Handbook, *The Trade Cycle* (1958), is still one of the best introductions to this inherent characteristic of capitalism.

One of his most influential articles, 'The saving function and the problem of trend and cycle', was published in 1955 in what Dennis Robertson called 'The Green Horror' (*The Review of Economic Studies*).

* Originally published in *Royal Economic Society Newsletter*, Issue No. 151, Octoter 2010, pp. 17–18.

Robin pointed out that James Duesenberry in his classic book on the consumption function (1949), had neglected the existence of ongoing productivity growth when he dated the onsets of the ratchet effect as the previous highest levels of income attained, rather than the previous lowest levels of unemployment. This is the sort of basic insight that the best economists make and then spell out their implications, in Robin's case, for the relationship between trend and cycle. The latter has become the most important base on which our understanding of the processes at work in capitalism is built, associated especially with the contributions of (late) Michal Kalecki and of Richard Goodwin (who was Robin's colleague at Cambridge in the 1950s and 1960s).

At much the same time, in *Economica* (1961), Robin wrote, using Keynes's liquidity preference theory of the rate of interest, one of the earliest and best accounts of what is happening in the banking and financial sectors of the economy when the Kahn–Meade–Keynes multiplier is working itself out in the real sector. Robin also showed how self-finance and 'other imperfections of the capital market' could be incorporated into the analysis. In 1964, with Frank Hahn, Robin published in the *Economic Journal* the famous survey of the theory of economic growth, the article which has been the role model for survey articles ever since. Though all three sections of the survey achieved high levels of exemplary scholarship, the second section on technical progress, which was primarily due to Robin, is the jewel in the crown of the survey. Its lucidity and clarity bring out the deep economic intuitions it contains.

Robin's most cited and admired article is his 1968 paper in the *Economic Journal* on why the UK had had full employment since the war. There, his great understanding of historical and political processes linked to his command of sound economic theory (not only that of Keynes) combined to produce a convincing set of arguments for why full employment was attained and maintained, a set of arguments that are so much more sophisticated and measured than the simple appeal of the then conventional wisdom to the application of Keynesian policies by governments in the post war period.

Robin himself thought he spent too much time on the treatise published in 1982, with Charles Feinstein and John Odling-Smee, on the causes of growth in the UK from 1856 to 1973, especially in the post war period to 1973, 'years of unparalleled growth in Britain, as in other countries'. The volume used a framework suggested by the editors, Moses Abramovitz and Simon Kuznets, for comparable studies of the experiences of other major industrialised economies. Be that as it may, it is easy to concur with the judgement of Feinstein and Odling-Smee that they wished 'to put on record that it was…Robin…, who made by far the most significant contributions to the design of the investigation, the analysis of the material and the writing of the final text'.

Robin always kept up to date with developments in economic theory and history and made sure that his teaching embodied them in a critical but fair manner. I vividly remember going to a fine set of lectures which Robin gave in 1980 to Cambridge undergraduates on macroeconomic and monetary theory and policy in the light of the contributions of Milton Friedman and Robert Lucas. Robin lucidly explained the gist of them; he extracted the positive aspects while maintaining the Keynesian foundations on which he had been brought up and to which he still adhered. As was noted, in later years he became more and more interested in the institutional and psychological aspects of the discipline, as befitted the holder of the Chair of Political Economy. One of his most insightful contributions was his review in the *Economic Journal* in 1977 of Fred Hirsch's engaging and fundamental volume, *Social Limits to Growth*. In it Robin coupled his high natural intelligence with his wide and deep understanding of theory and history. The review is the type of essay that the very best products of the Oxford PPE are uniquely fitted to write.

Robin's legacy to the Faculty at Cambridge through his writing and teaching will be a lasting one. As he ruefully was to admit, his attempts to reshape the ways in which that faction-benighted Faculty went about its business were not successful. Moreover, in retrospect, he felt that his aims in this regard were probably mistaken anyway and that his own comparative advantage lay much more with scholarship than with attempting to change administrative structures.

Robin had an austere presence but he was basically a friendly and kind person, extremely supportive of the young, both students and colleagues. He was excellent company, with a dry wit. He enjoyed tossing about ideas and old-fashioned gossip.

Part VIII
General Essays

21
Cambridge Economics (2008)*
with Catherine Walston

Maynard Keynes called Thomas Robert Malthus, 'the first of the Cambridge economists'. He provided a brilliant description of Malthus's approach:

> Malthus was above all, a great pioneer of the application of a frame of formal thinking to the complex confusion of the world of daily events. Malthus approached the central problems of economic theory by the best of all routes. He began ... as a philosopher and moral scientist, ... brought up in the Cambridge of Paley, applying the *à priori* method of the political philosopher. He then immersed himself ... in the facts of economic history and of the contemporary world, applying the methods of historical induction and filling his mind with a mass of the material of experience ... finally he returned ... to the pure theory of the economist proper, and sought ... to impose the methods of formal thought on the material presented by events, ... to penetrate these events with understanding by a mixture of intuitive selection and formal principle and thus to interpret the problem and propose the remedy.

This approach has characterised Cambridge economics at its best ever since. (In recent years there has been a concerted effort to make teaching and research in Cambridge carbon copies of the corresponding procedures in leading United States economics departments. The relevance

* Originally published in Peter Pagnamenta (ed.), *The University of Cambridge: An 800th Anniversary Portrait*, London: Third Millennium Publishing, 2008, pp. 168–71.

of differentiated products, comparative advantage and historical legacies and tradition has been heavily discounted.)

The study of political economy at Cambridge started within the Moral Sciences Tripos. (Keynes wished it had stayed there.) Alfred Marshall (Professor of Political Economy 1886–1908), the next great figure after Malthus, started the separate Economics Tripos in 1903. Marshall's writings, teaching and pupils dominated Cambridge economics up until at least World War II. Two major strands emerge from his tradition. One was first most associated with his chosen successor, A. C. Pigou, the other, with his most illustrious pupil, Keynes. Some of their successors have contributed significantly to both strands, most notably, James Meade but also Richard Kahn, Nicholas Kaldor, Austin Robinson, Joan Robinson, and Tony Atkinson. The most important infusion of modern approaches to economic theory came with the appointment of Frank Hahn in the early 1960s and then as a Professor in the 1970s. Robert Solow over does it by claiming that Hahn alone dragged Cambridge economics kicking and screaming into the twentieth century but he was a great intellectual influence from the 1960s on.

We should also record the extraordinary importance of two 1920s papers by Frank Ramsey, the mathematician and philosopher, who tragically died in his late 20s. His work on optimum taxation and saving was to influence at least one of our subsequent Nobel Prize winners, James Mirrlees (1996). Standing apart in some dimensions, yet integral to the major developments that occurred, was Piero Sraffa (1898–1983). Sraffa came to Cambridge in 1927 through Keynes's initiative; he edited the works and correspondence of Ricardo (1951–73) (in collaboration with Maurice Dobb) over many years, and wrote the single most important critique of the conceptual foundations of neoclassical economics, *Production of Commodities by Means of Commodities* (1960). It was at the same time a rehabilitation of the classical and Marxian approach to economic theorising.

Marshall provided two major theoretical developments – the theory of value and distribution, of relative prices and quantities, and the theory of money and monetary policy. He bequeathed to the profession a method of doing economics and the philosophy that economics should both shed light and bear fruit, that is, should understand the functioning and malfunctioning of economic systems and attempt to improve them, especially the lot of the least fortunate, within the constraints imposed by liberal political and economic traditions.

Marshall provided us with a way of analysing the factors that determine the relative prices of commodities and the incomes of those who produce them, usually within freely competitive market structures. He developed a method for handling that fundamental but elusive characteristic of economic life, time, by distinguishing analytically between three periods – market, short and long for persons, firms and industries. Because he also developed what he called partial equilibrium analysis – looking at the behaviour of one individual, firm or industry, abstracting from their interrelationships with other individuals, firms or industries. These periods were rarely applied to the behaviour of the economy as a whole though he clearly understood the nature of the general equilibrium model of the latter. The periods were classified by which variables were allowed to change (by the analyst, not in reality) and which were constant, locked up in the *cet par.* pound. Thus, for the market period, supplies of commodities were given; in the short period, rates of production, but not total supplies of labour or capital goods, could vary. In the long period both supplies of labour and capital goods could vary but once the analysis started changes in methods of production could not vary.

Corresponding to these forces of supply were appropriate forces of demand and prices tended to be set at levels at which voluntary supplies and demand matched, constituting market prices, short-period and long-period normal equilibrium prices. Marshall believed all this to be a natural development of the concepts of market prices and (long-term) natural prices respectively of the classical political economy of Smith and Ricardo, a not uncontroversial view, especially for Sraffa and those who follow him.

The other major contribution by Marshall was the theory of the general price level (the Cambridge version of the quantity theory of money) which explained the central, long-term tendency of all prices taken together to attain a level primarily related to the quantity of money created by the monetary authorities. In the long term, the structure of individual prices and quantities was argued to be independent of monetary and financial matters – money was a veil which did not affect their structure and relationships. Exceptions, especially in the short term, were noted in, for example, theories of the credit and trade cycles. These were seen as fluctuations around the long-period position.

Keynes operated within this Marshallian monetary framework, though he increasingly stressed short-term happenings and policies to tackle them, until he wrote *The General Theory of Employment, Interest and Money* (which was published in 1936). It was the practical influence of the terrible unemployment of the 1920s in the United Kingdom and the 1930s in advanced capitalism world-wide and the critical response to his *A Treatise on Money* (1930), which brought about *The General Theory*. (*A Treatise on Money* was intended to be his *magnum opus*; it was written within the Marshallian tradition and for much of the time in collaboration with Dennis Robertson, who wrote seminal works on monetary and trade cycle theory.) In particular, the criticisms of his young Cambridge colleagues – Kahn, Meade, the Robinsons and Sraffa – and of Robertson, Hawtrey and Harrod were especially important for his transition to the structure of *The General Theory*. He changed us, as Meade told us, from looking at the world as a saving dog wagging an investment tail to an investment dog wagging a saving tail. The dichotomy between the real and the monetary was scrapped, with monetary and financial matters integrated in the analysis from the start. Especially relevant was the determination of the monetary rate of interest which in turn affected the amount of investment done through a comparison with the expected profitability of investment. Consumption expenditure was principally determined by Personal Disposable Income and its distribution between different income classes and was associated with the Meade–Kahn–Keynes multiplier principle. Keynes demonstrated that there was no necessary tendency for the economy to settle, in either the short or long term, at a full employment level, that voluntary saving and investment could be equated at levels well below full employment of the existing labour force and capital stocks. The quantity theory of money no longer explained the general price level which Keynes explained by adapting Marshall's theory of short-period competitive pricing to the economy as a whole. In doing so, he usually ignored, because he did not think it relevant for his central purposes, the other 'revolution' occurring in Cambridge in the 1920s and 1930s concerning partial equilibrium analysis and Sraffa's suggestion that price formation be analysed in the context of mini-monopolists operating in competitive environments. This became the theme of Kahn's *The Economics of the Short Period* (1929) and Joan Robinson's *The Economics of Imperfect Competition* (1933). In the post war period, Robin Marris built on these foundations, his highly original work on the economic theory of 'managerial' capitalism, Marris (1964).

During World War II Keynes applied his new theory to the analysis of situations of over full employment with accompanying inflationary processes, making his 'revolution' a general one. Though he mainly used a closed economy to illustrate his arguments, the theory was quickly extended to open economies and their interrelationships, not least by Joan Robinson and in the post-war period, especially by Meade (for which he received the Nobel Prize in 1977).

In the post-war period (Keynes died in 1946) his immediate contemporaries and colleagues at Cambridge, joined now by Nicholas Kaldor (who in the 1930s and 1940s at the London School of Economics, made seminal contributions to both mainstream and then Keynesian economics), built on this base to generalise *The General Theory* to the long period. That is to say, they analysed the long-term processes of distribution, accumulation and growth which had preoccupied the classicals and Marx, but now in the light of Keynes's new results.

In the world of economics itself there were two main approaches, both of which were also responding to Roy Harrod's pioneering writings on dynamic theory in the late 1930s and the 1940s as well as to the problems of reconstruction in post-war Europe and growing recognition of the problems of underdeveloped economies. The first approach, by those associated with a neoclassical emphasis, stressed the role of substitution in consumption, production and distribution in response to price signals and looked for the conditions which established and sustained steady rates of growth. The second approach, the post-Keynesian view, developed the relationship between saving and investment in the long term (and in some cases in the short term) to explain the distribution of the national income between profits and wages and the determination of the rate of accumulation and thus growth over time. Both approaches attempted to introduce the role of technical advances into their narratives. Kaldor's contributions were especially noteworthy but in later years he refuted them and developed instead his analysis of the complementary relationships between agricultural and industrial economies (and regions or sectors within one economy). He combined this with the concept of cumulative causation processes, of upward or downward spirals in systems, as opposed to mainstreams notions of equilibrating processes. Joan Robinson's contributions were especially influenced by those of Michal Kalecki who independently discovered the principal propositions of *The General Theory* but within a framework that was derived from Marx's schemes of reproduction. Kalecki not only provided a macroeconomic theory of distribution and a two-sided relationship between profitability and accumulation but he also developed a theory of cyclical growth. Eventually he scrapped the distinction between the determinants of trends, on the one hand, and of cycles, on the other, to argue that cycle and trend are indissolubly mixed (as did Richard Goodwin, another highly original Cambridge (both Cambridges and Oxford) economist).

Parallel with these developments (in which it must be said, that the neoclassical views came to dominate the profession) was the sustained critique of the conceptual foundations of mainstream theories of value and distribution, associated especially with Joan Robinson and Sraffa. (The post-Keynesian developments presented above were intended to replace those based on neoclassical foundations.) The critique concerned the neoclassical organising concept of price as an index of scarcity together with the need to measure capital in units independent of value and distribution, a method which used comparisons based on differences to analyse processes associated with changes, and the roles of ideology and 'vision' in the formation of theories. The main protagonists were at the other Cambridge, especially at MIT, but they had allies in Cambridge, England, for example, Hahn, Meade, Bliss (now in Oxford), and others. These issues are still unfinished business even though most of the leading Cambridge UK figures are dead. Luigi Pasinetti is the senior living heir, probably the last of the great system builders in our profession. His contributions combine the insights of the classicals with those of the Post-Keynesians.

Hahn and Robin Matthews provided the role model for survey articles ever afterwards with their survey of theories of economic growth in 1964. Hahn also, with Kenneth Arrow, wrote the standard monograph on general equilibrium theory which, starting with Walras and Irving Fisher, was brought into the modern world by Hicks, Debreu, Arrow, McKenzie and others. In the 1980s and 1990s Hahn, together with Kaldor and others, was in the vanguard of those attacking the theoretical propositions and policy recommendations of the monetarists and then the new classical macroeconomists based in Chicago.

Matthews also was associated with the pioneering developments of Cambridge economic historians – Phyllis Deane, Brian Mitchell, Charles Feinstein and others – who, building on Keynesian national income constructions, greatly changed our ways of looking at developments of both advanced and developing economies. Deane also made significant contributions to the history of economic thought, following in the tradition established by Sraffa and Dobb, with the edition of the Ricardo volumes and the critique of mainstream theory, in Dobb's case from a Marxist point of view. (Sraffa was much influenced by Marx as well.)

We must also highlight the sturdy tradition of often innovative applied work through the Department of Applied Economics (DAE) (1945–2005). This started under the leadership of the first Director, Richard Stone, in 1945. Stone was the second Cambridge Nobel Laureate in 1984, following his great friend Meade who received it in 1977. During the second World War they pioneered together the establishment of a national accounting framework for the UK economy and it was Stone's subsequent development of this at the international level that led to his Nobel Prize. Stone established the tradition that theory and measurement are mutually interdependent – robust empirical analysis depends on relevant theory, while it in turn depends upon reliable observations. When Stone ceased to be Director in 1956, he, with Allan Brown, developed the Cambridge growth project which integrated previous work at the DAE on demand analysis, input–output analysis and national accounts. The three following Directors – Brian Reddaway (who became Professor of Political Economy in 1970), Wynne Godley and David Newbery – had principal mentors in Marshall (all three) and Keynes (the first two). Reddaway presided over down-to-earth, no nonsense applied projects with policy implications. Godley drew on Marshall's concept of the long period and Keynes's analysis of the processes at work in modern capitalism and provided a logical framework of relationships incorporating double entry book keeping concepts, leading after many years to a huge jump in our understanding of the dynamic monetary macroeconomic processes at work both nationally and internationally. Newbery is a sophisticated Marshallian interested in applied microeconomic problems, developing countries and transition economies. All four were joined by the Department's own officers and Faculty teaching officers, especially Frank Wilkinson, Gabriel Palma and Ajit Singh.

Cambridge has been the source of important public policy advice through the seconding of leading Cambridge economists to government departments during World War Two (Keynes, of course, Kahn, Meade, Austin Robinson) and after, especially Kaldor.

Of our Nobel Laureates, both James Mirrlees (1996) and Amartya Sen (1998) fit into the Pigovian strand, with Mirrlees also much influenced by Ramsey on optimum taxation and saving. By training a mathematician, Mirrlees is precise and rigorous in what he has to say about optimum tax regimes, to which he marries the effects of asymmetries in knowledge and the relationship between principals and agents, in this case between governments and tax payers. He attempts to reach back over the attacks on Pigovian welfare economics by those who denied the existence of measurable cardinal utility and the possibilities of interpersonal comparisons, in order to produce results that at least offer guidance to practical policy. Sen is more committed to the general philosophy of being 'vaguely right rather than precisely wrong' (a Marshallian tenet). He tackled the difficult task of overcoming Arrow's 1951 argument that it was impossible to go from individual to aggregate social choices in a manner that gave unambiguous rules for social betterment. Sen's writings on social choice and its many applications to policy issues, especially relating to the poor and outcast, are both extremely rigorous philosophically, yet firmly in the Marshallian Pigovian tradition of fruit bearing. In the same vein many of Cambridge's brightest and best have worked on the problems of developing economies, exhaustible resources, climate change, social capital and the economics of the environment, searching for what economists can say with authority about what has happened and what ought to be done. Finally, game theory has come to play a large part in modern theory and Cambridge practitioners of it are up there with the leading lights.

Inevitably leadership in world economics has passed to the United States. Nevertheless, it is a Cambridge economist who is the author of the 'very short introduction' to economics volume in Oxford University Press's influential series of very short introductions. Partha Dasgupta has written a *tour de force*, enthusiastically endorsed by both Robert Solow and the Archbishop of Canterbury. By comparing the present and future lots of two ten year old girls, one living in a comfortable US suburb, the other in a poor African village, Dasgupta organises his discussion around 'some of the most urgent problems humanity faces today' combined with 'an account of the *reasoning modern economists apply*' – an approach centrally within the Cambridge tradition documented here.

22
100 Years of the Economics Tripos (2009)*

The Economics Tripos at Cambridge celebrated its centenary in 2003 with a number of brief lectures and, as is usual at Oxbridge, with food and drink.[†] My brief (in two senses) was to discuss some academic highlights of those first 100 years. What follows is a shorter version of my lecture. As background, may I point out that over this period, Cambridge economists made seminal, often classic contributions to welfare economics, employment and monetary theory, the theory of the firm and economic history, including history of economic theory?

I started with Pigou's *Wealth and Welfare* (1912) reviewed by Edgeworth in the March 1913 *Economic Journal*. 'Originality', Edgeworth writes, 'has set its unmistakable mark on Professor Pigou's work. [This is] not inconsistent with some resemblance to great predecessors ... The good which philanthropy and statesmanship should seek is defined in accordance with Sidgwick's utilitarian philosophy'. Pigou's theoretical means to achieve that end are 'the methods perfected by Dr. Marshall'. Pigou's 'most sublime' theoretical contributions assumed 'the form of mathematical reasoning', but with practical importance attached to other arguments taking the classical form of deduction from psychological generalisations.

Edgeworth, a wise old bird, writes that to assess the value of theory we should use the 'Aristotelian doctrine [of attending to] the ... pronouncements of the practically wise, who have acquired by experience a certain power of mental vision'. He poses the question: 'How far do our author's theories belong to the category of practical wisdom, or to that higher kind of science [which is] wonderful ... difficult but not useful

---

* Originally published in *Cambridge Economics Alumni Newsletter*, Issue Number 2, Autumn, 2009, pp 4–6.

for human purposes?' Mathematical economics is certainly useful but do further elaborations 'imply a correspondingly large contribution to the Art of Political Economy'? The analogy of mathematical physics does not help us to answer [so much for our physics envy]. Edgeworth therefore 'leaves to posterity the decisive answer'.

Cannan reviewed the first edition (1920) of *The Economics of Welfare* in the June 1921 *Economic Journal*. (Remember that he had been a candidate for the Chair of Political Economy that Pigou held). Cannan started with a complaint: 'In the presence of a thousand pages a reviewer feels somewhat of a worm ... like that despised being ... inclined to turn'. 'The sage who observed that of the making of books there is no end was a child in these matters. In ... Pigou's paradise an author will scrap his magnum opus ... superseding it with another twice its size every eight years.' Cannan sighs for 'a little of Malthus's "prudential restraint" '. He closes graciously, 'a valiant effort by a very gallant gentleman to increase our economic welfare'. Remember, though, that Captain Oates vanished into the Antarctic night, never to return.

A personal and professional tragedy was the intellectual falling out of Maynard Keynes and Dennis Robertson in the 1930s. Before this occurred, thank goodness, Robertson published in 1926 a seminal study – 'a theoretical skeleton' – of the relationship between real and monetary factors in the making of the cycle. *Banking Policy and the Price Level* was the 'horrible little younger son [surely brother?]' of *A Study in Industrial Fluctuations* (1915). The book was deliberately difficult and concise; the author thought it had merit because, as it was short, it was 'quickly over'.

Frank Ramsey's two famous papers, 'A contribution to the theory of taxation', in the March 1927 *Economic Journal* and 'A mathematical theory of saving' in the December 1928 *Economic Journal* were 40 years ahead of their time, spawning the later literature on optimum taxation and growth. Maynard Keynes in the March 1930 *Economic Journal* wrote of the second paper: '[It was] one of the most remarkable contributions to mathematical economics ever made, both in respect of the intrinsic importance and difficulty of its subject, the power and elegance of the technical methods employed, and the clear purity of illumination with which the writer's mind is felt by the reader to play about its subject.' Keynes referred to Ramsey's 'modesty'. This is borne out by Ramsey's assessment of the paper. 'Of course, the whole thing is a waste of time.' It had distracted him from "a book on logic" ... [because] it [was] much easier to concentrate on than philosophy and the difficulties that arise rather [obsessed him]'.

I turned next to Joan Robinson's *The Economics of Imperfect Competition* (1933), noting that it was preceded by Piero Sraffa's 1925 and 1926 articles Richard Kahn's 'The Economics of the Short Period' (1929), Gerald Shove's lectures and writings and Austin Robinson's classic, *The Structure of Competitive Industry* (1931). Keynes probably came closest to a correct assessment. He referred 'to the very considerable development of the theory of value in the last five years' and to the fact that there is 'no convenient place [to find] a clear statement of the nature of modern technique, or a summary of recent work...Mrs Robinson aims at filling the gap...has done it very well...The book will be for a little while to come...essential...for any serious student of the modern theory of value.'

The major landmark of Cambridge's contributions was *The General Theory*, published on 4 February 1936, the day after the Arts Theatre opened, 'two projects, linked by a common feeling, converging at a single moment in time' (Robert Skidelsky). When the Faculty celebrated its publication 50 years on, ours not being an exact science, we chose the wrong day in February. *The General Theory* is indisputably Keynes's work, but he was much influenced by the members of the 'circus' and by Kahn's 1931 multiplier article, 'Mr. Meade's relation', and Kahn's scepticism concerning the quantity theory, which still characterised *A Treatise on Money* (1930).

I drew on two reviews, one by Austin Robinson in *The Economist*, 29 February 1936, the other by John Hicks (JR as he then was), chosen by Keynes to review it for the June 1936 *Economic Journal*. Austin's was the only signed review ever to appear in that august journal (even then it only ran to initials, 'E.A.G.R.'.). Austin complained to Keynes about the narrowness of the title chosen – 'Mr. Keynes on Money' – and other alterations. Keynes told him it served him right for publishing in the Yellow Press. Austin's perceptive review has stood the test of time. He approved of Keynes's polemical passages: 'Like Horace's schoolmaster Mr. Keynes whips his pupils into agreement.' He deplored the comparative absence of the masterly, clear style of Keynes's earlier writing, the possession 'in unusual bounty [of] the gift of translating theoretical ideas into realities...conveying them in words of one syllable'. Austin used plain language to describe the existence of under employment rest states and the processes by which they may or may not be reached, drawing on his keen sense of industrial behaviour by explaining that the sub-profitable levels of output as a whole away from the rest states meant that the situations were not sustainable. He also had a clearer view of the equality of S and I and the roles it played than perhaps even the author.

Hicks's review article, though entitled 'Mr. Keynes' Theory of Employment', immediately evades this constraint by bringing in output, shifting equilibrium and money. Hicks chose employment (or rather unemployment) because it was then the most practical problem to which 'this sort of theoretical improvement' was relevant. It was a theory of output in general, Marshallian in inspiration in method but not confined to a single industry; 'a theory of shifting equilibrium vis-à-vis the static or stationary theories of general equilibrium ... of Ricardo, Böhm-Bawerk or Pareto'; 'a theory of money [in so far as it brought] money out of its isolated position as a separate subject into an integral relation with general economics'. For Hicks making S=I by definition was an important change in point of view – 'The changing, progressing, fluctuating economy has to be studied on its own ... it cannot usefully be referred to the norm of a static state'. 'From the standpoint of pure theory, the use of the method of expectations is ... the most revolutionary thing about the book.' Hicks identifies 'a proposition of fundamental importance' – *cet. par.*, the marginal efficiency of capital (*m.e.c*) will be lower, the greater the amount of capital goods already possessed – on which Keynes based his theory of trade crisis and a new theory of long-period unemployment, even more novel and startling.

Hicks concluded: '[We have] to change, not so much our methods of analysis, as some ... elements in the outlook ... inherited from the classics. [We] can have too much, even of economic virtues ... the nineteenth century could only afford Ricardo because it sinned so luxuriantly against Malthus. Today we must find a new sin, if it can give us a century before the day of reckoning it will have done well.' I must also mention the precociously insightful reviews by two of Keynes's pupils at King's, life-long friends and colleagues, David Champernowne and Brian Reddaway.

I closed the 1930s with two of my favourites – Maurice Dobb's *Political Economy and Capitalism* (1937), a classic that pays rereading, and Brian Reddaway's *The Economics of a Declining Population* (1939), the lucid arguments of which are becoming more relevant by the day.

For the 1940s I singled out James Meade's and Dick Stone's 1941 *Economic Journal* article on the national accounts of the United Kingdom. It was a by-product of Austin Robinson's favourable reaction to *How to Pay for the War* (1940), which convinced him of the need for reliable estimates of national income and expenditure on a continuing basis. He recruited James 'to get the logic right' and Dick 'for his remarkable familiarity with British economic statistics'. Austin always regarded this 'as his chief contribution to the war'. I also mentioned Joan Robinson's 1942 *Essay on Marxian Economics* which led Gerald Shove (in 1944) to give her an α on Marx but only β- on Marshall; and elicited a letter from Keynes addressed to 'Mrs. Austin Robinson', starting 'My dear Joan'. Keynes thought it 'as well written as anything you have done ... despite the fact that there is something intrinsically boring in [attempting] to make sense of what ... is not sense'. Keynes was left with the feeling that '[Marx] had a penetrating and original flair but was a very poor thinker indeed'. So now we know.

The 1950s saw at least four milestones: the Sraffa (in collaboration with Dobb) edition of Ricardo's works and correspondence (1951–55) for which Piero received the then equivalent of the Nobel Prize; the publication of volume I of Dick Stone's 'Red Books' on consumer expenditure in the United Kingdom, a magnum opus and veritable tour de force – Angus Deaton (1987) singles out for praise the explicit description of data, the 'masterly exposition of the theory of demand and revealed preference and [the] chapter on economic methodology which reads like a text until one realises that this is where the texts originated'; Joan Robinson's 'generalisation of *The General Theory* to the long period'; *The Accumulation of Capital* (1956), published 20 years on from *The General Theory* when Joan was the same age as Keynes in 1936; and Jan Graaf's *Theoretical Welfare Economics,* (1957), based on 'a Ph.D. thesis largely completed around 1951'.

Tibor Barna's review in the September 1957 *Economic Journal* was the most favourable and knowledgeable review of Joan's magnum opus. Using 'The Keynesian apparatus of thought and her reflections on competition and monopoly [she] applied them to classical problems and to the testing of classical answers.' For Abba Lerner in the 1957 *American Economic Review,* though, the 'most important parts are the errors and ingenious confusions which can give such first class exercises to graduate students (and professors) who could do with a tough work out and who can stand the tough cuteness of Mrs. Robinson's style'. For him '[the book] constitutes a pearl whose most conspicuous product is irritation.' For Lawrence Klein, writing in the 1980s, the introduction remains 'a truly masterful statement of economic principles [serving to lay bare] the fundamental aspects of our subject to beginners'.

Paul Samuelson described Jan Graff's book as 'a classic in our own time written by a brilliant South African [who] left his impress on the Cambridge environment but subsequently revealed a preference to be a non-economist'. Graaf concluded that 'the greatest contribution economics is likely to make to human welfare ... is through positive studies ... rather than through normative welfare economics'. For Samuelson Graff's nihilism was 'partly a matter of temperament ... one who [accepted] the universe in a cheerful David Hume way might state the same conclusions ... yet give quite a different impression'.

The year 1960 saw fundamental contributions to theory and to theory coupled to applied work, exemplified by Sraffa's *Production of Commodities* and Wilf Salter's *Productivity and Technical Change* (based on his Ph.D. of the early 1950s supervised by Brian Reddaway). For Ronald Meek, writing in the *Scottish Journal of Political Economy* in 1961, Piero's slim volume was 'a magnificent rehabilitation of the classical (and up to a point Marxian) approach to certain crucial problems relating to value and distribution ... [implying] rehabilitation of the labour theory of value in something ... like the form it assumed ... in Marx'. After following a similar intellectual pilgrim's progress to Piero, Krishna Bharadwaj perceptively entitled her review article in a 1963 edition of *Economic and Political Weekly* (*EPW*), 'Value through exogenous distribution'. Mourning Salter's tragically early death at the age of 34, Trevor Swan described his work as 'unfulfilled renown'. I still continuously meet people who are inspired by his book, superb intelligence and lucid analysis.

Robin Marris's highly original but difficult to read book, *The Economic Theory of Managerial Capitalism* (1964) was reviewed in the June 1965 *Economic Journal* by Charles Carter. Carter felt that Marris deserved 'much credit for a resolute attempt to write the theory of the firm in terms not wholly repugnant to common sense'. He worried that Marris's style obscured his 'essentially simple though powerful ideas', so that 'Mr. Marris's work ... will not have the influence which the originality and power of his ideas justifies.' Time has proved Carter's fears to be groundless; the book is a classic.

In December 1964 the Hahn-Matthews survey of growth theory, the role model for survey articles ever since, appeared in the *Economic Journal*. I also cited Nicky Kaldor's last will and testament to our trade, the 1984 Mattioli Lectures, *Causes of Growth and Stagnation in the World Economy* (1996) (published ten years after his death, edited by his biographers Tony Thirlwall and Ferdy Targetti). In them Nicky, the most obvious successor to Keynes in Cambridge, set out the reasons for his growing dissatisfaction with orthodox economics (Arrow-Debreu general equilibrium was his target), and with early and mid Kaldor, including his period as Jean-Baptiste Kaldor in the 1950s and 1960s developing macroeconomic theories of distribution and growth (this explains, not excuses, my omission of 'Alternative Theories of Distribution' in the

'Green Horror' in 1955–56). He then presented his latest (and, sadly, last) 'vision' of how the world works, emphasising complementarity, increasing returns, and the accompanying processes of cumulative causation that he derived from Smith, Allyn Young, his LSE teacher and mentor, and Myrdal. He closed with a 'package deal' of policies to save the world. That Nicky was ever an orthodox economist, albeit an internally critical one, is a mystery for the idea of a constraint on anything, especially himself, was completely foreign to his nature.

An important aspect of Keynes's influence is the seminal contributions of economic historians – Phyllis Deane, Charles Feinstein, W. J. ('Iain') MacPherson and Brian Mitchell – to our understanding of the first Industrial Revolution and to development generally, including in Phyllis's case, the evolution of economic ideas. Another major strand, to my mind, the wave of the future in theory, is the development of cyclical growth and multi-sectoral dynamic structural growth models by Michal Kalecki, Dick Goodwin and Luigi Pasinetti. Luigi is now the senior living heir to what I regard as the Cambridge Tradition.

There I stopped (except for brief mentions of our Nobel Prize winners and Marshall Lecturers), not because there have not been major contributions by Cambridge economists since then, but because time and space are scarce resources and maintaining friendships is a prudent choice, especially on gala occasions.

Note

[†] I thank but in no way implicate Stephanie Blankenburg, Mauro Boianovsky, Willy Brown, Prue Kerr, Geoff Mceks, William Peterson and Bob Rowthorn for comments on the draft of this necessarily highly personal statement.

Index